# The Danish Directors

## Dialogues on a Contemporary National Cinema

**Mette Hjort and Ib Bondebjerg**

**Translation by Mette Hjort**
*(in consultation with the directors)*

**intellect**™
Bristol, UK
Portland, OR, USA

First Published in Great Britain in Paperback in 2003 by
**Intellect Books**, PO Box 862, Bristol BS99 1DE, UK

First Published in USA in Paperback in 2003 by
**Intellect Books**, ISBS, 5824 N.E. Hassalo St, Portland, Oregon 97213-3644, USA

Published in Great Britain in Hardback in 2001 by Intellect Books, Bristol, UK
Published in USA in Hardback in 2001 by Intellect Books, Portland, OR, USA

Consulting Editor:   Robin Beecroft
Copy Editor:            Nicky Kinsman

A catalogue record for this book is available from the British Library

ISBN 1-84150-841-1

Printed and bound in Great Britain by Antony Rowe, Eastbourne

## Note on Editorial Practice

In the biographical notes and filmographies the titles of films by the interviewees are provided first in English and parenthetically in Danish. All subsequent mentions of these films within the interview in question are by English title only. If these films are evoked in other interviews, the first mention is by both English and Danish titles. Films that do not have official English distribution titles are identified by translated titles. In those cases in which the original title is in English the official Danish distribution title is nonetheless provided parenthetically. All other Danish films mentioned in the course of the interviews are similarly identified by their official or unofficial English titles and their official Danish titles. Films by non-Danish directors are mentioned only by official English and original foreign titles. In some cases the Danish films under discussion are based on literary works, and the same notational principles apply with regard to the titles in question.

Explanatory translator's notes have been added in a few cases. A short glossary of key terms at the end of the book helps to explain recurrent terms or institutional arrangements. The first mention of the relevant term in each of the interviews is marked with an *. The bibliography includes all cited texts, but also a number of key works or documents pertaining to Danish cinema, and some useful website addresses. Those entries in which the Danish represents an obstacle to basic comprehension have been glossed.

The first interview was conducted in June 1997 and the final one in March 2000. All directors have had the opportunity to comment on the relevant transcriptions and to update their interviews, either in writing or in a follow-up interview. All interviews are thus up-to-date at the time of going to press in June 2000.

# Contents

## Introductions

## Interviews

# List of Figures

# Acknowledgements

*The Danish Directors: Dialogues on a Contemporary National Cinema* is a belated response to the students who took Mette Hjort's 'Contemporary Danish Cinema' course at McGill University in Montreal, Canada. Malve Petersmann, Joanna Freedman and Andres Pelenur, in particular, heroically pursued their new-found interest in Danish cinema in spite of the paucity of relevant materials in English. Ib Bondebjerg signed on and agreed to assume responsibility for editing the Danish edition of the volume because of related experiences in a Danish context. Although Danish cinema commands considerable interest among indigenous audiences, the directors' views on their art and its place within various national and international contexts could until now primarily be gleaned from interviews that, by virtue of having been published largely in local newspapers, lacked accessibility and, in some instances, depth. This volume is an attempt, then, to encourage key film-makers to articulate their views in detail within the context of a sustained dialogue aimed at film scholars and film enthusiasts alike.

We've incurred a lot of debts of various kinds along the way. Special thanks are due to David Bordwell, who was one of the first people to believe in the project, which would have been stillborn had he not, with his inimitable warmth and enthusiasm, expressed interest in the idea. We would not have been able to carry out the project without the assistance of the Danish Film Institute: Vicki Synott provided facts, figures, publications and guidance at crucial moments; Bente Frausing supplied us with countless videos; Claus Horneman and Henning Sørensen generously arranged screenings of 16 mm films; Lene Boholm graciously allowed us to compile a set of complimentary stills from the Danish Film Institute's promotional collection; Ebbe Villadsen tracked down many of the official English titles and helped weed out inconsistencies and mistakes, and Lars Ølgaard provided various forms of library assistance. We are also happy to acknowledge a generous grant from the Danish Film Institute, which made possible an unabridged translation of the Danish edition. We are grateful to the directors, and especially Christian Braad Thomsen, for judicious advice, copies of films and books, and above all, for their willingness, not only to set aside time for the interviews, but to check and comment on the resulting Danish and English texts. Susan Hayward identified Intellect Press as a possible home for the book in the English-speaking world, and Robin Beecroft, our editor, deserves our heartfelt thanks for his remarkable efficiency, patience, flexibility and warm enthusiasm. Thanks also to Scott Mackenzie for his help with proofreading. Mette Hjort is grateful to Arnt Lykke Jakobsen and Helle Pals Frandsen, who solved a number of thorny terminological problems. She would also like to thank the Social Sciences and Humanities Research Council of Canada for a generous three-year grant in support of her research on national cinemas.

On a more personal note, Mette Hjort would like to thank Kirsten Hjort for editorial help early on. Our families have expanded significantly since we first undertook this project, and we'd like to dedicate this book to these newcomers and, we trust, future film enthusiasts – Siri, Jessika, and Magnus – as well as to Erik, who was there from the start, loves many of the films, and cheered us on.

---

## For Siri, Jessika, Magnus, and Erik

---

# Preface

## David Bordwell

Somewhere about ten years ago film journalists began declaring that cinema was dying. Faced with the rise of video and MTV, the dominance of Hollywood genre films, the death or silence of the masters who had sustained 1960s and 1970s cinema – Fellini, Bergman, Visconti, Bunuel, Hitchcock, Kurosawa, Antonioni, Bresson – many critics predicted that the seventh art would not last out its first hundred years. Yet exactly as this cry went out (most loudly from Paris), a new burst of creativity was flooding festival screens. Asian Cinema – represented by Hou Hsiao-hsien, Edward Yang, Wong Kar-wai, Takeshi Kitano, Hirozoku Kore-eda, Hang Sang-soo, and many others – captured the world's attention. Iran, the unlikeliest spot of all, sent us a cinema mixing old-fashioned humanism and bold reflexivity. Even Europe was producing the magisterial statements of Angelopoulos and Oliveira, and the more provocative work of Michael Haneke and the Dardenne brothers. Cinema is dying?

Interestingly, many of these works are coming from what Mette Hjort aptly calls 'minority cinemas'. Belgium cannot challenge France for the Francophone market, but its films top festivals. Taiwanese movie output is paltry compared to Japan's, but Taiwanese films are the talk of the international press (and are often financed by Japanese companies). Before the revelations of Kiarostami and Makhmalbaf in the late 1980s, who of us had seen more than a couple of Iranian films? If world film culture has revived, we should thank not the American 'independents' (though Tarantino, everybody's whipping boy today, surely deserves some credit) or the European conglomerates, but rather countries peripheral to the mainstream system. Film festivals have proliferated, creating many more venues for films which otherwise might languish in a single theatre or two in their country of origin. And with more screens and more screenings, discoveries can be made.

Such has been the case with contemporary Danish film. During the 1910s, this national cinema was one of the most powerful in the world; superb stylists like Urban Gad and Holger-Madsen flourished. For decades thereafter, Dreyer was the lone (and atypical) emblem of Danish cinema on the international scene. Not until the 1960s, as one of several 'young cinemas', did Danish film-making recapture international audiences. After another fallow period, the last dozen years have seen an explosion of Danish film talent.

For me, the revelation was not *Babette's Feast* or *Pelle the Conqueror*, which seemed tied to the sober European tradition of quality, but Lars von Trier's *Element of Crime*, which dared to be mesmerically stylised. Von Trier's career, along with the success of *Dogme*-affiliated directors, has only confirmed that this national cinema, like those of Asia and the 'minor' European countries, has a well-stocked storehouse of talent. How appropriate, then, that at the last Cannes Film Festival, *Dancer in the Dark* took prizes alongside the latest work of Edward Yang, Wong Kar-wai, and directors from Iran. (If we declare Denmark part of Asia, it would count as a complete rout.) And we ought not to underestimate the influence of these films. Two Hong Kong film-makers have told me that after seeing *The Celebration*, they intended to shoot their next movies in a similar way; and every student I told about von Trier's hundred-camera coverage of Björk thought that it was a very cool idea.

This book, then, performs a service we shall need more and more: it brings a scrupulous attention to those 'fringe' cinemas which are, at the beginning of a new century, firing our imaginations. It also represents a return to a simple but powerful research strategy: ask the filmmaker informed, intelligent questions. The first 'director's interview books' of the 1960s remain among the most-consulted and widely-read of all film publications, and this for a simple reason: they give filmmakers an opportunity to go on the record. They allow viewers points of entry into what might seem a forbidding body of work. They pick out films for us to follow up, and they take us behind the scenes into the creative process. The return of interview books, such as the in-depth Faber and Faber series, is another healthy sign that cinema lives.

Seldom, however, are we lucky enough to have such knowledgeable and sensitive interrogators as Hjort and Bondebjerg. Their questions are often fascinating mini-essays, and their appreciation of the specific qualities of each director's work elicits thoughtful replies. Every voice retains its own tone and temperament. The result is at once a reference work, an outline history of recent Danish cinema, and an enjoyable read. If the Danish cinema is becoming one model for other 'minority cinemas', these dialogues constitute one very inviting model for future film research.

# Danish Cinema:
# A Small Nation in a Global Culture

## Mette Hjort and Ib Bondebjerg

The history of Danish cinema, as both an art and an industry, includes periods of striking artistic innovation and economic growth, as well as decades of dramatic decline.[1] The key periods in Danish film history – silent film (1896–1930), classic cinema culture (1930–60), modern film culture after 1960 and the international breakthrough of the 1990s – each have their defining characteristics, both in terms of film art and film culture and in relation to questions of national and international success. The golden years of Danish cinema coincide largely with the era of silent film, and are intimately linked with the remarkable business acumen of the producer Ole Olsen, who founded Nordisk Films Kompagni in 1906. These years are also marked by the cinematic achievements of directors such as Viggo Larsen, Benjamin Christensen, August Blom, Holger-Madsen and Carl Theodor Dreyer, and by the emergence of the female star, Asta Nielsen, who played a strikingly vampish role in Urban Gad's *The Abyss* (*Afgrunden*, 1910). The advent of sound, combined with the negative effects of the First World War, had the effect of radically undermining Denmark's leading role within the international film industry, and during the period of classic cinema culture (1930–60), Danish film was reduced to a minor cinema produced by a small nation in an increasingly global world dominated especially by the US. The few Danish films that did manage to penetrate the international market during these years generated interest primarily as an expression of individual artistic talent, a case in point being the films of Dreyer. This period coincides largely with the articulation of the popular Danish genre formulae that were able at times to draw full houses and that helped to constitute film as Danes' preferred form of entertainment. However, the 1940s and 1950s also witnessed the emergence of aesthetically significant films marked by a more international mode of expression, and the key names in this regard are Johan Jacobsen, Ole Palsbo, Bodil Ipsen, Erik Balling and Gabriel Axel. The 1960s brought a crisis of Danish film culture entailed by the competition generated by TV, but also the emergence, much as elsewhere in Europe, of a modern film culture characterised by a new wave realism and greater artistic breadth. New figures, such as Henning Carlsen, enjoyed significant international recognition during this period. In the long run TV's ability to assume the role of preferred entertainment medium, combined with the dominance in Denmark of foreign and especially American films, had the effect of undermining Danish film on the national level. As a result, initiatives aimed at a national film policy were undertaken already in the 1960s, and by the early 1970s it was clear that the very survival of Danish film depended on the possibility of significant state support. The Danish Film Institute* was thus founded in 1972, and the film-makers who were able in the first instance to profit from the relevant state film culture would go on to lay the groundwork towards the end of the 1980s for the international breakthrough of Danish film in the 1990s. It is this

# THE VOW OF CHASTITY

I SWEAR TO SUBMIT TO THE FOLLOWING SET OF RULES DRAWN UP AND CONFIRMED BY DOGME 95:

1. SHOOTING MUST BE DONE ON LOCATION. PROPS AND SETS MUST NOT BE BROUGHT IN (IF A PARTICULAR PROP IS NECESSARY FOR THE STORY, A LOCATION MUST BE CHOSEN WHERE THIS PROP IS TO BE FOUND).
2. THE SOUND MUST NEVER BE PRODUCED APART FROM THE IMAGES OR VICE VERSA. (MUSIC MUST NOT BE USED UNLESS IT OCCURS WHERE THE SCENE IS BEING SHOT).
3. THE CAMERA MUST BE HAND-HELD. ANY MOVEMENT OR IMMOBILITY ATTAINABLE IN THE HAND IS PERMITTED. (THE FILM MUST NOT TAKE PLACE WHERE THE CAMERA IS STANDING; SHOOTING MUST TAKE PLACE WHERE THE FILM TAKES PLACE).
4. THE FILM MUST BE IN COLOUR. SPECIAL LIGHTING IS NOT ACCEPTABLE. (IF THERE IS TOO LITTLE LIGHT FOR EXPOSURE THE SCENE MUST BE CUT OR A SINGLE LAMP BE ATTACHED TO THE CAMERA).
5. OPTICAL WORK AND FILTERS ARE FORBIDDEN.
6. THE FILM MUST NOT CONTAIN SUPERFICIAL ACTION. (MURDERS, WEAPONS, ETC. MUST NOT OCCUR.)
7. TEMPORAL AND GEOGRAPHICAL ALIENATION ARE FORBIDDEN. (THAT IS TO SAY THAT THE FILM TAKES PLACE HERE AND NOW.)
8. GENRE MOVIES ARE NOT ACCEPTABLE.
9. THE FILM FORMAT MUST BE ACADEMY 35 MM.
10. THE DIRECTOR MUST NOT BE CREDITED.

FURTHERMORE I SWEAR AS A DIRECTOR TO REFRAIN FROM PERSONAL TASTE! I AM NO LONGER AN ARTIST. I SWEAR TO REFRAIN FROM CREATING A "WORK", AS I REGARD THE INSTANT AS MORE IMPORTANT THAN THE WHOLE. MY SUPREME GOAL IS TO FORCE THE TRUTH OUT OF MY CHARACTERS AND SETTINGS. I SWEAR TO DO SO BY ALL THE MEANS AVAILABLE AND AT THE COST OF ANY GOOD TASTE AND ANY AESTHETIC CONSIDERATIONS.
THUS I MAKE MY VOW OF CHASTITY.

COPENHAGEN, MONDAY 13 MARCH 1995

ON BEHALF OF DOGME 95

LARS VON TRIER        THOMAS VINTERBERG

*Dogme 95 Vow of Chastity.*

second international breakthrough that has led film scholars and journalists to speak of a return of the golden age of Danish cinema. State support and strong Nordic and European cooperation seem to have ensured that Danish film, at the outset of the new millennium, occupies a position of strength, both nationally, in terms of the commitments of indigenous audiences, and, to a growing extent, internationally.

## A new breakthrough for Danish film

Thanks to the founding of the National Film School of Denmark* in 1968, but also to a series of laws designed variously to provide state support for the art of film in Denmark from 1972 onwards, Danish film can once again lay claim to a significant number of outstanding film-makers whose works, in certain cases, are being hailed as milestones within the history of film. The most obvious case in point is the productive Lars von Trier, who has been compared to Dreyer, not only on account of certain perceived thematic resemblances in some of their works, but because critics consider their importance for the history of film to be somehow similar. Figures such as Nils Malmros, Henning Carlsen, Søren Kragh-Jacobsen, Jon Bang Carlsen and Jørgen Leth have been respected for decades by art film audiences who frequent the circuit of international film festivals that constitutes an important international forum for various European art cinemas. 1987 and 1988 are decisive years, however, for this is when Gabriel Axel and Bille August win Oscars for *Babette's Feast* (*Babettes gæstebud*) and *Pelle the Conqueror* (*Pelle Erobreren*) respectively. This is also when a new generation with greater breadth and a more focussed international orientation begins to announce itself: Lars von Trier, Thomas Vinterberg, Ole Bornedal and Nicolas Winding Refn have had the effect in the late 1980s and 1990s of generating a far more intense and much broader-based interest in contemporary Danish cinema. Film festivals, such as 'Northern Encounters' (Toronto 97) and 'Danish Cinema Then and Now' (The Lincoln Center 97) testify to this renewed international interest in Danish film, as does the number of prestigious prizes awarded to Danish film-makers in the 1980s and 1990s by, among others, the American Academy of Motion Picture Arts and Sciences, and the juries presiding over the Cannes and Berlin Film Festivals.

The 'Vow of Chastity' taken in 1995 by the film collective, Dogme,* which includes Lars von Trier, Thomas Vinterberg, Søren Kragh-Jacobsen and Kristian Levring, has contributed crucially to Danish film's current position internationally.[2] The remarkable success, for example, of Thomas Vinterberg's *The Celebration* (*Festen*, 1998) clearly shows that artistic innovation is fostered in certain cases, not by limitless resources and unbounded freedom, but by rigid constraints and restrictions. The implications of this film's success, not only for Danish film, but for European film-making more generally, are far-reaching indeed, for *The Celebration* proves that quality film-making with a broad appeal does not presuppose the kinds of astronomical budgets that are feasible primarily within a Hollywood context. *The Celebration* and the larger project to which it contributes further underscore the fact that the real challenge faced by film-makers in the smaller European nations is not that of finding a direct inroad to Hollywood, but rather, that of expanding and strengthening the possibilities of an indigenous context of production, supported perhaps in the Danish case by a form of Nordic and European cooperation that would help to counteract the emergence of mechanisms linked to overly national forms of film-making. Vinterberg puts the point as follows in an interview included in this volume: 'My collaboration with Lars von Trier has taught me that he is able to make Denmark big, without leaving Denmark, and this, for me, is the ultimate ideal. The idea is not to go international and become famous, but to think oneself beyond certain typically Danish mentalities.' (p. 275)

Danish cinema towards the end of the 1990s and at the beginning of the new millennium is not only a story of international success, for Danish film currently occupies a privileged place within the local, or national, imaginary. Danish films' share of the market has at times been very small, and what has been striking in that regard is the dominance of American film and the difficulties encountered by films from other

European countries in finding a niche. In the 1970s and early 1980s Danish films' share of box office returns was over 25 percent and some years almost 30 percent. However, by the end of the 1980s and early 1990s the relevant figure was under 20 percent (see Frands Mortensen in Bondebjerg et al., eds, 1997: 310–11). 1995 was the worst year of all, for Danish film secured only 8 percent of the market while American film accounted for 81 percent of earnings (anon, 1998: 5). But from 1995 onwards Danish films have improved and consolidated their market position, both nationally and internationally. The Danish share was 17 percent in 1996 and 19 percent in 1997, and the most recent figures from 1999 confirm Danish films' new-found prominence with 28 percent. Also, for the first time in many years income generated abroad stands out as a significant factor.

This renewed national interest in Danish film is undoubtedly the result of many different factors, including an increased awareness on the part of some of the younger Danish film-makers of the importance of situating their cinematic works in relation to certain indigenous genre conventions, such as those of popular Danish comedy,* while appropriating and indigenising certain international genre formulae where relevant. The turnaround clearly occurs in 1996, the year in which a more internationally orientated and genre-aware generation begins to manifest itself. Ole Bornedal, one of the key figures of the Danish new wave, makes the following remark in this volume about his film, *Nightwatch* (*Nattevagten*):

> I think *Nightwatch* had a much greater impact on Danish film than you actually might think at first – although it may be rather self-centred of me to talk about this. There had been two big box office successes before *Nightwatch*. One was *House of the Spirits* (*Åndernes hus*), which was the film that our parents and grandparents went to see. That film was able to appeal to everyone, because it was a Bille August film with lots of big stars. The other film, *Waltzing Regitze* (*Dansen med Regitze*), was classic Danish film art at its best. It effectively conveyed a fine story that simply appealed to a wide audience. *Nightwatch*'s impact was somewhat different. It was in many ways more modern and appealed to a younger generation. *Nightwatch* made use of a contemporary cinematic language while mobilising the classic thriller genre, and it was driven uniquely by a strong sense of narrative desire, by a tight dramaturgical set-up. What is more, it pursued certain entertainment values almost shamelessly. I don't think the film is a great work of art, but it did help to legitimate the idea that even European film art can make good use of generic stories (p. 233–34).

Another important factor is the emergence in recent times of a number of young actors (Sidse Babett-Knudsen, Kim Bodnia, Sofie Gråbøl, Thomas Bo Larsen, Paprika Steen, Ulrich Thomsen and Iben Hjejle) who are capable of capturing the imagination of the younger generations and redirecting their attention towards Danish film in what at times suggests a revival of the Danish star system that existed during the period of classic Danish film culture. At the same time, as is frequently the case in the context of minor cinemas produced by small nations, international success has significantly increased the amount of media attention that Danish films and film-makers enjoy nationally. The result, as Morten Piil (1998: 8) notes is that at no point since the era of silent film has the promise of Danish film seemed greater.

## Public recognition and enhanced state support

The growing national commitment to Danish film is reflected not only at the level of ticket sales, but also in terms of enhanced state support. In April 1998 Henning Camre and Ib Bondebjerg presented a detailed four-year plan of action on behalf of the recently restructured Danish Film Institute. The report outlined, among other things, a set of initiatives designed to enable the Institute to increase the number of new Danish films produced, to enhance the impact of Danish films at the Danish box office and on the international market, and to sustain and further develop the quality and breadth of Danish film. The document was positively received by key politicians and had the effect of significantly increasing the state's budget for Danish film. The total amount of state support for Danish film is to be increased by 75 percent over a four-year period (1999–2002). Support totalled 200 million Crowns in 1999 and 350 million Crowns have been budgeted for 2002, which amounts to an increase of 150 million Crowns compared with earlier annual budgets. These new resources are released as annual increments over the entire period. The Danish Film Institute thus received an additional 50 million Crowns in 1999, an additional 100 million Crowns in 2000, and can expect a further 150 million Crowns in 2001 and 150 million Crowns in 2002. In a press release dated August 25, 1998, the Minister of Culture, Elsebeth Gerner Nielsen justified the new budget by referring both to the quality of contemporary Danish film and to its role within a general politics of identity:

> Danish film has entered a wonderful phase, supported by great talent and international success. It has really become apparent that Denmark has a way with film. We have the talent, we have the Film Institute, and a Film School that has never been better. We should therefore strike while the iron is hot. In supporting film, one is simultaneously promoting a very broad cultural effect. Film and television increasingly influence the way we understand the world. At the same time film is the root of developments in the area of other electronic media. Danish film is therefore more capable than any other medium of contributing to the preservation and development of Danish culture and identity.

In the same context, Henning Camre (1998), the Director of the Danish Film Institute, similarly focussed on notions of success and cultural identity in his account of the government's enhanced investment in Danish film: 'The new grants should be viewed in the context of the success and impact of Danish film in recent years; they are meant to ensure that film's role as a cultural factor is maintained and further developed.'

The general optimism surrounding Danish film in recent years is reflected in a number of specialised publications. Examples of critical works include *Dansk film, 1972–97* (Bondebjerg et al., eds, 1997), Peter Schepelern's *Lars von Triers Elementer – en filminstruktørs arbejde* (1997), *100 års dansk film* (Schepelern et al., eds, 1997), and *Nordic National Cinemas* (Soila et al., eds, 1998). The release of a striking number of recent Danish films has more or less coincided with the publication of film-makers' diaries or specialised anthologies devoted to the production history of the films in question: Christian Braad Thomsen's *Sygdom forvandlet til skønhed* presents a series of meditations linked to the realisation of his most recent film, *The Blue Monk* (*Den Blå Munk*, 1998); *Omkring Barbara*

(1997) is an anthology designed to shed light on historical and cinematic issues relevant to Nils Malmros' adaptation of Jørgen-Frantz Jacobsen's canonised novel, *Barbara*; and Lars von Trier's *Idioterne* (1998) includes both the script for the second Dogme film, as well as a series of intensely personal reflections in the form of a film-maker's diary. Thomas Vinterberg's *Festen* (1998) includes the script for his Dogme film, diverse reflections on its production history and an interview with the director. Together these works testify to the enhanced interest in increasing widespread public awareness of Danish film.

## The film-makers' perspective

What is lacking, however, is a volume that enables a group of distinguished Danish film-makers to situate their views on their craft and cinematic achievements within a larger historical and institutional context. This collection of interviews seeks to fill this lacuna by foregrounding the film-makers' conceptions of the emergence and development of contemporary Danish cinema, and of the role that particular individuals and works have played in the construction of a national cinema. The emphasis is placed on feature-length works of cinematic fiction, but other types of film-making are explored where relevant. The Danish documentary tradition is, for example, evoked in the interview with Henning Carlsen, who was trained by the important Danish documentary film-maker, Theodor Christensen (1914–67), and who made some 45 documentary films, including several modern classics, before embarking on a career as a feature film-maker. A similar strategy is employed in the interviews with Jon Bang Carlsen and Jørgen Leth who have both contributed significantly to the development of new trends within documentary film-making. A book dedicated uniquely to the Danish documentary film-makers would in itself be a worthwhile project, but the emphasis here is on the fiction film. The volume makes a contribution to the existing literature on Danish film inasmuch as it attempts to bridge the gap between critical, interpretive discourses and the views of the practitioners: what we have here is the film-makers' responses to the kinds of questions that have preoccupied scholars of national cinema for some time now.

An underlying assumption of much critical work on film is that the critic, by virtue of certain specialised skills, is better placed than the film-maker to identify and interpret the significance of a given work's key features. The idea is that practitioners rely primarily on the kind of tacit knowledge that emerges as a result of a longstanding engagement with a given set of practices, and remain focussed on a number of micro-level problems and solutions, rather than on overarching interpretations and symbolic meanings. Yet, as Johannes Riis (drawing on David Bordwell) points out in 'Toward a Poetics of the Short Film' (1998), the practitioners' views are important resources if the point of second-order, critical reflection is to provide an account of certain craft practices rather than to articulate general interpretations of a given film's hidden meanings. The view motivating this collection of interviews is clearly similar to the one endorsed by Riis, for the aim is not to encourage the pursuit of various forms of symbolic interpretation, but rather to promote an understanding of how, exactly, specific films are constructed and with what intentions. The interviewers have thus assumed throughout that a serious engagement with film requires some understanding of the film-makers' intentions. There can be little doubt that it is the film-makers themselves who have privileged access to precisely these intentions.

The idea that the intentions of film-makers should figure centrally in our attempts to come to grips with particular works was considered wrongheaded for decades but is gradually regaining some ground. It should be noted, however, that the trivialising of film-makers' intentions was characteristic only of a specialised critical response to film, for the reception of film by popular or non-specialist audiences has always included an element of intense fascination for the personalities of film. Nor is this fascination merely the result of an industry's cynical attempts systematically to produce a series of intriguing *auteurs* for purely commercial purposes. Rather, the popular response reflects the typically Romantic view of the artist as a being who is intensely attuned to the moral sources that shape our lives. As Charles Taylor has argued at great length in his groundbreaking work, *Sources of the Self: The Making of the Modern Identity* (1989) and in 'The Politics of Recognition' (1992), identity is inwardly generated in the modern period, rather than socially derived, as was the case in the pre-modern era. That is, modern identities are no longer automatically established at birth by particular forms of social belonging, but gradually discovered and consolidated as our lives unfold. Artists, claims Taylor, occupy a privileged place in the landscape of modernity precisely because they are perceived as capable of articulating and hence clarifying the largely implicit moral frameworks that shape our modern identities. An eloquent spokesperson for this view within the context of Danish cinema is the remarkably prolific film-maker, Jørgen Leth, whose oeuvre includes a number of films about outstanding artistic figures and sports figures, examples being *Peter Martins: A Dancer* (*Peter Martins – en danser*, 1978) and *Stars and Watercarriers* (*Stjernerne og vandbærerne*, 1973). In the interview included in this volume, Leth points out that the films in question were attempts to unsettle the typically Danish idea that all instances of excellence must be submitted to the law of levelling that enshrines equality as an overarching value. In Leth's films attention is drawn to the ways in which the lives and accomplishments of outstanding figures can be understood as generally enriching, precisely because they depart from the ordinary.

Whereas an externalist, critical perspective on the history of Danish film registers primarily a series of shifting emphases on various genres and visual styles, the kind of internalist perspective afforded by this collection of interviews has the effect of foregrounding some of the psychological dimensions of the shifts in question. Henning Carlsen's interview is particularly revealing in this respect, for his statements shed light on the dynamics of intergenerational agon in the context of a small nation, where resources necessarily are limited. Carlsen goes so far as to claim that his latest film, *I Wonder Who's Kissing You Now?* (1998) finds its origin and inspiration in a series of dark, brooding fits of jealousy provoked by the successes of a younger generation devoted, among other things, to a visual style shaped importantly by hand-held cameras. While young graduates from the National Film School secured generous state funding for their films in the late 1980s and 1990s, Henning Carlsen, the director of such classics of the cinema as *Hunger* (*Sult*, 1966), was left to contend with a series of rejections that effectively barred him from film-making for almost a decade. (*Wolf at the Door*/*Oviri*, Carlsen's film about Gauguin and his Danish wife, Mette Gad, was released in 1986, and *Two Green Feathers*/*Pan*, the film-maker's next film, in 1995). *I Wonder Who's Kissing You Now?* is Carlsen's attempt not only to explore in detail the nature and effects of jealousy, but to transform what is essentially a negative and destructive emotion into a source of creative inspiration. Carlsen's reflections on this film movingly foreground the extent to which new tendencies within a modern art world dedicated to innovation are purchased at a price.

The interviews collected here take seriously, then, not only the revived interest in intentional analysis, but the popular conception of the artist. As a result emphasis is placed both on questions of craftsmanship and on the deeper values and convictions motivating the commitment to various forms of contemporary Danish film-making. The deeply moving narratives of courage, stubborn conviction, passion, disappointment and sheer hard work are as important here as are, for example, the reflections on camera work, cinematic style and generic conventions.

## Film as art, industry and institution

Yet, if these interviews are about artists and their art or about craftsmen and their craft, they are also about the culture industry, for film-making is both a business and an art. Together the interviews shed light on the evolution of the Danish film industry during the second half of the twentieth century, a period that embraces veterans such as Gabriel Axel and Henning Carlsen and young luminaries such as Thomas Vinterberg and Lotte Svendsen. Key historical developments become apparent as the views and voices of younger directors are brought into dialogue with those of reflective older film-makers capable of situating their work in relation to crucial shifts, tendencies and institutional arrangements. The interviews also help to identify the specificity of contemporary Danish film as a product of both private investments and various forms of state intervention and support. Finally, the volume explores a number of enduring issues and challenges related to Denmark's status as a small nation-state. Inasmuch as questions of language, audience and influence are framed in terms of an opposition between small nations and large nations, the film-makers' responses provide insight into the specificity of the film-making of a small, but privileged nation (Hjort, 1996).

A key difference separating various generations of Danish film-makers has to do with the nature of their original training in film. A veteran film-maker such as Henning Carlsen, who celebrated his 50th anniversary in the Danish film industry in 1998, was trained on the job during his years as an assistant to the renowned Danish documentary film-maker, Theodor Christensen. Gabriel Axel, another prominent veteran, came to film via theatre and TV. The apprenticeship model still constituted a viable and salient path into the world of Danish film during the late 1960s, the early years of the National Film School's existence. The generation of film-makers born in the 1940s thus includes figures who opted for the apprenticeship model (e.g. Morten Arnfred), as well as some of the first graduates from the National Film School (Christian Braad Thomsen and Anders Refn). It also includes the complete auto-didact, Nils Malmros, and versatile artists such as Erik Clausen and Helle Ryslinge, whose ability to secure State funding for their initial film-making projects was based, not on formal training in the art of cinematic production, but rather on their established profiles within other artistic domains.

The National Film School was established in 1966 and suffered from an initial lack of leadership and vision. By the mid-1970s, however, this institution was set on the course

15

that would make it a key element in the renewal of Danish film in the long run. At this point, the Film School is viewed as contributing directly to the recent successes of Danish film. What is more, it is now widely regarded by aspiring young film-makers as an institutionalised entrance ticket to the national film industry. Yet, the central role played by the National Film School by no means commands unambiguous approval, for loyal proponents of the now virtually defunct apprenticeship model are sceptical, not only of the school's gate-keeping function, but of the normative grids it employs to discipline the creative energies of young film-makers. Erik Clausen reveals himself in his interview to be a particularly eloquent opponent of the Film School's dominance.

The Film School is a central part of the Danish film industry's ongoing process of professionalisation, or, less controversially, an expression of changing conceptions of what qualifies as professional film-making. The relevant shifts in attitude find a parallel in the Danish Film Institute's emphasis from 1989 onwards on script development, seed grants and more professional distribution and marketing mechanisms. Interestingly, the growing emphasis on standardised methods and procedures has had the effect of constituting some of Denmark's most successful film-makers as novices incapable of meeting the norms imposed by a complicated vetting system. Helle Ryslinge points out that she was able in the mid-1980s to secure funding from the Danish Film Institute for her first feature film, *Coeurs flambés* (*Flamberede hjerter*, 1986) on the basis of a one-page project description. The assumption now is that quality is best guaranteed by a system of assessment that requires film-makers to submit detailed treatments and fully developed scripts as part of their application for state funds. In this sense the Danish Film Institute and its policy-makers clearly support the view espoused by Angus Finney (1996) and others, who identify poor script development as one of the causes of the crisis faced by many of the European film industries during the last few decades and prior to the more positive developments in the mid-1990s. At the same time, film-makers such as Helle Ryslinge and Christian Braad Thomsen argue passionately that the current situation favours one conception of art over another inasmuch as an intensely visual mode of expression is held ultimately to be wholly grounded in the kind of literary expression that scripts necessarily must be. Ryslinge takes her critique one step further when she contends that the present arrangement in fact betrays the spirit and letter of the Danish Film Act, inasmuch as what is actually supported is the film industry, rather than film art. However, interestingly this traditional opposition between film as industry and film as art is somewhat less sharp in the minds of the younger Danish directors, who also seem committed to blurring the boundaries between the popular genre films and the more narrow art films. The interview collection thus brings to the fore a number of striking shifts in the very understanding of film as a form of artistic and cultural expression.

## National film culture and internationalisation

The interviewers' questions systematically foreground changing definitions of Danish film, the role that natural language plays in sustaining cultural identity and the question of what kind of Danish should be promoted or utilised in Danish films. When Christian Braad Thomsen began his career as a film-maker in the early 1970s, he took issue with what he perceived to be the stilted, overly theatrical use of the Danish language in film.

What he rejected, essentially, was the pattern of speech that was preserved and transmitted by the Royal Danish Theatre, which was where most successful Danish actors received their training. The challenge, as far as Braad Thomsen was concerned, was cinematically to capture the genuine diversity of Danish speech cultures and idioms. It was a matter, more specifically, of recognising the extent to which the Danish nation is comprised of citizens whose speech departs radically from the allegedly neutral high Danish that finds its historical origins in the capital and is mediated through the national educational system and official public institutions.[3] Braad Thomsen's admirable project was to record various forms of spoken Danish and thereby to reveal the extent to which the nation's citizens are marked, not only by national culture, but by regional differences and oppositions between rural and urban areas. Regional dialects and a variety of urban sociolects thus figure centrally in Braad Thomsen's work, but also in the films of directors belonging to the same generation, Jon Bang Carlsen, for example, and not least Nils Malmros, whose cinematic universe, linguistically, socially and culturally, is rooted in the provincial town of Århus.

Interestingly, the situation faced by young film-makers today is virtually diametrically opposed to the one identified by Braad Thomsen in the 1970s. Thomas Vinterberg, for example, now claims that the challenge is to make room for eloquence and linguistic precision in Danish film. The speech patterns associated, not only with informal communication, but with certain life-worlds now function as one of the norms that innovative film-makers can and allegedly must contest as they seek to renew indigenous forms of cinematic expression. Many of the younger Danish film-makers remain committed to everyday speech patterns and various sociolects, including, increasingly, the characteristic linguistic tendencies of new Danes of immigrant background. Yet Vinterberg foregrounds the need for greater clarity and the kind of nuanced expression that makes possible a sincere and penetrating exploration of various forms of interiority. In this sense Vinterberg appears to be pursuing something like the 'new inwardness' that has been identified by Lars von Trier in connection with Zentropa's and TV2' revival of the sentimental novels by Morten Korch and return to a more theatrical tradition.

The institutional framework for Danish film-making has changed considerably over the last ten years or so, with the introduction of a number of specialised programs and budget lines. The interview questions repeatedly identify the relevant policy changes and programs, thereby allowing film-makers to articulate their views, for example, on the internationalisation of Danish film, various co-production and co-financing arrangements, the Film Institute's low budget program, New Fiction Film Denmark,* and the so-called '50/50' or '60/40' policy.* As a result the interviews provide a clear indication of how film-makers perceive the policies that constitute the general context of production for contemporary Danish film.

The internationalisation of Danish film is typically associated with the creation of Eurimages in 1988 and the Nordic Film and TV Fund in 1990, but it is also directly reflected in the Danish Film Acts'* liberalisation over the years of the very definition of a Danish film. The 1972 Film Act explicitly specified that a film could qualify as Danish, if and only if, it made use of the Danish language and of primarily Danish artists and technical personnel, and this requirement could be waived only after a special dispensation from the Ministry of Culture. The 1989 Film Act, on the other hand, introduced an important disjunction that makes possible, for example, English-language Danish films. More specifically, the requirement is that a film can qualify as Danish if it makes use of the Danish language or makes a special artistic or technical contribution that helps to promote film art and film culture in Denmark.[4]

The cinematic internationalisation of the late 1980s and early 1990s was in many respects an example of what Ben Lee and other members of the Center for Transnational Studies in Chicago (1992) have referred to as 'corporate multiculturalism', for the process was driven to an important extent by strategic or economic motives. The overarching goal, more specifically, was to secure the kinds of funds needed to compete with big-budget films being produced elsewhere, especially by Hollywood. If 'internationalisation' once had a positive ring to it, many now find that the term grates on the ears, and as Henning Carlsen and Susanne Bier point out, the emphasis is now placed, not so much on a concept of co-production as on a notion of co-financing that keeps financial and cultural questions separate. There has been a shift, then, from corporate multiculturalism to what, following Lee and his fellow researchers, might be termed 'critical multiculturalism'. The project of internationalisation has, in other words, been reframed in properly cultural terms, for it is now widely recognised that attempts to subordinate matters of cultural expression to questions of finance tend to produce films that are problematic precisely because they lack recognisable or plausible cultural identities.

The shift from the strategy of co-production to that of co-financing was in large part a result of critical reactions to a number of films that were perceived to have failed in similar ways. These instances of failed internationalism have been referred to informally as 'Nordic puddings' or 'Europuddings' on account of their confusing conflation of national styles, idioms and identities. Failed cinematic internationalism is thus frequently identified with a view from nowhere, for the films in question convey neither a national nor a local perspective, just as they fail to express a consistent artistic vision. Films, it is now argued, must come from somewhere, that is, must have a recognisable origin. In this volume accomplished film-makers such as Henning Carlsen and Susanne Bier reflect probingly and frankly on some of their less successful films in an attempt to clarify the limitations of the earlier approach to international film-making. At the same time, they point out that the early period of internationalisation had a number of positive effects, which prepared the ground for a less haphazard and more reflective form of transnationalism. Bier, in particular, emphasises the emergence of transnational networks and the articulation and circulation of multicultural narratives that begin to focus attention, not on national identities, but on supranational identities and a dialogue of cultures.

There is considerable agreement at this point among film scholars and members of the Danish film industry that Danish cinema, in the foreseeable future, will exhibit at least two tendencies. In his cogent contribution to *Dansk Film 1972-97* (Bondebjerg et al., eds, 1997), Jesper Andersen from the Danish Film Institute convincingly argues that big-budget film-making based on extensive collaboration between a considerable number of co-financing partners will be anything but an exclusive or dominant trend in Danish film, for emphasis will also be placed on relatively inexpensive films that can be financed primarily nationally, that is, with state monies earmarked for film. Two recent initiatives on the part of the Danish Film Institute are particularly important in this respect. New Fiction Film Denmark was established in 1994 and is an independent form of support based on cooperation between the Danish Broadcasting Corporation, TV2 and the Danish Film Institute, and has as its mandate the funding of films lasting no more than sixty minutes. In 1997 a special grant from the Ministry of Culture made possible the creation of a low-budget fund administered by the Danish Film Institute and designed specifically to support films with a production budget under 5 million Crowns.[5]

Another important feature of the institutional landscape of contemporary Danish film is the 50/50 policy, which was originally envisioned in the 1989 Film Act and subsequently transformed into a 60/40 policy in 1997. This policy was introduced in order to ensure that the construction of a Danish national cinema is guided, not only by artistic considerations articulated by specialised members of an educated elite, but also by popular tastes and inclinations. Whereas funding from the Danish Film Institute could only previously be granted following a positive assessment on artistic grounds by one of the six appointed film consultants,* the 50/50 policy provided the possibility of effectively bypassing these gatekeepers. The policy in question involves an assessment in terms of both intrinsic dramatic qualities and audience potential by independent experts. A central premise is the possibility of securing at least half of the financing in advance from private sources, for government contributions are limited by a ceiling of three million Crowns (subsequently changed to five million with the shift to the 60/40 percentages). The policy was initially rather controversial, for it was used to fund some notoriously unsuccessful films, by any standard of success. At this point, however, it is clear that it has had the desired effect of renewing Danish film by means of a commitment to breadth and pluralism. Some of the most successful recent Danish films, in both artistic and box office terms, received government funding via this policy. Examples include Ole Bornedal's *Nightwatch* (1994), Jang Winding Refn's *Pusher* (1996), Susanne Bier's *The One and Only* (*Den eneste ene*, 1999) and a series of family entertainment films produced by Regner Grasten Film from 1992 onwards. Together these films have significantly enhanced Danish films' share of box office returns. The consultants do, however, continue to dispose over larger budgets and many of the more artistically significant Danish films that have been able to command international recognition received Danish monies via the consultancy system. This is true, for example, of all of Lars von Trier's films, as well as of Nils Malmros's, Søren Kragh-Jacobsen's and Bille August's films. The new policy has, however, had the effect of significantly expanding the range of Danish film and of calling attention in the Danish context to the important link between generic conventions and audience appeal. In his interview Bornedal clearly foregrounds the positive features of the relevant hands-off policy that is designed to promote popular, mainstream film-making. The renewal, quality and breadth of Danish film is thus ensured by means of a balance between policies that bypass artistic assessments and policies that rest precisely on artistic evaluations by changing consultants.[6]

The interview questions focus on another set of issues having to do with Denmark's status as a small, privileged nation involved in the production of what might be called a 'minor cinema'. According to Miroslav Hroch's (1985) influential account, small nations are characterised by a history of foreign rule that generates a structural relation of subjugation. On this view, Denmark belongs, not to the category of small nations, but rather to the category of large nations, which is defined by the rule of co-nationals and, in some instances, by the subjugation of foreign nations. Yet, as Ernest Gellner (1996) incisively points out in a critique of Hroch's views, 'Danes appear to be consigned to the "large nation", which can hardly be correct in some simple numerical sense'. The 'numerical' issues that Hroch ignores are indeed worth taking seriously inasmuch as they generate a specific set of challenges and problems. Underwriting many of the interview questions, then, is the assumption that Denmark can be usefully viewed as a small nation involved in the production of a minor cinema for the following reasons: 1. The size of its population is too small to sustain a commercially based, indigenous film industry. 2. The language spoken by the nation in question, Danish, is understood primarily by Danes, making it difficult to expand the market for Danish film through exports. 3. A key problem for the indigenous film industry is the ongoing influx of American films. The film-makers are thus consistently asked to reflect on questions having to do with target audiences, language and the construction of a national, cinematic culture in an internationalised film industry shaped importantly by Hollywood.

In the context of Denmark viewed as a small nation, the relation between certain films and already established discourses of Danishness is particularly important (Hjort, 2001). These discourses may be anchored in key historical events, in the lives of figures who are considered to be central to the nation's self-understanding and cultural specificity or in canonised literary works (Hjort, 2000). In some cases it seems to be a matter of using already established cultural discourses as a leveraging device to secure in advance a certain national audience for a given film. Yet, as the interviews with Bille August, Søren Kragh-Jacobsen, Anders Refn and Jørgen Leth make clear, the mobilisation of already existing discourses of Danishness is never purely a matter of pragmatic considerations. Nor is this kind of project necessarily aimed at further enshrining certain monumental figures within the relevant national heritage. Indeed, in many cases existing discourses of Danishness are reanimated with a critical intent. For example, Leth's remarkable films about the Danish Bournonville tradition of dance or about the outstanding dancer, Peter Martins, are designed to make room for notions of excellence within a culture committed fervently to radical equality. In his period films, Anders Refn draws on literary works by the Danish writer Gustav Wied in order precisely to challenge the conception of country living that is expressed in the popular Morten Korch films, Denmark's contribution to the heritage film genre.

Another recurrent issue linked to small nation status is the question of language. Natural language in Danish film is a complicated phenomenon that has been insufficiently explored in critical discussions. It is first of all a matter of clarifying the diverse implications of an asymmetrical relation between major and minor tongues that to some extent underwrites the choice of English in, for example, Lars von Trier's *Element of Crime* (*Forbrydelsens element*, 1987) or Bille August's *House of the Spirits* (1993). More interesting, perhaps, is the complicated interplay within the small nation-state of Denmark of high Danish, various forms of regionalised Danish, and a range of sociolects reflecting, among other things, class differences. Danish film has been largely dominated by the high Danish (*rigsdansk*) that is associated with the capital and official culture and that is disseminated by the media and through the state school system.[7] A case in point is Erik Clausen's *Carl, My Childhood Symphony* (*Min fynske barndom*, 1994) which features high Danish although it is a partially fictionalised account of key years in the life of the famous Danish composer, Carl Nielsen, with special emphasis on his roots in the provinces. Whereas some film-makers view the consistent gravitation towards high Danish as nothing more than a convenient convention, other film-makers, such as Nils Malmros and Lotte Svendsen, are clearly attuned to the deeper political issues involved in the imposition of a high culture in the name of a folk culture, or the consistent dissemination of the linguistic cultures of the capital throughout the regions and provinces of the nation-state of Denmark. Nils Malmros' stubborn insistence on using the provincial *århusiansk* in most of his films can thus be seen as a way of contesting certain dominant, national identities, as can Lotte Svendsen's decision to use *bornholmsk* in her most recent film, *Gone with the Fish* (*Bornholms stemme*, 1999). Of interest in this respect is also Christian Braad Thomsen's earlier project of capturing and preserving the Jutlandic dialect through film.

Finally, the interview questions are designed to clarify Danish film-makers' understanding of their relation, not only to certain indigenous or national cinematic traditions, but also to European and American film, especially Hollywood. The relevant self-understandings vary radically and reveal strikingly different attitudes towards the very idea of a national cinema, just as internationalisation clearly has created new relations to especially American film. The generation that emerges in the 1970s is typically very critical of earlier periods of Danish film and tends to regard the Danish genre films from particularly the classic period as examples of a mainstream film culture without artistic merit. As far as directors such as Christian Braad Thomsen, Erik Clausen, Anders Refn, Morten Arnfred, Nils Malmros, Søren Kragh-Jacobsen and Bille August are concerned, Danish film as an artistic tradition was virtually non-existent in the 1970s. These figures, it appears, saw themselves as initiating, rather than continuing, the project of serious film-making in Denmark, and the European art cinema of the 1960s was for them a key source of inspiration. But in the case of some of these directors – Anders Refn, for example – it was also a matter of appropriating aspects of various American genre film traditions.

The younger generation of directors who emerge in the 1990s follow a rather different tack, both with regard to their international affiliations and national commitments. Lars von Trier's films, for example, reveal a deep respect for Dreyer and key figures in European film, such as Tarkovsky. However, as is the case for the entire generation in question, his films are also dialogues with the American and Danish genre film traditions, which are considered anything but trivial. Trier has consciously sought out and tried to renew genres such as film noir, the melodrama and the musical, with constant reference to Hollywood, but on his own terms. What is more, the Korch project that von Trier and Zentropa have initiated is a provocative revival of what in intellectual and artistic circles functions as the most vilified element of Danish mainstream film culture. Generally speaking members of the younger generation, which includes Thomas

Vinterberg, Lotte Svendsen and Ole Bornedal, express a more positive relation to the tradition of popular Danish film and American film, even as they affirm the commitment of earlier generations of Danish film-makers to European art cinema. Bornedal, for example, is thus both a great admirer of Bergman and of the American genre film tradition. The interviews suggest that Danish film at the outset of the new millennium has found ways of dealing successfully with some of the limitations and inferiority complexes that attach to a minor cinema produced by a small nation in a significantly globalised cinematic culture. Danish film-makers at this point are emphasising indigenous genres while connecting with a wide range of national and transnational traditions in ways that have proven capable of commanding interest and respect both nationally and internationally.

1   For a brief overview of the history of Danish cinema, see Engberg (1990). Schepelern et al., eds (1997) provides a more detailed account of the various decades of Danish film. Contemporary Danish film from 1972 onwards is explored in aesthetic, institutional and statistic terms in Bondebjerg et al., eds (1997).

2   So far five Danish Dogme films have been released: Thomas Vinterberg's *The Celebration* (*Festen*, 1998), Lars von Trier's *The Idiots* (*Idioterne*, 1998), Søren Kragh-Jacobsen's *Mifune* (*Mifunes sidste sang*, 1999), Kristian Levring's *The King is Alive* (2000) and Lone Scherfig's *Italian for Beginners* (*Italiensk for begyndere*, 2001).

3   See Brink and Lund (1975).

4   The willingness to loosen the criterion of Danishness in the Film Act was very much a result of developments in the area of Nordic and European co-productions. But another key factor was undoubtedly the fact that Lars von Trier's films, starting with *The Element of Crime* (1984), could not be legally accommodated and thus required a special dispensation. Today English-language films by Danish directors are normally accepted as Danish if they satisfy the clause that emphasises a special artistic contribution to Danish cinematic culture.

5   The money in question was a source of considerable controversy between the Ministry of Culture and the Danish Film Institute. The earlier Minister of Culture had, without consulting the Film Institute, virtually promised the money to the Dogme directors. Yet, as far as the Danish Film Institute was concerned, such a promise thwarted the Institute's sovereign right to determine which films are worthy of support. The Institute thus insisted that the Dogme directors be required to follow standard procedures in their bid for monies. They, on the other hand, refused to apply on these terms. The monies from the Ministry of Culture were as a result used to fund a number of other low-budget productions. The Dogme project was instead funded by the Danish Broadcasting Corporation following a judicious intervention on the part of the program director, Bjørn Erichsen. New leadership at the Danish Film Institute did, however, subsequently make various forms of support for the project possible.

6   The point of limiting the consultants' contracts to three years, and of assigning three consultants to the area of feature film-making and another three to the area of short films and documentaries, is to ensure that producers and directors have a certain amount of leeway and to attenuate the risk of a given set of tastes dominating in the long run.

7   There are a number of historical exceptions to the norm of high Danish in Danish film. Certain Danish comedies from the 1930s and many of the Korch films cultivate dialects that are reminiscent of certain peasant comedies, especially Holberg's *Jeppe of the Hill* (*Jeppe på Bjerget*) and *Erasmus Montanus*. Relevant films in this regard are *Rasmine's Wedding* (*Rasmines Bryllup*, 1935) and *Bolette's Wedding* (*Bolettes Brudefærd*, 1938). See also the comic roles in the Korch films, especially Peter Malberg's role as the ever faithful helper figure.

# Four Generations of Danish Directors

## Ib Bondebjerg and Mette Hjort

When Gabriel Axel, the first and eldest representative of Danish directors to be included in this volume, made his debut as a film director with *Nothing but Trouble* (*Altid ballade*, 1955) Lars von Trier was not even born. This provides some indication of the historical and generational scope of this book, which encompasses four generations of directors with dates of birth ranging from 1918 to 1969. These dates establish a spectrum from the dominance of silent film to the decade in which Danish film became wholly dependent on a cultural politics of state support. Together the directors' debuts chart a number of key phases, including the classic Danish film culture of the 1950s, the European new wave of the 1960s, the modern, realistic decade of the 1970s and the internationalisation of Danish film in the 1990s.

Gabriel Axel is a product of a film culture that received virtually no state support. In that context popular Danish comedies and erotic farces provided the commercial basis for a mainstream film culture that occasionally produced more artistically ambitious films. While Axel here represents the oldest generation of Danish film-makers, which includes the accomplished Astrid Henning-Jensen and, not least, the unsurpassed Danish master of popular film, Erik Balling, he has also played a key role in Danish film's most recent international breakthrough. Whereas most of the directors belonging to this early generation were firmly rooted in Danish culture and traditions, Axel pursued a dual career in Denmark and France. And Axel's internationally oriented films – *The Red Mantle* (*Den røde kappe*, 1967), *The Prince of Jutland* (*Prinsen af Jylland*, 1994) and *Babette's Feast* (*Babettes gæstebud*, 1987) – variously prefigure the internationalisation of Danish film in the 1990s. The eldest of the represented directors, who is still active and in the process of shooting yet another film, can thus be said to have prepared the way for the youngest generation's international trajectory.

The next generation is represented by Henning Carlsen and Jørgen Leth, whose decisive breakthrough marks the emergence of a modern Danish film culture in the 1960s, concurrently with and as a response to the European new waves. The breadth of their work is similar, for they have both contributed to the development of modern Danish documentary film-making and to the artistic renewal of Danish fiction film. Their points of departure and artistic temperaments are, however, quite different, which may to some extent be a reflection of the ten years that separate them. Carlsen's training occurred in the film industry where he found a basis in classic documentary film-making. Yet, his documentary films initiate and mark the transition from the classic documentaries of the 1940s and 1950s to the more open, observational documentaries of the 1960s (Bondebjerg 1996). His remarkable feature, *Hunger* (*Sult*, 1966) articulates key tendencies within the 1960s new wave realism, and has played a decisive role, along with later films, such as *Wolf at the Door* (*Oviri*, 1986) and *Two Green Feathers* (*Pan*, 1995), in situating Danish film on the world map of cinema. With his background in concrete poetry, Leth is intimately connected with the artistic experimentalism that is part of the

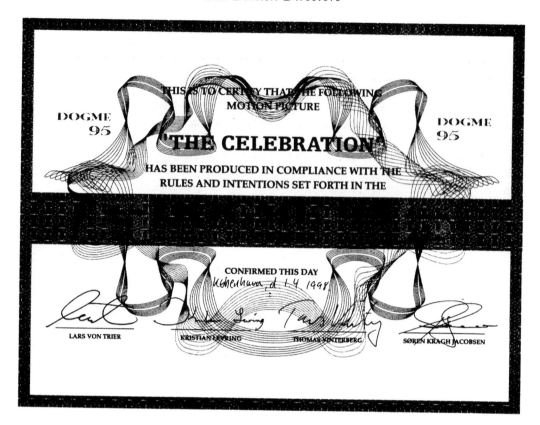

THIS IS TO CERTIFY THAT THE FOLLOWING
MOTION PICTURE

DOGME 95

'THE CELEBRATION'

HAS BEEN PRODUCED IN COMPLIANCE WITH THE
RULES AND INTENTIONS SET FORTH IN THE

DOGME 95

CONFIRMED THIS DAY

København, d 14 1998

LARS VON TRIER     KRISTIAN LEVRING     THOMAS VINTERBERG     SØREN KRAGH JACOBSEN

*Dogme 95 Certificate*

modernism of the 1960s. Leth's oeuvre includes a large number of experimental short films, documentaries and features. He is also a well-known TV personality, not only on account of his films about sports, but also as a result of his skilful commentaries on the Tour de France. Leth's film topics and public persona express a cosmopolitanism that involves roots in a distinct national context as well as a broad international horizon.

The directors belonging to the third generation featured here were all born in the 1940s and established themselves as professional film-makers in the course of the 1970s, with the exception of Helle Ryslinge whose directorial breakthrough came in the mid-1980s. But Ryslinge, Jytte Rex, Christian Braad Thomsen, Erik Clausen, Anders Refn, Morten Arnfred, Nils Malmros, Søren Kragh-Jacobsen, Bille August and Jon Bang Carlsen are all part of the generation that was able to profit from new and enhanced forms of state support for Danish film as well as from new vocational opportunities. Yet, a salient feature of this generation compared to the subsequent one is that only half of the relevant film-makers opted for training at a specialised film school such as the National Film School of Denmark.* On-site training in the industry or alternative routes involving other artistic activities still play an important role for this generation. This is a generation that was heavily immersed at key moments in alternative culture, left wing politics, the women's movement and the youth revolt, and this is clearly reflected in the central place that socially committed forms of cinematic realism occupy in the film-makers' cinematic production. At the same time there is no monolith here, for together the film-makers' work includes many different tendencies. Rex and Ryslinge both found a point of departure in feminism, but ended up travelling along very different aesthetic tracks. As a visual artist Rex is concerned with symbolic modes of expression, whereas Ryslinge combines comedy and satire with gender politics. Much like Rex, Bang Carlsen has been less interested in film as narrative than in film as a form of symbolic, visual expression. He has over the years developed a largely original form of staged documentary film-making which he has brought to bear on both national and other milieux and cultures. Much like Ryslinge, Clausen came to film, not via the industry or some film school, but via other artistic activities. Clausen is a painter, popular satirist and comedian, and his contribution as a film-maker has been to inject new social issues and political concerns into Danish comedy. The left-wing intellectual, Braad Thomsen, has for decades been an acerbic critic of various tendencies within Danish film culture and of related policies of state support that could be seen as somehow catering to commercialism and popular tastes. In both his fiction and nonfiction film-making, Braad Thomsen has cultivated themes of social realist inspiration as well as issues inspired by Freudian conceptions. Anders Refn, who was part of the second cohort to attend the Danish Film School, has had a two-fold impact on Danish film: his period films and literary adaptations constitute significant innovations within the Danish heritage film tradition and encourage a more socially aware engagement with the cultural past; his dialogue with a rather slender Danish crime genre tradition amounts to a significant internationalisation of national conceptions.

The many faces of realism in contemporary Danish film have been articulated by four of the directors belonging to this third generation: Arnfred, Kragh-Jacobsen, Malmros and August. Like many others of his generation, Arnfred found a starting point in the anti-authoritarian youth film of the 1970s. In his earlier films he explored, among other things, working class culture and aspects of country life, and in the course of the 1990s he, much like several other Danish directors, turned towards a more internationally oriented form of genre film-making. Kragh-Jacobsen's strengths similarly have to do with the depiction of the lives of children and adolescents. In his case, however, the relevant realities are explored through aesthetic styles ranging from social to magical realism. Kragh-Jacobsen's participation in the Dogme* project bespeaks a commitment to cinematic renewal, and his own Dogme film, *Mifune* (*Mifunes sidste sang*, 1999) was a major international breakthrough. Malmros, a genuine auteur and perhaps the greatest psychological realist of Danish cinema, has dedicated himself largely to film-making in a national, even regional vein, for his accounts of the psychological and sexual development of children or depictions of tragic female figures are in most instances set in his home town, Århus. August is this generation's most internationally established figure, and his career is marked by phases that largely coincide with the evolution of Danish film as a whole since 1972. His early films (1978–84) are socially committed representations of some of the welfare state's weaker citizens and tend to emphasise the

*Björk as the Czech immigrant, Selma, in Lars von Trier's* Dancer in the Dark

plight of women, children and young people. Together with his TV productions, these films contributed significantly to the realistic wave of the period in question. August's *Pelle the Conqueror* (*Pelle Erobreren*, 1987) is the first of a number of internationally acclaimed Nordic co-productions. It won the *Palmes d'or* at Cannes (as did *The Best Intentions/Den goda viljan*, 1992), as well as the Oscar for Best Foreign Film, and helped to prepare the ground for Danish film's international breakthrough in the 1990s. During the 1990s August increasingly emphasised mainstream film-making and, more specifically, the adaptation of canonised novels or contemporary bestsellers.

Lars von Trier functions as a somewhat older mentor figure and model for the fourth and youngest generation in this volume, although the directors who emerge in the 1990s and were born in the 1960s have not necessarily looked to his films for aesthetic or stylistic inspiration. But it was von Trier, born in 1956, who first began to reject the dominant modes of expression associated with Danish national film culture in the 1970s and 1980s, and this critical reckoning became a point of departure for the most recent generation of film-makers. Indeed, the rejection of realism as a norm and affirmation of a general orientation towards European art cinema and American genre films are characteristic not only of von Trier, but of most of the more recent directors. Dogme 95, which was initiated by von Trier, has served further to enhance this director's impact, both nationally and internationally. At the same time, this project helps to build bridges between the generations inasmuch as the film collective in question includes Søren Kragh-Jacobsen.

This volume includes interviews with younger directors who represent three important tendencies within contemporary Danish cinema. Ole Bornedal represents a trend involving the valorisation of some of the more desperate and spectacular action genres of international inspiration and an American-style depiction of the city and its subcultures. Susanne Bier, Lotte Svendsen and Jonas Elmer are all associated with various attempts to renew the Danish comedy tradition. Bier has worked deftly with modern romantic comedy; Svendsen has opted to pursue a more surreal form of social comedy; and Elmer has used improvisational techniques to produce comedy with a distinctive poetic quality. Last but not least, Thomas Vinterberg's work combines various elements. His first feature *The Greatest Heroes* (*De største helte*, 1996) in some ways parallels films by Bornedal and Nicolas Winding Refn in its focus on two desperate young men and their journey through Sweden in one of the few road movies of the new Danish cinema. Vinterberg has also revived and renewed a dramatic and to some extent magical psychological realism that brings together traits from various Scandinavian, European and American traditions. Key films in this regard are his short film *The Boy Who Walked Backwards* (*Drengen der gik baglæns*, 1993) and his Dogme film, *The Celebration* (*Festen*, 1998).

*The Danish Directors: Dialogues on a Contemporary National Cinema* evokes four generations of Danish film history as seen through the eyes of a series of leading directors. It clearly establishes that Danish cinema is many things and that the film culture of this small nation emerges through intense interaction between national and international impulses and embraces many different tendencies in much the same way that the film cultures of larger nations do. The films of the Danish directors reveal certain constants across the generations, but at the same time there are also decisive differences, some of which have to do with the changes that the institutional parameters of Danish film-making underwent in the course of the second half of the twentieth century. Whereas, for example, international recognition was an isolated phenomenon in some of the earlier periods in question here, the younger directors associated with the new wave of the 1990s operate within a context that is characterised by global orientations and an optimism that is importantly fuelled by a recent international valorisation of Danish film. Many of these younger directors clearly feel a strong attachment to various indigenous cultures, but they are also children of an increasingly global reality involving a reconfiguration of relations among national (Danish and American) and supranational (Nordic and European) elements. Some of these directors have chosen at times to work outside Denmark, whereas others have opted to travel beyond the borders of Denmark in spirit alone. Yet, in both cases there is evidence to suggest that we are dealing here with a generation that finds its roots, not only in national culture, but in cosmopolitan, international and global connections.

# Gabriel Axel

## 1918–

Gabriel Axel was originally trained at the Royal Danish Theatre School. Prior to his breakthrough as a film and TV director, he worked as an actor in both France and Denmark. He is one of the most productive directors of the early period of Danish TV theatre, having produced some 50 televised plays between 1951 and 1970. These productions include both classical and modern plays, as well as the first Danish TV series, *Rainy Weather and No Money* (*Regnvejr og ingen penge*, 1965). Axel's contribution as a film director is varied and embraces films in a realistic vein, erotic comedies, popular comedies, and epics based on classic works of literature. His first feature film, *Nothing but Trouble* (*Altid ballade*, 1955), which focuses on a working class family, is one of the best Danish realist films of the 1950s. *Golden Mountains* (*Guld og grønne skove*, 1958) is a subtle social satire about provincial Danes' encounter with the modern world during the post-war period, and is one of the

Gabriel Axel

finest Danish comedies of the 1950s. *Crazy Paradise* (*Det tossede paradis*, 1962) was the first in a series of erotic comedies that was to establish Axel internationally. The sheer range of Axel's creative talent is evident in the modernistic and symbolic *Paradise and Back* (*Paradis retur*, 1964). Axel's first major attempt at a historical epic, *The Red Mantle* (*Den røde kappe*, 1967), did poorly at the Danish box office and was almost uniformly dismissed by the Danish critics. Interestingly, the film's reception was quite different elsewhere in the world. In 1977 the Danish Broadcasting Corporation informed Axel that they had no use for his talents during the upcoming year. As a result he moved to France where he went on to enjoy a highly successful career in French TV. He was, for example, awarded the prestigious Balzac prize for *The Night Watch* (*La Ronde de nuit*, 1977). In 1987 he made a strong comeback in Danish film with his adaptation of Karen Blixen's short story, *Babette's Feast* (*Babettes gæstebud*) which was the first Danish film ever to win an Oscar as Best Foreign Film. The road movie, *Christian* (1989), was poorly received, as was *The Prince of Jutland* (*Prinsen af Jylland*, 1994), which draws on Saxo Grammaticus' account of Amled and features established English-speaking actors in the leading roles.

## Feature films
1955, *Nothing but Trouble (Altid ballade)*
1957, *A Woman not Wanted (En kvinde er overflødig)*
1958, *Golden Mountains (Guld og grønne skove)*
1959, *My Helen (Helle for Helene)*
1960, *Flemming and Kvik (Flemming og Kvik)*
1962, *Crazy Paradise (Det tossede paradis)*
1962, *Oskar*
1963, *But We're Fine (Vi har det jo dejligt)*
1963, *Three Girls in Paris (Tre piger i Paris)*
1964, *Paradise and Back (Paradis retur)*
1967, *The Red Mantle (Den røde kappe)*
1968, *Danish Blue (Det kære legetøj)*
1970, *Amour*
1971, *With Love (Med kærlig hilsen)*
1975, *The Gyldenkål Family (Familien Gyldenkål)*
1976, *The Gyldenkål Family Breaks the Bank (Familien Gyldenkål sprænger banken)*
1977, *Going for Broke (Alt på et bræt)*
1987, *Babette's Feast (Babettes gæstebud)*
1989, *Christian*
1994, *The Prince of Jutland (Prinsen af Jylland)*
2000, *Laila the Pure (Laila Den Rene)*

## TV productions, Denmark (from a total of 49)
1951, *Death (Døden)*
1953, *Bear (En bjørn)*
1954, *A Celebration (En mindefest)*
1955, *A Woman is Superfluous (En kvinde er overflødig)*
1956, *Miss Julie (Frøken Julie)*
1957, *Forced to Wed (Det tvungne giftermål)*
1960, *The Eternal Husband (Den evige ægtemand)*
1965, *As They Like It (Retten på vrangen)*
1965 *Rainy Weather and No Money (Regnvejr og ingen penge*, episodes 1–4)

## TV productions, France
1977, *A Crime of Our Times (Un Crime de notre temps)*
1977, *The Night Watch (La Ronde de nuit)*
1979, *Curé de Tours (Le Curé de Tours)*
1979, *The Rooster (Le Coq de Bruyère)*
1979, *The Fishing Net Maid (La Ramendeuse)*
1981, *Antoine and Julie (Antoine et Julie)*
1981, *The Children's Blue Bird (L'Oiseau bleu)*
1984, *Heaven's Columns (Les Colonnes du ciel*, episodes 1–5)

## Acting roles

1953, *We Who Go the Kitchen Route* (*Vi som går køkkenvejen*, directed by Erik Balling)

1954, *Royal Visit* (*Kongeligt besøg*, directed by Erik Balling)

1954, *The Joys of Sharing* (*Det er så yndigt at følges ad*, directed by Torben Anton Svendsen)

1954, *The Sky is Blue* (*Himlen er blå*, directed by Svend Aage Lorentz)

1954, *Jan Goes to the Movies* (*Jan går til filmen*, directed by Torben Anton Svendsen and John Hilbert)

1954, *Karen, Maren and Mette* (*Karen, Maren og Mette*, directed by John Hilbert)

1955, *The Bride from Dragstrup* (*Bruden fra Dragstrup*, directed by Annelise Reenberg)

1955, *The Day Came When* (*Der kom en dag*, directed by Sven Methling)

1956, *Puss in the Corner* (*Kispus*, directed by Erik Balling)

1958, *Officer Karlsen* (*Styrmand Karlsen*, directed by Annelise Reenberg)

1961, *Peter's Baby* (*Peters baby*, directed by Annelise Reenberg)

1962, *He, She, Dirch and Dario* (*Han, hun, Dirch og Dario*, directed by Annelise Reenberg)

1963, *Three Girls in Paris* (*Tre piger i Paris*, directed by Gabriel Axel)

1965, *A Friend in Need of Housing* (*En ven i bolignøden*, directed by Annelise Reenberg)

1966, *Virtue Goes Overboard* (*Dyden går amok*, directed by Sven Methling)

1967, *I, a Nobleman* (*Jeg – en marki*, directed by Mac Ahlberg and Peer Guldbrandsen)

1971, *With Love* (*Med kærlig hilsen*, directed by Gabriel Axel)

1972, *Up and Coming* (*Nu går den på Dagmar*, directed by Henning Ørnbak)

1976, *The Gyldenkål Family Breaks the Bank* (*Familien Gyldenkål sprænger banken*, directed by Gabriel Axel)

1977, *Going for Broke* (*Alt på et bræt*, directed by Gabriel Axel)

**Bondebjerg:** You were trained at the Royal Danish Theatre School, and you were initially much more oriented towards theatre than film. You were employed in the Theatre Department at the Danish Broadcasting Corporation from 1951 to 1968, where you directed no fewer than fifty performances. What, for you, is the key difference between theatre, TV and film, and why did film and TV win out over the 'real' theatre in your case?

**Axel:** I don't feel that film and TV won out over theatre in my career. On the contrary. I've really used what I learnt through theatre in my film and TV work, namely, how to direct actors. When you've been an actor yourself, you know how actors feel. Most actors enjoy talking to a director who, with precision and without shouting, can identify what was good and bad about a given performance. Even stars and great actors like Michel Bouquet are grateful for incisive criticism. Actually, the more severe you are, the happier they are. So I don't know what I would have done without my training in theatre. Actors perform best if you, with just a few words, can help them to find the right feeling and expression. Louis Jouvet, my great teacher, said that the actor's great virtue is that he or she doesn't have to think, but rather feel and sense. If each of the actors in an ensemble begins to 'think' and interpret his role, then it becomes impossible to create a uniform tone and style. Take Stéphane Audran. She only needs a few words. As we were getting ready to shoot the scene in *Babette's Feast* where she's been down to the boat to collect her ingredients for her feast and is walking back through the village, she asked me what she should be like and what she should be feeling. 'Am I happy?' she asked. 'No, Stéphane, you can't be happy *before* you create your feast, but you are "serene" because you have all the ingredients you need in order to practise your art.' In her case that one word, serene, sufficed for an entire series of shots, from her walking through the village virtually to the conclusion of the dinner. If you give the actors the right words at the right moment, and if you establish a sense of trust, then they feel secure.

**Bondebjerg:** How did you end up in TV theatre and what, for you, is the key difference between TV and film?

**Axel:** It was very exciting. Jens Frederik Lawaetz had invited me and some other people to a meeting in the Radio House. There were about thirty of us, and we were told that TV would soon become a reality. Lawaetz then handed everyone a copy of *Politiken* and *Berlingske Tidende* and asked us to underline something that was of interest to us, for example, music, news, theatre, children, and so on. He collected his newspapers the following week, and on the basis of our indications he then decided who would be in the Drama Department, the Music Department, the News and Current Affairs Department, the Children's Department, and so on. I was placed in the Theatre Department and you can't possibly imagine what the conditions were like during those first years, or how primitive the techniques were. It was a unique experience, to say the least!

But the differences between TV and film are probably not that great. If you're going to tell a story within the small frame provided by TV, you compose the image differently. A striking difference is that you're more inclined to use close-ups in TV, but that's really the main one. There are also some technical differences. In the case of TV, the pace has to be really fast. A video camera is capable of a lot, and you can cut from one thing to the next while in the studio. You work without any clear light sources and you end up with a diffused light that lacks atmosphere. As a result it's tempting to overuse the zoom. That is, you tend to pull the actors or objects forwards and the entire background as well. A film camera that is on tracks can move towards the actor, and that makes for an entirely different kind of effect. Then there's the difference in format: the small screen versus the large screen. This has an impact on the aesthetics of the two media and their reception.

**Bondebjerg:** *Nothing but Trouble*, your first feature film, is based on a script by Leck Fischer, who drew on a Norwegian film from 1954 by Edith Calmar. *Nothing but Trouble* is, it seems to me, still one of your best films. It's also a very unusual film in the context of Danish film culture of the 1950s, for its depiction of a working class family is unsentimental, realistic, and in no way moralistic. *Nothing but Trouble* deals with the need for solidarity and love during a difficult period prior to the emergence of the welfare state. In this sense its message resembles that of many of your other films. What, exactly, is the origin of this film, and how do you see it today?

**Axel:** As a result of my work for TV, film companies like ASA and Nordisk started contacting me. Nordisk invited me to make *Nothing but Trouble*. I had children myself, including a little five year old boy, my first child, and parts of the film were of course shot from a child's point of view. In that film we also tried to create the mood and atmosphere that neo-realism, and especially de Sica, had evoked. In a way we also anticipated some of the things that the Dogme films are doing today. I told my cameraman that we needed what I called 'a little French sloppiness.' He'd give the camera a shove every now and again, so things would be less polished here and there. And one of the things we did in order, for example, to recreate the boy's perspective was to place the camera on the same level as his tricycle. We tried to recreate the authentic atmosphere of the Nørrebro area of Copenhagen. We shot the film in an apartment that was one metre from the train tracks, because we really wanted people to be able to feel the atmosphere. The atmosphere in a film stems from the hundreds of things that you can't see, but which you'd miss if they weren't there. Dreyer's films are saturated with atmosphere, not because there seem to be a lot of things in the image, but because nothing distracts from what's essential. At the same time it's more gratifying to try to create a realistic atmosphere in a black and white film. You avoid the danger of producing something resembling a postcard, which is the effect that colour can have. In order to foster the realism I was after, I'd use authentic experiences from my daily life in the scenes involving, for example, the mother and the little boy. At one point he's on the potty and he shouts: 'Mummy, I'm finished, it was just a fart.' My son had said precisely that earlier that morning and I simply used the sentence. It was wonderful and very inspiring to work with the little fellow. He was a real find, and Sigrid Horne Rasmussen was also a real find for her role. She was able to express the warmth and feelings of that hard-pressed working class wife. And Jørn Jeppesen made for a fine policeman. I miss him.

**Bondebjerg:** Many of your films belong to the genre that is often rather condescendingly referred to as 'Danish popular comedy',* but within that genre you've produced a number of films that have met with success at the box office and at times with critics. Your third feature film, *Golden Mountains*, received several international awards and is at this point acknowledged to be one of the finest examples of the genre in question. What, for you, was the original point of this story, and how would you describe the film's narrative form and style in relation to both Danish and international traditions of comedy?

**Axel:** One of the film's themes is, of course, the encounter between Danish and American culture. The film is about these islanders who think they've found oil. Then the Americans show up with their wealth and their Coca Cola and suddenly everyone is supposed to march to their drum. The film exploits the comic possibilities that are implicit in that kind of situation. The film was made during the Marshall-plan years when American mass culture was really making inroads in Denmark. The film reflects this reality. *Golden Mountains* is about two fathers who are opposed to an untraditional love affair. The film is about prejudice, rivalry and power struggles, and the fact that the story unfolds in a small island society involving two communities who feel superior to one another really helps to underscore these phenomena. A girl from Ærø doesn't marry a boy from Omø, and fishermen and peasants are very different kinds of people. I wanted to depict the particular atmosphere that exists in that kind of island community because it crystallises and foregrounds certain common human traits. I don't think there's anything like a viable formula for comedy in a Danish or international vein. I simply tried to find the satirical and amusing tone in Johannes Allen's script.

**Bondebjerg:** I'd like to pursue the discussion of Danish popular comedy. The Gyldenkål Family films, which you made in the 1970s, did fairly well at the box office. The tone and style of these films are rather different, however, for the satire is a lot coarser, it seems to me, than in *Golden Mountains*. Were the films an attempt to find a formula that was just as viable as that of the Olsen Gang films, or did you have other models in mind? How would you yourself characterise these films' style and mode of narration?

**Axel:** I'd almost say that if there's any commedia dell'arte anywhere in Danish film, it's in the Olsen Gang comedies. They established a norm for acting, and both the audience and the producers expect everyone who's trying to make similar comedies to meet it. You can't get Kirsten Walther, who plays Yvonne in the Olsen Gang films, to budge one inch. Kirsten Walther and all the other actors in the two Gyldenkål Family films came straight from the Olsen Gang films, so I didn't have much choice but to let them keep on acting in that style, which was what everyone expected them to do anyway. I said to my cinematographer, Henning Kristiansen: 'You know, it's not Shakespeare, but we're going to put as much effort into it as we would if it was.' You have to try to maintain a certain professional standard, even in those kinds of films, and in a sense you need the same techniques whether you're dealing with Gyldenkål or Hamlet. It's, of course, true that *Golden Mountains* has its own tone, style and atmosphere. Somebody once pointed out that it was a bit like the films of the Czech new wave, like Milos Forman's early films, for example. But I didn't consciously look to any other films while making it. But the Gyldenkål Family films emphasise a fairly coarse satire whereas *Golden Mountains* in many ways is quite poetic. The former are almost a parody of the genre. The producer said we needed to come up with something that could compete with the Olsen Gang. But we only made two films based on the concept: *The Gyldenkål Family* and *The Gyldenkål Family Breaks the Bank*. By then we'd pretty much exhausted the story.

**Bondebjerg:** Your French background may partly explain why many of your films belong to the subgenre of romantic comedies, which isn't, of course, that far removed from a certain important Danish as well as American genre tradition. It all begins with *My Helen* which is based on a French boulevard comedy. *Oskar*, which you shot in both France and the US, is similarly based on a French play. Kjeld Petersen appears in *My Helen* and Dirch Passer and Ove Sprogøe are both in *Oskar*. Their presence automatically connects these films with the Danish farce tradition. But are you also influenced by French and American romantic comedies?

**Axel:** *My Helen* is based on a French play that I'd staged for the Betty Nansen Theatre. *Oskar* is based on a real French boulevard comedy with an amusing story, which we for various reasons had to situate in Denmark, but we did give it a bit of a French atmosphere. Although I made use of Danish farce actors, the idea was to try to produce something that was less heavy than the Danish popular comedies and farces. The latter are quite amusing, but they quickly become rather clumsy when compared with the French comedies. I wasn't, on the other hand, at all influenced by American comedies. I've never tried to imitate the Americans. I've had a number of offers from over there. I received a lot of scripts from the US when I won my Oscar in 1987, but I said 'no' to them all. I'm on home ground in France and I'm on home ground in Denmark. The Americans sometimes produce wonderful things, but we shouldn't try to imitate them. It's my firm conviction that we should be ourselves from start to finish, and the reason I'm inspired by things French is precisely that France is my other home.

**Bondebjerg:** In your comedies you quite naturally deal with the place of love and eroticism in people's lives. You've explored this same theme in films of a more explicit erotic nature, both before and after the legalisation of pornography in 1969. *Crazy Paradise*, for example, combines a powerfully erotic theme with some of the satirical elements of Danish popular comedy. Eroticism is also a central theme in your two later and very different films, *Danish Blue*, which combines fiction with a documentary style, and *Amour*, which is an episodic film about love from Viking to contemporary times. Do you see these films as piquant entertainment, as attempts to make Danish film more liberal, or as both things at once?

**Axel:** *Danish Blue* was quite clearly an attempt to answer questions such as 'What, exactly, is pornography?' Until I decided to make it, I'd never seen a porno film in my life, but I'd met this man who had the second largest collection of erotic films in Europe (the largest collection belonged to the actor, Michel Simon). So there I sat watching these porno films. What I really found erotic was the image of a small Japanese woman's eyes and the expression of genuine pleasure on her face. Eroticism is in the mind.

    *Crazy Paradise* was a big success worldwide. It was seen by two million Swedes and it cleared 18 million German marks in German sales alone. It only cost us 700,000 Crowns to make, so it probably generated more money than any other film at that time. In that film I also used an island society as an image of society more generally, just as I'd done in *Golden Mountains*. The film was amusing and was an attempt to evoke a distinctly Danish provincial atmosphere. The erotic was a dramatic element here inasmuch as it helped to sustain the action. Ole Juul's novel also had a good deal of social satire. A naked body can also be beautiful and Hans V. Pedersen was rather charming and endearing in his role as the erotic stud. *Crazy Paradise* is also the only film in which Dirch Passer manages to do justice to a serious role. His career is in many ways a tragic one. He was a world-class clown and a fantastic film comedian, but in the long run he relied on clichés, and that destroyed him. *Danish Blue* is a documentary film that provocatively combines fictional and factual elements in order to highlight just how ridiculous the porn legislation was. I talked to priests, to judges, to doctors, to all kinds of people, and the film did contribute to the legalisation of pornography. The film also enjoyed considerable success at various festivals around the world, and it was also shown at Cannes, in the *Quinzaine des réalisateurs* series. Both conceptually and stylistically *Amour* is inspired by the tradition of piquant French postcards. I tried to recreate the style and the charm of those cards cinematically. At the same time the film is an exercise in three different kinds of style: a silent film style, a style inspired by the Romantic writer Alfred de Musset, and a style that resembles that of my own film, *The Red Mantle*. That film also did very well abroad. Metro-Goldwyn-Mayer sent someone over here, and he totally believed in the film and bought the world rights to it, and it was shown at Cannes that same year.

**Bondebjerg:** Normally your films are characterised by a classical narrative form and a realistic style, but one of your films, *Paradise and Back*, which is based on a script by Peter Ronild, is distinctly experimental, symbolic, and modernistic, both at the level of theme and cinematic language. Critics identified the new wave, among other things, as a source of inspiration.

**Axel:** *Paradise and Back* is a love story between a mismatched couple, a bourgeois woman and a working class man. The emphasis throughout was on the symbolic. The action takes place before and during the occupation (up until the liberation), and is expressed symbolically. The gulls, for example, were the German planes, while an overturned sentry box stood for the end of the war. But I never once thought of the new wave while making it. I thought only about the story and about how wonderful it was to be allowed to make a black and white film. My theatre training was also visual, and was the most excellent and rigorous that you could possibly dream of getting in the last century. Louis Jouvet was an absolute pioneer and it was he who breathed new life into the French theatre and definitively broke with naturalism. I learnt absolutely everything I know from him. Ronild was a representative of the new, modernistic generation, and I had to do battle with him on numerous occasions. He had so many settled ideas, so I finally had to say, 'Look, if you're going to keep this up, then you can make the film yourself. If I'm going to make it, you're going to have to give me some space.' I think Balling also talked to him and told him that he had to express a little confidence in the director, but he was constantly proposing changes to the script and all kinds of other things. It was quite inspiring in some ways, but also exhausting. So I promised myself that I'd never do that again. I found it interesting to make a film that was so abstract and symbolic, but it's certainly a lot easier to say things directly, to call a spade a spade. It was exciting to have a go at composing radically different images and at developing an alternative mode of narration, but once was enough. Most directors actually end up making the same film over and over again. At this point, though, I have fond memories of making the film. And Lise Ringheim was wonderful.

**Bondebjerg:** In addition to realistic films, popular comedies and romantic comedies, you've also made a couple of films that reflect an intense interest in the medieval Danish monk, Saxo Grammaticus. I'm thinking, of course, of *The Red Mantle* and *The Prince of Jutland*. The former is based on the legend about Hagbard and Signe, as retold by Saxo, while the latter draws on Saxo's Amled story. In the credits to *The Prince of Jutland* you actually thank your mother for having taught you to love the ancient Danish legends. What is it that fascinates you about this ancient material and what, in your mind, can it convey to contemporary audiences?

*Babette (Stéphane Audran) with the ingredients for her feast (*Babette's Feast*/*Babettes gæstebud*). [Photo: Peter Gabriel]*

**Axel:** Yes, my mother taught me to love legends, as well as folk stories and fairy tales. My father read to us, which was something I enjoyed more than anything else, and these things have remained with me. I'd at any point rather hear a good piece of fiction than something about everyday life. My bookshelves are full of ancient legends and tales, and I think they all have at least as much to teach us as any contemporary story. Those ancient narratives all have a message. I'd almost go so far as to say that there's a message in every dramatic situation, in all exchanges involving people. That's why I've never made films with the message writ large. You can say it all quite differently, because it's all there in the ancient legends and tales. I think those tales have some very basic dramatic and narrative qualities that give them a kind of simplicity and force that's hard to find in most contemporary texts.

**Bondebjerg:** You worked on *The Red Mantle* with Henning Bendtsen, who's one of the most outstanding of Danish cinematographers. You shot the film in Ultrascope and it's clear that the film's cinematic style is the result of very deliberate choices involving colour, the relations between landscapes and people, close-ups, shots of everyday life, long shots, and dramatically edited sequences with fighting. What are the guiding principles underwriting the film's style and aesthetic? Were you influenced in this regard by any particular Danish or international traditions or examples?

**Axel:** We consciously kept things simple. We wanted to tell the story in as powerful and simple a way as possible, so that nothing would get in the way of what was essential. We chose Iceland as a location, because it had black beaches, seas foaming with white froth, grey skies, and lots and lots of shades of grey. I tried to keep everything within the spectrum of shades of grey, with the exception of the red mantle, which was to be that beautiful reddish-brown colour. These were things that Henning Bendtsen and I talked about and experimented with back in the 1950s, which was when we first talked about making *The Red Mantle*. We used *Oskar* as a means of experimenting with this idea of working with various shades of grey. Everything in the film was black and white, even the dog, a Great Dane. Only the women's jewellery and the men's ties had colour. I've remained faithful to that idea of simplicity ever since, also during my years in France. In a film a lot of colour can be too much. Iceland was a magnificent location and we made very deliberate use of it. The scenes involving fighting were very carefully choreographed, with an emphasis on simplicity. Four men against one, and he kills them one by one. Kurosawa was important here. We'd take shots of a sword, a man who reaches out to touch his arm, and an arm that lies on the ground. At no point does that man figure in the image at the same time as his attacker. This kind of fighting style was very much dictated by our inability to pay for a special effects man. Afterwards you can always produce whatever blood and gore you need. It's that simple. A sword here, cut, followed by a shot of a limb there, and the eye believes it's seen a dismemberment. I generally admire Kurosawa for the simplicity of his effects. I also value Truffaut for his honesty. Those are the two directors whom I admire the most. If you have something to say, then you should at least try to say it as simply and beautifully as you can.

**Bondebjerg:** The film is not only remarkable on account of its pregnant visual style, but also as a result of its very minimalistic and modernistic music, which was composed by Per Nørgaard. What prompted you to explore this combination of ancient and modern elements?

**Axel:** I told Per Nørgaard that I really wanted him to compose the music, but that I didn't want anything that was too typical of him. At first he didn't think he could do that, but as it turned out, he could. Nørgaard looked to ancient melodies and instruments for inspiration in the case of both *The Red Mantle* and *The Prince of Jutland*, and he, of course, also wrote the music for *Babette's Feast*. He received a certain amount of money to produce the music for *The Red Mantle*. The idea was really to emphasise quality, so he had a Stradivarius and the four best musicians he could find. But the music wasn't quite right, so I wrote him a letter in which I explained that the music wasn't meant to underscore anything, but rather to complement other aspects of the film. It was supposed to give the film a new dimension. He then redid everything without demanding an extra penny. That's a *Mensch* for you. He then composed that wonderful music that nobody can hum along to. It's really very special and it isn't, in fact, that typical of Nørgaard's work. I sometimes think he might be ahead of his time. He's certainly a great musician, and a wonderful human being. The music he composed for *The Red Mantle* is as minimalistic and simple as it could possibly be. It plays a purely supporting role, and neither rapes the viewer nor stifles the dialogue in any way.

**Bondebjerg:** On the whole *The Red Mantle* was very poorly received in Denmark. But it was included in the competition for the *Palmes d'or* at Cannes and was awarded the *Prix technique* for its atmosphere and stylistic unity. It subsequently enjoyed a good deal of success outside Denmark. How do you explain this?

**Axel:** Only the tabloid *Ekstra Bladet* had something positive to say about it. The reviews in all the other publications were unrelentingly critical. But in the US it received reviews that could really go to your head if you happened to have tendencies along those lines. Perhaps there was too much bragging about the film before the Danish premiere, with the result that expectations in Denmark were simply too high. I don't know whether the critical responses had anything to do with the law of Jante,[1] but it's not uncommon in Denmark to want to tear down someone who's perceived as reaching too high. It's also possible that a film simply has to appear at the right time. *Babette's Feast* appeared at just the right time, just after Pollack had drawn attention to Blixen with his *Out of Africa*. *Babette's Feast* was quite simply the right story with the right people at the right time. You can't predict anything in film. *The Red Mantle* appeared at the right time and earned millions in the US, and *The Prince of Jutland* probably appeared too late.

**Bondebjerg:** You had, of course, established an international reputation for yourself well before *Babette's Feast*. Yet, this Blixen adaptation is clearly the highpoint of your career. It was also your first Danish-language film after a ten year hiatus following your departure for France in 1977. You'd dreamt of making the Blixen film for some 14 years. Why were you so interested in precisely this particular Blixen story and why did it take you so long to realise the project?

**Axel:** My wife persuaded me to read the short story by Blixen during one of our summer holidays. She said it was really beautiful, so I read it, and I thought the story was fantastic. All of my four children were on holiday with us, so I read them the story, and each of them responded differently to it. They picked up on different things, ranging from the story's more comical aspects to its sadder elements. The fact that these four children had four different views on the story told me that it would make for a wonderful adaptation because it was bound to move a lot of different people. Karen Blixen was brilliant and I have a lot of respect for her, but when I first read the story and simply immersed myself in it as literature, it didn't occur to me just how difficult it would be to concretise it on the screen. All the contrasts and writerly devices that she disposes over as an author can't simply be transposed to the screen. For example, when she says that the town in which the story unfolds, Kjerringöy in Norway, resembles a brightly coloured toy town, you simply accept her claim, but when I shot some footage of the town, it resembled some kind of open-air museum. Everything was historically authentic, but the images resembled what you'd expect to find in a tourist brochure. So it turned out that the town that Blixen actually had in mind was useless for our purposes. It was like something on a postcard, and that was completely wrong. Everything had to be grey, drab and sombre, and then suddenly at the end there was to be that feast. You need the grey tones as a contrast to the feast, which is all in colour. So we moved the entire film to the west coast of Jutland, and the big grocers in Berlevaag became that little man with a rowboat on the beach, who sells Babette some plaice, and the shop owner who sells Babette a pound of bacon, two onions and half a pound of sugar. We had to transform Blixen's milieu into something much more modest, into a place where the women wore their ordinary, everyday clothes. We needed a small society with only a few inhabitants who lived in humble white houses and huts with black seaweed on the roofs. On the other hand we did absolutely everything to ensure that the actual feast was truly grandiose. We ordered everything from Paris, so all the porcelain and silver were completely authentic. Everything was to be authentic, on just this one occasion. The food included real caviar, real *cailles en sarcophage* with truffles and authentic sauces. But we toned everything else down, because you have to begin modestly if you're going to conclude with such élan. So we painted all the sets grey and used Frederiksberg castle with its powerful colours as a point of contrast. Film language is all about reference. If you want to create a sense of stillness, then there has to be a dog barking in the distance, or something else. If you want to film a deserted street, there has to be a piece of paper blowing in the wind, or a cat prowling around, or a shadow on a wall. In order to create the impression of an empty room, you need a mattress and a table, maybe even a stool. These are all things you figure out as you go along, and that takes time. I'm quite envious of the younger film-makers who've attended the National Film School.* One of the reasons Bille August and all the others are able to speed ahead is that they learnt everything they needed to know in film school. For the older generation film was a craft that was to be learnt practically, through trial and error, but we also ended up inventing a lot of things. For example, during the Blixen production we were trying to make people's faces a certain kind of ivory colour, and we discovered that we could do this if we painted the sets pink and then later effaced the pink in the laboratory. We recounted that anecdote in Hollywood during the Oscar awards, and I assure you that everyone in that room clapped, because that wasn't some modern Hollywood trick, but primitive old craftsmanship. We had to make a lot of concrete changes in Blixen's story in order to recreate it cinematically, but the aim throughout was to be faithful to the spirit of her tale and to make it work on film. I also used a narrator so that film viewers would be able to hear Karen Blixen's own language. Out of respect and deference for the storyteller, I had the narrator draw attention to the fact that the viewers were about to hear a good story. The words are all Karen Blixen's, although they're excerpted from the Danish version of the story, which she of course translated and reworked herself. But there's no further need for the text once the viewer is comfortably settled in the saddle. Babette speaks French, the Swede speaks Swedish, and the others speak French and Danish to Babette until she learns Danish. There would be no point to the film had we dubbed everything into one language. Denmark is a small country and there are only some five million people who speak Danish. In that kind of context it's crucial that people cherish their language, for language is an expression of a culture. You move differently, you walk differently when you're speaking your own language.

**Bondebjerg:** Your background, both personally and professionally, is both Danish and French. On a number of occasions you've identified a need to strengthen various forms of cinematic collaboration within Europe. European audiences are generally uninterested in European film, and tend to favour their own national cinemas and American film. How do you explain this and what, for you, are the qualities of European film that are worth protecting and further developing?

**Axel:** The situation is changing throughout Europe. Once a number of good directors have established themselves, there will be others who will inevitably look up to them. This generates competition about issues of quality, which is what produces certain standards, and standards are what's needed. All great periods of civilisation have had their pioneers, and those who've followed in their wake have frequently gone on to become just as good as, or even better than their masters. I've attended conferences where my role was to define European film, and on those occasions I've always criticised the idea that a film's nationality, the extent of its Europeanness, should be determined by means of some point system. You know, the idea that a film gets three points if the director is European, two points if the cinematographer is European, one point if the sound technician is European, and three points if the leading role is played by a European actor, and the film is then declared European once it's accumulated 12 points. I think this is completely wrong. The films end up becoming a complete hodge podge and having nothing to do with anything. In my mind a European film is a Danish film in Denmark, a French film in France, and so on. If we all nurture those differences, it will become a lot more exciting to listen to each other.

The fact is that frequently those European co-productions become more costly as a result of having to satisfy all the criteria for Europeanness. I've received support from Eurimages myself. They gave me eight million Crowns to make *The Prince of Jutland*. But in order to get that support at least four European countries had to be involved in the production. The studio was Danish, the music was recorded in Amsterdam with a Dutch orchestra, the sound was produced in Germany, the mixing was done in England and the editing in France. All this involved travel and food expenses that made the film two million Crowns more expensive. Also, it's hard to speak four languages while co-ordinating a large crew. European collaboration ought to be something quite different. It shouldn't be a matter of co-productions with all kinds of rules and requirements, but rather of co-financing. If we want to be international we first and foremostly have to be national. What the world needs is films that tell us something about how people live in Denmark, Sweden, France, Germany and so on.

**Bondebjerg:** You were virtually exiled to France from 1977–87, during which period neither the Danish Film Institute nor the Danish Broadcasting Corporation had much use for you. In France, on the other hand, you enjoyed considerable success. How do you see this period now and what's your relation to Danish film culture today? Do you see a big difference between working in a large European country like France and a small European country like Denmark?

**Axel:** Critics have the right to express their opinions honestly. I'm not opposed to that at all, and I don't feel any resentment towards the critics. The critic, Morten Piil, once said rather kindly that he'd seen *Babette's Feast* with *The Gyldenkål Family* in mind. That was, of course, a confession on his part, which I thought was very fine. But it also suggests why you can't be a prophet in your own country.

In France I received the most wonderful assignments from the outset, which is why I became known in France as someone who does quality work. Both success and failure have a spiral effect, the one upwards, the other downwards. Those are the conditions. You have to tell yourself that you're no better as a result of success, and no worse after a fiasco, because you have to start from scratch each time. In France I was one of a handful of directors who were able to dictate their own projects. Professionally it was probably the happiest period of my life, and the most instructive.

**Bondebjerg:** Would you care to talk briefly about your most recent film?

**Axel:** *Laïla the Pure* is a love story about a young Berber girl from a distant country in the south and a young carpenter, Niels, from a country in the far north. Their fates intertwine and it's love at first sight. But they don't share a language, which is why I use a narrator. The text, which was written by Bettina Howitz, is succinct. At times it's lyrically descriptive, at times informative or instructive, like a medieval ballad. I chose this narrative form in order to give the audience the pleasure of listening to a beautiful text that supports the characters' thoughts and feelings. 50 years in the business have taught me that the more simple a scene is, the more strongly it affects the viewer. The story is and remains the most important element in a film, and nothing should distract from what is essential, namely the action. All cinematic devices and effects have to be mobilised with great care. The music, for example, should not simply support the text. It should stand on its own and create its own atmosphere. Similarly, all the sounds, whether real or produced, should figure as independent elements, be it a matter of bird song, a donkey's braying or the rippling of a stream. A feature resembles a symphony in many ways. An *andante*, *allegretto* or *forte* help to ward off the danger of monotony, and a film's rhythm rarely has anything to do with the speed of the dialogue or action. As in music, it has something to do with shifts between movements. All the actors agreed that they had learnt a lot about their craft and about themselves as a result of having to act without dialogue. It was a matter of mobilising all possible resources in a concentrated form, and it was draining to have to express so much sorrow. For example, at a certain point, the actors who play Laïla's parents in the film were too exhausted to eat in the evenings. The actors identified very powerfully with their characters and discovered completely new aspects of themselves, including how far they could go emotionally. *Laïla the Pure* is in a way an experiment because it's a film without dialogue that harmoniously combines the narrator's text with music, various sounds and incredibly powerful acting. I hope to provide the audience with a really great experience, and I can't thank the Film Institute's consultants* enough for their moral, professional and economic support. I've always found people's confidence in me to be an enormous source of inspiration.

---

1    A satirical set of injunctions designed to undermine self-esteem, the law of Jante was articulated by the writer Axel Sandemose.

# Henning Carlsen

## 1927–

Henning Carlsen is one of the most central figures in modern Danish film as a result of his extensive production of both documentary films (45 in all) and feature films. Over the years he has also generously contributed his time and energy to key organisations and institutions linked to Danish film culture more generally. As director of the Dagmar Cinema (1968–81) he helped to underscore the importance of sustaining a commitment to quality art films in Denmark. His documentary film series *Old People* (*De gamle*, 1961), *Family Portrait* (*Familiebilleder*, 1964), and *Young People* (*Ung*, 1965) are classics of modern Danish documentary film and provide nuanced depictions of life forms and attitudes rooted in the Danish welfare society of the 1960s and of the generational conflicts that subsequently found expression in the youth revolt. His first feature film, *Dilemma* (1962), which is based on a novel by Nadine Gordimer, is marked by his

*Henning Carlsen*

documentary style, and was shot illegally in South Africa. It stands today as one of the early authentic cinematic depictions of racial conflict in that country. Carlsen's artistically most significant film and international breakthrough is his Knut Hamsun adaptation, *Hunger* (*Sult*, 1966). *Hunger* is a psychologically intense and cinematically powerful depiction of crises at the heart of modernity, and features an extraordinary performance by Per Oscarsson. Many of Henning Carlsen's feature films are adaptations of Scandinavian novels, examples being *People Meet and Sweet Music Fills the Heart* (*Mennesker mødes, og sød musik opstår i hjertet*, 1967), *We Are All Demons* (*Klabautermanden*, 1969) and *Two Green Feathers* (*Pan*, 1995), which are based on works by Jens August Schade, Axel Sandemose and Hamsun respectively. Carlsen has also helped to renew the tradition of Danish popular comedy* through his collaboration with Benny Anderson on *Oh, To Be on the Bandwagon* (*Man sku' være noget ved musikken*, 1972), among others, and in his most recent film, the romantic comedy entitled *I Wonder Who's Kissing You Now?* (1998). Carlsen's major international production is the English-language Gauguin film, *Wolf at the Door* (*Oviri*, 1986), with Donald Sutherland as Gauguin.

## Feature films

1962, *Dilemma*
1963, *Epilogue (Hvad med os?)*
1965, *Cats (Kattorna)*
1966, *Hunger (Sult)*
1967, *People Meet and Sweet Music Fills the Heart (Mennesker mødes, og sød musik opstår i hjertet)*
1969, *We Are All Demons (Klabautermanden)*
1970, *Are You Afraid? (Er I bange?)*
1972, *Oh, To Be on the Bandwagon! (Man sku' være noget ved musikken)*
1975, *A Happy Divorce (Un divorce heureux)*
1975, *When Svante Disappeared (Da Svante forsvandt)*
1978, *Did Somebody Laugh? (Hør, var der ikke en, som lo?)*
1982, *Your Money or Your Life (Pengene eller livet)*
1986, *Wolf at the Door (Oviri)*
1995, *Two Green Feathers (Pan)*
1998, *I Wonder Who's Kissing You Now?*

## Selected short films and documentaries (from a total of 45)

1954, *Welcome to Vendsyssel (Velkommen til Vendsyssel)*
1958, *The Cyclist (Cyklisten)*
1959, *Danfoss – Around the World, Around the Clock (Danfoss – jorden rundt, døgnet rundt)*
1959, *Knot Problem (Et knudeproblem)*
1961, *Limefiord (Limfjorden)*
1961, *Old People (De gamle)*
1962, *Clean Talk about Dirt (Ren besked om snavs)*
1964, *Family Portrait (Familiebilleder)*
1965, *Young People (Ung)*
2000, *The Portrait (Portrættet)*

## Books

1998, *Memoirs (Mit livs fortrængninger. Erindringer)*

**Hjort:** You were born in Aalborg to middle-class parents with hopes of seeing you enter the family brick business. An early encounter with the writings of Eisenstein and Pudovkin set you on a quite different course, and in 1948 you assumed a position at Minerva Film, as assistant to Theodor Christensen, the founder of the Danish post-war documentary movement and director of the important clandestinely produced resistance film, *Your Freedom is at Stake (Det gælder din Frihed*, 1946). You are at this point one of Denmark's most accomplished documentary film-makers and films such as *Limefiord*, *Old People*, *Family Portrait* and *Young People* are among the classics of Danish documentary film. Did the early years with Minerva Film, and the close collaboration with Christensen, have a lasting influence on your approach to film-making?

**Carlsen:** Yes, it certainly did. I worked with Theodor Christensen for many, many years, and we became very close friends. He was my 'film school', and I learnt all the most essential things I know about the medium from him, such as editing skills, but he also taught me that it's important to take a stance on the issues you deal with through this medium.

**Hjort:** Your film career is noteworthy on account, among other things, of its sheer range. You've directed remarkable films of different types and genres, but you've also played a key role within the Danish film industry more generally. In 1968, for example, you were granted a license to manage the Dagmar cinema in Copenhagen, which was once Carl Theodor Dreyer's cinema. Under your directorship the Dagmar cinema offered a steady flow of high quality films. During this same period you not only directed such films yourself, but started an import and distribution company together with Christian Braad Thomsen, who was equally passionate about the idea of introducing the Danish public to the best of foreign films. Could you reconstruct the context for your decision to manage the Dagmar cinema and start your own distribution company?

**Carlsen:** In a way, I suppose, my becoming the director of Dagmar was a bit of a coincidence. This happened just as I was finishing the film called *We Are All Demons*, which was to become my first real fiasco. But since I had my own cinema, I stubbornly kept on showing it there. The film was a resounding flop and I lost 600,000 Crowns, which was a lot of money in 1969. What is more, that loss simply multiplied the red figures in my Dagmar accounts. So I started my career as a cinema director with a heavy loss and without any capital of my own. That was the beginning of a tough battle that lasted 13 years.

The idea of starting an import company and of importing films came gradually to me and my colleague and friend, Peter Refn, who ran a different cinema called Camera, which was on Vesterbro (and who later took over the cinema called Grand). We'd imported a couple of films together and we then established Dagmar Film Distribution together with Christian Braad Thomsen. We thought we could afford to do this, because we were at the very least sure that the films would be premiered in our own cinemas. The films we imported were very experimental: Godard, Fassbinder, Truffaut and Japanese films that are rarely shown in Danish cinemas. They premiered in Dagmar and/or Grand and then they were shown in four or five other cinemas elsewhere in the country. We didn't need to import more than one copy of the films, but it never became a lucrative business. On the contrary. If we hadn't received support for the importation of the films from the Danish Film Institute, the entire enterprise would have been impossible.

**Hjort:** You were the driving force, along with Morten Arnfred, behind the creation in 1990 of the European Film College in Ebeltoft, which, interestingly, reflects the teachings of the theologian, Grundtvig, inasmuch as it is part of the Danish folk high school* system. The college has at times been described as a means of fostering European as well as Danish identities through film, with the critical intent, perhaps, of creating a certain resistance to Hollywood. Could you talk a little about the conception of national and transnational film cultures that underwrites the philosophy of the Ebeltoft college?

**Carlsen:** It all started with my being contacted by Knud Pedersen, whom I knew just a little bit from Aalborg, and who suggested that we establish a 'Common Market folk high school' in Denmark. At that point, towards the end of the 1980s, I had just helped to start up the European Film Academy in Berlin. We were very aware of what was happening on the other side of the Iron Curtain, which still existed then, and we were intent on seeing the countries on the other side of the Iron Curtain as European countries. I remember that the first person to receive a European Film Academy prize, a Felix, was Kieslowski, and he thanked us from the podium for having regarded Poland as a European country. As a result my immediate reaction to Knud Pedersen was that we should establish, not a Common Market folk high school dedicated to film, but rather a European folk high school dedicated to film, and that then became the guiding concept. It's in its eighth year now and operates at full capacity. The College can accommodate 107 students a year in courses lasting eight months, and about 50 percent of the students are Danish while the other 50 percent come from 26 other countries. We haven't limited ourselves exclusively to Europe, so we've also had students from South Africa, China and the US.

When we established the Film College, I was working under the assumption that its purpose would be to create the basis for a better, more informed audience for film. People who attended the College were to become better film spectators, and I do think that this is actually one of the roles it plays today. The students are made aware of a lot of different things that ordinary spectators simply don't think about, but at this point the College also serves a different function. We noted, for example, that of the 107 students who constituted the class of 1997, 50 were employed within the film industry, and in addition to those 50 students, 25 had been accepted to professional film schools in various places around the world. So our sense is that, although this was not the original intention, the Film College functions to some extent as a kind of pre-school for the film schools. It's very impressive that nearly 75 percent of the former students are working professionally with film. During the summer we set aside one month for two or three regular folk high school sessions in Danish for Danes, and they're very popular indeed. The remaining two months are dedicated to courses on different industry-related issues, and the target audience here is comprised of film professionals. At the moment we're emphasising the concept of distribution, because the big problem in Europe is the distribution of European film.

**Hjort:** How, more specifically, would you characterise that problem?

**Carlsen:** Essentially the problem, of course, is that Europe is divided along linguistic lines, and that we aren't interested in each other's films. How many Portuguese films are shown in Copenhagen, and how many Danish films are shown in Lisbon? Considering the number of films that get produced, it's rare for a Danish film to have a Swedish premiere, and the same is true of Swedish films in Denmark. We make films for our own little linguistic regions, and the result is that the region that in a way can lay claim to having a global language, namely English, ends up playing a dominant role. The American producers are immensely powerful and have an extremely well organised distribution apparatus at their disposal. The result is that they're clearly dominant to an extent that is simply unreasonable. It's really not reasonable that the Americans should be able to get anything into the European cinemas, good and bad films alike, while it's impossible for even the best European films to get released outside their country of origin. It's a huge problem and we're trying to come up with various solutions, but it's very difficult.

**Hjort:** Your first feature film, *Dilemma*, was produced under extraordinary circumstances. It's based on Nadine Gordimer's *A World of Strangers* and was filmed clandestinely in South Africa during the Apartheid years. Your cover was unexpectedly blown by a roll of film that had been sent to a Johannesburg laboratory at the request of Henning Kristiansen, your cinematographer. You and your crew went underground, managing to complete the film with the authorities in hot pursuit. You have throughout your career focussed on deeply ambivalent characters who oscillate dangerously between two poles or extremes. Ambivalence is the very essence of *Dilemma*. Could you reconstruct the film's original context and comment on the centrality of the theme of ambivalence in your work?

**Carlsen:** The idea of making a film in South Africa about Apartheid occurred to me because I'd been to South Africa in 1958 in connection with an industrial film that I made for Danfoss. Danfoss is a big Danish company specialising in refrigerators and thermostats and it's one of the largest industries in Denmark. Their 25th anniversary was coming up and they wanted to mark the occasion with a film. I proposed the idea of a film called *Danfoss – Around the Clock, Around the World*, and they liked it. I discovered Apartheid during those two trips to South Africa. It's important to remember that this was in 1958. Apartheid had existed for ten years, but the flow of information to the rest of the world was much slower then than it is now. In that kind of context, my sudden encounter with Apartheid was very overwhelming. I'd seen those benches with *Nie blankies*, or whatever it was, inscribed on them, the buses in which the races were segregated, and I'd been to a concert, a major performance of an important South African opera called *King Kong*, which was said to be one of the first performances in many years with a mixed audience. The mixed element consisted in all the whites sitting on the right hand side while everyone who wasn't white sat on the left hand side. The non-whites were then in turn divided into strictly segregated groups comprising Indians, on the one hand, and coloureds and blacks, on the other.

The experience of seeing how Apartheid functioned in practice was a very powerful one, and we encountered similar attitudes in connection with the shooting of our film. We needed the sound of a penny whistle and someone who could produce it. My cinematographer, Henning Kristiansen, and I had found a young man with a penny whistle and we'd taken him up to our hotel room. I shot the scene with him and while we were shooting we suddenly felt like having a beer. I called downstairs and ordered three Carlsbergs from room service, and the next thing we knew two Carlsbergs were brought to our room. I said, 'I asked for three.' The waitress then said that I'd have to speak to the receptionist about that. So I called the receptionist who said, 'You're not allowed to serve liquor to kaffirs.' I couldn't help but be shocked by that remark and I thought to myself, 'If I ever get the chance to make a longer film, a feature film, or a long documentary film, it's going to be about this.'

What then happened was that I inherited some money three years after I'd been to South Africa. The issues were still on my mind, so I spent my inheritance on making *Dilemma*. I prepared my commando raid by establishing contact with the authorities, to whom I explained that I wanted to make a film about refrigerators in the everyday life of the African housewife. This was presented as a sequel to the industrial film that I'd already made. I even managed to get the director of Danfoss, Mads Clausen, to write a 'To Whom it May Concern' letter along these lines. But at the same time I also contacted members of the ANC and Nadine Gordimer. She thought my project was interesting and wanted to help me. So as a result I ended up in both camps and I suddenly realised that I was behaving like the main character in Nadine Gordimer's novel, *A World of Strangers*. That's how I got the idea of making a film that was essentially based on her novel, but which also included documentary footage.

I then returned to Denmark in order to work out the financing and, purely by coincidence, I ended up not with one, but two cinematographers: Henning Kristiansen and the Swedish cinematographer, Arne Lagerkrantz. The authorities did, of course, figure out what we were up to two weeks before we were through shooting. Our visas had expired, and this was exactly when Henning Kristiansen had to return to Denmark, on account of an accident. I think they were confused by the fact that one of us ended up leaving the country. In any event we managed to keep things going for two more weeks. When I flew out of Johannesburg, there were more policemen than passengers in the departure hall, and they kept examining my luggage. In Salisbury I met up with a man who'd very discretely left South Africa with all of our sound tapes, so that they wouldn't be confiscated. The next day the Swedish cinematographer left the country, and he'd arranged to have all of our equipment sent. He'd just sent it by regular mail, but it happened to be on the very same aeroplane that he was on. Nobody noticed this though.

**Hjort:** Your first Hamsun adaptation, *Hunger*, won a number of prestigious awards and established you internationally as one of Denmark's leading directors. Per Oscarsson, for example, who played the role of the self-absorbed and self-deceived young author, won the prize for Best Male Actor at the Cannes Film Festival in 1966. The prevailing wisdom had somehow been that it would be an impossible task to adapt Hamsun's *Hunger* (*Sult*) to the screen. Your *Hunger* continues to this day to serve as an example of outstanding cinematic adaptation in a context of national production where adaptations long have played an important role. You wrote the script for *Hunger* together with Peter Seeberg. Could you describe the process of adaptation as you remember it?

**Carlsen:** I can begin by saying that the adaptation exists on account of a coincidence. *Hunger* was one of the first grown-up books I ever read. I'd read it when I was twelve or

13, and had then completely forgotten it. However, I later made a film in Sweden, *The Cats,* and there were 15 actresses and one male actor, Per Myrberg, in that film. He was incredibly thin and every day I found myself wondering how he could be that thin until one day I suddenly realised that if a good actor could be that thin, then it ought to be possible to make an adaptation of Hamsun's *Hunger*. That's how it all started. I then re-read *Hunger*, while I was still in the process of making *The Cats*, and I thought the idea of an adaptation was just marvellous. I wrote to Tore Hamsun, Knut Hamsun's eldest son, who administered the rights, in order to ask whether it would be possible to purchase the film rights. My idea was to make the film as a Danish, Norwegian, Swedish co-production, the first ever. I think that idea appealed to Tore Hamsun, because the atmosphere surrounding Knut Hamsun in Norway wasn't exactly neutral or positive, and that's putting it mildly.[1] I think that Tore felt that if Denmark and Sweden were willing to make a Knut Hamsun film based on *Hunger*, that is, if these two countries deemed his work worthy of adaptation, then that in itself might help somewhat to resurrect Hamsun. I would imagine that that's why he let me go ahead with the project.

I then started collaborating with the now late Peter Seeberg, because I was really starting to grapple with a canonised text the size of Mount Everest on the map of world literature. I had long conversations with Peter, where it was a matter of determining which passages we wanted to use from the book, and how we wanted to use them. The problem with the book is, among other things, that it comprises seven or eight chapters, all of which are largely identical. At the outset of each of them the main character is absolutely famished, and then we learn about his many trials and tribulations, and finally each chapter concludes with him getting his hands on something to eat. This basic structure gets repeated in each of the chapters, with the exception of the final one, where he manages to escape the vicious circle. But in a film, that kind of structure would involve repeating various segments and sequences, and that doesn't really work. So we devised a general structure for the film, and made use of the incidents that we felt were appropriate by fitting them into an integral whole that didn't have those constant interruptions that were linked in the novel to his needing something to eat, and so on. I realised that you can't turn a book into a film without really doing violence to the book. The other thing I realised was that what I wanted to adapt was my own experience of the book, rather than the book itself. That difference established quite a nice distance, and I've used that principle ever since when making a film based on a book – and that is, after all, something I've done quite a number of times. It's the first impression of the first or second reading of a book that you should be looking to adapt.

Our biggest problem was that *Hunger* is a first-person novel, because the question is: How do you turn a subjective book into a film? We're familiar with the concept of a subjective camera – when the camera sees what a character sees, it's described as a subjective camera. I had, of course, seen a number of long, long scenes that made use of a subjective camera style, and some people have even tried to make a whole film with a subjective camera, but it's never worked. We slowly discovered that we could kind of construct a triangle consisting of the camera, Per Oscarsson and the audience. Gradually we settled on the idea that there should be virtually no scenes in the film (there are only a few exceptions to this) that didn't focus either on Per Oscarsson or on what Per

Oscarsson sees. His ongoing experiences, the one piled on top of the other, became a substitute for the novel's first person narrator. The other thing that replaced the narrator was, of course, the possibility of identifying with Per Oscarsson. So in that respect it actually became a very subjective film.

We ran into a lot of other difficulties, because we had a hard time getting the images to look as though the events were unfolding in 1890. So we ended up doing a lot of trial takes. Finally we succeeded because we discovered that when you start using telephoto lenses, the images you produce prompt a certain sense of temporal displacement. I can't really explain why. I have a theory that the longer the telephoto lens is, the more the spectator is inclined to believe that the represented events are taking place in the postulated time period. The book was originally set in the present and there was nothing exotic about it when it was first published, but there is, of course, always something a little bit exotic about historical costume films. That's why we decided to try to downplay the exotic elements as much as possible. The idea was to arrange everything in such a way as to avoid anachronisms, but the historical dimension was in no way to be underscored. We made sure that everything corresponded to the historical period in question, and then we simply forgot about the issue. That principle turned out to be quite a good one.

**Hjort:** *The Cats* is based on a play by Walentin Chorell and focusses, much like Lillian Hellman's *The Children's Hour*, on the scapegoating of a figure accused of lesbianism. The woman in question (Eva Dahlbeck) is the manager of a laundry, where the represented events occur. *The Cats* has been described as a kind of precursor to Ingmar Bergman's films from the late 1960s. The stark, carefully controlled, and highly charged, black-and-white images in, not only *The Cats*, but *Dilemma, Hunger* and *We are all Demons* make comparisons with Bergman or Dreyer inevitable. How would you yourself describe your relation to these two film-makers with whom you frequently are compared?

**Carlsen:** Yes, how shall I describe it? My relation to Dreyer is ancient, because I was 16 when I saw *Day of Wrath* (*Vredens dag*), and that's a film that I must have seen as many as 40, perhaps 50 times. I've always been deeply fascinated by Dreyer as an image maker, and I've also seen *The Passion of Joan of Arc* (*La passion de Jeanne d'Arc*) countless times. My relation to Bergman is more ambivalent. By the way, *The Cats* was produced by the producer who'd made some of Bergman's earliest films. He'd produced four films by Bergman. I don't think the early Bergman films are successful and I think it's wonderful that a director is allowed to make as many as ten films as an experiment aimed at discovering a style and form of his own. That's a luxury that only very few people get to enjoy. Bergman is possibly a greater writer, a greater *auteur* than Dreyer is, but I still think that Dreyer is a greater film director than Bergman is, if it's a matter of comparing them. I also have a bit of trouble with Bergman's ongoing obsession with religious questions because I'm deeply anti-religious myself, which, by the way, I believe Dreyer was too.

*Summer Interlude* (*Sommarlek*) made a great impression on me when I saw it in Oslo as a young film man. Having left the cinema I found myself walking around the block I

*Donald Sutherland as Gauguin in* Wolf at the Door (Oviri). *[Photo: Rolf Konow]*

don't know how many times. At that point I hadn't yet started making feature films myself and at some level I felt that everything had already been done, that there was nothing more to be said. However, I don't actually think that I'm especially influenced by Bergman. There is on the other hand no doubt whatsoever that I'm deeply influenced by a quite different director, namely Jacques Becker, because his *Golden Marie* (*Casque d'or*) is simply the most beautiful, the most powerful, the best film I know of. I thought about any number of different things while I was making *Hunger*, but never about *Golden Marie*. Nonetheless when I see *Hunger* nowadays I notice all kinds of similarities with *Golden Marie*. I made a trip to Paris in 1955, with the intention precisely of studying what I thought was an adaptation of a Maupassant story. But I was then told that the script was an original one and that it was based on real events. That came as an enormous surprise to me, but didn't in any way detract from the film. It's a wonderful film that has definitely influenced me a lot, but quite unconsciously. In fact, I only realised the extent of the influence in question several years later when I saw *Golden Marie* again and thought, 'Goodness, it's just like *Hunger*.' But *Golden Marie* was, of course, made many years before *Hunger*.

**Hjort:** *Wolf at the Door* is a biographical film and focusses on two intensely disillusioning years in the life of Paul Gauguin, who is played masterfully by Donald Sutherland. It's a matter, more specifically, of the period between 1893 and 1895, when Gauguin, having returned from Tahiti, faces cold indifference towards his numerous paintings and intense conflict with his Danish wife, Mette Gad. *Wolf at the Door* is in many ways a fascinating film, not least because it takes issue with standard conceptions of Gauguin. Your defence of Gauguin, for this is of course what *Wolf at the Door* is, is also a condemnation of those aspects of Danish culture that the painter reviled. What was it, exactly, that motivated you to make *Wolf at the Door*?

**Carlsen:** Once again, coincidence played an important role here. During an interview, I once rather glibly said, 'I don't choose my topics, they choose me', which is something that Louis Malle has said too, I later discovered. However, *Wolf at the Door* finds its starting point in 1980 when I was hospitalised in Svendborg for a few weeks and actually hovered between life and death for a while. One night, around half past three or four o'clock in the morning, I woke up, and it was exactly as though there was a projector behind me, and this projector was projecting a scene with a charabanc driving through a forest onto the wall. As the charabanc reaches the curve in the road it comes to a standstill and out gets Paul Gauguin, who raises his hat and takes his leave. He's speaking Danish, and then he simply walks away in the direction of the hospital windows while the charabanc drives in the direction of the hospital door. What I saw there on the wall was the clearest of visions. I knew immediately that it was Gauguin. At that point I'd never even seen a picture of Gauguin and I knew almost nothing about him.

But the morning after my experience in the hospital I said to my wife 'I'm going to make a film about Paul Gauguin. Go to the library and borrow whatever books you can find on him.' She returned with two books, both written by Gauguin's youngest son, Pola Gauguin, who was born just before the family moved to Denmark, and who was about five months old when Gauguin left Copenhagen. These two books had been uncritically appropriated by the entire international art history community, which simply neglected to pay much attention to the fact that Pola could barely have had any real recollections of his father, since the latter left the country when Pola was still a baby. All the impressions he had of his father stemmed from Mette, who was naturally deeply bitter. Drawing only on this one-sided bitterness, Pola Gauguin writes his two books, which are then appropriated uncritically by art critics all over the world. I found that to be an absolute scandal, and that's the context in which I became immersed in Gauguin. Gauguin wasn't more of a drunkard than so many others have been. He was deeply committed to his family and felt a profound sense of responsibility for them.

I felt that if I was going to make a full-length film about Gauguin, then first of all it shouldn't be the kind of traditional birth to death biography. That wasn't interesting and, in any event, a number of TV programs had already dealt with precisely that. Together with my friend, the script writer Jean-Claude Carrière, I decided very early on to find some way of delimiting the subject. We found the delimitation we were looking for in Gauguin's return to Paris after his first visit to Tahiti. During his stay in Paris he tries to achieve success, but faces total failure instead and ends up leaving again. The period in question lasts 18 months. The time frame was clearly delimited as was the action, and so, as a result, was the biography itself. My relation to that film is such that every second time I see it I think it's an absolutely wonderful film and the other times I think it's garbage. It has a number of positive qualities, there's no doubt about it, and I have a book here on the bookshelf behind me that focusses exclusively on films about artists, and the claim is that *Wolf at the Door* is one of the more significant in the genre. But the film was an absolute fiasco in Denmark. When we showed *Wolf at the Door* in Venice, we – that is, the film, Donald and I – received a standing ovation that lasted a full ten minutes. I know because I timed it. The applause was simply deafening for ten minutes. It got to the point where it was embarrassing. Then the next day the world press pronounced on the film, and for the most part the responses were negative. After that I didn't make another film for ten years.

**Hjort:** *Wolf at the Door* could easily have been produced as a so-called 'natural co-production'. That is, it is not difficult to imagine a properly bi-cultural *Wolf at the Door* that reflects the Danish and French sources of funding in much the same way, for example, that the bi-cultural *Pelle the Conqueror* (*Pelle Erobreren*) reflects Danish and Swedish funding. You decided, however, to have the actors, some of whom were Danish, speak English throughout the film. What was the basis for this decision?

**Carlsen:** Originally the idea was that the film would be a 50/50 co-production involving my own company and Gaumont in France. Gaumont was very pleased with the script we handed in, but the discussions about who should play the various roles were endless. When Jean-Claude Carrière and I wrote the script in French, we modelled Gauguin on Donald Sutherland without for a second imagining that he would ever play the role. But I finally proposed Sutherland after all and he was very accommodating. In fact, I'd called him in England and he read the script that very same night. The next day he said that he thought it was a good script, but that he'd like to make a quick trip to Paris, where his family was. He said he'd be leaving that weekend, and then we could talk once he got back. I thought Donald Sutherland spoke French, and I hadn't for one second thought about the language issue, which was, of course, rather naive on my part. But I did, on the other hand, think: 'He had a role in Bertolucci's *1900* and in Fellini's *Cassanova*, so why not in my film?' But after having visited his family he called me in order to decline the role because he'd tried out some of the scenes in French with his wife as a spectator and she'd laughed her head off. I then suggested that we could resort to dubbing, but he didn't want any part of that. When I subsequently called Gaumont, they suggested that we make the film in English. That had never occurred to me. So I called Donald back, who said that at that point he'd need to see an English script and preferably as soon as possible because he needed to make a number of other decisions too. This was just before the Cannes Film Festival, so every serious translator was already completely booked up. We were able to find an American student who'd spent a couple of years studying at the Sorbonne. When she was through with the script I made my way to Donald's place in Paris and handed over the script while expressing all kinds of reservations about it. No sooner had I returned to my apartment on the other side of Paris than the phone rang. It was Donald calling to ask why I'd had so many reservations about the script. He said he thought it was a wonderful script and that he'd love the part.

However, two years went by before we got things underway in 1985, and in many ways it was an unhappy production. There were so many power struggles during the making of that film, and that was something I just wasn't used to. There were power struggles between me and the cinematographer, between Donald and myself, and all along I had to do battle with the Danish Film Institute in order even to be allowed to make the film. It wasn't a pleasant production. But Donald and I became very close and he came over to observe the editing. So that's the reason why the film is in English. It was of course a little paradoxical to be making the film in English, when all the shooting was to take place in Copenhagen, and 95 percent of the action, which concerns a French artist, was supposed to occur in Paris. Everything was done in Denmark. There's nothing, not a single shot, from France; the entire Parisian milieu was constructed in a studio in Valby. There are a couple of shots that are supposed to be of Brittany, but we took one of those down in Stege harbour and the other, which is a landscape shot, we took down on Møn. The only thing that takes place in Copenhagen is actually the charabanc ride, which was the first thing we shot, and then there were a few scenes in Mette's home. They, by the way, are purely fictional. At no point did he visit her in Copenhagen during the period in question. We had him visit Mette as a way of replacing an exchange of letters with something more visual. But otherwise the film is very truthful, because it's very faithful to things that Gauguin himself wrote, including his correspondence.

One of the problems we had to deal with arose three weeks before we had to start shooting. Donald suddenly approached me and proclaimed the script to be a piece of garbage that needed to be entirely rewritten. In his script he'd made a number of marginal notes, 'there's sex here', 'there's sex here', 'there's sex here' and that kind of thing. He'd identified all those moments in the film where there was something just slightly frivolous about the story. Yet, frivolity wasn't, of course, something that was alien to Gauguin, but Donald suddenly insisted that it all had to go. So we hired Christopher Hampton, who was well versed in Gauguin because he'd just written a script that was an adaptation of Somerset Maugham's novel *The Moon and Sixpence*. He asked me whether his hands were free and I said 'No, they're not. Your hands are free as long as you stick to the sets because we've already started constructing them, and to the locations, because we've already found those, and to the existing cast of characters, because we've already hired the actors. Other than that, you can do as you wish.' He then wrote a new script which largely respected those basic parameters. The paradoxical thing was that when the film was finally finished Donald felt that it lacked a certain coarseness. He felt that his character had become too refined, but that's bloody well his own fault.

**Hjort:** Could you talk a bit about the archival work you did in connection with *Wolf at the Door*? You just mentioned that Pola Gauguin's biographies were of no use to you.

**Carlsen:** Jean-Claude Carrière, who's a very good friend, had agreed to help write the script, which he got me to write in French, with the assistance of my wife, Else, who is perfect in French. I wrote the sequences after having spent six months researching the material every single day at the *Bibliothèque Nationale*. The *Bibliothèque Nationale* had all the sources and all the information that art historians in my mind should have explored carefully, and I also found plenty of evidence of what I was discussing earlier. So the film is very much the result of original archival research. I did a lot of research, but I also relied heavily on Gauguin's own books, primarily *Before and After* (*Avant et après*) but also *Noa-Noa*.

**Hjort:** Expensive co-productions are increasingly seen as one of the means of sustaining a vigorous Danish film industry. Whereas Danish directors and producers typically seek co-production partners among the Nordic countries, you have produced two Danish-French co-productions, *Wolf at the Door* and the earlier *A Happy Divorce*, starring Jean Rochefort and Bulle Ogier. Do the advantages of enhanced budgets, in your experience, outweigh the specific problems and challenges associated with transnational productions?

**Carlsen:** I certainly think that there were a lot of problems connected with the early co-productions. We now tend to talk more about co-financing, bilateral agreements and other collaborative financial arrangements, but the big drawback, one might say, of co-productions was that they to a certain extent effaced the nationality of the films. Take a film like *A Happy Divorce*, for example. It was actually quite a successful film. It did well, both in France and Denmark. It opened the Cannes Film Festival in 1975 while being an entry in the competition, which was unheard of. But what happened in the case of that film, which is the only film I've ever made in French, was that it was perceived as Danish in France and as French in Denmark. The Danish Film Institute has never promoted it abroad as an example of contemporary Danish film production. I've had exactly the same problem with *Two Green Feathers* which was mostly a Norwegian production, although some Danish money was involved too; I'd also invested some of my own money in it. So the Institutes simply decided to classify *Two Green Feathers* as a Norwegian film with a Danish director. But the Norwegian Film Institute has never promoted it internationally, because when it's time to send out a film that represents Norway, they always opt for a film with a Norwegian, rather than a Danish, director. There's a way in which films simply die as a result of being co-productions.

There's so much talk about the need to produce co-productions because it is felt that then we'll somehow be able to make more films. That is, of course, utter nonsense. If, for example, you look at the three Scandinavian countries, and they each have, let's say, a budget of 100 million Crowns, then you have a total of 300 million Crowns for the production of films. Whether you make films to the tune of 100 million Crowns in each of the three countries separately, or you spend 300 million Crowns on films in Scandinavia as a whole makes very little difference. Actually the only difference is that you get less for your money if you opt for co-productions, because a co-production is always more expensive to produce. There's a tendency in the context of co-productions always to opt for the most expensive solution. What is more, co-productions involve a lot of expenses having to do with travel, fees and lawyers. And the process of actually securing the co-production monies can itself be very expensive. I know, for example, that in the case of Lars von Trier's *Europa* it cost four million Crowns to get the five million Crowns they got from outside sources. I don't actually believe that co-productions provide a solution to anything. They certainly don't solve any problems at the level of film production more generally, although they may in some cases provide a solution to problems associated with a particular film.

**Hjort:** The Norwegian author, Hamsun, has been of enduring interest to you. Almost thirty years after *Hunger*, you returned to Hamsun's work, and the result is *Two Green Feathers*, a co-production involving Norwegian, Danish and German monies, as well as support from the Nordic Film and Television Fund and Eurimages. Interestingly, *Two Green Feathers* is not based uniquely on Hamsun's novel *Pan*, but incorporates the short text entitled *Glahn's Death* (*Glahns død*). What is gained, cinematically, by fusing the two narratives in this way?

**Carlsen:** It's important to point out that the postscript entitled *Paper on Glahn's Death* (*Papir om Glahns død*) has been integrated into the novel. That is, it's included in all the editions of *Pan*, although it was written two years before *Pan* and had been published independently. I suspect that Hamsun re-read it when he was looking for a new theme and trying to figure out what his next book might be about, and he probably discovered that the story about that lieutenant and the fine lady up there in Northern Norway was rather good. At that point he sits down and writes *Pan*. Having finished *Pan*, he possibly feels that he's written something that's a little maudlin, although very poetic. Somewhere in one of his letters he wrote: 'I'm not in the process of writing a novel. I'm in the process of writing a poem.' He possibly felt that the novel needed to be spiced up and that may be why he had the short story reprinted, because its language and style are completely different. It's very sober and the narrator is someone entirely different. The fact is that we can only speculate about his reasons for including it. A lot of literary scholars have been rather displeased with the addition of the postscript, although I always thought its inclusion was rather interesting. When I was contacted by an American, who asked whether I would consider making the film, I rediscovered that postscript, which I'd completely forgotten, much like everybody else. I don't know how many people I've spoken to who've forgotten the final short story that takes place in the jungle. I'd decided that I would only make an adaptation of *Pan* if I could find a new angle, one that hadn't already been used in one of the four existing adaptations of the novel. That's why I decided to integrate two episodes, the one from the beginning of the novel and the other from the final short story, where Glahn receives a letter. Basically, the two episodes with the letters recount the same story: Edvarda seeks out all the new foreigners, in the hopes of getting one of them to help her to get out of the remote corner of the world in which she lives, and this is also exactly what the young native girl living in the jungle does. She too would like to turn her back on her wretched existence, and she hopes that one of those Englishmen will help her to engineer an escape. The sense of claustrophobia and longing is the same in both cases. That's why I decided to place Glahn in India, from where he then writes what he writes in *Two Green Feathers*, so that we're only talking about a single letter that someone received. I felt that that strategy helped me to solve a lot of problems, and, conversely, I felt that in retaining the Indian dimension, I somehow underscored a natural contrast between the claustrophobic atmosphere of the jungle and the sense of agoraphobia associated with the Norwegian mountains. But at the same time I decided that it was important to ensure that *Two Green Feathers* didn't resemble a tourist film or a nature film. You can't film Hamsun's descriptions of nature. You can't compete with them, so it's best to tone them down completely. That's why we've included only a very limited number of nature images in that film.

The most difficult aspect of that film had to do with finding Edvarda. I considered a lot of wonderful, talented and beautiful Norwegian actresses, but they all had a certain 1995 look. Sofie Gråbøl has that unusual, almost archaic face, and then she's the only actress I know of who can be incredibly beautiful one minute and incredibly ugly the next as a result of an inner transformation. That was exactly what I needed for the role of Edvarda. The film was a great success in Norway, but it did poorly in Denmark, except for the fact that it received some favourable reviews. I have, of course, suffered from the whole story of *Hunger*. No matter what I came up with, people would say, 'That's not bad, Mr. Carlsen, but *Hunger* was after all better.' Only with *Two Green Feathers* have I had the experience of somebody saying, 'It's almost as good as *Hunger*', and at that point you can't do much better.

**Hjort:** You've just completed a tragi-comedy about marital conflict entitled *I Wonder Who's Kissing You Now*? Could you talk a bit about your reasons for making this low-budget film?

**Carlsen:** The film is financed by means of the 50/50* policy. It received no funding from any of the major TV stations, and the consultants at the Danish Film Institute didn't wish to fund it either. So gradually it began to dawn on me that I had a good script on my hands. So we produced the film by means of the 50/50 policy. The Danish Film Institute matched the 3.5 million Crowns that we provided, and then we got some additional money from the Nordic Film and Television Fund and from TV 1000. That's how we financed the film, but it was produced for less than eight million Crowns. It's a kind of comedy, with bitter undertones, about jealousy. It's based on a novel by Ib Lucas, *Silhuetter* which is about a man who writes five letters to his doctor and gets three in return. That was the book's organising principle, and it amused me enormously when I first read it. I then set the book aside and didn't think about it again. The reason I'd bought it at all was that I'd become very interested in the concept of jealousy. I hadn't, of course, made any films during all those years following *Wolf at the Door*. I felt that *Wolf at the Door* had received unfair treatment, and I was also filled with jealousy towards the younger directors who were able to make lots of films and who were enjoying enormous success. I was really in the grip of jealousy, which I didn't like at all, and I thought to myself, 'The only way you're going to be able to deal with this is by trying to make a film about jealousy.' I tried to find some material that would be appropriate and I read quite a number of studies on jealousy. Three months after I'd read the novel, it suddenly occurred to me, that it wasn't the novel's form that was interesting, but what it was about. So I called Ib Lucas, whose number I found in the phone book, and we decided to meet, and the chemistry between us was marvellous right from the word go. He's a secondary school teacher, so he had a fair bit of time on his hands during the summer months. So we were able to write the script together during that first summer. We had a lot of fun writing it. We produced nine versions all told, and the ninth version was published as a book at the time of the film's premiere. I'm actually very pleased with that film. It's both funny and serious at the same time, and Tommy Kenter, who's an incredibly good actor, and on whom we'd modelled the main male character, actually ended up playing the part, and very successfully so, I think.

I had trouble finding a Danish actress of the right age. I needed someone who was about 38 years old. That's why I ended up choosing a Swedish actress, Marika Lagercrantz, who was in Bo Widerberg's last film, *Love Lessons* (*Lust og fägring stor*). She was a great success. She was incredibly good. I really, really enjoyed working together with her, and we only needed to change the script slightly to accommodate her being Swedish. The film relies heavily on Tommy Kenter and Marika Lagercrantz, but Morten Grunwald, Lars Knutzon and Lotte Andersen have interesting smaller parts. I'm very pleased with that film.

1    Knut Hamsun, Norwegian writer (1859–1952) and Nobel Prize winner (1920) influenced by Dostoevski and Nietzsche. *Hunger* (1890) was his first novel and *Pan* was published in 1894. Hamsun's popularity suffered seriously as a result of his sympathetic stance towards the Nazi occupiers of Norway during the Second World War. An account of his motives can be found in Hamsun's *Overgrown Paths* (*På gjengrodde stier*, 1949). See also Jan Troell's *Hamsun*.

# Jørgen Leth

## 1937–

Jørgen Leth studied literature and anthropology at the University of Århus and the University of Copenhagen, and has worked as a journalist for *Aktuelt* (1959–63) and *Politiken* (1964–67). Leth, who is both a poet and a film-maker, was a salient voice for Danish poetic modernism in the 1960s and a key figure in the 1960s' milieu of experimental documentary film-makers, especially the artists' collective ABCinema. Leth's most important contributions to experimental and documentary film-making are *The Perfect Human* (*Det perfekte menneske*, 1967), *Life in Denmark* (*Livet i Danmark*, 1971) and *66 Scenes from America* (*66 scener fra Amerika*, 1981). Leth has also developed a unique mythic or epic approach to the genre of sports documentaries, an approach that is best exemplified by *Stars and Watercarriers* (*Stjernerne og vandbærerne*, 1973) and *A Sunday in Hell* (*En forårsdag i helvede*, 1976).

*Jørgen Leth*

These films have helped to make Leth a much-loved and frequently used sports commentator for Danish television, particularly in connection with the annual coverage of the Tour de France. His wide-ranging production of short and documentary films includes several works about artistic figures and techniques, an example being his most recent film, *I'm Alive. Søren Ulrik Thomsen: A Danish Poet* (*Jeg er levende. Søren Ulrik Thomsen, digter*, 1999). In the area of feature film-making, Leth has developed a distinctive style characterised by experimental modes of narration. He has his own production company, Sunset Productions Inc., and has lived in Haiti since 1991.

## Feature films
1975,  *Good and Evil* (*Det gode og det onde*)
1983,  *Haiti Express* (*Udenrigskorrespondenten*)
1989,  *Notes on Love* (*Notater om kærligheden*)
1992,  *Traberg*

## Short films and documentaries
1963,  *Stop for Bud* (*Stopforbud*)

1965,  *Look Forward to a Time of Security (Se frem til en tryg tid)*
1967,  *The Perfect Human (Det perfekte menneske)*
1968,  *Near Heaven, Near Earth (Nær himlen, nær jorden)*
1968,  *Ophelia's Flowers (Ofelias blomster)*
1968,  *The Deer Garden Film (Dyrehavefilmen)*
1969,  *Jens Otto Krag*
1970,  *The Search (Eftersøgningen)*
1970,  *Without Kin (Frændeløs)*
1970,  *The Deer Garden, the Romantic Forest (Dyrehaven, den romantiske skov)*
1970,  *Motion Picture*
1971,  *Life in Denmark (Livet i Danmark)*
1972,  *Chinese Ping Pong (Kinesisk bordtennis)*
1973,  *Stars and Watercarriers (Stjernerne og vandbærerne)*
1974,  *Klaus Rifbjerg*
1975,  *The Impossible Hour (Den umulige time)*
1976,  *A Sunday in Hell (En forårsdag i helvede)*
1978,  *Peter Martins: A Dancer (Peter Martins – en danser)*
1979,  *Kalule*
1979,  *A Midsummer's Play (Sanct Hansaften-spil)*
1979,  *Dancing Bournonville (At danse Bournonville)*
1981,  *Step on Silence*
1981,  *66 Scenes from America (66 scener fra Amerika)*
1983,  *Pelota*
1986,  *Moments of Play (Det legende menneske)*
1986,  *Notebook from China (Notater fra Kina)*
1989,  *Danish Literature (Dansk litteratur)*
1993,  *Michael Laudrup: A Football Player (Michael Laudrup – en fodboldspiller)*
1995,  *Haiti, Untitled (Haïti. Uden titel)*
1999,  *I'm Alive. Søren Ulrik Thomsen: A Danish Poet
        (Jeg er levende. Søren Ulrik Thomsen, digter)*

## Books
1962,  *Yellow Light (Gult lys)*
1964,  *Canal (Kanal)*
1967,  *Sports Poems (Sportsdigte)*
1967,  *Happiness in No-man's Land (Lykken i Ingenmandsland)*
1969,  *Smooth, Inflated Cushions (Glatte hårdtpumpede puder)*
1971,  *The Adventure of Ordinary Sights (Eventyret om den sædvanlige udsigt)*
1971,   *It Passed Me By (Det går mig forbi)*
1976,  *Like Something in a Dream (Det er ligesom noget i en drøm)*
1979,  *The Film Machine (Filmmaskinen)*
1987,  *How They Look (Hvordan de ser ud)*
1994,  *The Dogs are Barking (Hundene gør)*
1994,  *The Yellow Jersey in the High Mountains (Den gule trøje i de høje bjerge)*

2000,  *What the Picture Shows* (*Billedet forestiller*)

**Hjort:** You're an unusually versatile figure. Not only do your films span a number of genres, your career as a whole embraces a wide variety of activities. Indeed, in your case, one is almost tempted to speak of a series of parallel, yet interconnected careers. You've published numerous volumes of poetry and essays. When you were in your twenties you worked for *Aktuelt* and *Politiken* as a journalist with a special interest in jazz, sports, film and theatre. More recently, you've become a much-loved national figure as a result of your unique commentaries on the Tour de France for Danish TV and radio. One thing you cannot lay claim to, however, is formal training in the art of film-making. How exactly did you get started as a film-maker?

**Leth:** I started writing early on. I'd worked as a journalist and had written poetry before I made my first films, but I'd always thought a lot in images. This is clear already in my first collection of poetry, *Yellow Light*, which I published in 1962. Poetry is often visual, and my poetry is particularly visual. So mentally it wasn't much of a shift for me to start making films. I had some good friends, with whom I collaborated artistically, and we simply agreed that we would make a film. At the same time we had a very intense relation to various cinematic conventions and wanted to change things. We wanted to simplify things. That in a sense is an idea that has motivated much of my work in film; I wanted to work very directly with the medium, just as one does when writing poetry. I wanted to avoid the technical traps, to avoid giving centre stage to technology. In some ways there's a direct parallel here with today's Dogme* concept. We threw ourselves into our first film, which we financed ourselves; in fact, we did absolutely everything ourselves. We borrowed equipment and made a virtue of every necessity; the fact that we simply couldn't produce synchronic sound became a virtue. We recorded the images and sound separately. The film is called *Stop for Bud* and we made it in 1963. That was my first film and it gets around. It's distributed worldwide by a French distributor and was made in the context of a congenial artists' collective consisting of Ole John, Jens Jørgen Thorsen and myself.

The next film, *Look Forward to a Time of Security* was even more radical, from a purely formal point of view. I made it together with Ole John, in Spain, where I was living at the time. We simply put images and sound together in the most incongruous ways, transgressing every manner of cinematic convention. That, then, was our first major attempt to develop a quite different take on film form, and it was to a certain extent an education in itself. We simply made the film and knew only what we felt we needed to know about film technique. At the same time I was writing for the Danish daily *Aktuelt* and had the occasion to interview Antonioni, Godard, Bo Widerberg and a series of Danish directors, so film journalism was also part of my cinematic education. The films had an impact on my poetry, and my entire career has been marked by a certain interaction between writing poetry and making films.

In 1966 we had the opportunity to make a professionally produced film, *The Perfect Human*. It was a great success, won a number of prizes at festivals, received the Danish Bodil* and any number of other awards. I suppose one might say that it provided the entry ticket to making films on professional terms. As a result I've simply skipped all formal film training, but the ironic point is that I did apply to the National Film School of Denmark* a couple of years later, unsuccessfully. By then I'd already made at least five films, but I was gently refused. The argument was that I already knew the craft of making films and therefore would be too overwhelming a presence among the other students. I was actually rather relieved to hear this!

**Hjort:** You're one of Denmark's most important documentary film-makers and many previous interviews and critical discussions have focussed on the precise nature of your documentary practice. Some critics have described your documentaries as lyrical, and you yourself have repeatedly underscored the importance of a kind of 'ethnographic wonder', as well as your desire, not to prove a particular point, but rather to show realities in an open-ended and thought-provoking manner. At times, the documentary spaces you create seem designed to provoke certain alienation effects. I'm thinking, for example, of your use of song lyrics to comment on the utterances of the hippies in Nepal, who figure centrally in *Near Heaven, Near Earth*. In Tómas Gislason's masterful documentary about you and your work, *From Heart to Hand* (*Fra hjertet til hånden*), you equate Jean-Luc Godard with poetry, and François Truffaut with prose. Is your view on the tasks and challenges of documentary film-making shaped by Godard, and thus also, indirectly, by Brecht?

**Leth:** I'm glad you've included the reference back to Brecht, for it's true that he had an enormous influence on Godard and therefore also indirectly on me. In the 1960s I often felt that Godard and I were travelling along parallel trajectories. I've never, with the exception of the interview I did with him, exchanged thoughts with Godard or known him as a colleague or friend, but I've always loved his films and I've taught courses based on his work at the Danish Film School. I've also written about Godard's films – *My Life to Live* (*Vivre sa vie*) and not least *Two or Three Things I Know About Her* (*Deux ou trois choses que je sais d'elle*) – describing his pseudo-anthropological approach to reality, which is also my own. It's a question here of adopting a stance towards reality that is marked by wonder, questioning and to some extent naïveté, while at the same time adopting a stance towards film that makes possible a probing, analytic and experimental relation to the language of film and its capacity to describe reality. This is the same kind of *Verfremdung* we find in Brecht and the idea is that language in itself, the very way of posing the questions, is important. Although Godard has been a key source of inspiration, the influence of, for example, Andy Warhol and Marcel Duchamp has been at least as important. I often feel that I've been inspired primarily by developments in the other arts, typically painting or music. During the early 1970s I worked closely with some Danish painters, including Per Kirkeby. So developments in painting, the modes of perception associated with painting, have been very important to me, and if the artist Duchamp has been important to me, so has the composer, John Cage. Cage's philosophy of emptiness, the way he utilises temporal duration, have left definite traces in my films. It's a matter of having confidence in simplicity, in every single minute, in time as it passes. Cage's ideas are reflected in the confidence I invest in the long take, where the contemplation of time and events within a single frame goes on for quite a while.

**Hjort:** In 1970 you co-directed *The Deer Garden, the Romantic Forest* with the important Danish painter, Per Kirkeby. The film is a visually remarkable exploration of the changing faces of a park that occupies a unique place in Danish culture. Could you describe the nature of the collaboration in question? I'm interested, of course, in the ways in which a painterly perspective might have shaped the visual language of the film.

**Leth:** Kirkeby and I were actually friends and artistically we had a lot in common. We worked together as part of the artists' collective, ABCinema, in the beginning of the 1970s. The driving force in that context was the idea that artists from different schools and from across the arts should be able to make films together. I was invited to make the film about the Deer Garden and it seemed perfectly natural to ask Per Kirkeby to be part of the project. The reason I wanted him to be part of it was that art historically he is anchored in and has a tremendous passion for romanticism and the Danish Golden Age.[1] And it seemed to me that the Danish Golden Age provided an excellent aesthetic angle on the Deer Garden. From a compositional point of view we thought of the Deer Garden in terms of a series of large Golden Age paintings, and the depiction of the seasons is also very much inspired by a Golden Age aesthetic. There's a great deal of stillness in the film and at certain points the romantic conception of things finds vivid expression.

**Hjort:** You studied literature and anthropology at the Universities of Århus and Copenhagen, and your films are in many ways dialogues with key anthropological thinkers. I'm thinking, of course, of *Notes on Love*, which includes a sequence that situates your filming of primarily Melanesian women within the context of Malinowski's work on the Trobriand islands just North East of Papua New Guinea. You point out that Malinowski was working here some seventy years earlier, that his project at that time was 'to describe love' and that he is your 'hero'. *Notes on Love* even includes images of black and white photographs taken by Malinowski. Most contemporary anthropologists associate Malinowski with positivistic beliefs, and favour instead some version of anti-realist anthropology, which remains sceptical about our ability ever to grasp the truth of a foreign culture. At times, you seem closer to this kind of literary anthropology, which foregrounds the poetic, writerly activities of the anthropologist, than you do to the realist anthropological theories of Malinowski. Could you talk about your relation to Malinowski, and your self-understanding as an anthropologist?

**Leth:** I see anthropology and especially Malinowski as tools that I can use in my films; they provide a kind of aesthetic attitude. The point is by no means to establish myself as a disciple of Malinowski, or something like that. What fascinates me about Malinowski is actually his use of language and the distance – the very precise distance – he establishes in relation to his subject matter. A lot has happened in anthropology since then and I'm interested in people like Michel Foucault, whom I've also read, but I can't use his work in the same way, although his ideas are perhaps closer to my own way of thinking than

Malinowski's are. I sometimes refer to Foucault in my manuscripts. However, I can use Malinowski. I can use his way of seeing and I find the very idea of describing sexuality as a phenomenon deeply inspiring. So I keep going back to his major work, *Sex and Repression in Savage Society*, which in some ways is my bible, not on account of its propositional content, but on account of its method. What moves me is his almost naive relation to what he describes. His straightforwardness and way of describing things make him the romantic incarnation of the anthropologist sitting in a tent and looking at the natives. That approach has been deeply inspiring throughout my work. I've wanted to be someone who looks upon life with a sense of wonder, someone who somehow asks the most awkward questions. We're dealing here with an aesthetic attitude rather than some position in anthropology. I have a frivolous relation to anthropology, for I simply use it as a tool. My references to Malinowski go all the way back to *Life in Denmark*. That is, when I line up the women in that film, I'm drawing on Malinowski. Indeed, there's actually a hidden reference to Malinowski; it's almost a citation. The subtitle reads 'Women from a Provincial Town', and both the composition and title recall Malinowksi.

**Hjort:** The concept of the exotic seems to be central to your conception of documentary film. Why?

**Leth:** It's true that I'm very interested in making the banal exotic. A good example is *Life in Denmark*, where I try to view the familiar with a stranger's eyes, try to adopt an analytic stance towards what is most natural, obvious and mundane. That's the aim, what I try to discipline my mind into achieving. In a way I attempt to charge the most obvious reality with meaning. When I write poetry, for example, I may determine that everything is a matter of choice, even the possibility of ruling out certain options. My approach has frequently been to rent a summer house somewhere and to isolate myself entirely from everyday obligations and intercourse in order simply to sit and describe the most immediate view: what I can see on my table or through the window. The driving force here has been my conviction that things or reality can be charged that way, can be somehow re-enchanted, to use an old-fashioned romantic term. I am perhaps related to the romantics in that I believe that it is possible to describe the things we see so simply and realistically, and at the same time so intensely, that they become charged and enchanted. I think this method makes possible a certain transcendence, to speak a little mystically. It's possible to adopt a certain perspective on reality which changes it and allows it to be viewed with a sense of profound ethnographic wonder. In this way the most obvious realities are called into question as everything is dissected in an almost experimental manner, and reassembled in new ways. These are the ideas that have motivated many of my more experimental films, from *Life in Denmark* to *Good and Evil*. In those films it was a matter of removing things from their normal contexts and placing them in an empty room where they could be scrutinised.

**Hjort:** Many of your films have focussed on Danes and Denmark. In films such as *Dancing Bournonville* and *Peter Martins: A Dancer* you provide a cinematic interpretation and record of outstanding moments in the cultural life of the nation. In *Life in Denmark* you isolate some of the driving concerns of ordinary Danes. Films like *Ophelia's Flowers* and *The Deer Garden, the Romantic Forest* are lyrical explorations of aspects of a specifically Danish nature. Could you talk a little about the intended audience for these national films? Are these films directed primarily at a national public, or at an international audience? Lurking behind these questions is the issue that is at the heart of current debates about the future of Danish film: are international audiences interested primarily in that which is always already international, or rather, in that which is experienced as other, as different?

**Leth:** I rarely think of the audience when I make my films. That's perhaps a point of view that few would share, but I really don't think about the audience. The same is true when I write poetry. I don't think about the reader. This sounds coquettish, but it's actually true. That is, if I'm interested in something, if the subject matter interests me enough to make a film about it, then I simply make the film and assume that someone will want to see it. My view more generally is that not all films necessarily have to have a large audience, just as a poetry collection can't have lots and lots of readers, compared to novels. At the same time it's clear that poetry is important, and perhaps even necessary if literature is to survive. It has an inherent power to inspire people and retain its vitality across time. The same is true of film, in my view. This, ideally, is how I like to see things. I think that there's an unfortunate tendency to focus on what in the television business is called 'viewer ratings' and to measure films in terms of their box office success. I do, of course, realise that film is different from poetry in that films cost money, but since we are fortunate enough to have a system that legally guarantees the development of film art in Denmark, I think it's important to make the films one wants to make, without thinking in terms of what may or may not be popular. That's my alibi for making films and my political position on questions of cultural production. It's important to be able to make films in much the same way that poetry is written. That is, it's important to be able to experiment with the language of film, to question cinematic conventions, constantly, so that the language of film can be revitalised by means of a probing and experimental stance.

As far as the relation between the national and the international is concerned, I would want to say that I've been fortunate enough to see my films appreciated abroad. My films' success at festivals, that is, in the eyes of a discriminating audience, has in part enabled me to continue making films in Denmark. If my films were to be measured in terms only of how many viewers see them in the cinema, and that kind of thing, everything would quickly grind to a halt. However, it happens to be the case that Denmark has had a wonderful distribution system for documentary and experimental films. In this sense the National Film Board is really a kind of popular library for documentary film; it's had the effect of making these films very accessible, and they're in fact much more widely utilised and viewed than most people happen to think. At the same time I've also had the pleasure of knowing that many of my films actually have been shown in cinemas and were made in cinema format, that is, 35 mm. As a result their chances of being shown at festivals have been good and many of them have been internationally distributed. If we focus on the concept of international film, I have to say that I go to the cinema less and less, and feel less and less satisfied by the experience when I finally do. The kind of hybrid product that can be referred to as an 'international production' is of course the most boring thing imaginable. We're talking about a product of the most average quality, the result of any number of dramaturgical deliberations, market analyses and so on. This has to be deadly boring and I'm certainly not interested in going to the cinema in order to see that kind of thing. I don't believe in the idea of aiming at that kind of film. A market is of course a market; that can't be denied, but I also believe that there's something called film art, which has its own conditions of development, its own imperatives and trajectories which run parallel to the market mechanisms or depart from them entirely. There are of course also a lot of directors whom I value highly today, who have made very successful films. I'm thinking, for example, of Martin Scorsese, Jim Jarmusch, Quentin Tarantino and Lars von Trier.

**Hjort:** You're intensely interested in love and, by your own admission, a great lover of women. Yet, the view on love that emerges in, for example, *Notes on Love* is anything but the standard, romantic conception. In this film the viewer witnesses a series of sequences in which a man examines the face of a woman, not gently and with compassion, but in an almost unbearably clinical, dispassionate and self-absorbed manner. The solipsistic and unilateral nature of the interactions is fully expressed in the following statements, which are made by one of the men, and repeated in a subsequent sequence: 'I can tell you very clearly what I'm doing to you. I'm holding you in my arms. I'm kissing you. I'm pressing your body against my body and won't let you go. That's what I'm doing to you.' Are you, in fact, deeply sceptical of romantic conceptions of love? If not, then what, exactly, were you trying to convey with these sequences?

**Leth:** That's a difficult question to answer because making that film was almost like writing a poem; I'd almost want to say that it was made instinctively. It's actually hard for me to interpret the film, to say exactly what I wanted to convey with it. It's a *film cru* in the sense that it almost spells itself through its material. I'm fascinated with this idea of performing an action while at the same time observing myself doing it. There's a kind of 'schizophrenia', if you will – which is perhaps part of life too – in both my poetry and my films. It's a matter of intensely observing the most basic activities while also engaging in a form of self-scrutiny. This self-reflexivity was very extreme at that particular point in time, because I was at a certain stage in my life; I was very introverted and my descriptions of love in that film are almost macabre; they're like dissections. However, if you look at my poetry, you'll find a lot of erotic images. I actually think that it's primarily the tone that's different in that film and in my poetry. I'm driven to describe with great precision what I see, what I feel, what I observe myself and others doing. This motivating force is almost like placing a magnifying glass in front of the eye in order to observe reality, both feelings and their expression; but it's also a matter of expressing a very frightening depth that is part of love's essence. This approach is perhaps extraordinarily clinical and observational compared with ordinary forms of acting, but I think that many of the actors with whom I worked felt that the experience in question was unique. The actors had to be completely naked, both literally and

65

metaphorically, and this involved delving deep into themselves in search of certain resources, since my stance towards them was almost ethnographic. My aim was to try to transfer the ethnographic perspective from a really exotic and distant world to a proximate world, to our own, thereby transforming the relevant realities into equally ethnographic objects. The idea behind the film was to turn love into an ethnographic object; in itself a powerful thought. I was in a very particular state of mind when I made *Notes on Love*, and I wanted to proceed in a really radical way, which has made it one of my most extreme films. It was actually intended to be more ironic, more lighthearted, but it ended up becoming a very dark film. But I'm very pleased with it, because while I was making it I felt I was carrying out the project as a kind of personal intellectual experiment. I wanted to peel away everything that was superfluous, to remove everything that might sweeten the film or make it gentler, more comprehensible, if you will. In that sense the film is as dark as a poem, I think. I was also delighted to work together with Per Kirkby.

**Hjort:** The concept of narrative occupies a central role in both your art and your life. In *Haiti Express* you foreground the issue of narrative in a series of voice-over statements that thematise the difficulties involved in beginning a story. You've frequently talked about your love of Haiti in terms of narrative. Your claim has been that in Haiti you're constantly in the thick of unfolding stories, the beginnings and ends of which seem mysterious and obscure. A narrative, for you, is clearly something quite different from the rational construction with a beginning, middle and end that Aristotle envisaged. What, exactly, is your view on narrative, in art and life?

**Leth:** The question becomes very powerful when you mention both art and life. I think of myself as a storyteller. I won't pretend otherwise, but I don't tell stories in the way that is expected. I've exploded that particular narrative mode in my films, and I've done so on purpose. First of all because I rarely have what might be called a 'message' in my documentary films. There's rarely something I absolutely want to prove, and I also find it boring to tell a story in a conventional way. I don't find it boring to see films by other film-makers who tell stories that lead somewhere, but I find it tedious to have to concern myself with the idea of having some anecdotal point. I've never been tempted to tell stories in a conventional way. I do on the other hand find it inspiring to work with narrative if I can use a certain aesthetic method and philosophical concepts as a starting point. In *Haiti Express*, which you refer to, I take on the question of narrative directly. I construct the narrative in such a way that we don't know where it leads or ends. In so doing I turn the very form of the feature film, the narrative, into a game. It's a matter of playing with the concept of reality, of never hiding the scaffolding or techniques and of making them manifest instead. At this point I find *Haiti Express* a deeply pleasing film. It was brutally received when it first appeared and for many years I was very hurt by the negative responses it received and I didn't see it again for a very long time. In recent years I've seen it on several occasions with quite different people and I'm really quite pleased with what I did with it. My aim in *Haiti Express* was to work with a collapsable fiction that we moved around in reality. That is, I had some actors whom I wanted to place in some real situations, and then I wanted to write up the scenes based on those situations.

I'd obviously made up my mind about a lot of things in advance, and I had lists of the scenes I wanted to shoot, but much of the time the actors were simply placed within a given chunk of reality, where they were expected to make sense of their stories. *Haiti Express*'s story was developed on a set that was real. This was true merely as a result of choosing Haiti, whereas the producer had a clear preference for a more controllable location. He suggested Guadeloupe or Martinique, but I was fascinated by the idea of Haiti, quite simply because Haiti was a banana republic, full of strange and surprising things, a surreal political reality. It's a question of letting yourself be challenged. I've always felt that it was more exciting to undertake something that was difficult and challenging, something that wasn't that straightforward or easy to grasp. That's why I've never written a complete script. I don't think it's interesting simply to reproduce a script on film. I think it's more exciting to work with some sketches, which can then be developed in relation to actual circumstances. Real circumstances are very important to me, tremendously inspiring. There's this sense of having some sketches, some angles, and also some narrative elements, which can then be moved around and played with. I like to retain that kind of openness in the actual process of making a given film.

There are aspects of *Haiti Express* that I find deeply gratifying. For example, the interview with Roberto D'Aubisson in El Salvador in the beginning. Arranging that took some doing. He was after all an incredibly dangerous man, the leader of the death squads and so on. It was a coup that we managed to arrange that interview. In fact, we conducted it under false cover, as a real TV crew from Denmark, but we used 35 mm film. We managed to get access to him and we'd consulted some of our most expert colleagues before the interview, Raymond Bonner from *The New York Times* and Chris Dickey from *The Washington Post*. We'd asked them what we should ask D'Aubisson. They suggested that we should ask the most probing questions. Was he behind the murder of the four nuns? Had he ordered the murder of archbishop Romero? And so on. The task in question was a very, very unusual one for an actor. Imagine this Danish actor who shows up and has to try to be a journalist, or is given the task of representing a journalist. However, Henning Jensen did a wonderful job of his role and once he'd taken four valium pills on the way to the interview he asked those questions in a terrifying atmosphere, surrounded by bodyguards and so on. I'm very proud of the fact that we were able to work so directly with reality.

Here we have that concept I want to propose, the idea of collapsable fictions, fictions that you can somehow unpack and unfold; and then the story simply continues. I do after all tell a story, a rudimentary one perhaps. It's an old existential story about a journalist in this case, an intellectual, who somehow loses himself, loses his identity or his sense of self in a reality that becomes less and less perspicuous. This is a well-known literary plot and I don't make any effort to complicate it, so it's very rudimentary in the film. However, every single scene, on the other hand, interests me enormously, or rather, every scene is a story in itself. Actually, it's really a matter of a series of tableaux that have been arranged contrastively, but everything in the film is real, including the interview with the minister towards the end, and I'm very proud of that. I had requested an interview with the

Minister of Information and Jean Claude 'Baby Doc' Duvalier, but we were told that they wouldn't be able to meet with us, although they'd be happy to answer our questions. Therefore I sent in written questions and we got written answers back. So that's the dialogue in the scene; we're actually using the Haitian government's responses.

**Hjort:** You've made a series of documentary films about larger-than-life figures, individuals whose extraordinary natural gifts are matched only by their intense ambition to realise this potential fully. I have in mind, clearly, your bicycle trilogy – *Stars and Watercarriers*, *The Impossible Hour*, *A Sunday in Hell* – and *Peter Martins: A Dancer*. You've frequently expressed contempt for the small-minded nature of certain typically Danish attitudes. In Denmark a radical, anti-authoritarian commitment to equality leads easily to a dogmatic and debilitating refusal of excellence and its enriching influence. Your position, quite clearly, is that the quality of our lives can only be enhanced, not diminished, through contact with exceptionally gifted persons. The lives led by these individuals embody, somehow, some of the very moral sources and virtues that we, in our inept ways, are constantly struggling to contact. Are the films in question an extended meditation on the virtues of certain forms of distinction and hierarchy, as compared to misguided interpretations of equality?

**Leth:** Yes, your question actually articulates much of what can be extrapolated from those films. When I make films about great figures, wonderful, brilliant performers, it is because I feel a certain fascination. Frequently my starting point is a kind of polemic against dominant tendencies of the time. In the 1960s I made *The Perfect Human*, which in itself is a kind of polemic against imperfection, the cultivation of mediocrity. The sports films were made during the same period in which I wrote my sports poems. The latter were very controversial in 1967 because they cultivated the sportsman as a hero, as a model, as someone who's capable of moving us. A great sports performance is like theatre, where we can see the qualities of our lives explosively displayed in purified form, which in turn enables us to situate ourselves in relation to our ideals. Outstanding sports accomplishments resemble Greek theatre, where all kinds of characters and traits were put on expressive display – heroes, villains, virtue and vice. We owe it to the great performers to respect them for this aspect of what they do. At the same time, my interest has been in the mechanisms underwriting the accomplishments of these particular individuals. My stance, once again, has been an anthropological one involving ethnographic curiosity about how the various elements fit together. It's not enough, in my mind, simply to admire a given achievement. My aim is to ask how and why. What does the workshop of Peter Martins, the dancer, look like? I'm interested in peering inside and the film is very much driven by my own curiosity. That is, there's something that I myself want to know.

I knew absolutely nothing about ballet when I first started working on the Martins film, but I was fascinated by his charisma, by what he was able to give us. What I saw in Martins, which is also what I saw in the sports heroes, was the charisma, the ability to facilitate or transmit certain experiences. These kinds of experiences are transcendental; the experience of a great performance is something that enriches our lives. That's why

*Elements in Leth's so-called 'existential catalogue'* (Good and Evil/Det gode og det onde).
[Photo: Henning Camre]

we congregate around it, but my stance involves describing the work that goes into these performances. My aim is to penetrate and reveal what it is exactly that these remarkable individuals do, the mechanisms underwriting their accomplishments. I maintain admiration and respect as my starting point. But my aim in the films has been to explain, to reveal, to examine, to get to the heart of the relevant processes, in order perhaps to enhance our understanding of them. I'm not motivated by moralising intentions. I simply want to explain something. However, it's true that there's a polemical dimension, a response to the perhaps very Danish cultivation of mediocrity, which I find disturbing and sterile.

**Hjort:** Some of your documentary films experiment interestingly with the relation between word and image. I'm thinking, for example, of *66 Scenes from America*, which presents a series of almost hyper-real, postcard-like images of America, that are identified, in a series of significantly *delayed*, laconic and minimalist comments. The longest sequence is that of Andy Warhol fastidiously eating a hamburger. Having completed this exercise, Warhol delivers the following line: 'My name is Andy Warhol and I just finished eating a hamburger.' What, exactly, is the purpose of the intentionally strained and awkward relation between images and words in *66 Scenes from America*?

**Leth:** I'm delighted you've noted the delays and timing with such precision, because that's a very powerful element in the film. I'm deeply fascinated by the relation between word and image, which I've explored in various ways from one film to the next, using commentators, that is, voice over, but also subtitles. In my mind word and image needn't go together. I'm interested in how the individual image is perceived or read. This goes back to my fascination with the fact that films consist of several separate elements: sound, image and text. I'm fascinated by the possibility of pushing the way in which the image is read in different directions. For example, by placing the music in unexpected places, which is something I do a lot, sometimes following stochastic principles. Here again there's a reference to John Cage, Warhol and Marcel Duchamp. The principle of chance is very important to me. That's frequently how I make a decision and I often leave it to the film's editor to organise the various elements into a sequence. The concept of a sequence is entirely arbitrary as far as I'm concerned. I never insist on a specific sequence of scenes. In fact, I can easily imagine throwing them all into a box and retrieving them at random. I did precisely that in several of my films. *66 Scenes from America* is typical in that respect. The material is organised following different concepts. There are landscapes in which one sees a house, there are flags, there are people. That's how I organised the material and after that it was the principle of chance that determined the order in which the categories appeared. As far as the film's text is concerned, I became fascinated by the fact that the very gesture of providing information can have the effect of categorising an image.

That's a fascinating idea. In *Life in Denmark* the subtitles are a very dynamic and controlling element of the viewing experience itself, but in *66 Scenes from America* I've reduced the verbal aspect to a minimalistic phrase. That is, I sort of empty the film, empty each individual scene of content, by putting a label on it. I played around with the effect of providing the relevant information earlier or later in the scene. There's another interesting aspect: the people who do the talking in the film have to introduce themselves after they've performed their actions. In the Warhol scene I received an involuntary and perfectly wonderful gift, which precisely makes me believe in the magical significance of chance. When I similarly situate the music in different places, I do so because I myself am curious to see what happens as a result. I think that doing this kind of thing has a very stimulating effect, just as the utterance in the Warhol scene does. He is told that he has to say his name and that he should do so when he has completed his action, but what happens is that the action takes a very long time to perform; it's simply agonising. I have to admit that I personally adore that, because it's a pure homage to Warhol. It couldn't be more Warholesque. That's of course why he agreed to do it. He's also almost sculptural in his way of placing things, of handling them. It's quite wonderful and at the same time there's something movingly fragile about him, so much so that one becomes quite concerned for him. At least I find that I'm deeply moved by the image of his fragility. However, the scene has other chance gifts. First of all there's the temporal duration itself, which makes it a pure John Cage scene. Time passes and things happen, and the action in question is very simple and at the same time very expressive and full of plasticity. Then some light falls through the window, a sunray changes the image twice by altering the light on Warhol's face. This is a pure gift, something I have absolutely no control over. Finally, Warhol happens to misunderstand what he's supposed to do, so there's a long pause after he's finished eating his hamburger during which time he simply sits there, ready. His eyes flicker around and he doesn't utter the sentence immediately after he's finished eating as I'd expected him to. He sits there and we see the concern in his eyes; the suspense almost kills us, although we feel compassion too in a way. At last, after a noticeable pause, he says the phrase and the explanation for the delay is that he was waiting for a cue. Now, this delay gives the scene a quite different dimension, I think. I like to think of many of these things, which are inscribed within the film, as comprising a kind of mysterious trace; that is, at some level, as I've already suggested, I really believe in a kind of magic of the film material. I think Magritte is a major source of inspiration, for as you know he accompanies his images with incorrect information. I mean, the effect of this is incredibly stimulating. It's pure surrealism. I'm interested in this idea of claiming that something is something other than what it in fact is. I'm interested in the effect of these kinds of claims. Just as music can colour the atmosphere in a given scene. I've been committed to the idea of controlling things up to a certain point. And beyond that point I prefer some uncharted territory, so that chance and circumstance can play a role. That openness is tremendously important, because it also explains why I, at some deep level, refuse to operate with banal dramaturgical principles. It's very important to me that my films be moved by a different kind of spirit, that their pulse be different. The thing is that I'm sometimes criticised because people don't find my films sufficiently representative of the phenomena they explore, but my aim has never been to be representative. I think it's rather boring to have to exhaust a topic, to have to hear all sides of the story, as it were. I completely reject the idea that documentary film-making should be educational in a rational sense, the idea that it has certain obligations along these lines. I don't think that film art should be educational, but rather that it should expand some horizons and make possible certain experiences that people might find enriching or useful. However, the use value in question can't reside in some narrowly single-minded concentration on where one is going or what one should be trying to say with one's images. The stories I tell have a life of their own which cannot be translated into use value. There is of course a very reductive conception of documentary film-making in many parts of the world, and I'm one among a small number of documentary film-makers who make their films exactly the way they want to, insisting that this is how they tell their stories.

**Hjort:** You're one of a handful of Danish film-makers who have worked with a number of different genres of film-making. What sets you apart from your colleagues, however, is your willingness also to blur the boundaries between, for example, the genres of fiction film and documentary film. *Traberg* is particularly interesting in this respect as it documents a period in the turbulent political history of Haiti, while at the same time developing a fictional narrative about the real-world journalist, Ebbe Traberg. What, exactly, were you trying to achieve with this interesting blending of fictional and documentary elements?

**Leth:** I discovered afterwards that *Traberg* in a certain way is a remake of *Haiti Express*, although it's very different. It's less stringent than *Haiti Express*, but I wanted to make a film with a fictional story that would capture a good deal of my fascination with the exotic and the qualities associated with banana republics. I really enjoy watching detective films myself, so I dreamt of making a kind of detective film and of perhaps adopting a playful stance in relation to the genre. When I was writing up the project together with Dan Holmberg we talked about how the hero should be a worn figure, a kind of Elmer Leonard hero, someone whose life had been full of rather dubious affairs. He should, we decided, look like Traberg, who has been my good friend for years and years, so we thought, why not use Traberg? We thought the idea was wonderful, so that's what we did. We then created this set-up that had him starting out in Spain, where he actually lived, in order to find someone or other. Holmberg, my gifted photographer, and I actually agreed that we'd be very relaxed about the nuts and bolts of the intrigue, that is, how to get from one place to the next. Traberg just needed a reason, the envelope and so on. We decided that we'd feel no sense of obligation towards, and would relate only vaguely to, the demands of the genre. *Traberg* is not, of course, a documentary film about Traberg. Some people thought that it was, especially some of Traberg's acquaintances, but it's not. It's a fiction film, that's the intention. However, what happens then is that during our stay in Haiti all hell breaks loose; Haitian reality simply explodes and a lot of very dramatic things occur. As the observer of life and reality that I am, I become absolutely fascinated with what's going on and feel that it should be included in the story. I feel that I can't simply tell a story that entirely circumvents the unfolding events. Instead, my view was that these events should break into the already very flimsy story. My sense was that chance, once again, had made us a gift. In a way the idea here picks up on that of *Haiti Express*. Reality is now so violent – there were those attempted coups – that we have to include it. Then it turns out that the reality in question is so overwhelming that it takes over the film, almost takes over the Traberg story. Traberg becomes peripheral, a marginal frame around a depiction of what is happening in Haiti at the time. I don't know whether *Traberg* is as interesting as *Haiti Express*, but there's a lot of extraordinarily powerful documentary material in it, I think. In that respect it makes sense that *Traberg* should be the way it is.

**Hjort:** Many of your films articulate a kind of anthropology of religious sentiment. You have systematically focussed on human activities that involve the kinds of intense interaction that Durkheim associated with religious feeling. In *Stars and Watercarriers* you mobilise religious terms to explore the realities of cycling. In your Haiti films you return, again and again, to voodoo. Viewers watching the rather marginal, collectively produced film entitled *The Search* witness a number of different religious symbols and situations, including a crucifixion. Why this emphasis on religion?

**Leth:** My attitude towards religion is in all respects voyeuristic. Religion or religiosity is a strong and central element in people's lives, and it is only as such that I have encountered it, that is, as material. It's not that I've sought it out. Take voodoo in Haiti, for example. It's clear that one encounters voodoo if one is interested in observing life in Haiti. It's also clear that it's incredibly exciting to see it, explore it, and depict it on film, but it's a matter of curiosity. I do not have religious leanings myself.

**Hjort:** Your bicycle films are extraordinary in this way, and so are your films about dance. I was reminded of a conversation I had with Anders Refn about *The Flying Devils* (*De flyvende djævle*) in which he said that what moved him and excited him about that film was this idea that you can't be a trapeze artist unless you really trust the other people with whom you are performing. There is the same kind of insight in your films, I think, into these irreducibly social phenomena. You really foreground something that a lot of people are largely unaware of.

**Leth:** The idea of sacrifice or total commitment is a crucial element in my films. It plays a very important role in my description of people's efforts and achievements, of the challenges they undertake. We are of course dealing here with concepts that have religious resonances. My films are frequently about sacrifice, both actual and symbolic, and it makes perfect sense to me that the language in question would be coloured by religious concepts. I sort of use that kind of experience as a lever. I'm not reticent or in any way embarrassed about using a language that is so heavily charged or that may have religious overtones. I have the feeling that when I described those aspects of bicycle racing and dance, I really wanted to shift to another level. My own experience of these things is very sensitive; I see things that lie beyond our immediately accessible reality, which I would like to share.

**Bondebjerg:** Your most recent film, *I'm Alive. Søren Ulrik Thomsen: A Danish Poet* has just received the Best Portrait Film prize at the Odense Film Festival. The focus in this film is on the poet as singular individual and his pursuit of the kind of unique, poetic language that is capable of disclosing the world. You yourself are an exceptional poet and you've dealt with central Danish poets in some of your other films, in *Klaus Rifbjerg* and *Danish Literature*. You've objected vehemently to the tendency to use film merely to illustrate poetry and literature more generally. As a result the portrait of Rifbjerg also captures the poet in his daily existence, in his workshop, as it were, and makes present both the poetic text itself and the creative individual behind it. Your distillation of Danish literature is similarly based on the idea of foregrounding the poetic text, at times by means of the poet himself. Do you see these literary films as part of a larger series of films about outstanding individuals? Do you see yourself as using the same techniques and approach here as in your films about great sportsmen or about Peter Martins?

**Leth:** No, I don't see the films as parts of a series, but I don't mind if others do, because of course the starting point is the same: a fascination with excellence, with the truly exceptional. I don't use the same techniques in all the films in question, but the basic perspective is certainly the same. It's a matter of witnessing the ultimate achievement, something sublime, while exploring the disciplined work that underwrites it; it's a matter of penetrating a given milieu. Films about literature are unique in the sense that they require an almost surgical precision. I hate the trivialisation of literature, and there's certainly a lot of that in film. I'm allergic to it. I remember that when I was making the film about Klaus Rifbjerg I was terrified by the idea that it might become a lot of unstructured talk, so I devised some tableaux, where I felt the author could appear as a

73

clearly defined image of himself, thereby eliminating the illusion of an interview. I think the result was a little rigid. *Danish Literature* is inspired by formal issues, by the challenge involved in the arrogant thought of being able to provide a cinematic presentation of all of Danish literature in 40 minutes. That is, the motor force here was the idea of abbreviation. What inspired me was the dizzying thought of wrestling with such an enormous topic under strict formal constraints. I think it worked. It was also a film-maker's dream involving a personal selection of texts by authors both dead and alive, and a set of clear rules. That was what was decisive. And one of the rules of the game was: no illustration of texts.

That rule was also decisive for my collaboration with Søren Ulrik Thomsen. I hate it when poems are illustrated with images. Film simply cannot compete with the suggestive power of poetry's imagery. I don't like it when a film intrudes on a poem and appropriates its language. What is required is a much more controlled strategy. Søren Ulrik Thomsen had himself expressed a desire to see me make the film about him. I was nervous in the beginning, because I didn't know whether our chemistry would be right, but everything worked out very nicely. I'm very pleased with that film. It's as though I was offered that project at exactly the right moment. Søren Ulrik's poetry and personality have inspired me and my collaborators to make something very powerful and pure. Dan Holmberg, my photographer, has produced some of the most beautiful work he's ever done, and the same is true of Camilla Skousen, my editor. I dare say that the poems inspired us to make a film that itself is a kind of poem. Søren Ulrik came to Haiti so that we could talk about the project, and the first thing he said was that it was important to him to know that I would make a film that I would be pleased with from an artistic point of view. I presented a potential problem to him, the fact that I refuse to illustrate poems, although I did want to be able to make use of a lot decontextualised images from his poetry. He solved this by simply giving me *carte blanche* to cannibalise his poems as I saw fit. He repeatedly said that he was sure that my cool aesthetic distance in relation to what he called his 'overheated' poetry would lead to something good. I think he was right. The stories he tells in the film, about his childhood and his method, he had those in his head right from the start. He outlined several of them for me in Haiti a year before we started. Those were things he wanted to give to the film, I clearly understood that, and I also regard them as a gift. The fact that the stories in question were so polished and complete also helped to establish the film's style. Søren Ulrik Thomsen as a person and poet was fully present and at the same time at a comfortable distance. I felt like making a film with emblematically clear images. So I asked myself: What do I have? I have the poet's poetry, I have him as a physical person, I have what he wants to say and I have his concrete environment, his tools and immediate milieu. Those are the elements. No mediating, connective tissue, just the pure goods. I think the film reveals Søren Ulrik Thomsen's stature as a poet and his generosity as a person. That's not nothing.

1    Refers to a generation of painters associated with the professors C.W. Eckersberg and J.L. Lund. Key names include Christen Købke, Dankvart Dreyer, Constantin Hansen, Jens Juel, Johan Thomas Lundbye, Jørgen Roed, Martinus Rørbye and P.C. Skovgaard. The fertile period in question dates from 1820 to 1850 and emphasises portraiture, genre and landscape painting, realism, national historical themes and Danish nature.

# Christian Braad Thomsen

## 1940–

Christian Braad Thomsen was one of the first students to graduate from the National Film School of Denmark,* where he was trained as a director from 1967–69. In addition to producing a wide-ranging cinematic oeuvre, which includes both short, documentary, and feature-length films, Christian Braad Thomsen established himself as an incisive culture critic and film writer already in the sixties. His stance on policies relating to film and culture more generally has frequently been uncompromising and he has always been a passionate advocate of alternative film art. These commitments are evident, for example, in his book *The Non-Reconciled* (*De uforsonlige*, 1988), which focusses on a number of his favourite film directors. His artistic and political leanings are also reflected in his books on Fassbinder, Hitchcock and the French new wave directors. Braad Thomsen's passionate interest in psychoanalysis is foregrounded in a collection of his film criticism entitled

*Christian Braad Thomsen. [Photo: Jan Buus]*

*Snapshots: Film, Politics, and Psychoanalysis, 1968–93* (*Snapshots. Film, politik og psykoanalyse 1968–93*) and in his Freud biography, *Sigi the Conqueror* (*Sigi Erobreren*, 1984). Braad Thomsen has also played a crucial role in Denmark as an importer and distributor of art film. His features include the realist *Dear Irene* (*Kære Irene*, 1971), the more tragi-comic *Ladies on the Rocks* (*Koks i kulissen*, 1983) and *The Blue Monk* (*Den Blå Munk*, 1998). Braad Thomsen's interest in recollection and central Freudian concepts informs some of his features, especially *Children of Pain* (*Smertens børn*, 1977), *Dreams Don't Make Noise When They Die* (*Drømme støjer ikke når de dør*, 1979), and *Stab in the Heart* (*Kniven i hjertet*, 1981). Similar concerns are evident in his documentary autobiographies, *Wellspring of My World* (*Herfra min verden går*, 1976) and *Flowers of Memory* (*Hvor mindets blomster gror*, 1991). Two of Braad Thomsen's most recent films – *Karen Blixen: Storyteller* (1996) and *Morten Korch: Every Cloud Has a Silver Lining* (*Morten Korch – Solskin kan man altid finde*, 1999) – provide two very different cinematic portraits of key Danish authors.

## Feature films
1971,  *Dear Irene* (*Kære Irene*)
1977,  *Children of Pain* (*Smertens børn*)
1979,  *Dreams Don't Make Noise When They Die* (*Drømme støjer ikke når de dør*)
1981,  *Stab in the Heart* (*Kniven i hjertet*)
1983,  *Ladies on the Rocks* (*Koks i kulissen*)
1998,  *The Blue Monk* (*Den Blå Munk*)

## *Short films and documentaries*
1971,  *The Squatters* (*Slumstormerne*)
1971,  *Things Could Be Better, My Friend* (*Det kan blive bedre, kammerat*)
1972,  *The Nest Box* (*Stærekassen*)
1972,  *Dusan Makavejev*
1972,  *Rainer Werner Fassbinder*
1972,  *Joaquim Pedro de Andrade*
1976,  *Wellspring of My World* (*Herfra min verden går*)
1980,  *The One You Love* (*Den man elsker*)
1991,  *Flowers of Memory* (*Hvor mindets blomster gror*)
1996,  *Karen Blixen: Storyteller*
1999,  *Morten Korch: Every Cloud Has a Silver Lining* (*Morten Korch – Solskin kan man altid finde*)

## TV productions
1974,  *Flowers for Mona* (*Blomster til Mona*)

## Books
1971,  *Godard: From Gangsters to Red Guardists* (*Godard – Fra gangstere til rødgardister*)
1973,  *Political Film-Making* (*Politisk filmkunst*)
1983,  *Desire and the Law* (*Lysten og loven*)
1984,  *Sigi the Conqueror* (*Sigi Erobreren*)
1988,  *The Non-Reconciled* (*De uforsonlige*)
1990,  *Heritage and Debt* (*Arv og gæld*)
1990,  *Hitchcock: His Life and Films* (*Hitchcock – hans liv og film*)
1991,  *Fassbinder: The Life and Work of a Provocative Genius* (*Fassbinder – hans liv og film*)
1993,  *Snapshots: Film, Politics and Psychoanalysis, 1968–93* (*Snapshots. Film, politik og psykoanalyse, 1968–93*)
1994,  *The Camera as Pen: The New Wave in French Cinema* (*Kameraet som pen. Den nye bølge i fransk film, 1958–94*)
1998,  *Sickness Transformed into Beauty* (*Sygdom forvandlet til skønhed*)
1998,  *Pasolini* (*Pasolini*)
2000,  *Dream Films* (*Drømmefilm*)

**Hjort:** Your contribution to Danish film has taken the form of innovative film-making, but you have also played a crucial role as critic, some would say 'gadfly'. In order to take the pulse, as it were, of contemporary Danish film, and as a way of understanding your own cinematic project, I'd like to go back to your incisive and provocative diagnosis of the malaise of Danish film in the late 1960s and early 1970s. In a very interesting article published in *Aktuelt* (April 1966) you welcomed the decision to establish the National Film School of Denmark (1966). You argued persuasively that one of the shortcomings of Danish film at that point was its failure to promote what you call a 'Danish cinematic realism'. Your claim was that 'Danish film art' should be a matter of realistically depicting the way Danes 'think, speak, love and live.' Has Danish cinema gravitated towards the cinematic realism for which you called?

**Braad Thomsen:** Yes, it certainly has, but I've moved away from that realism. I remember watching the Danish films that were made in the 1960s and thinking, 'The language they're speaking isn't Danish; that's not how people speak in Denmark.' What was being spoken was a Danish theatre language and in that context it was necessary to call for a cinematic realism. I myself tried to articulate a new kind of realism when I made my first feature film, *Dear Irene*. Although I'd written a script of about 300 pages, we simply set it aside in many of the scenes and asked the actors to improvise their responses. They knew the relevant aspects of the situations in question and knew what the scenes were about, but other than that many of the scenes were generated through improvisation in order precisely to produce a certain kind of realism. I said 'actors', but they weren't actually actors, because back then my experience was that actors couldn't improvise. I thus chose to work with amateurs and good friends so as to be able to get at a more authentic Danish language. Today that kind of realism doesn't interest me as much. I'm much more interested these days in developing a stylised cinematic language.

**Hjort:** To illustrate your understanding of Danish cinematic realism, you referred to the now classic film, *Weekend* by Palle Kjærulff-Schmidt. Are there any recent films that exemplify the aesthetic in question?

**Braad Thomsen:** I could of course point to some very realistic Danish films that were produced in the course of the 1980s, but I think that would involve an overly restrictive concept of realism. I would rather point to a film like Lars von Trier's *Breaking the Waves* which in my mind has both the linguistic realism that I favour and an almost documentary camera style. At the same time Lars is able to give the film a more mythological dimension which has the effect of shattering the realism. I think that's incredibly well done.

**Hjort:** The conception of Danish film art that you articulated in 1966 is very interesting, for it supports a properly *cultural* definition of Danish film. Danish film, you suggested, must involve a cluster of elements, including, perhaps, the Danish language in one of its spoken forms, an exploration of Danish practices and traditions, and some representation of the land, sea and climate that have shaped Danish modes of life. Now, what is striking is that whereas the Film Acts* of 1972 and 1982 emphasised the Danish language, and thus defined Danish film in cultural terms, the later Acts of 1989 and 1997 articulated a definition of Danish film that is, on the whole, culturally neutral. How do you feel about this development?

**Braad Thomsen:** There's a noticeable and rather uninteresting tendency which involves Danish film becoming more and more internationalised, and thereby more anonymous, as part of an attempt to find a larger audience outside Denmark. I've never believed in that project, primarily because I believe that a Danish film has an obligation to be Danish, whatever that might mean. I've at least always believed that the films that do really well internationally are the films that are willing to reveal where they're from instead of trying to cater to a more anonymous, international film style. The films that have a certain national specificity are the most interesting and they're the ones that resonate internationally. Take my own films, for example. I didn't just make Danish films, I made Jutlandic films. Both *Wellspring of My World* and *Dreams Don't Make Noise When They Die* are very much defined by Jutland. Yet, at least *Wellspring of My World* became an unexpected box office success. Its success was surprising both because it was a documentary film and because it was so thoroughly Jutlandic that it was hard to believe it could be shown outside of Jutland. It was actually a bigger success in Copenhagen than in Jutland, and it went on to become a big festival hit all over the world, from Teheran to New York.

**Hjort:** You've described *Wellspring of My World* as a 'heritage film' (*hjemstavnsfilm*), a film about your native soil or home, which is Bjertrup in Eastern Jutland, where a regional dialect, *jysk*, is spoken. The dominant tendency in Danish film is to utilise *rigsdansk,** even in those cases in which the story unfolds in the provinces. Thus, for example, when Erik Clausen makes a film about Carl Nielsen, the famous composer from Funen, he nonetheless chooses to use *rigsdansk*, instead of the regional dialect, *fynsk*. I know that you're very interested in questions of language. I'm thinking, for example, of your remarks about your relation to German: Fassbinder, you've claimed, taught you to see beauty in a language that you'd previously associated only with authoritarian attitudes and oppression. What is your relation to the Danish language? How important do you think it is to make room for regional dialects within Danish film?

**Braad Thomsen:** I think it's terribly important. It bothers me when Erik Clausen makes a *fynsk* film in which nobody speaks *fynsk*; and it also bothers me when Morten Arnfred makes a *jysk* film in which the actors speak the kind of Danish that is associated with the Royal Theatre instead of *jysk*. I don't understand how anyone can do something like that, because as far as I'm concerned language is an incredibly important part of a film. I'd almost go so far as to say that all my films find their basis in reflections on language. Most directors would probably trace their films to visual considerations. I'm different in that respect because I've always wanted to film a particular language. In *Dear Irene* I wanted to film a more natural, improvised Danish. In *Wellspring of My World* I wanted to film the Jutlandic dialect before it disappears altogether. In *Children of Pain* I wanted to film a more pyschoanalytic, or at least, recollective language, and in *Ladies on the Rocks* I wanted to film Helle Ryslinge and Anne Marie Helger's completely wigged out, acerbic,

Copenhagen dialect. The starting point, really, has always been language. The task or challenge, of course, is to find the images that are relevant for the kind of language you want to film.

**Hjort:** I'm interested in your view on how Danish audiences typically react to the way in which Danish is spoken in Danish films. I have, for example, asked a number of people about their reactions to a film like Erik Clausen's *Carl, My Childhood Symphony* (*Min fynske barndom*) and most of them don't find the use of *rigsdansk* disturbing. They see it as nothing more than a convention connected to the fact that many actors are trained in Copenhagen, which is also where the Danish film industry is centred. People seem to ignore the *rigsdansk* which is actually spoken, and, in a process involving make-believe, they somehow supply the *fynsk* that is required by the story.

**Braad Thomsen:** I can't say anything about how Danish audiences more generally respond to this issue. I can only talk about my own response to the phenomenon, and I'm bothered by it. You're probably right that a lot of people don't even think about this. After all, German audiences don't seem to notice that the American films they see have been completely destroyed by the policy of dubbing all the voices into German. When I discuss this issue with my German friends, they say: 'But we don't even notice that – we find it perfectly normal. We do of course know they're actually talking American, but that doesn't worry us.' As far as I'm concerned dubbing completely destroys a film, because who can imagine a Robert de Niro film without the sound of Robert de Niro's voice, or a Marilyn Monroe film without the sound of Marilyn Monroe's voice? The Germans don't know what they're missing. As far as I'm concerned, dubbing is nothing short of a cultural scandal. I became very excited when I discovered something, which I really think is true, namely that dubbing was invented in the Nazi dubbing studios. Dubbing is a Nazi practice. What Hitler couldn't achieve on the battlefield he achieved in the dubbing studios, where all nations could be made to speak German. To deprive people of their own tongue is, in my mind, to subject the work of art in question to a form of fascist violence.

**Hjort:** *Wellspring of My World* is in many ways an autobiographical documentary, a film through which you, Christian Braad Thomsen, rediscover your roots. On a number of occasions you've referred negatively to the rootlessness of modern life. It's important, you've claimed, to have some sense of place. What about films? Should they also come from somewhere? Should they also be recognisably rooted in a given culture?

**Braad Thomsen:** The older I get, the more important I seem to think it is to inscribe oneself and one's films within a particular cultural tradition. This wasn't my view in the 1960s. Before I started making films myself, I was very fond of Jean-Luc Godard's films because they were so totally rebellious and iconoclastic in relation to all forms of tradition. For example, all of Godard's 1960s films completely undermine the cinematic tradition of Hollywood. Godard conducted those violent attacks on a tradition against which I also felt it was reasonable to rebel, but he wasn't rooted anywhere himself, and I believe that's why he ended up in a total vacuum, where he ultimately disintegrated as an artist. I think that it's important for even the most rebellious, anarchistic film-maker to feel connected to some place or other, otherwise there's a risk of being destroyed by one's own rebellion. Fassbinder, on the other hand, is, I believe, a very interesting example of precisely that combination of rebellion and rootedness. He was, of course, equally anarchistic and subversive in relation to his own country, West Germany, in relation to the bourgeoisie from which he stemmed, and in relation to the language of film. Fassbinder, as I learnt after his death, had discovered a very interesting tradition with which he could connect at some deep level. He looked to the exile generation in German culture, that is, to those artists who were forced to leave Germany in 1933 and the following years. People like Alfred Döblin, who wrote *Berlin Alexanderplatz* or Douglas Sirk, who of course was Fassbinder's big example. He was called Detlev Sirk in Germany, but he too had had to leave Germany. And there were some other writers who were forced into exile: Oskar Maria Graf, Bruckner and Bertolt Brecht. Before becoming a film-maker, Fassbinder staged Brecht. That is, he sought an identity in that exile generation that, just like himself, couldn't stand Germany.

**Hjort:** In 1990 you published your childhood memoirs, *Heritage and Debt*, which is the literary counterpart to *Wellspring of My World*. These two works provide a penetrating analysis of the *ambivalence* of inheritance. Inheritance involves gifts, but these gifts indebt the receiver. What is your view on this issue when it is transposed to a larger cultural sphere and becomes a question, for example, of a national heritage? What does it mean to be a Danish film-maker and to inherit the tradition of Danish film, the golden years of silent film, Dreyer and the popular comedies* of the 1950s?

**Braad Thomsen:** My problem is that I don't feel I have any particular relation to Danish film traditions, not to Dreyer nor to the popular comedies. In that sense I always felt that one had to start pretty much from scratch as a Danish film artist. That's also why I started out by emphasising the documentary genre. That is, I wanted to seek out the very Denmark that in my mind had yet to find cinematic expression. If I were to connect with any tradition at all, it would be with the tradition associated with Godard, who destroyed the language of cinema, that is, the conventional language of cinema, and the tradition connected with Fassbinder, who sort of reconstructed that language in his own way. Those are probably the directors who have meant the most to me.

**Hjort:** You've been an ardent critic over the years of what you saw as the Danish Film Institute's tendency to prioritise commercially successful film-making. The so-called 50/50* policy, which was introduced in 1989, was an attempt, precisely, to ensure that commercial film-making favouring popular taste cultures at odds with high art could receive state support. What is your view of the 50/50 policy (which went on to become the 60/40 policy)?

**Braad Thomsen:** My relation to that policy is very ambivalent, because I was actually in favour of it when it was first proposed, but my position back then was based on a certain definition of the policy that has nothing to do with the current situation. I supported the 50/50 policy because I was convinced that it needn't be purely commercial in its thrust, but could also provide favourable conditions for uncompromising, low-budget art films. The initial proposal was one that allowed directors, who were seriously committed to making innovative art films, to apply for monies.

Unfortunately the Ministry of Culture had a clause inserted which specified that the policy was earmarked for commercial films that were deemed capable of drawing full houses. That wasn't, however, the original proposal to which I and many others agreed. The original proposal was that not only commercial films, but also art films, could receive government funding, as long as the director or producer could provide half the necessary capital. Now, I'd be able to do just that, for example, if I were to forego my own salary as director, and if some of the other crew members were to do the same. If you were to stick to small budget films you'd actually be able to make films that way. That's why I supported the policy. At this point I think it's insignificant and an expression of a strange kind of hypocrisy. Government support for film was initiated here in Denmark because people had rightly understood that art films weren't viable on the commercial market and thus required public funding. In my mind the decision also to support commercial films is in violation of the Film Act, which never anticipated any such thing. The Danish Film Institute was supposed to provide an alternative to commercial film-making rather than to bolster the business in question.

**Hjort:** You've consistently claimed to pay no attention, in your film-making, to existing audiences, be they regional, national or international. Indeed, you've even maintained that the idea of a popular and aesthetically valuable film is a contradiction in terms. Would films such as Lars von Trier's *Breaking the Waves* or Bille August's *Pelle the Conqueror* (*Pelle Erobreren*) lead you to revise your views?

**Braad Thomsen:** That's not my position today. If that was my view earlier, then it was as part of a polemic towards the end of the 1960s. I don't think that was actually my position back then, because some of my favourite films are and have always been the great Hollywood films. Although I've been very critical of John Ford in many ways, I would still want to claim that he's made some of the most beautiful films I know. I'm thinking, for example, of *Grapes of Wrath* and also of some of his westerns, especially perhaps *The Man Who Shot Liberty Valance*. They're definitely commercial films, but they're also real works of art. At this point Hitchcock is the director I admire the most, because he has this ability to make films that target absolutely everyone whilst being unique artistic expressions. He manages to do this right in the monster's lair, as it were, right in the middle of Hollywood. I'm thinking here of his best films – *Vertigo*, *Notorious*, *Rebecca* or *Psycho*. This ability to combine the tastes of mass audiences with artistic integrity is perhaps what I admire more than anything else.

**Hjort:** One of your recurrent criticisms of the institutions of Danish film is that the consultants* charged with allocating government monies attribute excessive importance to detailed scripts. Godard, Fassbinder and Bresson, who tended to work without such scripts, would have fared poorly under Danish conditions. If you could change the behaviour of consultants, and the criteria by which film projects are judged, what would you propose?

**Braad Thomsen:** My assumption here is, of course, that just because someone can write a good script doesn't mean that he or she can make a good film. A good script is frequently defined as a script that makes sense when you read it, but at that point we might as well simply publish the script. What distinguishes the script from the final film is precisely what can't be accessed through reading. If it were only a matter of reading, there would be absolutely no point in making the film. So, in my mind, the more readable the script is, the less suitable it is as the basis for a film. The problem with my own scripts is that I can't articulate what the film is actually about in the script, and that's basically why I've had such a hard time getting my projects off the ground. I don't mean to suggest that I can't write, because I've written lots of books and have no problem expressing myself on the page. I can express myself in writing, but the real essence of a film is something that I've never been able to capture in writing. That's why I believe that the only reasonable way of allocating financial support involves careful consideration of the earlier films that a given applicant has made. I was very shocked to discover that *Ladies on the Rocks* didn't make it any easier to secure funding for my next project. It's not my favourite film, but it's my best film from a purely technical point of view. It's really very professionally made. I was nonetheless refused funding for my feature film projects until 1998, when I was able to make *The Blue Monk*. Having made a film like *Ladies on the Rocks*, I find that very strange. The rejoinder to this proposal might be that beginners would never be able to break into film-making if the relevant rule were to be consistently followed. The proposed rule being that the quality of earlier works is what determines whether one is allowed to continue or not. But beginners are never really beginners. They've always made films earlier, either in the context of the Danish Film Institute's Workshop in Haderslev or Copenhagen, or at the Film School. There's always some kind of practical work that they can be judged on, something other than a piece of paper.

**Hjort:** At this point you've made an impressive number of films spanning different genres. I believe that you consider your prize winning films, *Stab in the Heart* and *Ladies on the Rocks*, to be your most important cinematic achievements. Why do you particularly value these films over your other works?

**Braad Thomsen:** I'm particularly fond of them because they represent the two extremes of what interests me. *Stab in the Heart* is an amazingly rigorous, puritanical, black-and-white film involving a very subdued mode of narration, which I really love. *Ladies on the Rocks* is exactly the opposite: an effusive, lively, anarchistic, and outrageously funny film with a rapid pace of narration. At the same time it's both very funny and dreadfully sad, and that's actually what I like about it. That combination ultimately makes it a terribly sad film. I think that one of the most interesting things about film is this capacity to bring together polar opposites such as uproarious hilarity and profound sadness. That's also what I tried to achieve in the film about Karen Blixen, *Karen Blixen: Storyteller*. My

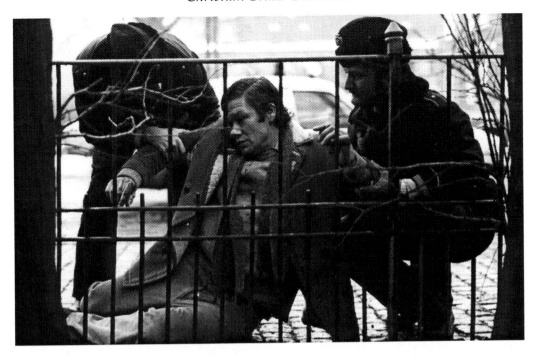

*Jesper (Stig Ramsing) is arrested for the murder of a young girl, Lillian (*Stab in the Heart/Kniven i hjertet*). [Photo: Fie Johansen]*

approach was different, though, because the intention in that film was to make the audience cry in the end. Documentary films aren't, of course, typically tear jerkers; we're much more used to crying during Hollywood films. But my aim was to make a documentary film – a film that was as factual and precise as a documentary – that also had the kind of melodramatic dimension we associate with Hollywood films. A lot of people really did have tears in their eyes as they left the cinema. I'd hidden behind a column so as to be able to see whether they had tears in their eyes, and they did!

**Hjort:** I would like to get you to talk now about issues having to do with sex and desire and their depiction in film. The relevant films here are, of course, your first feature film, *Dear Irene* and the controversial film about incest, *The One You Love*. You've described *Dear Irene* as an anti-pornographic film that squares off against the pornographic films that flooded Danish cinemas in the wake of the abolition of censorship in 1969. What is it about the depiction of sex and desire in *Dear Irene* that makes it, not simply non-pornographic, but anti-pornographic?

**Braad Thomsen:** The sex scenes in that film are heart-breaking because they express such desperation. There's no sense of happiness in them at all. They're cold because they don't involve love. By the way, when the film was first released it included more explicit sex scenes than the version you've seen. A few years after the film's premiere I actually shortened it by ten minutes. I edited the sex scenes a lot because I felt they were excessive, although they really were shot in a very anti-pornographic way. Soon after *Dear Irene* I actually developed quite an aversion to the very idea of sex scenes in film. I don't think that sexuality can be depicted cinematically. At this point I'm opposed to having sex scenes in films. I'd almost go so far as to say that I agree with another favourite director of mine, François Truffaut, who once said that when people kiss each other on the screen, it's as though someone suddenly turned the light on in the cinema because the illusion is shattered. Sexuality and kissing are such intimate things that you can't help but ask yourself 'Are they actors now or private persons?' There are certain limits here: you don't kiss a person unless you're in love with the individual in question.

**Hjort:** You once claimed that the abolition of censorship posed a real challenge for film-makers. As you so cogently put it, 'How far is one, from an artistic point of view, justified in taking things, when one legally has permission to go as far as one wants?' The key question, you said, is 'whether pornographic scenes can be integrated into a larger artistic context, in such a way that they no longer function as pornography, but as a form of extreme, everyday realism' (*Fyens Stiftstidende*, September 1971). There's a scene in *The One You Love* that initially strikes the viewer as pornographic. This is the scene that shows a woman being penetrated from behind by her lover as she cuddles her naked son who rests against her belly. Previously the woman has explained to the documentary camera that she and her son have a symbiotic relationship that involves his being distressed by her love-making, unless he is allowed to participate in the just described manner. Would you regard this scene as an example of a successful integration of pornographic elements into a larger artistic context?

**Braad Thomsen:** No, at this point I regret having included that scene. I would like to edit it out of the film. I think it fails. It fails because it so obviously contradicts what the mother has just said. That is, I believe the mother when she says that her son feels insecure when she screws a guy. There *is* some kind of symbiosis there. However, the scene in the film shows precisely that he doesn't accept the situation, because he actually tears himself away from his mother and expresses a desire to play with his elephant. One of the problems with that scene is that what he reacts to isn't actually the fact of his mother being with a man. That's what you think when you see the scene, but he's actually responding to the camera crew. My reason for retaining the scene – which is something I now regret having done – was that my old friend Sigmund Freud would find it interesting that the child drops his elephant and uses it as a pretext for getting away from his mother and her lover. The elephant, Freud would say, is of course a being with a long trunk, and we all know what that symbolises. So I kept the scene for reasons having to do with the play of symbols, but I should never have shot it.

**Hjort:** You're frequently described as a left-wing intellectual, yet your film-making is in no way a matter of political sloganising. You once described the image of the fat, bikini-clad girl who dances in Jytte Rex's and Kirsten Justesen's *Sleeping Beauty was a Lovely Child* (*Tornerose var et vakkert barn*) as the quintessence of political film-making on account of this image's ability to generate a growing sense of discomfort in a certain kind of viewer. Many of the images in *Dreams Don't Make Noise When They Die* are intensely disturbing. I'm thinking, for example, of the overwhelming sense of claustrophobia that is produced by the dream sequence in which we witness the old couple as newly weds before an altar framed by pews. Is *Dreams Don't Make Noise When They Die*, in your mind, an example of political film-making?

**Braad Thomsen:** Yes, but the film was a box office fiasco even though it was released during those very political years in the 1970s. The reason for this is that it explores a profound sense of disillusionment. The film focusses on a reactionary father and his ostensibly politically progressive son and suggests that the son's childhood limits the extent to which he can really act progressively. It's fair to say that the son's personal life is pretty much in ruins. When his wife is raped, for example, his response is to beat up the poor peasant who raped her. Had he been giving a theoretical lecture on the question of punishment, he would have advocated a quite different response to rapists, one that acknowledges that they too are victims. That's not exactly what he does in the film, and that's putting it mildly. I also think that he in his personal relationship with his wife repeats his parents' very cold relationship. He is, for example, incapable of holding her when she most needs him to do so. In that respect it's probably a political film. However, the film is about needing to be alert to the danger of repeating the very thing that one is trying to be an alternative to. That's a typical Fassbinder theme, but it's certainly also a theme that was prevalent during the 1970s in Denmark.

**Hjort:** Many of your films belong to a tradition of documentary film-making. *Wellspring of My World* is an autobiography framed as a documentary about the lives of peasants in Bjertrup. *Karen Blixen: Storyteller* uses the narrative techniques of documentary film-making to provide a compelling and at times Freudian interpretation of the life and work of the Danish author. *Children of Pain* involves an intriguing mixture of the fairy tale, travelogue and interview genres. *The One You Love* can uncontroversially be characterised as a documentary about the incest prohibition. Although these films all draw on some of the conventions of the documentary genre, they differ in important respects. To what extent do these films reflect an evolving sense of the tasks and possibilities of non-fiction film?

**Braad Thomsen:** Actually I've always had a problem with documentary film-making, and in some strange way it's against my will that I've made documentary films. I'm very fond of some of them. I like *Wellspring of My World*, and I'm really very fond of the Karen Blixen film, but it's a pure accident that they were made at all, because every single time I made a documentary film what I really wanted to make was a fiction film. When I made *Wellspring of My World*, I actually wanted to make *Dreams Don't Make Noise When They Die*. When I made *Children of Pain* I really wanted to make *Stab in the Heart*. When I made the Karen Blixen film I wanted to make a fiction film based on Thorkild Bjørnvig's book, *The Pact: My Friendship with Isak Dinesen (Pagten)*, and I still hope to do so some day. In that sense the documentaries have compensated for the fiction films I really wanted to make, because they were cheaper to produce than the feature films that I simply couldn't finance. I've always thought of the documentaries as research for a feature film on the same topic.

When I claim to have a problematic relation to the documentary genre as such, it's in part because it's not clear to me what the specificity of documentary film-making actually is. For example there are scenes in *Wellspring of My World* which are pure fiction, but you don't realise this because they're shot in a documentary way. There is, for example, a scene in which a story is narrated by means of the soundtrack only while the viewer contemplates an old dilapidated farmhouse on the screen. It's a terrible story about a farmer who hangs himself in his barn because the farm is sold behind his back. That story is actually fictional. Something similar happened in Bjertrup, but what really happened was so terrible that I couldn't film it without showing disrespect for the parties involved. That's why I came up with a fictional story that resembled the real one, inasmuch as it involved the same element of tragedy, while making it impossible to identify the figures involved. If you want to talk about the most terrible things, which is of course precisely what you want to do as a film director, then you have to have recourse to fiction, because basic human respect really limits how far you can go in a documentary. There's a limit to how close you can get to other people when it comes to their love lives and their relationship to death, and those are the only two things that really interest me in a film, love and death. Those are also the only two things that interest me in real life. When there's really something at stake, I begin to fictionalise, even in the context of a documentary. In my film about Karen Blixen I reveal Karen Blixen to be a real liar. What she presents as documentary truths in *Out of Africa* (*Min afrikanske farm*) turn out to be fictions that are held to manifest deeper truths. That is, if you want to tell the truth, you have to lie, or at least to create fiction. I'm delighted to have found permission to do precisely that in Karen Blixen's work!

**Hjort:** You once referred to *Ladies on the Rocks* as a 'popular comedy with substance' (*Midtjyllands avis*, November 1983). Yet, you've also been extremely critical of popular Danish comedies, which you associate with an all-time low in the history of Danish cinema. Why did you turn towards the genre in question? What, in your opinion, are the key elements that distinguish *Ladies on the Rocks* from more trivial instances of the genre?

**Braad Thomsen:** I hope that it distinguishes itself from them by mixing very conflicting emotions, by constantly using humour, not only as a source of laughter, but in order to talk about something that is terribly sad. The really sad things can, of course, only be told in a way that is light hearted and funny. The funniest film artist in the world is in my mind Buster Keaton, because he's the saddest. Some of Chaplin's earliest films are also funny precisely because they're so dreadfully sad, but I never laugh when someone tries to be funny for the sake of being funny. I'll never forget the first time I saw Stanley Kubrick's *Dr. Strangelove*, especially that scene in which the cowboy rides an atom bomb towards the demise of the world and waves his hat and says 'Yoohoo,' or whatever it is he says. We roared with laughter during that scene and there was this elderly lady sitting behind us, who jabbed us in the back and said, 'Now, now, just you wait, it won't be funny when it really happens.' I thought that scene was a brilliant example of how the most serious things can be depicted by means of the most deliriously surreal comedy.

**Hjort:** There are many textual links between your films. In *Wellspring of My World*, your mother tells the camera about the expenses involved in your father's funeral, and in *Dreams Don't Make Noise When They Die* the widow engages in a similar discourse. In *Dreams Don't Make Noise When They Die*, reference is made to a sexual incident between a son and his dying father, and a similar incident is evoked by one of the interviewees in *Wellspring of My World*. What is the purpose of these kinds of citations?

**Braad Thomsen:** The reason, as I suggested earlier, is that *Wellspring of My World* is research for *Dreams Don't Make Noise When They Die*. That is, my documentary films are always research for my feature-length fiction films. I've always naively believed that feature films would attract larger audiences than documentaries. That's why I thought I could take the liberty of repeating or citing certain things that I would like a larger audience to see. However, precisely the opposite has in fact been the case. *Wellspring of My World* was seen by many more people than *Dreams Don't Make Noise When They Die*.

**Hjort:** Your films include a lot of autobiographical elements, some of which are more obvious than others.

**Braad Thomsen:** Now, how would you know that? After all, you don't really know me!

**Hjort:** I was struck, for example, by the remarks in *Ladies on the Rocks* about the sad financial plight of many artists. Micha points out that she essentially lives on unemployment benefits, which she constantly risks losing because she spends her time constructively, on art. This is a complaint that you yourself have voiced in interviews focussing on conflicts between yourself and members of the Danish Film Institute. Are such autobiographical elements merely coincidental or is your cinematic oeuvre, as far as you are concerned, very much a reworking through art of your own histories and concerns?

**Braad Thomsen:** That kind of episode is, of course, completely autobiographical. Like all other Danish film directors, I have a rather complicated relation to the fact of being unemployed and receiving benefits. For the thing is that we directors just can't stop working although we're on the dole. We don't always get paid for the work we do, but it's still illegal to work. With reference to the question of autobiographical elements more generally, I would want to say that none of my films is autobiographical in terms of its narration, but they're all autobiographical at the level of feeling. The reason, quite simply, is that you can't depict an emotion that you haven't experienced.

**Hjort:** *Ladies on the Rocks* is a fascinating film for several reasons. I'm particularly intrigued by its evocation of the nation-state of Denmark. In this road movie, you show us the lives of two female performers, Micha and Laura, who are touring Denmark with their show. Unlike a film such as Erik Clausen's *Carl: My Childhood Symphony*, which effaces as far as is possible all references to a regionalised Denmark (while in fact claiming to be about regional culture), *Ladies on the Rocks* genuinely narrates the geography of the nation. The emphasis, it seems, is very much on foregrounding some of the diverse dialects and diverging practices that have a regional basis. Is *Ladies on the Rocks* to any important extent a film about the complicated relations between centre and periphery in the small nation-state of Denmark? More generally, perhaps, what is the intention behind the ethnographic elements?

**Braad Thomsen:** I've never thought of it that way, but it did of course occur to me that the entire film is about cultural conflicts as well as about cross-cultural understanding. I don't know whether you noticed the citation from *Wellspring of My World* in *Ladies on the Rocks*? It's in that scene in which Micha and Laura meet the old innkeeper. He says the same thing as my uncle in *Wellspring of My World*, namely that he loved the world of amateur theatre because it was like being part of one big family. He goes on to say that when you then have your own little family, you end up isolating yourself, and then the larger thing is all over. The women really understand what he's talking about, because they're torn between the theatre and their own families.

**Hjort:** So cultural conflict, but not necessarily between metropolitan and provincial cultures?

**Braad Thomsen:** Not necessarily, but that's connected to the fact that the two women are outsiders in the context of the capital and its privileged cultures. They're a couple of lousy comedians who can't really make it in the capital. In that sense they represent regional cultures in the capital.

# Jytte Rex

## 1942–

Jytte Rex, who was trained at the Royal Academy of Art, is both a painter and a film-maker. Through her films and paintings, which are characterised by an intensely personal, experimental and often feminist style, she has contributed significantly to debates about women's issues in Denmark. Rex has directed a number of films that blur the boundaries between documentary and fictional genres. Examples include *Sleeping Beauty was a Lovely Child* (*Tornerose var et vakkert barn*, 1971) and *Veronica's Veil* (*Veronicas svededug*, 1977), which both develop a symbolically charged cinematic language to explore primarily women's lives and dreams. The short film, *The Memorious* (*Den erindrende*, 1985), is, on the other hand, inspired by the literary universe of Jorge Luis Borges and involves a kind of meta-cinematic poetics that could be said to capture the essence of Jytte Rex' cinematic project. The feature

*Jytte Rex.*

films, *Achilles' Heel is My Weapon* (*Achilleshælen er mit våben*, 1979), *Belladonna* (1981), *Isolde* (1989) and *Mirrors of the Planet* (*Planetens spejle*, 1992), all involve stories that mix myths and symbolic dream images in a labyrinthine manner. In these films, unlike some of her earlier ones, Rex makes use of professional actors. Rex' most recent film, *Inger Christensen – Cicadas Exist* (*Inger Christensen – cikaderne findes*, 1998) is a more classic portrait film about the contemporary Danish poet, Inger Christensen.

## Feature films
1977, *Veronica's Veil* (*Veronicas svededug*)
1979, *Achilles' Heel is My Weapon* (*Achilleshælen er mit våben*)
1981, *Belladonna*
1989, *Isolde*
1992, *Mirrors of the Planet* (*Planetens spejle*)

## Short films and documentaries
1971, *Sleeping Beauty was a Lovely Child* (*Tornerose var et vakkert barn*)
1985, *The Memorious* (*Den erindrende*)

1998, *Inger Christensen – Cicadas Exist (Inger Christensen – cikaderne findes)*

## Books
1972, *The Women's Book (Kvindernes bog)*
1972, *Ash, Time and Fire (Aske, tid og ild – fra et glemt terræn)*
1978, *I Haven't Slept a Wink (Jeg har ikke lukket et øje – en billedroman)*
1986, *Family Trees (Stamtavler)*
1989, *Figure and Space (Figur og rum)*
1995, *Paintings, Drawings (Malerier – tegninger)*

**Hjort:** You were trained at the prestigious Royal Academy of Art, which you attended from 1963 until 1969. What motivated you to take up the art of film-making and how did you acquire the requisite skills?

**Rex:** I was interested in film already as a child, because I received free tickets to lots of films. In fact, I think I saw just about everything that was shown in Denmark at the time, and that wasn't just American films. There were many Italian, French and Eastern European films.

**Hjort:** How did you come by all these free tickets?

**Rex:** One of my mother's friends was a very successful sales agent for Tom's Chocolates and he was constantly in touch with the people running all the cinema kiosks, so he could always get tickets. He would show up on his big motor bike, all dressed in black leather, and hand us the tickets, so that's how I ended up seeing everything.

**Hjort:** When did you start working with film?

**Rex:** While I was still at the Academy I purchased a double eight film camera, which was exactly half the standard 16 mm format. It was a rather small camera with just three built-in lenses, and I would wander around shooting with it. Afterwards I spent many a day and night editing my 'scenes'. I played around with all the interpretive possibilities.

**Hjort:** A recurrent image and motif in your films is that of the labyrinth. Your thinking about the labyrinthine dimension of human existence is clearly influenced by your favourite author, Borges, who in many ways is a key figure in your work. Not only are your films visual meditations on Borgesian themes, one of your films – *The Memorious* – is an attempt to translate into images a number of Borges' highly conceptual stories. It might seem a lot harder to adapt Borges to the screen than other literary works of a more descriptive nature. Indeed, when Danish directors adapt literary works, they typically opt for texts influenced by a realist aesthetic and tradition. It must have been an extraordinary challenge to adapt Borges. How would you describe the process? What did you emphasise? What kinds of problems and opportunities do you associate with that project?

**Rex:** I've read Borges ever since I can remember. Or rather, ever since *Ficciones* was translated, and that was at some point in the 1960s. I was immediately fascinated by his books and by his world more generally. The root of the fascination has something to do with the many different levels he works with. Perhaps it's also related to my own childhood, which was full of images of, and sentiments about, Czechoslovakia, which is where my mother is originally from. She came to Denmark in 1938, just before the war. Her experiences left me with a feeling of being many different places at once, with a sense of emotional translucence. Borges' many complex levels seemed almost organically self-evident to me.

**Hjort:** Was it difficult to find a cinematic language capable of conveying the complex world of Borges' fiction?

**Rex:** Originally it had never occurred to me that Borges could be adapted. He is so unique, and the power of his work is so completely tied up with his use of language. At one point the National Film Board invited me to make whatever film I felt like making, and the first thing that flashed through my mind was, why not use Borges as a starting point, however risky that might be. I then settled on two short stories, both of which relate to memory in their own way. My films are usually based on my own texts, but in this case it was very liberating to have to think in terms of images based on Borges' texts.

**Hjort:** How did the public react?

**Rex:** Surprisingly enough, very positively. *The Memorious* was actually very well received.

**Hjort:** I believe it won a Bodil.*

**Rex:** Yes, and it played in the cinemas for three months, which is also very strange. It just goes to show that something apparently impossible and strange nonetheless can move a lot of people.

**Hjort:** The characters in your films frequently reflect on labyrinths. Whereas some perceive the labyrinth of existence as a prison-house of consciousness, others claim to perceive cracks in its walls, cracks that point the way to freedom and potentially authentic modes of being. One detects here a deeper philosophical message having to do with what makes life meaningful and worth living. What, more specifically, are you trying to convey through the persistent emphasis, both at the level of dialogue and image, on the figure of the labyrinth?

**Rex:** I'm trying to articulate the idea that the *path* followed in some imaginary or real labyrinth may ultimately be more important than the fact of reaching the goal or destination in question. What Borges underscores in several of his stories is that human agents' attempt to get to the heart of things, to find an answer, at times amounts only to a fateful cycle, a quest to resolve the riddle of the universe. As his stories demonstrate time and again, the labyrinth is constructed in such a way that it is either mistaken for reality, or the secret turns out to be that there in fact is no secret. I nod to Borges, if you will, or refer to him, in *Belladonna*, which includes a Borges citation in the part entitled 'The Garden of Diverging Paths', and the paths in the film really do diverge a lot. In one of my later films, *Isolde*, I again nod to Borges in the scene in which a young student visits the library in search of a particular book mentioned by the Argentine writer. The librarian is amused by the student and informs him that the book doesn't exist and is pure fiction. That is, the book itself is a fiction. It simply doesn't exist. Borges refers to a book that doesn't exist. The student stands there pointing to his notes and says, 'But it does exist. It says so here.' I refer to Borges in that kind of way, but otherwise I haven't worked directly with the labyrinth as a theme. Only in *The Memorious* where I use Borges' own texts.

**Hjort:** If Borges is the author who has influenced you the most, Gustav Mahler would appear to be the composer whose music you feel the deepest affinity for. In your films you make frequent use of Mahler's music, particularly his *First Symphony*. I am thinking, for example, of *Mirrors of the Planet*, *Belladonna* and *Veronica's Veil*. What is it about Mahler and his music that moves you?

**Rex:** Key passages in Mahler's music have almost the same significance for me as Borges' texts do – they provide a kind of direct access to transcending levels of reality. Mahler starts a theme and then shuts it down, while allowing earlier themes to shine through as though they were materially present. By the way he's from Bohemia, and I think that something in the timbre of his music provoked a kind of recognition when I first heard it as a nineteen year old. Whether this sense of recognition – imagined or real – was prompted by the inner images I'd created of the landscapes of Bohemia or by my mother's songs, I don't know.

**Hjort:** Your sense of belonging was complicated. Home, for you, was not just Denmark.

**Rex:** Very much so, because my mother got divorced during the war, and I wasn't very old at the time. As a result I experienced her sense of loss very intensely, and it was very much connected to being an outsider in a foreign country. Her stories about Czechoslovakia and the mountains became a natural part of my world, a point of longing.

**Hjort:** In *Veronica's Veil* there are images from a trip you took to Czechoslovakia with your mother.

**Rex:** Yes, I was expecting my own child then. My mother had not been back to Czechoslovakia in all those intervening years, 35 years in all. Some of the people who had gone back earlier had been abducted or had simply disappeared without a trace. However, at that point in the 1970s the situation seemed better, and in a way there was a circle that needed to be completed, and that's why she wanted to go back. She wanted among other things to see whether she could find her mother's grave. I followed in her footsteps and filmed various events along the way with my super-eight camera.

**Hjort:** I'd like to discuss the role of music in your films more generally. Although many directors use music to underscore or actually to provoke a particular mood, your use of music tends to foreground its narrative potential. As many critics have remarked, the stories told in your films are anything but conventional narratives based primarily on stable characters and their utterances. Is music particularly important in your films, precisely because you choose not to develop your stories in a conventional manner?

**Rex:** Yes, definitely. In fact I use all sound as a language in and of itself that doesn't simply have to illustrate the unfolding events. That is, in terms of sound, the fact of hearing a door being opened and closed can be marked in many ways other than that of a purely ordinary naturalism. In my mind sounds contribute actively, although differently, to the mode of narration. That's why choosing the right kind of music is very important to me. I've never really had the courage to ask a composer to compose music for my films, because then I wouldn't be able to determine freely when the film's various elements are to intersect in just the way that is required. How exactly the elements are to be combined is something that I first discover as the film achieves its definitive form in the editing room. The tonality of different musical recordings can be absolutely decisive. For example, in the case of *Mirrors of the Planet* there was only one particular recording of Pachelbel's *Canon* that was appropriate, one characterised by the darkest of moods and a contrapuntal structure that is almost physically present.

**Hjort:** Opinions about your films are mixed. On the one hand, you are considered by many to be one of Denmark's most courageous and creative film-makers. Those who praise your work do so on account of its intensely personal style and visual complexity. On the other hand, you have received rough treatment over the years at the hands of predominantly male journalists who have claimed that your films, particularly the earlier ones, are amateurish and fail to tell a coherent story. Yet, your films, quite clearly, are not simply random or purely non-narrative assemblages of images, for they do, in fact, tell stories. What is your conception of cinematic narration? Has your view of cinematic narration changed over time?

**Rex:** My early work was characterised by a very anarchistic relation between the script-writing phase and the actual shooting of the film. *Belladonna* marks a departure from this approach, because from that point on – and thus in the case of both *Isolde* and *Mirrors of the Planet* too – I spend a lot of time working through the scripts. During the final stages of script writing I also work with other people. However, with *Isolde* I had the feeling that certain scenes 'merely' had to be filmed so that the story could proceed, and I wanted to avoid that kind of situation in the future. In my mind every single scene should be cinematically innovative, and as a result I ended up going to the opposite extreme in *Mirrors of the Planet*. The story or plot was under-prioritised, and this had the

*Isolde (Pia Vieth) embraces the lover, played by Kim Jansson, who will inadvertently become her assassin (Isolde). [Photo: Hannelise Thomsen]*

effect of generating a number of gaps in the film's suggested continuity. On the whole the story is conveyed by the scenes that centre around images, which together function almost like a messenger from some deeper spiritual level in the story. There are a lot of steadycam shots in *Mirrors of the Planet* and they provide a certain sense of physical materiality, just as my earlier super-eight shots did. The fact that the camera is actually carried by someone situates the eye on the camera's front line, which opens up a lot of cinematic possibilities.

**Hjort:** Would you like to comment on the two women with the gaudy clothing in *Isolde* and their role in the narrative?

**Rex:** They're librarians and every time we see them, they comment on the action. They're like a combination of a Greek chorus and Disney's Huey, Dewey and Louie. They're embodiments of slightly abstract figures, who can take all kinds of liberties. Sometimes they're very down-to-earth, almost petit bourgeois, and at other times they're very poetic; their speech consists of fragments from works belonging to the library's collections. They grab sentences that are somehow in the air, as it were.

**Hjort:** I seem to recall that you've used these kinds of liminal commentators in your earlier films too.

Rex: Yes, I've always had a bit of soft spot for them! These figures are a bit baroque and their status is indeed liminal. You could also say that they're like bulls in a china shop, for they're always slightly in the way. At the same time, they're able to comment on the action with great precision precisely because their language is so baroque.

Hjort: To claim, as certain critics have, that your films are intensely personal is to suggest perhaps that they are wholly original and bear no significant relation to the work of other film-makers. Yet, at certain points the influence of other film-makers becomes apparent. I'm thinking, for example, of the extraordinary moment in *Isolde* when Isolde (Pia Vieth) first meets the mercenary (Kim Jansson) who will become both her lover and her assassin. More specifically, the camera follows the circular movements of the two figures in a series of reaction shots. Something quite similar occurs in Fassbinder's *Martha* when Martha first meets the man who will become her husband and jailer. In that film, however, it is a matter, not only of the actors moving in a circular manner, but of the camera rotating too. The scene in *Martha* has been persuasively described by Christian Braad Thomsen as the most extraordinary cinematic expression of love at first sight, and your film seems to support this view. What is your relation to the work of other film-makers? Have you been influenced by particular films or film-makers?

Rex: Well, I've seen nearly all of Fassbinder's films and I really like his work a lot. Normally I don't cite other film-makers, but that scene is indeed a citation. That scene is precisely a nod to Fassbinder, just as I've occasionally nodded to Borges in my films. My scene isn't nearly as elegantly executed, though, for in Fassbinder's film the cameras rotate around the actors, while they in turn rotate around each other as they move forward. All of this happens with a kind of magical smoothness, for we never notice that the actors are constantly crossing tracks and wires.

Hjort: Would you like to say a bit more about your relation to other directors?

Rex: There are directors whom I'm very fond of, and I've seen all of their films, several times even – Hitchcock, Tarkovsky, Angelopoulos and Bertolucci, for example. But when I start working on a film, it's always on the basis of, and in continuation of, my earlier films. In my mind ideas can't develop properly if they don't spring from a personal source. My first films were closely related to my paintings, and I was also inspired by Andy Warhol's films, where the camera hardly moves. He's very extreme and shoots with an immobile camera pointed out of the same window for four or six hours on end. Absolutely nothing happens. Deep into the film a bird finally flies by, and that's it. Then there's his film *Sleep,* in which a sleeping man is filmed for a very long time. That's a provocative way of drawing attention to the idea that 'nothing' also can be a film. That idea certainly inspired me to allow very simple things to unfold in front of the camera, to let the image be or exist in itself, as it also does in painting.

Hjort: In 1972 you published a collection of interviews with women, entitled *The Women's Book (Kvindernes bog)*. Not surprisingly, this deeply moving book became a touchstone for many feminists in Denmark. The purpose of the book, you claimed, was to counter the idealised images of women circulating in the official public sphere with a series of realistic images involving attitudes, behaviour and looks not typically attributed to the ideal woman. Would you agree that the notion of counter-images functions as a guiding principle in much of your work?

**Rex:** Yes, although it was never an explicit goal, it's probably true that I've focussed on the idea of counter-images, which is connected of course to the period of social ferment during the 1960s and 1970s. At that particular point in time it made sense to explore one's own particular story, just as it later became important to take a stance against many of the attitudes motivating the women's movement when it reified into a platform for neo-marxism. There were a lot of painters who suddenly found themselves at odds with the official, feminist party line, and we were accused of being reactionary simply by virtue of the fact that our work was art. One had to agitate politically, which one of course rarely does as a painter, unless one works the way that *Red Mother* (*Røde Mor*) did, which I've never done.[1] As you suggested earlier, there were a lot of male critics who were very critical, but there was certainly no shortage of female critics who toed the very politically correct party line, so it's not the case that my work has been received positively by women and negatively by men. The responses have been divided fairly equally in that respect.

**Hjort:** You played a key role in the Danish women's movement and your work, be it a matter of photography, film, poetry or interviews, is consistently feminist in its thrust. What is more, you are credited with having developed a specifically feminine aesthetic. Thus, for example, in *Danske spillefilm, 1968–1991*, Peter Jeppesen, Ebbe Villadsen and Ole Caspersen (1993) claim that *Achilles' Heel is My Weapon* contributed significantly to debates about key differences between a masculine and feminine aesthetic. A key element in your specifically feminist or feminine film aesthetic would appear to be the recurrent utilisation of motifs and images that are inextricably linked to the lives and stories of women. Fabric, for example, plays a central role in many of your films. One of your films, *Veronica's Veil*, takes a very particular piece of fabric as its point of departure, the cloth that Veronica is alleged to have offered Christ and on which his face is believed to have left a lasting, divine imprint. In *Isolde* we find an interesting commentary on the many paintings, by Philippe de Champaigne and countless others, that depict the legend in question. In a way you create your own cinematic 'Veronica', one that transgressively replaces the face of Christ with the figure of Isolde. I am thinking of the shot in which Isolde is seated on a bed against a backdrop provided by a white cloth suspended from the wall. More traditional female activities linked to fabric also occupy a central place in your work. I have in mind, for example, *I Haven't Slept a Wink* where we find a series of pen and ink drawings depicting needles, thread, sewing, knitting and so on. What, for you, are the key elements in your feminine aesthetic?

**Rex:** I think that in a way some of the historically feminine aspects of everyday life have had greater significance for me as a result of the life of my mother, with whom I of course grew up alone. There was more of an emphasis than usual on the classic story of female suffering, which came to embrace many more levels than it typically would have on account of my mother's being foreign – that is, the element of isolation was significantly magnified. In addition to her regular job, which was very poorly paid, my mother worked until all hours of the night fixing other people's silk stockings in order simply to survive. My thoughts, dreams and fantasies throughout the 1940s and 1950s made all those situations of female survival part of my nervous system. Through fairy tales and myths they then became connected in my mind with, for example, the Nordic Norns, who sit at the tree of life with their thread, deciding over life and death. I lived on Købmager Street, just opposite Rundetårn, and the stairs were one of those dark ones with carved banisters, and the windows had a mosaic depicting the tree of life. These elements were further consolidated as I grew up, but at the same time I would want to underscore that at the level of imagery I don't think that my aesthetic, or use of cinematic language, is that different from any man's. One could find parallels in Fassbinder, who was intensely interested in women's realities, or in Tarkovsky's way of dissolving time and space. That's why I don't think the aesthetic in question is particularly feminine; not at all. However now and again I do perhaps focus on moments that could be said to have a female orientation; and it would be strange, after all, if those moments didn't take up more space in my films than in films created by men.

**Hjort:** Why is the Veronica legend so important to you?

**Rex:** It's a very powerful story that on a number of levels articulates an image of various aspects of the relation between men and women. In the film the cloth with all of its associative images becomes the connecting structure itself – the actual story.

**Hjort:** Some of the interviews published in *The Women's Book* also figure in *Achilles' Heel is My Weapon*. For example, the following story from the interview with Magdalene is recounted in the film in one of the documentary inserts: 'Oh yes, by the way, there's someone else I've been angry at, and that was my own husband. It happened one evening after we'd spent a lovely time in bed. He was always very nice afterwards. We always had to have a lot to eat afterwards. He got up to make the food, and then he said: 'you just lie there and enjoy yourself.' I'm not thinking about anything in particular; I'm just lying there with my eyes shut in the warm bed, without the covers. I hear him leave, close the door and so on. It doesn't occur to me that he might be so sneaky as to come in and place his fat ass right on my face. I can't forgive a man for doing something like that. I think it's simply abusive.' Is the woman we see in *Achilles' Heel is My Weapon* Magdalene? Did you in fact film all of the women you interviewed or was Magdalene an exception?

**Rex:** 'Magdalene' is a pseudonym. It was, of course, important that the woman who actually told me the story be anonymous. I used the story again in *Achilles' Heel is My Weapon*, because its violent images made it a ready accompaniment to the film's two main characters.

97

**Hjort:** A striking feature of your cinematic style is the tendency to focus intensely on the details of intricate designs, monuments and architectural constructs. Viewers, for example, may find themselves fascinated by a tilting camera that stubbornly refuses to provide an initial establishing shot and instead insists on slowly exploring the details of some sculpture, monument or flight of stairs. What role does the concept of the detail play in your thinking about film?

**Rex:** I think my use of details can be compared to the way in which I employ sounds. In reality the script very often finds its origin in a few suggestive images or settings, which are so compelling that I simply know there's an entire film hidden in them. Long before I find all the words or the plot, a guiding vision is mediated by these kinds of images – images that an entire film can be centred around.

**Hjort:** Per Aage Brandt, an important contemporary Danish philosopher of post-structuralist inspiration, has made a number of interesting claims about your work in an essay included in your *Paintings, Drawings* (1995, 34). The line of thought that particularly intrigues me is the following: 'The last of the texts in *Stamtavler* [*Family Trees*] is Jytte Rex's note on photography. Here we find, if we look thoroughly, a key to all of the rest, to all of her art. "The Imaginary Grey Space", a central expression for her, designates a specific kind of intermediate space that encompasses the shadows which conjoin space with space when "the wandering thoughts" move; painting the photograph, adding yet another space on top of a photographed space, entails following the shadows – these flaming, hard, airy, transformational forms: "On the threshold to other zones, through imaginary grey spaces, there are fire, diamonds and laser-vision. Stone. And white spots in the mind" (*Family Tree VI*). Colors, substantiality and visions arise in this imaginary threshold-field where from-within- and from-without-coming spaces meet one another" (translated by Dan A. Marmorstein).' What exactly do you have in mind when you speak of a 'grey space'? Can you give any cinematic examples of the process in question here?

**Rex:** This takes us back to your question about Borges and my brief comments about the issue of translucence. In the imaginary grey space there are virtually no shadows. There may be some shadows, but the landscape in question is kind of misty. Hammershøi's paintings look as though they're grey, but he actually uses the entire colour spectrum in order to achieve precisely those grey effects. On closer examination, his paintings turn out to comprise quite a lot of red, green, blue and yellow. I think those imaginary spaces can be compared with precisely that aspect of his work. If you look at the planets through a telescope, at Venus, for example, you see a lot of colours that are constantly changing, just like mother of pearl. The things that are truly essential disclose themselves through those kinds of colours, material spaces and misty landscapes. It is from those spaces that the settings required by some particular project spring. An imaginary space can prompt a vision that outlines only those very images that are important in a given context. To me it's always been a question of peeling away everything superfluous and unnecessary.

**Hjort:** You're not only a successful film-maker, but also an accomplished painter and photographer. It could be argued that your cinematic style clearly reveals your interest in still photography. In many of your films it's a matter of giving expression to inner states, be they conscious or unconscious, by means of a series of discrete images that bear no obvious relationship to each other. Some of the cinematic images appear as photographs accompanied by poems in the volume *Ash, Time and Fire*. Examples are the images of the stunning crater with which *Mirrors of the Planet* begins, or the images of the woman in the bright red cape who appears at different moments in the same film. You also use paintings and photographs to articulate or define the significance of a given cinematic moment. In *Isolde*, for example, the viewer watches a hand paging slowly through a book with pictures of Hammershøi's paintings. Could you talk about your conception of the relationship between the different media with which you work? More specifically, how has your interest in still photography and painting affected your cinematic style?

**Rex:** Hammershøi is a good example of something very meditative and mystical in painting. For example, Vejen Art Museum has Hammershøi's painting of a woman in a baker's shop. She stands with her back to the viewer, in front of a table and facing a wall. The loaded stillness and mysterious atmosphere in Hammershøi's painting is comparable to what can be found in an entire Tarkovsky film.

**Hjort:** What, exactly, is the point of including shots of Hammershøi's paintings in *Isolde*.

**Rex:** The scene in question takes place in the library, where there's a metal, grid floor, so that the floors above and below are visible, and shelves upon shelves of books. Isolde stands daydreaming in front of a window as she pages through a book of Hammershøi's paintings. It's very quiet; the only thing we hear is some doves cooing outside. What is created here is a condition of transparency. Past and present coincide, and it's as though things have always been like this, like this space between Hammershøi's stillness and Isolde's. Then the door opens and the two women wearing gaudy clothing come in and comment on the situation as they typically do. The stillness and sense of anticipation associated with this space is an image of Isolde's own inner stillness after having returned to work following a suicide attempt. Accompanied by the doves' cooing and Hammershøi's paintings she quietly starts afresh, on her own terms and in the grey nothingness that can be found in Hammershøi's paintings, which nonetheless are always full of colour.

**Hjort:** Superimposition is a technique used frequently in your films. For example, in *Mirrors of the Planet* a moment of conflict between Adam Morgenstern and his new lover is followed by images of a book of black and white pictures, which we see through crystal clear water. What is the significance, for you, of this particular cinematic technique?

**Rex:** Once again, it's a matter very concretely of making two levels transparent to each other, of letting them persist and reside in each other for a moment, thereby making an entirely different level visible. Film, I would imagine, is the medium best suited to explore the possibilities involved in this merging of images, the pauses between them, and the way in which they influence each other.

**Hjort:** The language spoken by characters in your films is frequently poetic and somewhat elusive. A good example is the exchange that takes place on a riverbank between Adam Morgenstern (Ole Lemmeke) and the dancer (Cher Geurtze) in *Mirrors of the Planet*. One is reminded, perhaps, of the language spoken by characters in Virginia Woolf's *The Waves*, for the individuals in question do in fact communicate dialogically, but they do so in a way that sets them apart from most ordinary speakers. What, exactly, is the purpose of systematically gravitating towards a highly literary and philosophical mode of expression?

**Rex:** A lot of people find this aspect of my films really problematic, and the actors frequently have to twist their tongues significantly in order to produce their lines. I think it's also interesting to make use of the possibilities that are inherent in speech. The strangest of tongue twisters have to be uttered in the most naturalistic way possible, in the same tone of voice as when we, for example, say 'What's for dinner tonight?'.

---

1   Founded in 1969 the purpose of this group, which includes Dea Trier Mørch, Troels Trier and Erik Clausen, is to create political, proletarian art.

# Erik Clausen

## 1942–

Erik Clausen came to film as an experienced left-wing political satirist. Indeed, he and his faithful partner, Leif Sylvester Petersen, were a vital part of Danish left-wing political culture in the 1970s. In *Clausen & Petersen's Show* these popular performers combined elements from an ancient commedia dell'arte tradition with rough political satire and rock music. Popular humour, comic genres and raw social realism are characteristic of Clausen's TV sketches, *Clausen's Garage* (1983), and of most of his films and film roles. A characteristic feature of Clausen's cinematic production is that he himself frequently plays one of the main roles. Popular comedy and rock music figure centrally in his debut film, *The Circus Casablanca* (*Cirkus Casablanca*, 1981), which is about a travelling circus, and in the related *Rocking Silver* (1983), which depicts the decline of a rock group and its attempt to recapture earlier successes. These films were viewed as renewing the rather worn Danish popular comedy* by means of a

*Erik Clausen during the shooting of* Carl, My Childhood Symphony (Min fynske barndom). *[Photo: Johan Johansen]*

contemporary idiom and content. Social themes are also foregrounded in films such as *Felix* (1982), which explores loneliness, and *Fish Out of Water* (*De frigjorte*, 1983), which deals with the effects of unemployment and crises in the Danish workers' movement. *Fish Out of Water* won a Bodil* as Best Danish Film of 1983. Clausen explores a more experimental visual style in *The Dark Side of the Moon* (*Manden i månen*, 1986), a story about a man's search for the daughter he's never known following his release from prison after serving a sentence for the murder of his wife. The visually inventive *Rami and Juliet* (*Rami og Julie*, 1988) draws creatively on Shakespeare's *Romeo and Juliet*, situating the classic love story in the context of ethnic conflicts in an emerging multicultural Denmark. The ambitious feature film, *Carl, My Childhood Symphony* (*Min fynske barndom*, 1994), is a lyrical cinematic biography and an evocation of the dawn of democracy in Denmark.

## Feature films
1981, *The Circus Casablanca* (*Cirkus Casablanca*, appears as Charles)
1982, *Felix* (appears as Svend Erik)
1983, *Rocking Silver* (appears as Frank)
1986, *The Dark Side of the Moon* (*Manden i månen*)
1988, *Rami and Juliet* (*Rami og Julie*)
1989, *Me and Mama Mia* (*Tarzan Mama-Mia*, appears as Helmuth)
1993, *Fish Out of Water* (*De frigjorte*, appears as Viggo)
1994, *Carl, My Childhood Symphony* (*Min fynske barndom*)
2000, *Set the Horses Free* (*Slip hestene løs,* appears as Bent A. Pedersen)

## Short films
1997, *Tango* (appears as Ole Jensen)

## Acting roles
1978, *Me and Charly* (*Mig og Charly,* directed by Morten Arnfred and Henning Kristiansen)
1984, *In the Middle of the Night* (*Midt om natten,* directed by Erik Balling)
1985, *The Flying Devils* (*De flyvende djævle,* directed by Anders Refn)
1991, *The Great Day on the Beach* (*Den store badedag,* directed by Stellan Olsson)

## TV productions
1983, *Clausen's Garage*

**Hjort:** You didn't start making films until you were in your forties. It was only at that point, you've claimed, that you had the self-confidence needed to knock on the doors of the Danish Film Institute. It's hard to believe that an application to the Danish Film Institute could be the first or even most important step in a Danish film-maker's career. How, exactly, did you get started? What was it that made you and your plans to make *The Circus Casablanca* seem worthy of support to the consultants* at the Danish Film Institute?

**Clausen:** I'm a phenomenon from the 1960s and 1970s, the kind of artist who doesn't believe in separating the media. To me self-expression is a fundamental need. The cultural revolution in the 1970s was a matter of common concern, which was a source of enormous strength. I painted a lot, and we took to the streets, where we performed street theatre. We didn't feel like working with guilt or the Lutheran Strindberg tradition. Instead we drew on the commedia dell'arte tradition, which was what made sense to my friends and I in terms of our working class backgrounds. The mental *Weltschmerz* that is cultivated, for example, in the films of Ingmar Bergman and Lars von Trier, is unknown among the working class, or among peasants. In Denmark it's a small Copenhagen phenomenon, supported, of course, by the critics. We, on the other hand, worked with rock music and rock shows and toured throughout Scandinavia. We worked very anarchistically and rarely spent time on scripts or rehearsals; we expressed ourselves directly. We consciously made use of a language and dialect that were far removed from the official idiom of high culture. But there was no condescension. We produced political theatre camouflaged as popular hits, and we had a significant impact. Then at a certain point I felt like making a film. I'd gone to the cinema a lot as a child. I found the Italian neo-realists an extraordinary experience. American films in the 1950s were even more narrow-minded, puritanical and idiotic than they are today. Then the neo-realist films appeared, and they were a revelation. Suddenly I could recognise a lot of my family and neighbourhood in these films. They didn't seem Italian and exotic to me, but universal, and it's brilliant when art captures something universal. Popular art often makes use of archaic forms – the fat and the thin person, the good and the evil person, beauty and the beast – and these have also been of interest to me. I had no film experience when I started making films, but I had a lot of experience as an artist. I had a sense of form, and I was very angry about social injustice. I wanted to represent those who'd been overlooked and forgotten, the simple-minded, the people who are so naive as to believe in a down-to-earth future. This isn't on account of compassion, but because I actually believe that they as people are more interesting since they pay a price for their stance towards life. It may be a matter of a wrinkled face or much more directly of completely downtrodden, lost and down-and-out people. I can depict that, because I don't work on inspiration, but on indignation. That's perhaps very moralistic, but so be it.

However, that business about how it's difficult to make films, that's just something the established folks claim in order to keep film for themselves. The new cameras – and here I'm thinking of the High Eight video cameras we have today – are in my mind revolutionary, and they'll further erode the mystique surrounding film-making. What's happening is absolutely incredible. Young people today need only a reasonable budget to make their own films. I shot my last film, *Tango*, with a High Eight camera. I shot it in a very political milieu in South America, and it was very much to our advantage not to look like a film crew, but rather like some stupid Scandinavian tourists. That enabled us to film in some places where we normally would have needed permission to film.

**Hjort:** Many Danish film-makers, it seems, are reluctant to talk about their relation to other film-makers. You're clearly an exception in this regard, for you've made a point of making your likes and dislikes clear. You've cited the positive influence of a number of Italian, Czech and Polish film-makers, just as you've distanced yourself from figures like Bergman and Woody Allen. Do you see yourself as somehow dialoguing with other film-makers through your work?

**Clausen:** My films are, of course, influenced by other directors. My weakness is probably that I don't have a particular identity as a film-maker. This means that I shift styles from one film to the next, depending on what the film is like. Other film-makers, much like painters, are concerned with having their own style. I intend to devote my later years to working towards a more subjective and personal style. Whether this is a form of individualism that has crept into the picture, I don't know, but I've become very interested in formal issues. Danish film is characterised by two things: for the most part a thorough-going naturalism, which is dreadfully boring, and, second, a bourgeois ideology involving a puritanism that is hostile to art, a neo-Protestant tradition. Although I claim to be a Marxist, my tradition isn't Marxist, but Protestant. That Protestantism is part of us and the result is that 95 percent of our Danish film tradition is extremely petit bourgeois. If you look at films from other countries, you'll find a tradition of experimental and intellectual art. Yet, Danish film is virtually hostile towards intellectual statements and the experimental.

However, we have a strong documentary tradition, which includes some very talented and courageous people who've opposed that petit bourgeois mentality, which is in such stark contrast with other aspects of Denmark. I'm thinking here of our democracy, which has really developed a lot, and our open-mindedness about debate, minorities and, not least, sexuality. Yet, all of this is virtually absent from Danish film. The film milieu has succeeded over the years in producing film directors who go directly from secondary school to the Film School. Those kinds of film directors become like fish in an aquarium. They're not on the open seas, they're never at risk, and they're not desperate. They may produce some brilliant films, but what I miss is the authenticity that we other film-makers have and that you find in a Jack London or a John Huston. Authenticity is a very, very big thing for me. I think it's amusing to listen to someone tell me about the moon, but I think it's even more amusing to hear the story from someone who's actually been there. I think it's amusing to listen to someone tell me about love and the great female figures in world literature, but I find real experiences of love more interesting. If I were to organise a curriculum for film students, I'd make them work on freight boats, in nursing homes, prisons, factories, and on the construction of bridges, and I'd urge them to listen to the amazing stories that are told in these places. However, society is best able to control art by creating academies and schools.

Let me return to my relation to other directors. We humans have a sense for equivocal images, and many images are predictable and unambiguous, and that's not interesting. That's why I've been very influenced by European directors, for they're dialectical. They have the courage to represent a beautiful woman and at the same time to suggest that she has a character flaw somewhere. They have the courage to represent a priest who talks about the great, divine revelation while being a horny goat. That duality, which is part of the European tradition, is something I like a lot. I'm very inspired by directors like Milos Forman, especially during his Czech period, and by Fellini of course, but otherwise directors as such don't interest me that much. I think of myself as an independent artist, and when it comes to film, I'm clearly an auteur. I try to construct my own universe in my films, which I both direct and act in. I work with the language of everyday life. In Mike Leigh's films there's a wonderful use of everyday language. Ordinary people frequently use language defensively. They're defensive, no matter what they say. Even if they're just asking for directions, there's a defensiveness in the way they speak. Mike Leigh is able to capture this.

**Hjort:** In 1986 you became Chair of the important Danish Directors' Association *Sammenslutningen af Danske Filminstruktører*. In an interview with Helle Høgsbro (1986), you identified a number of film-related issues that you felt were particularly urgent at that time. I'm interested, for example, in the following remarks: 'We need to revive the cultural debate that started already in the 1930s with forceful figures such as P.H.,* Hans Kirk and Theodor Christensen. It was very different from the low-grade polemicising that's going on nowadays, where it's a matter of doing battle with the film consultants and otherwise playing the role of the misunderstood film genius.' What exactly is it about the culture debates of the 1930s that you consider important? Did you manage to achieve at least some of the goals you set yourself as Chair of the association?

**Clausen:** When I became Chair the association was quite split. We weren't organised. It's important to be united and also to have an organisation where there's an ongoing debate about issues that only concern directors. This has something to do with better contracts, enhanced influence, discussions about final cut, and all those things. It's a good association, an artistic association when that's what we want it to be, and a union when that's what we feel we need. The Danish Film Act is the result of an initiative in the 1960s on the part of directors such as Henning Carlsen, Annelise Hovmand, Astrid Henning-Jensen and others, who ensured that film became a public cultural affair. The Film Act was initiated by the Directors' Association, not by academics, although they'd have us believe otherwise. What I miss nowadays in Denmark is a passionate debate about culture, and by 'passionate' I mean unreasonable, desperate. The conversational approach is ironic, instead of humorous, it's sarcastic instead of poetic. I foregrounded the 1930s debate because back then people knew their dialectics and could talk about themselves while also talking about politics; both things were part of the picture. Our problem as film directors is that we're not writers, but image-makers. I have no writerly tradition I can draw on. My tradition involves story telling and debating. This is where I miss the intellectuals. We need debate, because debate is what produces better films. For me vigorous debate is like a work-out while also being an expression of what we stand for. We owe the public a debate about what it is we're trying to achieve with our films.

**Hjort:** Much like your colleagues Christian Braad Thomsen, Jytte Rex and Søren Kragh-Jacobsen, you've been very critical over the years of the way in which the importation of foreign films is handled in Denmark. Kragh-Jacobsen seems to have a point when he insists that a viable Danish film industry presupposes the possibility of collectively educating the Danish public in such a way that it is capable of appreciating modes of cinematic expression that depart from the commercial norms of Hollywood film. However, clearly, Danish directors cannot be solely responsible for providing the kind of education that is required here. What needs to change? What does the ideal Danish public look like and how is it to be produced? Has the recent international focus on Danish film significantly changed the nature of the Danish public?

**Clausen:** Film is also cultural warfare. Who's to be part of the picture? Film is identified with the things we experience. Fortunately there's no scientific proof for that, because art's not something you can define. Art is undefinable, it's a sensuous experience. It's something ambiguous, like grandmother's stories, where you're both repulsed by the ugly troll and drawn to it. It may also be a feeling that is part of your erotic fantasy. For me art and film generally have something to do with the unconscious. It's hard to describe, but we people have a need to mirror ourselves in something, otherwise we can't see ourselves.

Let me return to the question of film in relation to society. Of course the politicians and Capital know that art is dangerous. Artistic experiences are sometimes transformed into action, and in Denmark's case this often happens in connection with popular movements, examples being the anti-authoritarian movement in the 1960s and the women's movement. The latter has had the effect of ensuring that women who are over 50 today still have their pride and are very, very beautiful, whereas my grandmother was finished by the time she was 50. Here I think that hero-figures in the world of art, including film, have played an important role.

I don't know whether we should try to educate the audience, but art is very important, because as I mentioned, we have this need to see ourselves in something other than our own reflection. Art is universal and a matter of fantasy and that's why it's what's closest to the unconscious. That's why it's so incredibly exciting, uncontrollable and politically dangerous. If we produce the kind of art that, without denying life's risks and the danger of defeat, is able to represent life as a sensuous experience, a real pleasure, something that's worth fighting for, then art and film can help to undermine the fear that society tries to inculcate in us. The images that society imposes on us have a real grip on us, in much the same way that those statistics we create do. These statistics are presented as objective and build on negative facts only. There are no statistics measuring happiness and pleasurable sensations. Yet there are lots of statistics about substance abuse, alcoholism, suicide rates, child mortality rates and unemployment. There are no statistics on erotic satisfaction, and none on the pleasure that mothers take in their children. This is where art comes in. Art is by nature artless and unsuspicious. Art is by nature optimistic. The fear that Danes experience is not of a social, but rather of a mental character. Art has a mission here, but it must never become pedagogical. The more useless art apparently is, the more useful it ultimately is.

**Hjort:** You don't pull your punches when it comes to Hollywood film. I'm thinking, for example, of the following remark: 'We're in the process of allowing ourselves to be inundated with Yankee shit that morally speaking appeals to what's most base in human beings and operates on a spiritual level similar to that of Donald Duck and Co.' (interview with Helle Høgsbro, May 1986). In an interview with Helle Hellmann (*Politiken*, March 1988), you claim that the required opposition to Hollywood involves the development of a quite different aesthetic and alternative mode of narration: 'In my film I allow myself the luxury of narrating several stories at once, that is, a complex mode of narration. We're so used to being pulled around by the nose by an effective American narrative technique.' *The Dark Side of the Moon* won international acclaim for the beauty of its images and critics responded favourably to the stylised nature of the narrative developed in *Rami and Juliet*. Could you talk about your views on film aesthetics and narrative in relation perhaps to these two films?

**Clausen:** We have the same relation to American film as intellectuals have to football. It's a love/hate relationship. Intellectuals understand the collective value of sports and at the same time they applaud the outstanding individualist, the stars, and the strong man. We think that the people who go to football are idiots and at the same time we think that the fact that football can unite the entire nation is fascinating. This is the kind of relation we have to American film. We love to hate American films and at the same time we admire people like Marlon Brando. Whether American film can be separated from American society is an interesting question. I'm not sure it can. American film is just as intimately linked to the American system of power as Soviet cinema or Riefenstahl's films were connected to the Soviet state or to Hitler's regime. Films are often an expression of what is going on in society, and the films we see here, which in some cases have certain artistic qualities, a certain honesty and authenticity, are only a small part of American film. Frequently they're made outside of Hollywood. When Spike Lee starts making films, he does so for the same reasons that I do. Films generate profit, and the producers look at the profit before examining the contents. They can swallow a political film as long as they earn a couple of million dollars on it.

For me American film is Chaplin. If you read his memoirs, you'll find a paradox. As he becomes more successful, as the audience's enthusiasm for Chaplin's films grows, he finds himself facing more and more difficulties behind the scenes. We always think it's the other way around: now that you're popular, things must be working well for you. In the end he's thrown out of the country, which shows the limits to the tolerance of the American system. Yet to reject American film would be stupid. I can only say that I don't associate any great experiences with American film. Hollywood is a jungle, and they have to import some meat from the outside in order to feed the machinery, but Hollywood films are not artistically interesting. They're politically interesting, because in my mind they're part of the American propaganda apparatus. Some of the American films that are showing here in Copenhagen are trivial and others are good. We do, of course, admire the self-confidence and megalomania of the Americans, but I'd prefer them not to be responsible for defining the content of film art. If they were to define it, it would become so boring that I, for one, wouldn't be interested in making films any more. I think the Americans could learn a lot from the art forms of other countries. They could learn from African art and South American music, more so than from American film, and many of the more interesting directors are, of course, imported from Europe or influenced by tendencies from over here.

**Hjort:** You're arguably one of Denmark's most beloved public figures. Indeed, as far as Søren Kragh-Jacobsen is concerned, you're one of the few actors and directors capable of motivating a significant percentage of the Danish public to go and see a Danish film. What's striking, however, is that you frequently suggest that you somehow stand outside the imagined community that is the Danish nation. Let me remind you of some of your previous statements: 'We didn't understand a word of the patriotic songs. We couldn't connect the feelings expressed in those high-blown songs with what we experienced in our own neighbourhoods. In a way we weren't part of the cultural identity. What we could identify with was the green grocer pulling out his accordion and singing 'I'm a gypsy' or the old sailors' songs, or the tango that made our parents leap up and dance around during a courtyard party. I wonder when I'll reach what they call Denmark, the

*Erik Clausen as Charles in* The Circus Casablanca (Cirkus Casablanca). *[Photo: Roald Pay]*

place where King Christian still stands leaning up against a mast' (*Kristeligt Dagblad*, August 1990). Could you say a little more about national identity and your relation to dominant notions of Danishness?

**Clausen:** I think that national perspectives are the stupidest thing in the world, and I think they're uninteresting. I feel at home most places. I might be sitting in the middle of Istanbul and suddenly I'll find myself thinking, 'I wouldn't mind living here.' The only problems would be finding work and learning the language. I've sat in the middle of Montreal and suddenly realised that I already had friends and acquaintances, and that I could easily just stay on. If you have that national feeling, then you're chained to a place, to a neighbourhood, to a street. I watch the young people who are unemployed or the young intellectuals who spend years of their lives waiting to get into university. Inside I'm screaming, 'Leave, for God's sake, go anywhere, go to some place where you're welcome. If you want to become a doctor, you ought to be welcome to study medicine, and if you're interested in hard physical labour, there must be some place in the world where you're welcome.' As far as I can tell, the nationalism of today's Europe is as great a tragedy as Nazism was. When we've gained a certain distance from the things that are happening these years, we'll see that they've cost a lot of human lives and that there have been other costs too.

Danish cultural life – what we at the Danish universities and in the Danish folk high schools* call 'Danish culture' – is dominated by a very small part of the population. I am, of course, putting this bluntly. There's a subculture in every country, but what counts as good is determined by those who are established. In the case of film, they've decided that Dreyer is a good director who expresses Danish cultural life. Sometimes artists are misused, which is what happened in the case of Carl Nielsen. His roots are in the peasantry. He depicts the light, the dawn of democracy, and he has an incredibly impressive sense of form. His compositions, his way of dissolving the old harmonies, are extraordinary. He's then pulled in, stolen, and made part of official culture. When it's a matter of describing Danish cultural life, it's always the high points that are emphasised. And that doesn't interest me that much. What's interesting is when an artist tries to change the agenda. Someone like Tove Ditlevsen managed to do this, for she gave the workers an identity. And there was no condescension here, for she worked with the structures of feeling that are embedded in the neighbourhoods she knows so well.

**Hjort:** Marginal figures and their social problems are often central to your films. I'm thinking of your treatment of loneliness in *Felix*, where the widow Inger Marie Måge attempts to deal with her sense of isolation by advertising a reward for the retrieval of her cat, which doesn't actually exist. In an interview published in *Filmfaust* (1987), you claim that your aim is to create a series of cinematic counter-images (*Gegenbilder*). This concept is clearly linked to the marginal status of your central characters. What, exactly, is it that is being countered in your films, and what, more positively, do you see as the ideal *effect* of your cinematic images?

**Clausen:** The ideal for me in film is when an ugly person is made beautiful and a beautiful person ugly. We can do this in film because of the close-up. This is the first time in the entire history of art that this possibility exists. I do, of course, know that there's such a thing as the art of portraiture, but it's frequently been practiced in such a way that the painter's approach was orchestrated by the person paying for the image. The cinematic image allows us to study each other closely; we can sit in the dark and look directly at someone. In reality we're creatures of discretion, and film, and especially the close-up, allow us to get beyond that sense of modesty. A face tells its own story. For example, if I make a beautiful woman lie on the screen, the result is a delight to watch, because she's been raised to think of herself as a sweet girl. She's the one who takes dancing lessons and who has all the Barbie dolls. She's liked by all her aunts. Yet, now she is lying to her mother. You can depict that contrast cinematically, but virtually only with the help of the close-up.

The second thing that's important to me in film is making sure that some of the images are saturated with meaning. The problem with the cinematic image is that it's often very unambiguous. When I produce a painting, there's always a painting behind the painting. At the very least, I can always let some of the brush strokes be rough, so that the image behind the image becomes the classification of the image as a painted image. It's difficult to do this kind of thing with the cinematic image. That's why I've had trouble with some of my films, with *The Dark Side of the Moon*, for example, where we see the world through the eyes of a paranoid man. It all becomes very artificial, and I think that's really linked to the problematic nature of the cinematic image. Yet it seems a bit artificial to revert to black and white images in order to resolve those kinds of representational problems, or to grainy images, or a hand-held camera.

So for me images of people, that is, close-ups, are important and so are saturated images. Other than that, what's interesting is the fact of being able to use reality as a set. You can provide a horrible depiction of a rich neighbourhood and a beautiful depiction of a poor neighbourhood, which is what we did in *Felix*, a film that was set in Sydhavnen, where I grew up. Or you can represent the actual reception of President Clinton in Denmark as a form of insanity. I think the great advantage of film is that it's a mass medium that nonetheless allows for a mode of representation that is as subjective as that of a first-person novel. I use the term 'counter image' to indicate that it's a matter of counter publicity. Instead of reproducing the official images of the rich, healthy, sick and poor, my films represent situations and stories in which the losers win. However, some of us are so stupid and innocent that we immediately spend what we win, which means we're back where we started from in no time. The narrator tells us they lived happily for the rest of their days because the fairytale somehow has to be brought to a close. Yet we know that's a lie. We know the man's going to look at another woman the very next day and that they'll be fighting a week later.

**Hjort:** In 1989 you directed *Me and Mama Mia*, which was an extraordinary success. Indeed, this film for children and adolescents sold more tickets in Denmark than a successful foreign film such as *Batman*. In *Wide-eyed: Films for Children and Young People in the Nordic Countries*, Ida Zeruneith (1995) claims that she, in her capacity as children's film consultant, approached you with the specific request that you consider making a film for young people. The result, *Me and Mama Mia*, focusses on the 11 year old, motherless Rikke, who longs for a horse, in part because she has been taught at school that Pegasus, the winged horse, was believed to be able to fly to the kingdom of the dead. Rikke's dream comes true when she wins a horse through a Cornflakes lottery. Given the success of *Me and Mama Mia*, one cannot help but wonder why you didn't explore this genre further. Why is there to date only one children's film by Erik Clausen?

**Clausen:** I think specialists are one of the great evils of our time. Specialists are idiots. If you make films all the time, you become a specialist. As a director, you need to go out and experience something, you need to reflect, you need to take part in life. I do think that I could have made other children's films, and this may still happen, but directors need to do other things. The most difficult thing about making a film for children and adolescents is the language. Language is a living organism that changes all the time, so when the children spoke the lines I'd written for them, they sounded completely wrong, like an advertisement.

**Hjort:** There's much talk these days about the need to internationalise Danish film, and I would like to discuss this issue in relation to *Carl, My Childhood Symphony*. *Carl* is a Nordic co-production involving Danish, Swedish and Norwegian funds. What's interesting is that the overall 'look' of *Carl* is quite different from that of your earlier films. Indeed, the aesthetic effect of *Carl* is much closer to that of Gabriel Axel's *Babette's Feast* (*Babettes gæstebud*) or Bille August's *Pelle the Conqueror* (*Pelle Erobreren*) than it is to *Rami and Juliet* or *The Dark Side of the Moon*. *Babette* and *Pelle the Conqueror* are, of course, films that are oriented, not only towards Danish, but also towards Nordic and international audiences. *Carl*, it seems to me, is similarly governed by a strategy of multiple address. The geography of Denmark has been rendered virtually unimportant and this makes it easier for international audiences to identify with the narrative. You've also chosen to do without the regional dialect, *fynsk*, that is an integral part of the historical narrative that is the basis for your fictionalised treatment of Carl Nielsen's childhood years. Is *Carl, My Childhood Symphony*, in your opinion, an example of the internationalisation of Danish film?

**Clausen:** The visual dimension is inspired by the painters from Funen[1], who were Carl Nielsen's contemporaries and part of that cultural revolution that took place in the 1880s. Carl Nielsen was also part of that cultural revolution, just as I'm part of the cultural revolution that took place in the 1960s and 1970s. As the film shows, a popular revolt occurred in Denmark towards the end of the century. The Church and schools were suddenly perceived as oppressing children's souls, and people wanted to change this. The free schools[2] were created, and they exist to this day, and this is where democracy in Denmark emerged. Playing music in public had been forbidden and suddenly that interdiction was removed. This made possible the beginnings of a musical movement, just as in the 1960s when we developed our own music. The painters from Funen were a collective movement consisting largely of painters who were craftsmen and who helped each other socially, so that they were also able to paint. People in Copenhagen looked down on them, but they were excellent painters, so they've had a tremendous impact on popular culture in Denmark. However, the film is too naturalistic. Although we have a camera and millions of Crowns at our disposal, we can't do what the painters from Funen can do with water colour. As for the dialect question and the business of speaking *fynsk*, that's simply impossible. That would be a form of nationalism. The fact that they speak *fynsk* is not that interesting. Had it been a matter of a real minority who spoke a different language, the situation would have been different.

Neither we nor the producers were focussed on a strategy of internationalisation in connection with this film. I think that discussion is wrongheaded, for it's the very national or very Danish films that are successful internationally. I'm thinking, for example, of Nils Malmros' wonderful film, *The Tree of Knowledge* (*Kundskabens træ*) which isn't simply Danish, but *århusiansk*. That film has been shown all around the world. The same is true of some of the foreign films, including the American ones, that do well here; they're often very local. You could also use the term 'subjective'. I must admit, though, that the naturalism in *Carl* was a mistake. The film is mainly inspired by the painters, because at some level I think it's a matter of vanity to believe you can provide a representation of a composer. Music has a range that film just doesn't have. In some ways, I'd also want to say that it's not that important to provide a representation of a composer. Or, if that's what you want to do other things should be emphasised. What I wanted to point out with the film is that Carl Nielsen isn't only some elite figure. Rather, he was a product of his environment, which he was always faithful towards and inspired by, and which he consciously treasured.

**Hjort:** Your films are all very much about Danish realities. What's more, the approach adopted towards these realities is that of the social realist, with additional elements from the tradition of Danish popular comedy. *Fish out of Water* deals with some of the typical causes and effects of unemployment in Denmark. *Rami and Juliet* focusses on the plight of refugees in an increasingly multicultural Denmark. I was intrigued by your most recent film, *Tango*, which was made under the auspices of New Fiction Film Denmark.* In this humorously ironic fictional documentary, we meet Ole Jensen (played by Erik Clausen), who's enjoying early retirement benefits, having been unemployed most of his adult life. The sluggish Ole Jensen interacts primarily with his social worker who, in a final attempt to awaken her protege from his slumbers, encourages him to take tango lessons. During his first class, Ole Jensen steals an airline ticket that protrudes temptingly from a dancer's pocket. He uses the ticket and soon finds himself in Uruguay, where he learns how to dance and how to respond with passion to life. Although Ole Jensen learns much about Uruguay and its troubled political history, the film is very much about Denmark throughout. Virtually all the information conveyed about Uruguay serves to highlight some aspect of Danish life about which you're critical. Thus, for example, the military dictatorship in Uruguay is contrasted with the alleged Danish situation where oppression takes the form of self-censorship throughout the population at large. Does it make sense to think of *Tango* as an interestingly ironic and innovative instance of the genre known as *Danmarksfilm*?

**Clausen:** Yes, I think of *Tango* as a kind of satirical *Danmarksfilm* because if you're going to depict Danes, you have to do so via others. I think the renewal of Danish art will come from some of the immigrants. I just know there's a young 13 year old immigrant somewhere in Århus or Tåstrup who has the same rage that I had when I was 13. If someone is going to write a new *Pelle the Conqueror* (*Pelle Erobreren*)[3] I don't think it will be someone by the name of Jens or Andersen. In *Tango* I tried to work with political satire, and a mixture of fiction and non-fiction. On the one hand, we have a country that's so rich that people are paid not to work. We pay 200,000 people for *not* interfering with the sphere of production, and we don't have any concrete oppressors. Yet there's less debate here than in Uruguay, even during the military dictatorship. There's less political art here than there, and we have fewer confrontations, although conflict could cost them their lives. The mental oppression that occurs here is primarily self-inflicted, and this is what I want to draw critical attention to. I'm glad that so many people have been inspired by the film and that what I say has angered a lot of people. From the point of view of formal issues, it was an exciting film to shoot. There were certain social and moral difficulties involved, because I couldn't make fun of the people I was interviewing, although I was working in a satirical vein.

When the film premiered in Uruguay the Cinémathèque was full, and we received a standing ovation that lasted a full five minutes. As the producer over there pointed out this was because the film was good, and also because it didn't do what other films typically do, which is to look at Uruguay from a European or North American, anthropological perspective, and as a third-world country. In *Tango* Uruguayans are represented as equals. The film was shot with a High Eight camera because it would have been difficult for me to finance it otherwise. We shot a lot of footage, had no script, and didn't spend time rehearsing. The film was to a large extent made afterwards, and it took us three to four months to do the editing and to produce the sound and music. I'm sorry it's not a bit longer. But this was the length that the TV people and New Fiction Film Denmark wanted, and I actually felt that was ok. I still have a lot of good material, especially concerning the women. The women in the film are incredibly strong. I'm not that happy, though, with the actual satire. In Denmark we talk a lot about people from the 1960s and 1970s who were revolutionaries and now have corporate positions or, at the very least, positions in some state institution. Yet, this isn't true. Most of them are lost. Most of them are disappointed people. Nobody wants to listen to them, and certainly not their children. Many of them are unemployed, they smoke too much hash, they drink too much beer and they're insufferable. They've paid a very high price for their ideals and their commitment. They've been forgotten. I know a lot of people who are in exactly the same position as Ole Jensen.

**Hjort:** In my opinion you're one of three or four Danish directors producing films that can be characterised as intercultural in their thrust. *Rami and Juliet*, it seems to me, does not merely represent a clash of cultures, but aims actually to open up a dialogue between cultures. Are you interested in communicating across cultures?

**Clausen:** Yes, I think that the multicultural tendency is one of the best things that's happened to Denmark in recent times, in the wake of the anti-authoritarian movement and subsequent women's movement. People from countries other than America and Germany have come to Denmark, and this has helped to highlight the limits of Danish tolerance. As a result we've discovered that while we're a very rich, democratic country, we're also mentally a very impoverished, undemocratic nation. However, as time passes, the newcomers will automatically start to intervene in everyday life, and people will get to know each other, and I do think I'd be able to represent this cinematically.

I sometimes find we Danes very pale and inbred. Yet, the ongoing multicultural developments will soon influence our art and music. The politicians problematise the process, but an exchange of views is already going on. There are music projects, where we play together; there are a lot of things. Again, you never see any of this on TV. However, the multicultural developments that are taking place around the world are very, very exciting, and we shouldn't think they're not happening in Denmark, because they are. A lot of young Danes are leaving. Many of them don't want to have to wait to get into university. If I were a young, unemployed worker today, I wouldn't wait around. I'd leave, or I'd open a kiosk or a pizzeria. I wouldn't sit around waiting for fate, or for some pale-faced social worker to show up with a project or some recommendation that I take tango lessons. I'd grab hold of life here and now. That's the 'to be' part in 'to be or not to be', and the working class has never had the luxury of worrying about the second part of that dilemma.

**Hjort:** *Rami and Juliet* mobilises canonised narratives associated with large nations: Shakespeare's *Romeo and Juliet* and Bernstein's *West Side Story*. What's the advantage of framing your narrative in these terms? Is the calculation here in part strategic? That is, does the utilisation of such narratives make it easier for the products of a minor cinema to penetrate a larger, international market?

**Clausen:** At that point I felt like making a very theatrical film, and then I discovered, as an adult, just how wonderful Shakespeare is. I hadn't read him earlier, and I simply put these two things together. Some stories are eternal, and the one about Juliet is. There was an American filmed version of the story recently, in which two white families were feuding. I thought that was weak and wrong. They should have brought two different religious traditions into conflict, a Muslim tradition against a Protestant one, or a Protestant tradition against a Jewish one. However, I found it exciting to work with Shakespeare and with a stylised film, in which, with the help of special lighting techniques, we were able to use the concrete constructions in the suburbs as stylised sets. It's beautifully made, but the public isn't interested in seeing the film. All the films that have referred explicitly to theatre in recent times have been problematic. In theatre the use of *Verfremdung* effects is elementary; you find this in commedia dell'arte. However, *Verfremdung* is problematic in film because it introduces a certain arrogance, and I wasn't expecting that. I can't say that I wouldn't use a theatrical style again, but I'd want to draw on something closer to the commedia dell'arte tradition – which is what I did in my first film, *The Circus Casablanca* – instead of citing Shakespeare, because somehow that involves too much pathos. As far as I can tell, I've been proven right, for the classics are indeed thriving in the suburbs. When I go to some grill bar in Tåstrup for lunch during a shoot and see a young immigrant with his blonde girl, I know that the problems they're up against in principle are the same as Romeo and Juliet's, although they may be less dramatic. *Rami and Juliet* is a beautiful, stylised and theatrical film, and if you look at what other directors have done, you'll see that they've all made a theatrical film at some point, especially the European directors. Let me tell you, *Rami and Juliet* is very famous in the Arab world, because we consciously chose to say, 'Here's their perspective and here's ours.' Western films tend to have an inbuilt imperialism. When we look at other countries, at other parts of the world, we do so at the very least with anthropological eyes, and usually as part of an imperialist tradition. We're used to setting the agenda; we're used to being in control. The Turks feel we don't accept them, not because we oppress them, but because we're not interested in them. The most insidious means of political oppression is not violence, it's indifference. There's greater oppression involved in my making you invisible than there is in my hitting you.

1   Painters from Funen. Johannes Larsen, Fritz Syberg and Peter Marius Hansen, trained by Kristian Zahrtmann and associated with a new realistic view of rural life and nature on the island of Funen towards the end of the 19th century. Contributed to the emergence of impressionism in Denmark.

2   Schools run according to principles that are elaborated independently of the state school system. The Free School Act of 1855 guarantees the relevant schools specific liberties derived from the parental right to determine how a child should be raised and educated and from the constitutionally enshrined rights of minorities to educate their children according to conviction. Free schools receive substantial state support.

3   Novel by Martin Andersen Nexø (1869-1954), first published in 1915.

# Anders Refn

## 1944–

Anders Refn is the son of the stage designer, Helge Refn, and the father of the film director Nicolas Winding Refn. Anders Refn began his career in film as a prop assistant and assistant director, but went on to be trained as a director at the National Film School of Denmark,* which he attended from 1967–69. His first feature film, *Copper* (*Strømer*, 1976), set a new standard for realistic crime fiction in Danish film, and Jens Okking, who played the role of a cop caught in the system, won a Bodil* for his remarkable performance. The TV sequel, *Once a Cop* (*Een gang strømer*, 1987), is characterised by spectacular action sequences, a solid, realistic story, and careful casting, and similarly provided a new measure for modern Danish TV crime fiction. Refn's innovative approach to TV is further evident in the series *Taxi* (*Taxa*), which he conceived of, wrote the script for (together with Stig Thorsboe) and partially directed (episodes 1–3 and 15–18). Refn has

*Anders Refn.*

adapted two classic Danish novels to the screen. *The Baron* (*Slægten*, 1978) and *Black Harvest* (*Sort høst*, 1993), which are both based on novels by Gustav Wied, and are social melodramas in a visually interesting cinemascope format. These films depict powerful drives and social contradictions in a patriarchal manor house milieu at the turn of the century and feature several of Danish film's most established actors in outstanding roles. *The Flying Devils* (*De flyvende djævle*, 1985), which was inspired by a short story by Herman Bang, is a Danish-Swedish, English-language co-production with non-Danish actors. This beautifully filmed circus melodrama won five Robert* awards, including Best Danish Film of 1985 and Best Cinematography in recognition of Mikael Salomon's achievement. Unfortunately, however, the film failed to attract a large audience, which had serious economic consequences for a number of the people involved. Refn has also worked as an assistant director and editor on a considerable number of films by other Danish directors. He received a Robert prize in 1996 for his editing of Lars von Trier's *Breaking the Waves*. His most recent film, *Seth*, won the prize for Best Fiction Film of 1999 at the Odense Film Festival.

## Feature films
1976, *Copper* (*Strømer*)
1978, *The Baron* (*Slægten*)
1985, *The Flying Devils* (*De flyvende djævle*)
1993, *Black Harvest* (*Sort høst*)

## Short films
1999, *Seth* (*Seth*)

## TV series
1987, *Once a Cop* (*Een gang strømer*, episodes 1–6)
1995, *The Village* (*Landsbyen*, episodes 24–29)
1998, *Taxi* (*Taxa*, episodes 1–3, 15–18)

**Hjort:** In Denmark the name 'Refn' is intimately linked to the arts. Your father, Helge Refn, was responsible for the set design in *The Man Who Thought Things* (*Manden der tænkte ting*) and he served as artistic consultant on one of your films, *The Baron*. Your brother, Peter Refn, was for many years the director of the venerable Copenhagen cinema, *Grand*, and directed *Violets are Blue* (*Violer er blå*). *Pusher* established your son, Nicolas Winding Refn (Jang Refn), as one of Denmark's most promising young directors. When did you first realise that film would be your passion and metier? What's it like to be able to share that passion and metier, not only with a sibling, but with your child?

**Refn:** I think one of the reasons I've never been involved in theatre is that my father primarily was a man of the theatre. He was what used to be called a stage designer. I've always wanted to make my own way in the world, so I naturally sought out some territory that he hadn't charted and didn't have any influence over. When I started out in the film industry as a prop assistant – which is about as low as you can get on the ladder – I never mentioned my surname. I didn't want any special treatment just because my father was a well-known theatre personage. Originally I wanted to be a jazz musician and I did become a semi-professional musician, but I wasn't good enough, so I dropped that.

While I was preparing for the Danish equivalent of 'A levels' I made a couple of eight mm films together with a friend who was a photographer and had bought a camera. Having passed my exams, however, I started studying sociology at the University of Copenhagen. I had to do something and I thought sociology was interesting. I didn't thrive at all in that milieu, though, so after 18 months I took the leap and went into film. First I wrote a letter to Bo Widerberg in the hope of being included in the production of one of his films, but that didn't work out. At that point my brother, who'd already established himself as a director's assistant, was working for Flamingo Film. I didn't want to have to rely on him to open doors for me, so it was one of my brother's good friends, Jens Ravn, the director of *The Man Who Thought Things*, who got me a job as a prop assistant at Palladium in Hellerup. I started working there in 1965 and I was both an assistant director and an assistant editor to Sven Methling, among others. The

National Film School of Denmark was established in 1966 and I applied that very first year but was turned down, along with a lot of other hopeful people. I continued working on the floor at Palladium, and also at Saga and Laterna Film. And then I got into the Film School the following year, and was there from 1967 until 1969. I've always loved my metier, which is very important, I think, if you're going to survive in a business that's as strange as the Danish film industry is. You can't really make a living as a film director in Denmark. You have to do something else on the side. I've edited a lot of films and have worked hard at becoming a good editor. I actually know how to do most aspects of film-making. I work as a script writer and as an editor, and I've also done a lot of assistant directing. It's of course true that I've also done these things because I think they're a lot of fun. I think it's really, really important to want to be part of a team. You may not be wielding the baton each time, but you're at least part of the band, which means that you're keeping your instrument properly tuned. For example, I edited Lars von Trier's *Breaking the Waves*, which was a lot of fun and an amazing experience for me, artistically and otherwise.

However, I think you should only make films when you can't help yourself. I don't think you should make films in order to stay busy. The decision to take on the heavy responsibility as a director is often a fateful one, because you become your films and they become you. Being a director is a horrible job. You're under constant pressure. You're constantly grappling with your own fears and with other people's expectations, with fear of failure and nightmares, and you're so vulnerable to all kinds of accidents that can ruin your film. All in all the job of film director isn't particularly attractive. You have to have incredible will power, passion and a lot of affection for whatever project you initiate, and you have to be able to defend it all the way through, and afterwards too. I've turned down a lot of big feature film projects because they just didn't move me. Sometimes the scripts were fine, but they just didn't resonate within me, or with my way of seeing the world.

As far as being from a film family is concerned, I used my father as a consultant on *The Baron*, which was my second feature film, and he was wonderful. This is more apparent to me now that I'm older. Back then I was more guarded, because I wanted to be in control. The work he did for me was very touching and I fear I may not have thanked him enough for it while he was alive. That's why I dedicated *The Flying Devils* to him. In many of my films there's a pronounced element of rebellion against father figures. It's often a matter of strong men who break down, or of children who rebel against their authoritarian parents. The family has always been an interesting universe to explore, and other people have thought as much too: Shakespeare, O'Neill, Strindberg and Ibsen, for example. The family is in a way the fundamental element, the basic molecule.

There are so many unhappy examples of people who've tried to follow in their father's footsteps. So I've interfered very, very little with Nicolas' choices, although I did urge him to become something other than a film director. He did give film acting a try, but quickly discovered that he had no desire whatsoever to become an actor. So I was very, very happy when his first film worked out so well for him. I think *Pusher* is a very successful film and, interestingly, there's a strange parallel between his debut and my own. When I was making my first film, *Copper*, there was this convention in Denmark, which ruled out realistic stories about crime. Nicolas has taken a rather unsympathetic and little admired pusher and turned him into an interesting character. I have, of course, given him advice when he's asked for help, but other than that I think he has his own temperament, his own cinematic language and background. He grew up in the States.

**Hjort:** Nicolas is an avid moviegoer who tends to describe his cinematic vision by means of references to the history of cinema. You've been less eager over the years to discuss your admiration for particular films or film-makers. Could you name some of the film-makers who've inspired you?

**Refn:** If I haven't talked about my relation to other directors, it's probably because nobody has ever asked me to do so. I've been influenced a lot by the history of film. My brother, Peter, who's dead now, spent many years of his life running the Danish art-film cinema, *Grand*. We used to devour films when we were young. We'd see three films a day if we could. Sometimes we'd be able to make the seven o'clock screening, the nine o'clock screening, and the midnight screening. It's the great directors like Buñuel, Kurosawa, Bergman and Visconti who've intrigued me. I think I'm especially indebted to Visconti. Both *The Leopard* (*Il Gattopardo*) and *Rocco and His Brothers* (*Rocco e i suoi fratelli*) are films that made a deep impression on me. It's clear to me now, after the fact, that I've cited them on various occasions. I've also drawn on René Clair's *Our Freedom Now* (*À nous la liberté*) without realising it. *Copper* ends with an inauguration ritual that resembles that of Clair's film: they inaugurate the factory, which has been decorated with garlands, and a number of distinguished people give speeches; and then the moment of embarrassment occurs. The resemblance had never occurred to me, but it's clear that you borrow and steal shamelessly from other directors. I could keep on naming names: Cassavetes, John Huston, Stanley Kubrick, François Truffaut. The French directors and the new wave made a deep impression on us and so did the Czechs, people like Milos Forman and Jiˆí Menzel, and Nordic directors, like Bo Widerberg and Jan Troell. Alf Sjöberg's *Miss Julie* (*Fröken Julie*) also made an enormous impression on me. Then there's Dreyer, although it's hard to say where I've stolen from him. I've always admired especially *Vampyr*, *The Passion of Joan of Arc* (*La Passion de Jeanne d'Arc*) and *Day of Wrath* (*Vredens dag*), and I'm one of the few people who actually quite liked *Gertrud* in spite of its theatrical and somewhat old-fashioned style. At some level it had a great feel to it and a certain masterfulness that you don't find in a lot of Danish films. It was clear that this was a somewhat dull film by a great director. You couldn't just discount it, which is precisely what the Danish critics did. Most of them thought it was ridiculous. A very theatrical style often seems a bit hollow and can be off-putting. This is true of *Babette's Feast* (*Babettes gæstebud*) which also has uneven acting if you listen to the Danish. Yet people love it elsewhere in the world, for those nuances don't register once the film moves across the border. So it's received very differently abroad.

**Hjort:** You're a great admirer of the Danish author, Gustav Wied. Indeed, two of your four feature films are based on novels by Wied. I'm thinking, of course, of *The Baron* and

*Black Harvest.* In an interview published in *Månedsmagasinet Agenda* (November 1993), you suggest that your interest in Wied has to do with his ability to capture certain national traits: 'He had an eye for a certain Danish meanness, where it's a matter of completely taking someone apart in an apparently friendly manner. That meanness really exists and Wied is one of the few authors who has been able to depict it in a moving and gripping manner.' Is your interest in these turn-of-the-century novels primarily historical, or do you feel that these works continue to reflect crucial aspects of Danish culture?

**Refn:** They certainly do. I wouldn't have spent time on those films if they hadn't depicted feelings and characters or explored moral and existential problems that I myself find important. Those films aren't motivated by a historical perspective, but by the idea that Wied touches on something absolutely fundamental in the way in which we behave towards each other. In Denmark, Wied is often staged in a somewhat parodic and theatrical manner. There's a tendency to emphasise the humorous dimension, and this diminishes him significantly. I think he has an amazing ability to cut right to the bone. We Danes often rely on self-righteousness and irony in an attempt to take a certain distance from things. Yet, Wied's novels – *Blood Line* (*Slægten*) and *Black Harvest* (*Fædrene æde druer*) – recount the most terrible tales of self-deception. *Blood Line* is about a man who tries to buy his way to happiness. He purchases a wife for himself because he wants to strengthen his position within local society, and he believes that he can determine the conditions for his own happiness. It turns out that reality is at odds with what he wants. And as a result he ends up in a dark spiral, for he thinks that he can harness reality with brute force. The theme of *Black Harvest* is completely different. It's about a man who refuses to limit his own desires and who believes that he can take whatever he wants without assuming responsibility for anything. In the last scene, which is full of irony, he suddenly becomes devout, after having destroyed absolutely everything. He's completely destroyed his family, he's lost his estate, his daughters have become alcoholics or have committed suicide – and he then turns to the Lord and finds salvation...! There are some very clear moral assertions in those stories.

**Hjort:** Could you say a little more about the relation between film and national culture?

**Refn:** I don't know whether it's possible to make a national film. My cultural background is clearly Danish, but although the conflicts I depict have a Danish content, they're also general moral conflicts. There's perhaps a Scandinavian tone in my visual style. I've always gone for a soft backlight and I've always been drawn to the idea of producing beautiful images, because I see them as providing a contrast to the brutal stories I tell. How Danishness otherwise is reflected in my films is something I haven't really thought through. I've often been accused of using an essentially American narrative mode, one that's dynamic and action-oriented. I don't, however, know what to make of that claim, because I think that Kurosawa, for example, also makes use of a wonderfully dynamic and expressive mode of narration. It's a matter of being able to bring intensity and energy to the screen. I've never been interested in a sluggish Danish visual style, although I suppose there's nothing inherently Danish about that kind of style except for the fact that it's a recurrent feature of Danish cinema. My TV series, *Once a Cop*, was chock-full of all kinds of violence, but had a very clear moral message, namely that violence doesn't solve any problems. I felt that it was important to develop an alternative to American crime series, one that made use of the genre's dynamic mode of narration while mobilising suspense, action, brutality and violence in a morally responsible manner. I do think it's very important that Danes be allowed to mirror themselves in an image of reality that is Danish. I've emphasised that a lot. All the stories in *Once a Cop* and in my first feature film have a basis in reality. Everything was very carefully researched. The stories about corruption, violence and car chases have their parallels in Danish reality. We didn't just sit around copying American films. The stories were genuine and we discussed them with various policemen. We then used their stories in an artful way, integrating them into ours in an effort to reflect Danish realities and mentalities. My films are also different from American mainstream films inasmuch as my characters are much more complex and have both a dark and light side; they're not simply good or bad. Nor do the good guys simply beat the bad guys in the end. In fact, in my films the bad guys often get off while the good guys somehow get destroyed. That's of course sad, but it's also an appeal to the audience to make sure that this doesn't happen to them. As a director you have an enormous responsibility in terms of what you want to convey with your stories.

**Hjort:** At first blush *The Baron* and *Black Harvest* look like good candidates for inclusion in the genre known as heritage film. The salient features of this type of film have been cogently described by Andrew Higson in his *Waving the Flag: Constructing a National Cinema in Britain* (1995), which identifies the Merchant-Ivory productions as key British examples of the genre. According to Higson, the defining feature of a heritage film is its tendency to reinvent and reproduce 'a national heritage for the screen.' Typically, such films are based on canonised novels. The stories they tell tend to take place in 'stately homes' and involve lavish 'period costumes' (26). Now, what is fascinating is that while *The Baron* and *Black Harvest* make ample use of stately homes and period costumes, they probingly critique, rather than instantiate, the genre of heritage film. These two films take issue with the nostalgic Morten Korch* adaptations, which is where we find full-blown examples of Danish heritage films. Could you say a little about the critical relation between your films and those associated with the writer, Korch? What's your view of the renewed interest among younger film-makers in Korch? I have in mind the directors associated with Lars von Trier's/Zentropa's Korch project.

**Refn:** I was supposed to have been involved in the TV series *Quiet Waters* (*Folkene i Dale*), but I said 'no'. I've always, throughout my career, tried to produce something that was different or somehow new. My Wied adaptations were indeed costume dramas and an attempt to explore the heritage genre, as you call it. I was terrified once I'd completed my first feature film. All directors are afraid when it's time for the premiere. You've given the film your utmost and then you simply have to await the verdict. Even if you don't have the greatest respect for the reviewers, because you know how haphazard the process can be, it's a terrible moment. Now, in the case of *Copper* I was lucky. It was favourably

*Pete Lee Wilson, Jean Marc Montel and Karmen Atias in* The Flying Devils *(De flyvende djævle).*
*[Photo: Flemming Adelson]*

reviewed, did well at the box office, and was awarded a Bodil as Best Danish Film of 1976, a Bodil for Best Supporting Actor and a Bodil for Best Supporting Actress, so a number of people felt that I ought to make a sequel. However, that was precisely what I didn't want to do. I felt that I ought to use my good fortune to make a 180 degree turn and head off in the opposite direction. Inspired in part by *The Leopard* and related stories, I'd dreamt of making an erotic melodrama, and I now wanted to realise that dream. This was in the 1970s and erotic melodramas weren't exactly in style back in the heyday of social critique and Marxism. The timing of *The Baron* was by no means as good as that of *Copper*. The reviewers had divided opinions about *The Baron*, which did reasonably well at the box office, although the figures were nothing like *Copper*'s. It did fairly well, though, and still brings in quite a bit of money. It was important to me to ensure that *The Baron* didn't continue the tradition of the phoney, quasi-romantic, Morten Korch or Ib Henrik Cavling films. I tried to bring real feelings to the screen, and to adopt a stance of solidarity vis-a-vis my characters; I didn't turn them into stereotypes, but instead made them as complex as possible. I had the added inspiration, of course, of having met Jens Okking, for whom *Copper* had been a major breakthrough. I felt that I hadn't explored Okking's character fully enough in *Copper*, so I was delighted to be able to offer him a role for which he was perfect in *The Baron*. It was really quite a challenge to take up the heritage genre at that point in time, and both *The Baron* and *Black Harvest* ended up becoming not only explorations, but critiques of the relevant Danish tradition. Wied is, of course, also a dubious figure in the literary landscape, but not in quite the same way as Korch.

**Hjort:** Could you expand on that?

**Refn:** Wied's not quite sophisticated enough. He's not accepted in the same way that a Herman Bang is, nor is he the brilliant stylist that certain other writers are. He's a little too vulgar and his literary devices are a bit too blunt. Dan Turrell, who was my consultant on *Black Harvest*, said something rather amusing about Wied. He said that he was a very strange author because he always seemed intent on emptying out all the drawers. He just takes all kinds of stories and then he works with them in what is almost a collage-like fashion. He'll have a brilliant chunk of dialogue that can be used verbatim in the script, followed by some almost journalistic descriptions or something resembling slapstick. His work is full of contradictions. Wied has always been a bit on the margins of the literary establishment. He was a thorough-going misanthropist, and he ended up killing himself.

**Hjort:** The acting in *The Baron* and *Black Harvest* is outstanding. I'm thinking, for example, of Jens Okking's remarkable performance as the cuckold in *The Baron*, and of Poul Reichhardt's stunning interpretation of the role of the lascivious, atheistic priest in the same film. In previous interviews you've foregrounded the importance you attribute to working carefully with actors: 'You need to use your best energy on the actors. A poor image of a brilliant performance is to be preferred over a clear image of a bad performance' (*Månedsmagasinet Agenda*, November 1993). Could you talk a little about your method of working with actors?

**Refn:** That's the most interesting thing of all, but it's also a little bit difficult to talk about. I've worked as an assistant director to a lot of other directors, so I've stood there in the semi-darkness and observed them work. As far as I can tell there's no fundamental principle that works for everyone. Every new actor is a new challenge. That's why it's so important to cast your crew at the same time that you do the casting for the roles. It's the film crew behind you that constitutes the band in which you're ultimately playing. It's crucial that the director be able to trust his crew to the point of being able to turn his back on them and concentrate his energies fully on the actors. It's the acting that has to generate the authenticity that is the film's emotional tenor, and strangely enough, nearly all actors are afraid of the camera. It's black and dark and may suddenly approach you in order then to pull back again. It's very difficult to let go and to express your feelings towards something as undefinable as a black hole; the actors really have to have a lot of courage. As a director you have to encourage your actors to take those risks and to expose themselves. It's also important to make good use of your human musicality. If an actor isn't properly 'tuned' you have to be able to bring that person into the ensemble, so that he can play in the same key as the others. The smaller roles are, of course, especially difficult. The actors playing the central roles can build up their characters over an extended period of time, and you end up developing something like a shared language, but the smaller roles are just as important. Everything counts. It only takes one bad actor to destroy a scene. I have extensive experience with the metier, the language of cinema, and the various manipulations that it makes possible. I do of course make sure to shoot certain sequences that will allow me, if necessary, to get around a bad performance without the audience noticing.

As far as the director is concerned there's a major dividing line in a film production. The first phase embraces the genesis of the idea, the decision to make the film no matter what, the script writing process, the casting, and the search for locations, money, and a team to work with. During that phase you constantly have to build things up, make them bigger than life. Then once you start shooting you constantly have to transform the elements, enrich them, and nuance them. You have to take risks. Then the point comes when you thank your crew and the actors and walk into the editing room. That moment marks the beginning of the second phase and a lot of directors have trouble adjusting to it. As the director you're steaming with adrenalin. Everyone has been looking to you for guidance, you've been working like a madman, and you've put all your passion and your every ambition into that film. Suddenly you're in the editing room. Suddenly you have to look through the other end of the binoculars and start peeling things away. Now it's a question of analysis, and of figuring out what you actually got out of the earlier process. The decisions you make are absolutely decisive. It's easy to destroy something if you're not very, very sensitive and if you don't have a sense for authenticity and a feel for the acting. That's why the game that unfolds at the editing table between the editor, the director, and that silly little screen is so sensitive. You're constantly talking to and criticising the actors – or praising them if they happen to have performed brilliantly. And then suddenly you find that you can manipulate an utterance. By cutting out a pause, for example, you're able to make an utterance sound natural and just right, or you can attach the line to a smile instead of something else. There's an amusing example of that in *Breaking the Waves*. It's when Bess sees Jan naked for the first time. She's sitting there on the bed and he takes her hand and puts it on his penis. We edited in an image of her blowing her hair away. It was from an entirely different take, but produced a comic effect in this other context. So you can improve an actor's performance during the editing stage, but this does, of course, presuppose that you have some material to work with in which the actors have expressed the requisite feelings. That's why it's so important to love the actors and to enjoy their company. You have to have a clear sense of the qualities of the people you employ. Those actors who claim that they can play anything because they've been trained at a theatre school are idiots. Film is an incredibly revealing medium, so the roles that an actor can play are clearly limited by his or her physique and charisma.

**Hjort:** Your third feature, *The Flying Devils*, did poorly at the box office, and has to date sold only some 9,281 tickets. At the same time, this film was praised by critics and awarded the Robert prize for Best Danish Film of 1985. The story deals with the lives of circus performers and takes place in a number of different countries. The characters in the film communicate in English, which most of them speak with heavy accents. Although the choice of English and changing locations is wholly in harmony with the story, these elements, combined with the lack of audience appeal, have led certain scholars to classify *The Flying Devils* as a Europudding. Large-scale co-productions are increasingly important in the context of minor cinemas produced by small nations. Yet, such co-productions seem to involve a standard budget of problems that directors and producers only sometimes can solve. Did you fail to solve some of these problems in *The Flying Devils*?

**Refn:** That was the first production of its kind in Denmark. I'd met a Swedish author, who'd written a script about a six-day bicycle race, and I was supposed to help direct it. Unfortunately that didn't work out. However, I'd had that Herman Bang story called *Four Devils* (*Les quatre diables*) in the back of my mind for a while, for I felt the work of the trapeze artist provided a beautiful symbol of the extent to which people are mutually dependent: if they don't catch each other up there under the roof, everything goes all to hell. I also found the dream of flying and of achieving the unachievable to be a beautiful theme. When I made my police film, I spent time at various police stations. This time I travelled around Europe with that Swedish author and saw as many circus performances as we could find. We soon discovered that Herman Bang's story didn't stand up to scrutiny, so we dropped it, but retained the setting. *The Flying Devils* was a long and painful production. We were plagued by accidents and bad luck at every turn. But the goal was to tell a story about the circus milieu which would capture both the poetry of the resemblances between the performers' itinerant existence and the behaviour of migratory birds, and the fact that the circus is a dying art form. The circus, we realised, wasn't as glamorous as we might have thought, but the milieu in question was in many ways very beautiful and exciting. The facade has to be perfect, but behind the scenes you find incredible poverty and a very, very brutal struggle for survival. I found that contrast fascinating. My reason for using the manor house as a model in both *The Baron* and *Black Harvest* is that it's such a dramatic construction. It's excellent as such because you have a complete social hierarchy within a very manageable geographic unit. The same is true of the circus. I've always been interested in hierarchical systems. I've always found them to be good dramatic engines that make possible some very basic kinds of conflicts. The goal was also to make a road movie that involved following the performers as they fled from the cold and moved further and further south so that they wouldn't have to heat up their tents. The story concludes in Italy where the miracle finally happens, but nobody notices it. That's the film's poetic and moral idea. At the same time the story is about a father who is ultimately severely punished for having exploited his family terribly in an attempt to realise his ambitions through his children.

Ingmar Bergman's son called me not that long ago and told me that he'd just seen *The Flying Devils* on Fårö together with his father. They'd seen it twice. His father, who sent his regards, had said that he thought it was a wonderful film. Apparently he didn't understand why it hadn't been a huge success. He felt it had all the elements of a box office hit. However, a lot of terrible things happened in connection with that film. We were constantly over budget and my producer declared bankruptcy just after the premiere. We did manage to sell the film to an American distributor, but that turned out to be quite problematic. We'd also intended to post-synchronise Mario David, for his English is lamentable, and that's putting it mildly. The Babel-like mixing of tongues is, of course, an important feature of the milieu in question. And we felt there was something dramatically effective about that strange 'no-man's tongue' that everybody kind of crippled along with in various heavy accents, but I know that a lot of people found it offensive. But we didn't have enough money to do the post-synchronisation, which I still think is a pity. We didn't select actors from here, there and everywhere in order to get money from a variety of countries. We had no such motive. I chose Erland Josephson because I felt he was the best person for the role as circus impresario, and the same holds for all the other actors, including those playing the young trapeze artists. The idea of relying only on Danish actors was out of the question. Nobody would have found a Jørgen Reenberg hanging under the tent roof the least bit credible. I think those excellent, unknown actors brought a certain authenticity to the film. A lot of people were amazed at how good they were at the trapeze, but that effect was achieved by means of tricks and stunts. Mikael Salomon, who was the cinematographer and is a good friend of mine, deserves a lot of the credit. He's in Hollywood now and has just directed his first feature film. *The Flying Devils* was a very risky production, and we're both proud and happy to have landed on our feet. Although it entailed some rather serious economic consequences for a number of people, including myself in that I lost two years' worth of salary, I have no regrets whatsoever. I'm very, very fond of that film. I've shown it at a lot of festivals and have enjoyed it in many ways. It's the only one of my films that I don't co-own, which I find rather sad. I hope that I'll be able to purchase the rights to it at some point.

**Hjort:** The police drama, *Copper*, was a tremendous success and was followed in 1987 by a TV series entitled *Once a Cop*. In previous interviews, you've claimed that it's the responsibility of Danish directors to articulate narratives that are rooted in properly Danish realities. You've suggested that both the feature film and its spin-off are a matter of using certain American genre conventions as the scaffolding for Danish narratives: 'We've had a series of shootings since *Copper*'s release in 1976 and *Once a Cop* reflects this fact. It has everything: shootings, chase scenes with motor boats and cars. It has all the things we're familiar with from the American series even though it remains close to Danish realities' (*Thisted Dagblad*, October 1987). This mixture of Danish and American elements has had an important influence on Danish film, and has been further pursued by some of the younger Danish directors, such as Ole Bornedal and Jang Refn. Could you sketch a larger context for this relation between a Danish realism of everyday life and American genre conventions in *Copper* and *Once a Cop*?

**Refn:** After having made *Copper* I felt like moving in a different direction, which is why I made *The Baron* and *The Flying Devils,* but then Henrik Iversen from the Danish Broadcasting Corporation asked whether I'd like to make a TV series. It was actually Okking who suggested that we ought to take up the character of the cop again, and I was initially very sceptical. Then I talked with Flemming Quist Møller, with whom I'd originally written the script for *Copper*, and he said that it might be amusing to take the cop out of the sanitarium and place him back in the real world, but ten years later, so that we could explore changes in Danish society. We thought that was an interesting concept to work with, and, morally speaking, we could go in two directions: either he'd have to triumph over evil or else he'd have to die. We also wanted the new story to show that crime had become an international affair and that violence had escalated in an absurd way. Okking was to play the role of someone who'd once fought idealistically for justice and had been burnt so badly that he wanted nothing to do with it any more. As far as he's concerned people can shoot at each other as much as they want as long as they don't shoot at him. He's given up and refuses to take a stance on anything. As his counterpoint we chose a new-style yuppie policeman, played by Jens Arentzen, who fights for justice, but also for his own career.

Earlier I'd always turned down offers to work for TV, because I felt that it involved such a strange little black and white image. But for one thing TV screens were getting bigger and then it was a matter of a series, which is something that TV has really cultivated. It was a challenge to try to tell a story in six episodes. Our approach to televisual narration was to see TV as a medium for the restless zapper. This meant that the pace of our narrative needed to be faster. We also decided we'd mobilise all the genre's characteristic devices. The series opens with a shooting episode in a bar, so we start at full speed. That had never been done on Danish TV before, and a lot of the reviewers felt that it was a bit much, but people loved the series. 2.7 million Danes watched it. It's the greatest success since *Matador*. Our narrative approach kept people glued to the screen, but our story also had a moral dimension, for it was all about taking a stance. Everything in the series is based on reality and involved careful research. Realism is my trademark. I have a lot of respect for people who work in other ways, but realism is my way of telling a story. Not some one-dimensional social realism, but a psychological realism. I allow myself a lot of stylisation and symbolic language. It's not just a matter of recording some everyday occurrences. As a film artist you have to manipulate reality shamelessly, but for me it's important that a film have a realistic point of departure and a basis in reality.

**Hjort:** *Copper* was the subject of lively debate in the Danish popular press when it was first released. Although you'd researched the film carefully, members of the Danish law enforcement agencies took issue with your conception of their profession and activities. In their view, the film was anything but a realistic depiction of police activities in Denmark. The debate here is not unlike the one generated by your son's film, *Pusher*. According to some critics, the emphasis on violence and criminality in *Pusher* is much less a reflection of Danish realities than a symptom of the director's fascination for film-makers like Quentin Tarantino. Do you see *Copper* and particularly *Once a Cop* as precursors to the somewhat violent, American-style films being produced today by some of Denmark's younger film-makers?

**Refn:** Good film art reflects the reality it's made in. I'm absolutely certain that *Pusher* is inspired by all the films that Jang (Nicolas) has absorbed, including those by Tarantino, who is actually a wonderful director in my mind. I think there's a tone and a nerve in *Pusher* that makes it very much an original work. My generation is responsible for the emergence of realism in Danish film. Then there was a period in which there was a need for stylisation – I'm thinking of Lars von Trier, among others. That's how it's always been in the history of art; a constant oscillation between the figurative and the non-figurative. In that sense the wheel keeps on turning. Now we've kind of returned to the realistic pole again. However, I'm not a fundamentalist, for I do like all kinds of films. Still, my cinematic language is, after all, what it is.

**Bondebjerg:** Last year you enjoyed considerable success, together with Jens Martin Eriksen, in connection with your short fiction film *Seth*, which won the prize for Best Fiction Film at the Odense Film Festival. How did you end up making that film?

**Refn:** Jens Martin approached me with his short story and asked whether I'd be interested in filming it. My initial response was 'no'. I hadn't made a short film since film school and just didn't feel that that was a format I wanted to work with. Yet, somehow that story got under my skin, so we decided to make a research trip together to the place where the story takes place, Fjerritslev. As usual reality had a real impact on me, and I began to see the film in my mind. The story is quite simply about a stranger who arrives in a small town on the west coast of Jutland at some point late in the summer. He gets himself a room in the local inn and then an absolutely demonic power game between him and the locals begins. He's using a false name, he's suspected of a murder in the region and his actions become ever more frightening and incomprehensible, but nobody dares do anything. The film is a study of the mechanisms of complicity and impotence in a small repressive society. We wrote the script together in the space of a few weeks and then got the green light from the consultant* Jørgen Ljungdalh at New Fiction Film Denmark. It was in many ways a happy production. I had a fantastic cast again, we shot the film in ten days with the same two-camera technique that I'd used in *Taxi*, and we came in under budget, so we were even able to make a 35 mm copy for the purposes of the Odense Film Festival and a subsequent theatrical release. The only sad thing that happened was that the actor Benny Hansen died shortly after we'd finished shooting. I'd worked with Benny before, on *Black Harvest*, and always felt that he was a really talented character actor, who far too rarely received the roles his talent deserved. I'm delighted that he performed so stunningly in *Seth* before it was too late. It was very strange to go straight from his funeral to the editing room, where I could bring him back to life by simply pressing a button. Generally speaking I find it strange to watch my old films, because it's unfortunately the case that more and more of the actors are alive only on the screen. But then one of the wonderful things about our art is precisely the fact that it has that kind of memory.

# Helle Ryslinge

## 1944–

Helle Ryslinge started out in fringe theatre during the 1970s. She produced the satirical women's cabaret called *Female Attractions* (*Dameattraktioner*) together with Anne Marie Helger, and this show was to become the inspiration for the film-maker Christian Braad Thomsen's satirical comedy *Ladies on the Rocks* (*Koks i kulissen*, 1983), which is based on a script by Helger and Ryslinge. Since 1974 Ryslinge has had roles in many films, including films for children and adolescents and women's films directed by Jytte Rex. Her debut as a director was the comedy *Coeurs flambés* (*Flamberede hjerter*, 1986) with Kirsten Lehfeldt in the main role. The film was hailed as a major breakthrough in the cinematic treatment of gender issues. Ryslinge's probing, satirical take on contemporary social and cultural milieus also finds expression in *Sirup* (1990). In her most recent feature film, *Carlo and Ester* (*Carlo og Ester*, 1994), Ryslinge explores with gentle irony passion amongst the old and related generational prejudices.

Helle Ryslinge.

## Feature films
1986, *Coeurs flambés* (*Flamberede hjerter*)
1990, *Sirup*
1994, *Carlo and Ester* (*Carlo og Ester*)

## Short films
1997, *The Beer Monkey* (*Ølaben,* appears as the ethnographer)

## Acting roles
1974, *The Girl and the Dream Castle* (*Pigen og drømmeslottet*, directed by Finn Henriksen)
1974, *Prince Piwi* (*Prins Piwi* directed by Flemming Quist Møller)
1976, *The Gangster's Apprentice* (*Gangsterens lærling*, directed by Esben Høilund Carlsen)
1977, *Veronica's Veil* (*Veronicas svededug*, directed by Jytte Rex)

1979, *Achilles' Heel is My Weapon* (*Achilleshælen er mit våben*, directed by Jytte Rex)
1981, *Stab in the Heart* (*Kniven i hjertet*, directed by Christian Braad Thomsen)
1981, *Rubber Tarzan* (*Gummi Tarzan*, directed by Søren Kragh-Jacobsen)
1981, *Belladonna* (directed by Jytte Rex)
1983, *Ladies on the Rocks* (*Koks i kulissen*, directed by Christian Braad Thomsen)
1987, *Tootsiepops and Candyfloss* (*Negerkys og labre larver*, directed by Li Vilstrup)
1989, *Happiness is a Curious Catch* (*Lykken er en underlig fisk*, directed by Linda Wendel)
1989, *The Knight of Justice* (*Retfærdighedens rytter*, directed by Jesper W. Nielsen)
1990, *Spring Tide* (*Springflod*, directed by Eddie Thomas Petersen)
1991, *The Hideaway* (*Møv og Funder*, directed by Niels Gråbøl)
1998, *The Blue Monk* (*Den Blå Munk*, directed by Christian Braad Thomsen)

**Hjort:** You directed your first feature film, *Coeurs flambés*, in 1986, after about twenty years of acting, both in film and on stage. You play the role of ethnographer in your latest film, *The Beer Monkey*, which was funded by New Fiction Film Denmark.* More recently, you've played the bartender, Helle, in Christian Braad Thomsen's *The Blue Monk*. What's it like to wear both caps? Do you feel your experience as an actor makes you a better director?

**Ryslinge:** Acting and directing are two separate things. When I agree to act in a film, I basically accept to do a certain job. After all, there's another director in charge, who has some idea of what he or she wants to do with the film. So I simply try to provide what the person in question is looking for. I'm not good at dealing with a situation in which I'm both director and actor. I can handle a small role like the one I play in *Carlo and Ester*, where I appear briefly as the alcoholic daughter-in-law. I lose sight of the general picture, though, when I act in my own films. *The Beer Monkey* is, of course, a different story – there I'm Helle Ryslinge, not some fictional character. I can't, however, do what Woody Allen or Erik Clausen do when they play major roles in their own films.

**Hjort:** What exactly is it that prompted you to become a director in 1985? How did you get started?

**Ryslinge:** When I was little, I didn't know what I wanted to be. I'm someone whose life has been determined largely by circumstance, chance and passion. That can be both good and bad. When I was little, I wanted to be a potter at a certain point. I think it was because I had an uncle who was a great potter. Having spent some time in his workshop, it became apparent that I was really rather good at it, so I wanted to be a potter. It was wonderful to touch the clay and that sort of thing, and I happened to be good at it, but that's not what happened, right? I didn't do any of the things you'd do if you really wanted to become a potter. Instead I was trained as a school teacher, because I was a very immature teenager, who took a long time to become independent. My parents were bourgeois and very overbearing, and they felt that I simply had to have a proper, decent education. I just wanted to get away from home, so I agreed to go to teacher's college, so that I at least could rent a room somewhere. I hardly ever went to class, and I've only been a school teacher during shorter periods right after graduating when I needed to earn some money. I wasn't cut out to be a school teacher, so I went through the training program like a sleepwalker. At the same time I instinctively sought out those milieus where there was music and something going on. That pointed me towards the road that I ended up traveling and which involved my always messing around with something or other creative. So I got into theatre very early. I could actually just as easily have become a potter, if I'd happened to have had friends who were potters. My friends, however, were into theatre and that's how I ended up working in theatre for many, many years. I did mostly fringe theatre, or at least, I didn't perform in the big, established theatres. Then I got a couple of film roles and at a certain point I started to stage shows together with Anne Marie Helger. The director Christian Braad Thomsen wanted to make a film called *Ladies on the Rocks*, and since we were about to shut down the show we accepted roles in his film, which we ended up being very much involved in. That experience was very important. Christian did do some of the script writing, but the script is to a very large extent mine and Anne Marie's. Yet it's his film, because he's the director. He'd seen some of our shows and was crazy about them, and he wanted to make a road movie about two girls who travel around with their show. The film is not biographical. When I had to hand in a *vita* to Zentropa in connection with Braad Thomsen's *The Blue Monk*, the person I spoke to revealed that she understood *Ladies on the Rocks* to be a film about our show or about us, but that's nonsense. The film is pure fiction. It's about two girls who travel around with a show, and we devised acts especially for the film. We did, of course, incorporate some aspects of an act that we'd already developed, but that was it. It's Christian's film, however, and I found that very frustrating, because it was my first attempt at writing a film script. It was Christian who called the shots and that's when I thought, 'Damn it, I'm going to make my own films.' That kind of in-between situation, where the film is very much yours and also entirely someone else's is just dreadful. That's why I started making films.

**Hjort:** Could you talk about your method for working with actors?

**Ryslinge:** I try to prepare everyone really well. Once you're on the set you can't waste time on weird questions that might suddenly pop up because the actors don't already have a clear sense of why they're supposed to behave the way they do. If that happens, you end up with thirty odd people standing around waiting and that costs a hell of a lot of money, so all those kinds of things have to be worked out in advance. That's why I spend a lot of time on reading rehearsals, because I need to feel that both the actors and I are well prepared when we start shooting. If the groundwork is done well enough, then there aren't that many problems on the set, at least not if the actor is good. If the actor simply is wrong, then you have a problem no matter what. Normally you discover that beforehand, but not always. That's not good, but it happens. It's happened to me too. Actually, it's awful when that happens, but otherwise, if you understand each other, everything falls into place. Actually understanding is what it's all about, aside from the preparation I've been talking about. If you're dealing with a good actor, then I really believe that you communicate the same way you would if you were to find yourself with the same person in an entirely different context of work. It's of course also a matter of a lot of technique, which is not my strength. I rely very heavily on the communication and chemistry being in order. I've experienced terrible things because I don't have those technical, pedagogical tools that perhaps provide other directors with a way of dealing with actors and getting the best out of them. I have to rely very much on my own instincts and intuitions and my own temperament. I'm not a good director in the technical sense of the term.

**Hjort:** I'd like to talk a bit about casting in connection with *The Beer Monkey*. We see only a few authentic beer monkeys. Most of the drunks are played by actors.

**Ryslinge:** The real beer monkeys don't have a lot of lines, but they're included precisely because of their authenticity.

**Hjort:** In a way the role of beer monkey isn't that appealing, which brings to mind the kinds of difficulties that Lars von Trier encountered in his search for a male actor who was willing to lie immobilised in a hospital bed during most of *Breaking the Waves*. Could you talk about what you were looking for when you did the casting for *The Beer Monkey*? Was the casting in any way problematic in this instance?

**Ryslinge:** Well the whole idea was to adopt the standard conventions of nature programs. If you make use of well known actors, then the whole thing is ruined. That is, the most important challenge was to find people we never see on the screen. You really have to look hard in various nooks and crannies, and the actors in question have to be given very thorough screen tests. Also, they can't be too good looking, because then they're not suited for the role. Søren Skjold, who plays Ole, has that marvelous beer belly, and we constantly had our eyes peeled for people who looked sufficiently pickled and haggard. You can't just rely on make-up, because you can really tell the difference. Most actors show up with their white teeth, their nice figures and that sort of thing, but that just won't do. It was a quite an undertaking. The inevitable upshot of our search was a mixture of semi-professionals, professionals and genuine beer monkeys. That scene, for example, in which there's a couple fighting in a pub, is a damn good scene. I think they're just so incredible. She's an alcoholic, she's never been in a film before, and she looks great. He's done a lot of different things, but at some point he completely lost it and ended up hitting the bottle. He's back on track again now. He doesn't drink at all, but it's cost him. He's brilliant. It would be a lot easier to find actors for the film about the briefcase beasts that I'd initially planned to make as one of four episodes in a series. The task would be similar in the sense that you can't use any of the known figures because the format is that of a nature program. However, it's probably easier to find a number of good looking people, and the briefcase beast, after all, is oh so good looking.

**Hjort:** *Coeurs flambés* was an enormous success. Indeed, a number of the film's scenes have become veritable touchstones of national belonging. I'm thinking, of course, of the scene in which the charming young nurse, Henry (Kirsten Lehfeldt), defies her sexist

*Henry (Kirsten Lehfeldt) entertains a renowned scholar from the US (*Coeurs flambés/Flamberede hjerter*). [Photo: Susanne Mertz]*

doctor lover, Löwe (Torben Jensen), by serving a carefully and obscenely arranged plate of pasta and sausages to Mr. Woodroof (Åge Hauglund), a renowned neurologist. *Sirup,* your second feature film, was slightly less successful, perhaps because viewers felt uncomfortable with what they perceived as the film's overly hostile take on men. Yet, to me, the two films seem very much of a piece. What has been neglected is the extent to which these two films begin to explore a realist feminist aesthetic. In *Sirup,* Ditte (Kirsten Lehfeldt) is shown in various states that are a far cry from the ideals of femininity. The viewer is presented with aspects of women's bodily life that typically remain hidden. For example, after a drinking bout, Ditte notices that she is bleeding and the camera subsequently lingers, as do the eyes of the disgusted Lasse Seerup (Peter Hesse Overgård), on the soiled underwear she was too drunk to remove before diving into bed. Would you agree that what is important here is not only the critique of men, but the realist depiction of women?

**Ryslinge:** If your first film is a major success, you pay for it for the rest of your life. It's the worst thing that can happen to you. After that everything you do has to be compared with that damned first film. No matter what you do, it shouldn't be quite the same, but in some ways it should be identical. It's just so unreasonable. In 1998 I happened to discuss *Sirup* with one of our young producers, someone who is the exact prototype of today's young producers. He's been to all the right schools, and he's learnt everything there is to know about dramaturgy. He says to me, 'The idea that you're not being allowed to make any films is utter nonsense. You just have to wake up and realise that we're in the 1990s. Welcome to the present.' To which I suppose I could respond: 'Well, fine, so I can't find my way in the industry that film has become, where you have to have figured certain things out before you can even get going on a project.' He felt that I'd transgressed the cardinal rule in *Sirup*, which is that your main character can't be a moron, or if he is, he has to be punished or exposed, for otherwise people won't be able to stand to watch the film. *Something* has to happen to him. I did, of course, know this when I made the film, and he's right. That rule is part and parcel of the dramaturgy with which we're very familiar. The most different kinds of men apparently felt targeted by the film. When the producer had finished reading the script, he claimed the film was all about him. I was flabbergasted. Again and again I've been told that the film couldn't possibly be commercially successful because it breaks that cardinal rule. The young producer then gave me the usual lecture: 'You just have to learn the rules of good dramaturgy.' However, perhaps that's not something I'm interested in doing. Perhaps I can't. I can't figure out where I'm supposed to turn to get money for my films. You don't get any money unless you mainstream your films, so you have to mobilise the standard dramaturgical model. After all, we're not really talking about film art here, but about the film industry. It's the market mechanisms that are decisive. The state monies that are allocated support, not art, but the industry, and I find that a real problem. I really don't know what to do with the cliché that says that I don't like men. That's just some label that's been stuck on me.

**Hjort:** So the Danish film industry has changed a lot over the years?

**Ryslinge:** Perhaps I was just lucky back then. I don't know. I do know, quite objectively, that everything has become very streamlined. When I first approached the Danish Film Institute* in order to apply for money for *Coeurs flambés* I handed in a single A4 sheet. I showed up with very little, a few vague thoughts, but the consultant* loved the idea and trusted me. He knew who I was. He'd seen some of the things I'd done and he loved *Ladies on the Rocks* and was crazy about our shows. I just don't know whether that would work today, whether you could just show up with a single A4 sheet. If not, I think there's a problem, because not all films can be fully described in advance.

**Hjort:** Your most recent feature film, Carlo and Ester, focusses on love as it is experienced, not by the young and beautiful, but by two 80 year olds. The film is unusual, not only because it foregrounds the extent to which passionate love is blind to age, but because it presents a non-idealised view of the elderly. Ester, for example, is anything but a sweet old lady. She destroys her backstabbing neighbour's beloved flowers, smuggles large quantities of alcohol across the German-Danish border, shoplifts and pouts jealously without good reason. All of your films target certain idealised conceptions of human interaction. Yet, in Carlo and Ester you make room for certain life-affirming passions and convictions. Do you see Carlo and Ester as differing markedly in tone and outlook from your other films?

**Ryslinge:** That film came to me as a single idea, but that's the way it's been every time. The idea here was a love story, a completely ordinary love story. I wanted the characters to be eighty, though, instead of twenty five. The idea, though, was that all their basic psychological mechanisms would be fully operative. Uncertainty, jealousy and all of those things are intact, so in fact it's just as though they were young. I don't, of course, believe that 80 year olds are like 25 year olds, but I do think a lot is intact, that many of the passions are still alive. Common sense or my intuitions about people tell me that this must be the case. Life isn't organised in such a way that people become indifferent about everything during the last years of their lives and no longer experience strong passions. So I started interviewing old people and my intuitions were confirmed again and again. I did a lot of research, especially on Altzheimers, in an old people's home, because I needed to know what I was talking about. It's a very difficult role to play. I took the actor with me and we spent a lot of time in the home.

**Hjort:** It would be fairly easy to point to a number of misanthropic elements in your films. Yet, it would be wrong to characterise your films as wholly misanthropic. This is especially true of *Carlo and Ester*.

**Ryslinge:** I've heard that some people find *The Beer Monkey* misanthropic. I'm not entirely sure what they mean. To a certain extent, though, I am a misanthropist, and the term 'misanthropist' is of course a label, and people love to be able to stick labels on others. You have to be classified, and I can't stand that, because we're after all so many different things. I do have to admit that I don't think the world is wonderful. The idea that we should be positive and upbeat all the time leaves me completely cold. I think life is too brutal for that, but that doesn't, of course, mean that I don't think that life is wonderful in many ways. I laugh at a lot of things, and I have faith in the goodness of people. There's clearly something very life affirming about making a film that is a love story about two 80 year olds, so the positive things are foregrounded in this case, although the characters do encounter a lot of resistance. I think the film is seriously flawed though. When I think about *Carlo and Ester* these days, it annoys me that I didn't include an additional element. There should have been some kind of backdrop, a crisis in society, a huge strike, for example. That would have changed the film's perspective in important ways because then the two old people would have been framed by something else, something bigger. However, all of this is irrelevant, because it didn't occur to me at the time. Perhaps a film is never really finished. It just has to be delivered to someone or other by a certain date.

**Hjort:** Would the perspective you have in mind have changed the very small-minded reactions to the old people's relationship?

**Ryslinge:** It would have had an impact on my own treatment of those reactions, which are probably a bit extreme. I don't think things are really that grim. There's probably a widespread feeling that it's just fine for old people to behave that way, that it's actually rather sweet.

**Hjort:** I gather from earlier interviews that you feel that the Danish media response to *Carlo and Ester* was wrongheaded. The film, in brief, was thought to have been motivated by political intentions.

**Ryslinge:** The response was dreadful and I thought 'How can I have been so stupid?', because I just didn't see it coming. The critics thought it was incredibly unusual and interesting, and they turned it into a series of claims about old people's rights, and I thought, 'But you're killing it.' They had the best intentions, because they really thought the film was interesting. The journalists did some research and found a couple of 75 year olds who'd recently fallen in love, and stuck them in a TV studio. They'd never been in a studio before and were completely nervous. It was just dreadful. I thought 'Why can't they just interview me, or the actors, which is what usually happens when a new film is released?'. I think that kind of response did a lot of damage. The journalist from *Ekstra Bladet* was crazy about the film, and her two-page article made it sound as though the film showed two 80 year olds screwing for about 30 minutes. That's really what it sounded like.

**Hjort:** Wasn't the response quite different elsewhere in the world?

**Ryslinge:** The film hasn't been widely distributed. It did get a prize in Chicago, but if the distributors don't smell money the film is shelved. That is, nothing is done to promote the film. That's how it works. When they do smell money, they put a lot of energy into it. It's all a matter of money. It's a horrible business because the medium in question is so expensive, which means that you're at the mercy of the various granting agencies, be they private or public. Because it's a matter of money, these characters want to see a return on their investment, so it becomes a business and the films become mere products. Films are referred to as products by the relevant parties in much the way that cheese or shoes might be. We're dealing with an industry, a business. This is really awful because the Film Act* specifies that what is to be supported is film art. What is in fact supported is the film industry.

**Hjort:** It's sometimes hard to understand the reasons governing the way in which government monies are allocated. Jonas Elmer, for example, was denied funding after having produced *Let's Get Lost* which was a major success. Something similar happened to Jang Refn after *Pusher*. Jang Refn recounted that his foreign contacts found it hard to understand how he could have been turned down. The idea was that if you'd proven yourself capable of producing something good, money for the next project ought to be readily available.

**Ryslinge:** That's how it should be. It would make sense for me to receive money every time I propose something. I've never produced garbage. The film about the 80 year olds hasn't been seen by a lot of people, but a lot of old people have seen it and they love it. Yet, that's not something that gets noticed. I also think it's incredibly unreasonable not to allow me to complete the nature series that was meant to start with *The Beer Monkey*.

Attitudes in this country are just so small minded. I just can't stand it. When I say this I'm told that there are a lot of countries where there's no government support at all for film. True enough, but at this point I'm really not sure what's worse, for the way in which the public funds are allocated isn't all good. There's no rhyme or reason to the process either. You can't get money for your next project although everything you've ever made was good. What is it they actually want to support? Many directors have to wait years before being allowed to move on to their next film. You can't maintain your craft if you don't get to practice it. Meanwhile you live on virtually nothing because the idea is that artists should be punished. Denmark treats artists very, very poorly.

**Hjort:** A lot of people would probably find that last remark quite surprising.

**Ryslinge:** Well, the Danish government's policies on art are very bad for artists. There are all kinds of funding arrangements and you can apply for lots and lots of grants. At the same time the will to support art really isn't there, although this isn't explicitly acknowledged. The problem has to do with the fact that the politicians themselves have juicy salaries and don't really understand what art is all about anyway. The same is true of all of those people who live off the film industry. Just think how many people there are in various offices, who earn good salaries by living off the films that someone else makes, and compare this situation to the generally rather impoverished condition of those who actually make the films. As a director you have to mess around with your scripts forever to accommodate what everybody and his uncle might have to say about them. They're all salaried; everyone is, except the director. Sometimes you even have to forego your own salary and goodness knows what else in order to get the final pieces of the financial puzzle to fall into place. It's inhuman. It's that same old song about the artist who is best off starving in an attic. That's the brutal truth. Denmark is a rich country and we could promote art and culture much better than we do. I just saw a program about Jørgen Utzon and it had me virtually in tears. I think the man is a genius. He's 80 now but he's still a beautiful man. The program was about his life and work and it also talked about the things he was never able to build. He's built very little in Denmark. Why don't we create some fantastic things instead of gravitating constantly towards mediocre compromises? A lot can be blamed on the Danish idea that 'it's best to be down to earth' and 'to keep one's feet on the ground'[1]. Those are the worst songs in the whole wide world and yet they're Danish national anthems and express the Danish national mentality, and the relevant attitudes are alive and well in the film milieu. Let's spend some money and make some mistakes. So what if some of it goes down the drain. You can be sure that some pretty remarkable things would get produced too. Everybody agrees that there isn't enough money. That's the only thing people in this business can agree on. Distributors, directors, producers, they all agree that there's not enough money. Everyone wants more money, but when it's time to spend it, they couldn't disagree more.

---

1    'Ved jorden at blive, det tjener dig bedst', last line of the first stanza in 'The Consolation of Denmark' ('Danmarks trøst', Grundtvig, N.F.S.); 'På det jævne, på det jævne', first line in the traditional song with the same title.

# Nils Malmros

## 1944–

Nils Malmros is without a doubt one of the most significant psychological realists of contemporary Danish film. His films are characterised by very precise, incisive depictions of childhood and adolescence using authentic images of everyday realities. Malmros' films draw on the director's memory of growing up in the provincial town of Århus and reveal an extraordinary visual ability to convey what those experiences were actually like. At the same time his portraits of a given period and of certain psychological dispositions stand as clear symbols of a more general human condition. His debut, *A Strange Love* (*En mærkelig kærlighed*, 1968), which was heavily influenced by Truffaut and the French new wave, was harshly received and disappeared quickly from the theatres. However, *Lars Ole, 5c* (1973) established Malmros as a director with a unique cinematic vision, which he has gone on to refine over the years. The film is set in the 1950s and focusses on the social and sexual games engaged in by both the male and female members of a given class in an Århus school. This theme is further developed in *Boys* (*Drenge*, 1977) which depicts a boy's development to manhood in three episodes. In *Tree of Knowledge* (*Kundskabens træ*, 1981) Malmros once again emphasises the idea of a group portrait, the subjects being boys and girls attending an Århus middle school in the late 1950s. The film's wrenching depiction of the loss of childlike innocence makes it a modern classic. *Århus by Night* (1989) makes use of autobiographical material, but in the

*Nils Malmros in conversation with Brian Theibel as Willy Bonde during the production of* Tree of Knowledge (Kundskabens træ).

137

form of a meta-film that ironically and precisely depicts the production of *Boys* and the troubling encounter between the inexperienced Århus director and his jaded film crew from Copenhagen. *Beauty and the Beast* (*Skønheden og udyret*, 1983) and *Pain of Love* (*Kærlighedens smerte*, 1992) shift the emphasis squarely to female sexualities and psychologies. And in his adaptation of Jørgen-Frantz Jacobsen's novel, *Barbara* (1997), Malmros successfully engages for the first time with a format of epic proportions and a more internationally oriented cinematic language.

## Feature films

1968, *A Strange Love* (*En mærkelig kærlighed*)
1973, *Lars Ole, 5c*
1977, *Boys* (*Drenge*)
1981, *Tree of Knowledge* (*Kundskabens træ*)
1983, *Beauty and the Beast* (*Skønheden og udyret*)
1989, *Århus by Night*
1992, *Pain of Love* (*Kærlighedens smerte*)
1997, *Barbara*

## Short films

1978, *Christmas Spirit* (*Kammesjukjul*)

**Hjort:** You're a unique figure in the context of contemporary Danish film. First of all, you're from Århus, rather than the Copenhagen area. More importantly, in spite of your success, both nationally and internationally, you continue to live in Århus. So central is the role played by this small town in your cinematic oeuvre that it becomes a state of being or state of mind, as Ib Monty incisively remarks. Indeed, you're one of a tiny number of film-makers who have insisted on using a heavily regionalised Danish in an industry dominated, linguistically and otherwise, by the capital. The desire to make room for other ways of speaking Danish is, it seems, also a matter of making room for other ways of being Danish. How would you describe the role played by *århusiansk*\* in your films? I'm interested here in a number of different issues: the nature of your original decision to make systematic use of *århusiansk*; the larger impact of your valorisation of *århusiansk*, as you perceive it; and the implications of your decision to work with *århusiansk* for your practices as a film-maker.

**Malmros:** The fact that my films are rooted to such an important extent in myself and my world is in many ways coincidental. It certainly wasn't my plan to chart my life when I first started making films. The explanation for this has to do with the way in which I got into film-making. After having seen *Jules and Jim* (*Jules et Jim*) in the cinema I felt that I too simply had to make a film just like it. I've always had a strong urge to imitate the things that excite me, so as to be able to internalise and understand them better. In that sense, my enthusiasm, for example, for modern furniture design led me to try my hand at making furniture. My encounter with *Jules and Jim* occurred right around the time when the Danish Film School\* first opened in 1966. I knew back then – and am still to this day completely convinced – that I didn't stand a snowball's chance in hell of getting in. I probably felt a little *noller*, which is the term used in Århus to refer to someone who is very careful and a little immature. I was probably also just afraid of making a fool of myself. So I began studying medicine after having applied, unsuccessfully, to the School of Architecture in Copenhagen. One advantage of medical school was that I could take on night shifts in the hospitals and earn some money. It was the only program that enabled students to earn money while studying. In addition, I continued to live at home, which also helped to make it possible to raise the small amount of capital that I needed to produce my own 16 mm feature film without government support. My father had a camera I could borrow. He was a neurosurgeon and used a camera to film his patients in the neurosurgical ward. So that was my first feature film, *A Strange Love*. That film also functioned as my personal film school, in that I had to reinvent not only film technique, but the language of film from scratch. The result of all this was something close enough to a real film that it could be shown in the theatres. It ran for three days in Århus and for two days in the Reprise in Holte near Copenhagen. The reviewer for *Berlingske Tidende* claimed that 'all those young people who dream about making films, of whom there are far too many, should make a pilgrimage to Holte so as to see for themselves just how wrong things can go.'

Coming to terms with that response took some time, but then quite coincidentally I happened to meet some old classmates from my middle school years. In talking to them I realised that I had an unusually detailed memory of my childhood and adolescence, and it wasn't just a question of factual details, but of the psychological games that were operative in class. I'd blithely assumed that everyone carried their past around inside them just as I felt I did, so I was surprised to discover that most of my classmates had almost entirely repressed various things that had happened. At the same time I realised that I'd identified a subject matter that I mastered reasonably well.

**Hjort:** Your early films, *Lars Ole, 5c*, *Boys* and *Tree of Knowledge* established you as a film-maker with a unique ability to unlock the drama of everyday life through autobiographical reflection. The film-maker, Christian Braad Thomsen, movingly describes this transfiguration of the commonplace that is so characteristic of your work in the program for *Boys*: 'Malmros' gift as a film-maker lies in his ability to use images to make us understand that all the things that seem fairly insignificant to us in fact make up our lives – and are more significant than we might think' (cited in Conrad 1991: 37). What was it that compelled you, for example, to recall, and reconfigure, your experiences as a pupil in the Århus school system?

**Malmros:** One reason is probably that I felt that I in *Lars Ole, 5c* had managed to transform my past into poetry, and had been able to do so precisely because I hadn't forced the poetry into the film through the front door, so to speak. The poetry has to come in through the back door, as Truffaut puts it. That is, poetry is not something that can be willed. The poetry in a film emerges as a gift, and only if the subject matter is dealt with honestly. I saw *Lars Ole, 5c* as a film about a certain mood, about a certain situation, namely that of being part of a fifth form. In that sense there was no real intrigue to the film. I then realised that my years at Århus Cathedral School had been quite turbulent in some ways. More specifically, I'd been involved in some events related to the form's most popular girl, who for seemingly incomprehensible reasons, suddenly was turned into a scapegoat and virtually expelled from the class. I had a very clear recollection of how and why all this had happened. Of course there were relationships I knew nothing about, because I couldn't possibly have been everywhere all at once. So initially I decided to do a bit of research. That is, I decided to talk to some of my old classmates so as to identify the 'missing links' and at the same time confirm that my own intuitions were right, and eventually this all became *Tree of Knowledge*.

Originally my plan was to shoot the film over a period of four years. I felt that it was impossible to make films of a certain magnitude at that point in the history of Danish film. However, if the director himself was stubborn enough to spend four years of his life on making his film, then that could in itself, I thought, lend the film a certain grandeur. The four-year time frame wasn't viable, it turned out, for reasons having to do with the film's production framework. On the whole I had a lot of trouble getting the film financed, among other things because Steen Herdel, who had produced *Boys*, had gone bankrupt. So the Film Institute* was very sceptical of him, and by extension of me, which I thought was completely unfair since I'd had absolutely nothing to do with his bankruptcy. The Film Institute wanted nothing to do with the project if I was the producer, so it ended up becoming a Per Holst Film, and I was quite happy with that arrangement. I was still allowed personally to shape the film here in Århus while Per Holst proved to be as patient as I needed him to be. However, we discovered that we did have to reduce the period of shooting to two years. Nonetheless, it was still possible to detect the fact that the children were actually growing in the course of the film.

In 1989 I made *Århus by Night*, which once again explores my memory of my past. At that point in my life my past was beginning to include some of my experiences as an adult. The film builds on my memory of what it was like to shoot *Boys*, and in addition it includes some sequences with episodes from my childhood, which had originally been part of *Boys*, but had been edited out because they weren't good enough. There were, for example, some visions of nurses in the dusk and of throwing clay through windows at naked ladies who were receiving light treatment; and then there were the images of the tunnels beneath the Århus municipal hospital, which were absolutely essential. I didn't ultimately include the tunnel scenes in *Boys* because I suddenly found myself worrying about the overly explicit symbolism involved in the secret tunnels as an image of the mind's labyrinthine workings. I then found that I could make good use of them in *Århus by Night*, partly because I'd become a better storyteller over the years and partly because I was less worried about their symbolic significance. At the same time I was able to recount the story of how I, as a young, immature director, found myself dealing for the first time with an unruly film crew from Copenhagen that was more interested in sleeping with all the girls in Århus than in helping me make my film.

**Hjort:** Numerous are the accomplished Danish film-makers with roots in other professions. What is unusual in your case, however, is your stubborn insistence on pursuing your medical studies for some 45 semesters, long after you'd established yourself as a film-maker. How do you see the relationship between these two professions?

**Malmros:** Those two universes have absolutely nothing in common. I find it enriching also to be able to live a life that is completely separate from the world of film. Besides it's healthy to be part of a hierarchical arrangement that places you at the bottom again. Clearly my position as a resident isn't quite the same as that of the young resident who's just starting out, but still. I'm the one who's constantly getting beeped and who has to rush around and deal with any number of different things. In the case of *Barbara* I was actually able to bring these two professions together in a reasonable way. When the film was deferred from the summer of 1995 to the summer of 1996, I took a position as substitute doctor at the Landssjukrahusid in Thorshavn. That was invaluable, because it enabled me to wander around quietly and do my research. And I was able graciously to win the trust of the Faroese who were going to help me make the film. Anyone who's seen *Århus by Night* will know just how out of hand things can get when a film crew is suddenly catapulted into a small community.

**Hjort:** Through your intense focus on children and adolescents, you've contributed significantly to a particular genre, that of the youth film, which occupies a central place in contemporary Scandinavian film-making. In an interesting monograph entitled *Drenge-drømme*, Karen Conrad compares the audience targeted by *Christmas Spirit* to the one aimed at by *Lars Ole, 5c* and *Boys*: 'Paradoxically enough the film [*Christmas Spirit*] seems to be weakened precisely because it targets children. *Lars Ole, 5c* and *Boys* also focussed on children, but the target audience wasn't primarily children, and as a result these films had a depth that this film lacks' (1991: 54). Interestingly, a film such as *Lars Ole, 5c* appealed, not only to different generations of moviegoers, but to audiences shaped by radically different cultures and histories. *Lars Ole, 5c* garnered multiple awards at an Iranian film festival already in 1974, the year before it won a Bodil* award as Best Danish film of 1974. You seem, in your films, to be addressing yourself to multiple audiences. Could you talk a little about your conception of the audience? I'm interested in your views on youth audiences, regional audiences, national and international audiences.

**Malmros:** When I was making *Lars Ole, 5c* I knew without a doubt that it wasn't a children's film. It's a film about childhood, but it's aimed at an adult audience. At the same time, I did, of course, hope that it might also be seen by children, but they weren't the primary target group. The same principle has been operative in all my other films. My films don't have the ingredients that one normally associates with a youth film, that catchy tune, for example, that ends up becoming a hit and has everyone singing along. Karen Conrad is right, though, to note that *Christmas Spirit* is a bit of an exception. It was conceived with a young audience in mind and was meant to develop a Christmas theme. It's also true that as a result the theme in that film is somewhat more superficial than those of my other films. However, on closer inspection, *Christmas Spirit* turns out to contain a fairly interesting theme after all, for it's all about the boy who would like to

141

*organise* and for that matter *direct* people's lives, his own and that of others. But *Lars Ole, 5c* established early on that it's precisely the local film that is universal. And the reason is, of course, that childhood is universal. The feelings experienced by a five year old child in China are the same as those experienced by a Danish five year old. Truffaut has talked about how the socialisation of individuals as national subjects only takes place around puberty.

**Hjort:** *Århus by Night* is a metafilm, which reflects on the cultural clashes that arose, during the making of *Boys*, between you and the professional film crew from Copenhagen. Whereas film-making for your alter ego, Frederik (Thomas Schindel), is an all-consuming passion, film-making is a job governed by precise rules and regulations as far as the film crew is concerned. To what extent are we dealing here with a clash between provincial and urban attitudes, rather than between the idealism of youth and the jaded stance of the experienced professional?

**Malmros:** I think the film is about both issues. It's true that it's about key differences between attitudes characteristic of Copenhagen and typical provincial behaviours, but it's also about what distinguishes being a child from being an adult. Indeed, it's about the conflict between childhood and the adult world. Frederik is able to move back and forth between these two worlds, thereby connecting them. One minute he's like a child as he plays cars with the little boy under the table, and the next minute he's taking part in the disputes over who beat up whom and why. Actually, *Århus by Night* is probably yet again about the loss of innocence, for this is what many of my films are ultimately about. It thematises the way in which we continuously lose our innocence as we move through life. Our every new insight is accompanied by a loss of innocence.

**Hjort:** Your early films were self-financed as a result of a series of rejections. You applied to the Film Fund, the precursor to the Danish Film Institute, for support for *Lars Ole, 5c*, and your three separate requests for funding were summarily rejected. The Fund refused to support manuscript development, the production of the film and the blowing up process from 16mm to 35mm film. These rejections ultimately became controversial and were finally discussed in Parliament, where the Minister of Culture, Niels Matthiasen, reluctantly admitted that 'it looked like it was harder for people from Århus to make films than it was for those who were born on the right side of Valby Hill' (Jørholt 1997: 244). Is the situation faced by aspiring young directors from the provinces noticeably different today, and has your success and your insistence on being a regional film-maker contributed to the relevant changes?

**Malmros:** I haven't personally had any problems along these lines since *Lars Ole, 5c*. I mean, I might have trouble getting exactly the amount of money I'd like, but that kind of constraint is fine. After all, there's a limit to how spoilt one needs to be. From *Lars Ole, 5c* onwards, though, all my projects have gone through. Actually I'm in the enviable position of having no unrealised projects, for I've made every film I've ever dreamt of making. I think that's quite unique in the context of Danish film. In his memoirs

*Eva Gram Scholdager as Elin, the scapegoat figure in* Tree of Knowledge (Kundskabens træ). *[Photo: Torben Stroyer]*

Henning Carlsen writes that what makes a director's hair turn grey is not the films he's made, but the films he never gets to make, and, in that sense, I ought to have no grey hairs at all. Part of the explanation probably has to do with the fact that I stuck to my own little corner of reality. I knew how to exploit the strength that was to be derived from remaining within the world of Århus. Whether young directors from Århus would find themselves in a situation that is comparable to the one I faced back then, I simply don't know. I do think that the Film Institute would tend at this point to be more attuned to the problem in question, since it's in their interest to avoid another parliamentary inquiry.

**Hjort:** You recently attended the ceremony during which the important producer, Per Holst, was awarded the LO prize (October 1998). Holst has produced four of your films, *Tree of Knowledge*, *Beauty and the Beast*, *Pain of Love* and *Barbara*. Holst is prized for his visionary ability to identify and genuinely support talented young film-makers. How would you describe your collaboration with Per Holst?

**Malmros:** I should hasten to point out that my relation to Per Holst is rather unique in the sense that he's much more my discovery than the other way around. When I was in the early stages of making *Tree of Knowledge*, Per Holst offered to produce the film on numerous occasions and I repeatedly turned him down. However, having dealt with the many hurdles that the Film Institute threw my way, I decided to bring Per into the picture after all, and, as I pointed out earlier, I was ultimately quite happy with the arrangement that emerged. I enjoyed not having to spend a lot of energy on the financial side of things. At the same time I was the lever that was able to pry open the coffers for Per Holst at the Film Institute, so the relationship has certainly been a mutually beneficial one. Per Holst needed me just as much as I needed him. The situation is clearly quite different in the case of the young directors who are emerging today. Here it's Per Holst who discovers the talent and nourishes it, and in that respect he's been extraordinarily prescient, I must admit. He has, of course, missed the target every now and again, but not very frequently. Zentropa tends to shoot with a much less accurate shotgun than Per Holst does.

What Per deserves credit for is his special ability to get the director to trust and insist on his own intuitions. He doesn't impose his superior conceptions on the film. There are times when he feels that the directors aren't incisive enough and that he, in a very pedagogical manner, has to try to open their eyes to the possibilities that exist in their own material, but he would never impose his position on the director. In *Barbara* we had a problem determining the extent to which the scene in Leynum led to an actual consummation of erotic desire. I was convinced that it didn't whereas Per Holst believed that it did, and I finally had to admit that he was right. When I went back over the relevant passages in the book, it became clear to me that Per's interpretation was implied by the text. So he'd known how to use certain pedagogical pointers to help me bring into focus certain important aspects of the book and, for that matter, of my own film. And Per's desire to include that erotic scene wasn't linked to crass commercial interests, but to a commitment to make the film better. As a producer Per would, of course, like to earn a lot of money, but he first and foremostly wants to produce good films.

**Hjort:** You're widely known to make use of a very particular approach to the directing of actors. Film scholars have made much of your ingenious ability to manipulate children into providing the facial expressions you desire. Your approach has not, however, always met with approval from adult, professional actors. Jesper Klein, who played the role of the father in your film about incestuous desires, *Beauty and the Beast*, experienced your directing style as intrusive and manipulative. Could you describe, very concretely, how you worked with the actors in *Barbara*, your latest film, compared with earlier films? I'm interested, that is, in your directing style at this point in your career.

**Malmros:** I'm going to have to refer back to what I said earlier about how I would make use of these very short scenes when I was directing children. I was really the one doing the acting, in the sense that I put all the pieces of the puzzle together. This was an approach to directing that I ended up developing out of necessity. The problem frequently was that the individuals acting in my films simply were incapable of developing believable characters. So the question I put to myself was: How can I intervene in the process and somehow control it? I thus developed that method involving those very short scenes out of necessity. Had the actors been believable in longer takes, then I wouldn't have had to proceed that way. In the case of *Beauty and the Beast* I chose to treat Jesper Klein the same way that I treated the children, because Line wouldn't have been believable if I'd directed her in any other way. And if the acting was to cohere, then my manner of directing the young girl and Jesper had to be more or less identical. I figured that this wouldn't exactly kill him, but he absolutely hated it. At the same time he was freed of all responsibility for the role. He did in fact give an interview just before the film's premiere in which he said that he'd merely been an instrument, in the sense that when the father peers down his daughter's blouse, it's not really the father, but rather Nils Malmros who does the looking. He did nonetheless win any number of prizes for his performance, and personally I don't think that Jesper has ever performed better, with the exception of his role in *The Ballad of Carl-Henning* (*Balladen om Carl-Henning*).

However, if you're involved in a big professional production, you can't lean on your actors in the same way. I tried to some extent to maintain my old approach in the context of *Århus by Night*, that is, I combined different methods and was directive primarily in relation to the actors from Århus. At other points in the film, when Flemming Jørgensen and Ronnie fight, for example, the actors were given free rein in a long take, and this gives the dialogue a certain fluid rhythm. At times I would nonetheless intervene and divide things up. If you're dealing with a big scene around a table, where it's a matter of rapid exchanges back and forth, it's almost impossible to do a full take of all the characters involved, or rather, doing so would require a tremendous amount of stock. It's also important to be clear on the fact that in the context of Danish film production the amount of film stock used represents a very significant part of a film's total budget. That's not the case in American film. In the US, the cost of film stock is about half a percent of the budget, but here it's about ten percent. If you look at the cost of film stock in relation to the investment of private capital, then it's really a significant budgetary entry. Being scrupulous about how much stock gets used is really a way of reducing costs considerably. That's why there are a number of scenes in *Århus by Night* that were made following my old methods. Many of the actors had a lot of trouble with that. Not, of course, in terms of their ability to perform, but in terms of actually being able to accept that they were simply required to utter a single line four or five times until they hit on the proper intonation. They felt that they were being humiliated. As Jesper Klein put it, 'I'm not an actor here, I'm a puppet.' That may be so, but I do think that a lot of actors, even in American films, have to put up with the idea of producing specific details by means of short takes. So I find actors who simply refuse to do this kind of thing rather unprofessional, but I've discovered a counter move: casting. So that's what I do nowadays. I think I screen tested about 70 women in order to find Barbara. I kept on looking until I found someone whose mode of expression was just right. In *Barbara*, then, we were able to work with long takes while shooting, and that was a pleasure, I have to admit. At times I would wonder whether I'd lost my old ear, because I couldn't hear any false notes. Then suddenly there'd be an actor who'd act in the old theatrical way, and I'd have to intervene and once again dictate the lines sentence by sentence. In the case of *Barbara* we'd also rehearsed most of the scenes and tried out the dialogue in Denmark, before we started shooting on the Faroe Islands, and during that process the actors had been able to make a number of suggestions and in some instances even partly rewrite the dialogue. Jesper Christensen is especially good at that sort of thing. He really tightened his part by cutting out something like a fifth of the dialogue I'd written or excerpted from Jørgen-Frantz Jacobsen's novel, but I was delighted with the result. Someone like Jens Okking does something completely different, which is a little more trouble for the rest of us, but otherwise legitimate enough. The minute he starts acting he rearranges the order of the words in his lines. That can make life difficult for the other actors, because they can't simply wait for a cue, but really have to be fully involved in his role. It doesn't much matter, though, if things go wrong, for after all we can always just shoot the scene again.

**Hjort:** *Pain of Love* is a moving depiction of a young girl's spiraling descent into manic depression and suicide. The film was very favourably received, both in Denmark and abroad. In this respect it is worth noting that Lars von Trier has referred to the character Kirsten (Anne Louise Hassing) as a source of inspiration for Bess in *Breaking the Waves*. You wrote the script for *Pain of Love* in collaboration with John Mogensen. What is the origin of this uncompromising portrait of self-destruction?

**Malmros:** Some of my films have involved precise reconstructions of events from my own life, but *Pain of Love* isn't one of them. The story is nonetheless one that draws on my own life history, and, very importantly, I'm not interested in the story because I happen to be a doctor. It wasn't a matter of consulting some medical reference book in order to ensure that all the symptoms were right. I do believe that the correct diagnosis of Kirsten would be manic-depressive, but my concern in that film was existential, not diagnostic. What we're dealing with here is, of course, a traumatic event from my own life which I needed to work through. For that same reason, I'd be reluctant to say much more about it.

You were asking about John Mogensen, who was also involved in *Barbara*. Actually, we'll also be working together on my next film. The division of labour between us basically assigns him the role of critic. In principle, he needn't invent anything or contribute anything, but he has to be at my disposal throughout the entire process and he has to be willing to discuss my ideas with me. Essentially his role is to be the person who constantly requires me to clarify my thoughts. He is, of course, allowed to provide some good suggestions, which he does, but he shouldn't feel that it's his duty somehow to present me with a lot of brilliant insights. I'm the one carrying the creative weight.

**Hjort:** Your first film, *A Strange Love*, was seen as an inferior copy of Truffaut's *Jules and Jim*. At later stages in your career, you've worked creatively, rather than slavishly, with techniques and styles employed by other film-makers. You've suggested, for example, that the concept of film style is absolutely central to *Boys*, which drew on Truffaut, Bresson and Cassavetes. Do you, at this point in your career, feel that you're engaged in a dialogue with other film-makers through your work?

**Malmros:** It's true that I was very much influenced by a number of directors when I was a young, impressionable film-maker. So much so that in the case of *Boys*, for example, I could trace each of the film's three sections to precisely the three directors you mentioned. At the same time the art of film continues to develop and acquire new modes of expression, which necessarily influence you at some level, but I feel no need to keep up with the latest cinematic fashions. However, I would automatically tend to express myself faster and with greater precision today than I would have when I first started out. I don't have the same patience that I used to, nor does my audience, so we need to get to the point faster. However, paradoxically enough, contemporary film language derives much of its power from a blurring of the image. Suspense is often generated by what we don't see. I'm not criticising here; I'm just pointing to what I take to be an important part of the secret of that blurred cinematic language. At the same time the music has become more intrusive. I can't help but be influenced by these kinds of developments. When I first started working on *Barbara* I felt that I needed to tell the story much more quickly than I normally do. Now when I watch the film, it's obvious to me that I did no such thing, and that's perhaps just as well, but I can't help but feel that my next film, which involves a story of certain epic dimensions, requires a rapid mode of narration, for otherwise it will end up being far too long.

**Hjort:** Ib Monty concludes his review of *Århus by Night* as follows: 'In Danish film he's the absolute master of a realism marked by intimacy and recollection, but that leap into deeper waters, which he once again prepares for here, is one that he continuously postpones.' Your latest film *Barbara* is the most expensive Danish film to date and an elaborate co-production involving studio filming in Stockholm, location filming on the Faroe Islands, and funding from Swedish, Norwegian and Danish sources, as well as Eurimages and the Nordic Film and TV Fund. The film is based on Jørgen-Frantz Jacobsen's novel, *Barbara*, which was first published in 1939. With *Barbara*, it would appear, you took the step that critics had been calling for, for what we have here is an ambitious international undertaking and a story that is based on a canonised work, rather than personal experience. Do you see *Barbara* as marking the beginning of a new phase in your career as a film-maker?

**Malmros:** Your question begins with that citation from Monty and I have to admit that I've since been very disappointed by him. I'd felt that his remark about deeper waters was basically correct, but I also felt that I was getting ready to take the leap with *Pain of Love*. I was quite shocked when Monty suddenly decided simply to pan that film. His was the only critical voice. The film was given five or six stars by all the other reviewers. Monty's was the only negative review, and it was totally negative and completely dismissive. In his mind, Kirsten was nothing more than a big gaping mouth. In real life, he claimed, nobody would be able to stand her for more than five minutes. That was it. There was nothing more to be said. As far as Monty was concerned the film represented a real moment of regression in my career. I feel the opposite is true. With *Pain of Love* I essentially took that leap into deeper waters. *Barbara* represents a leap in a purely technical sense and in terms of the size of the production, but it sticks to much safer ground, in part because it's based on a literary work. My decision to make *Barbara* was also linked to the fact that I'd heard the refrain about how I was forever studying my own navel just a little too often. At the same time I perhaps also felt that I'd somewhat exhausted my own material.

**Hjort:** What was, for you, the guiding thread in your adaptation of Frantz Jacobsen's novel?

**Malmros:** My approach was, of course, to try to awaken the feelings and sense of enthusiasm that I myself had felt when I first read the book. In many ways it's like another *Jules and Jim*. Unrequited love, love that can't be forced into existence, but which is all the more fascinating for that very reason. The novel has a very important and to me inspiring feature, which I noticed when I reread it, namely that it's actually incomplete. There are three chapters missing. Besides, very early on I recognised the interesting possibilities involved in letting the judge assume a more prominent role. In the novel, much as in the film, he's in love with Barbara but he doesn't dare declare himself, because he can't stand the idea of being turned down. That's why he adopts a kindly ironic stance and chooses to watch from the sidelines. The twist introduced by the film – and it's just a slight shift of emphasis – is that instead of assuming a purely passive role, he chooses to live his life vicariously, through Mr. Paul. That is, it is he who ensures that Barbara and Mr. Paul can get married. In the novel Jørgen-Frantz Jacobsen cheats, because we're never told who actually weds them. In the film it's the judge who arranges for the ceremony by putting pressure on his brother, the priest, Mr. Wenzel. Yet, the wedding itself is otherwise kept secret. The judge is thus he who *gives*. And when Andreas gets in the way of his plans by initiating a relationship with Barbara, he simply gets rid of him by writing his dissertation for him. In this sense he's also he who *takes*. He turns himself into Barbara's *destiny* and in this way he's able to feel that it is he who ultimately possesses her. However, to want to be someone's destiny without being willing to participate fully oneself is after all a deadly sin in Karen Blixen's sense. This is what he finally realises when Barbara, in our version, tragically disappears into the mist. In a letter addressed to Mr. Paul, he says: 'I too have heard rumours that Barbara has been seen in Copenhagen, but I don't believe them, for the truth is that she never reached the Fortuna. There will therefore be no divine mercy for me, not because I wanted to possess her, I knew that I never could, but because I instead nourished a vain desire to be her destiny, to be the one who gave and took. The truth is, dear Mr. Paul, that we are all like monkeys. What rages in our hearts is nothing but envy, greed, lust and vanity, especially vanity.' That last citation is from the novel, from an exchange between Mr. Paul and the judge. So Jørgen-Frantz Jacobsen has the final word, although his phrases have been recontextualised. These slight shifts of emphasis have the effect of inscribing the novel's depiction of mores within the context of a fateful tragedy, and for personal reasons, that element of fate was crucial. Indeed, it was the decisive reason for my wanting to make the film.

**Hjort:** Historical costume dramas present particular challenges, one of which is the task of identifying appropriate locations. You spent some time working in Thorshavn as a substitute doctor, in order to be able to research your locations. Could you describe the process in question?

**Malmros:** One of the fascinating things about the Faroe Islands is that there's a lot of untouched nature, but you also come across disturbing elements constantly, because the approach to the preservation of nature has been haphazard. The Faroe Islands are a strange combination of gifts and humiliations, but if you had the time you could walk around and find exactly what you were looking for, especially if you were able to add some things here and there. In that regard the rapid developments in the area of computer-manipulated images really helped us enormously. We were probably a little uncritical at the outset, because even though you can produce exactly the image you want with the help of the computer, you're frequently better served by adopting more traditional methods of telling the story. Although you can establish the geography of a place in a single image by digitally adding whatever is needed, montage – where it is a matter of bringing two locations together through editing – still represents a superior mode of narration. It's also important to recognise that it's not necessarily a good idea to opt for big establishing shots, although they can be produced digitally. In the case of the images of the three warships, the computer was invaluable. We only had one ship, and for economic reasons we produced our footage of it in the Caribbean. We then used cloning techniques to generate three warships, which the computer allowed us to situate in the Nolsø Fiord.

**Hjort:** Another challenge associated with the genre to which *Barbara* belongs has to do with the boundary that is easily crossed between art and romantic propaganda or tourist art. *Barbara*, I take it, was to capture the beauty of the Faroe Islands, but within the context of a fictional world of make-believe rather than in the manner of a tourist guide to the islands. Reviewers repeatedly mentioned the danger in question, and many of them claimed that your cinematographic style in *Barbara* deftly circumvents the pitfalls in question. How did you approach the filming of spectacular natural landscapes in *Barbara*? Henning Carlsen claims to have encountered similar challenges during the filming of *Two Green Feathers* (*Pan*).

**Malmros:** In his memoirs, Henning Carlsen points out that he's typically sought to avoid making use of a grandiose nature, especially in the case of *Two Green Feathers*, and I think that my own view basically resembles his. I certainly think that it's very important to make sure that you don't end up making a tourist film. Yet, in the case of *Barbara* I do think that the very special landscape that exists on the Faroe Islands has to be an important element in the overall atmosphere. That mixture of fog, flat verdant islands and enormous expanses is completely unique. In *Two Green Feathers* what's crucial is the sorcery associated with the forest, but on the Faroe Islands, there are types of landscapes that simply move us more than others. In my mind the Faroe Islands are a state of mind, and that's what I wanted to capture. I quite consciously steered clear of the tourist highlights, but nature is an integral part of reality up there. One of the overwhelming things about the Faroe Islands is that sense of sudden revelation. You'll be standing in the thickest fog and then suddenly everything will clear up briefly, and there are scenes like that in the film. For example, the one in which Barbara and Mr. Paul flee over the mountain in order to avoid Andreas. They're walking along in the fog and then suddenly the fog parts and they suddenly contemplate the immeasurably beautiful image of the island of Koldtur out there in the sea. At that point they clutch each other's hands and disappear back behind the hills. That's precisely the kind of experience you associate with the Faroe Islands and it would be wrong not to include it. What we're dealing with here is not a touristical highlight; it's the very soul of the Faroe people and their islands.

**Hjort:** The linguistic universe of *Barbara* is a complicated one, due at once to the nationalities of the participating actors, and certain historical realities that provide the context for the narrative. How did you approach the issue of language in this film?

**Malmros:** There's of course something rather interesting about those Nordic productions that somehow presuppose this idea of vacuuming the relevant literary canons in order to identify works that contain both Swedish and Danish, *Pelle the Conqueror* (*Pelle Erobreren*) being a good example. You'd have thought that *Barbara* had to be made in Danish, because Jørgen-Frantz Jacobsen only wrote in Danish. However, right from the start I decided that I'd let the actors speak their own language, and that's why my original plan was to find a Danish Barbara, or, better still, a Barbara from the Faroe Islands. The problem was that I wasn't able to find anyone who was convincing enough. A lot of the actresses were good, but it was hard to find the particular combination of traits that I was looking for. I was looking for someone who wasn't just a picture of Hollywood glamour, for someone who had a certain almost intimate charm and who also had the kind of primordial strength that was needed to row that boat, and it was very hard to find the right person. At a very late point in the process, someone recommended that I take a look at Anneke von der Lippe, and at that point I thought, 'Well, if she's to be Norwegian then the whole family should be Norwegian, including her cousin Gabriel.' It was Axel Helgeland from Northern Lights who'd recommended Anneke von der Lippe and he was also able to suggest a Norwegian Gabriel, namely Trond Høvik. Høvik had had a bit part in *Hamsun*, where he'd been a journalist. In that film the audience had only seen him from behind, but he'd shown a lot of promise nonetheless. I went to Oslo in order to cast them and they were both exactly what I was looking for. Initially the fact that they're both Norwegian might seem problematic, but in earlier times the Faroe Islands were actually more Norwegian than Danish. When I started looking into this more carefully it turned out that people used to speak something called *gøte-dansk*, meaning street Danish, on the Faroe Islands. It was a strange hybrid language which is very similar to the sound of Danish being spoken by a Norwegian, so that's what they speak in the film. The Faroe people think that this makes the film more powerful, and if that's the case, then we really can't complain. Barbara and Gabriel therefore speak *gøte-dansk* and occasionally some Faroese that they've learnt for the purposes of the film. The Danes speak Danish, the islanders speak Faroese and the Frenchmen speak French. In that context we're able to make a virtue of the fact that Mr. Paul doesn't initially understand what's being said.

# Morten Arnfred

## 1945–

Morten Arnfred is one of the reliable storytellers and realists of contemporary Danish film. His first feature film, *Let's Do It* (*Måske ku' vi*, 1975), left a decisive mark on the 1970s youth film, a contribution that was recognised when *Me and Charly* (*Mig og Charly*) won the Bodil* award for Best Danish Film of 1977. In the 1980s Arnfred developed an artistically persuasive form of social realism, and once again he won a Bodil award for his efforts, this time for *Johnny Larsen* (1979, based on books by John Nehm). The film carefully depicts the milieus relevant to the transition from a traditional working class culture to a modern welfare state culture, just as it paints a number of sensitive social and psychological portraits of young people in 1950s Denmark. Arnfred was also awarded a Bodil for his realistic and at times poetic film about the plight of farmers, *Land of Plenty* (*Der er et yndigt land*, 1983), which can be seen as a contemporary settling of accounts with the maudlin Korch* tradition in Danish film. In *Heaven and Hell*

*Morten Arnfred during the shooting of* Night Vision (Spår i mörket). *[Photo: Bengt Wanselius].*

(*Himmel og helvede*, 1988, based on a novel by Kirsten Thorup) Arnfred expands his aesthetic register to include elements of a more experimental cinematic style. In his most recent feature films, *The Russian Singer* (*Den russiske sangerinde*, 1993, based on a novel by Leif Davidsen) and *Night Vision* (*Beck 2 – Spår i mörket*, 1997), Arnfred draws on a number of mainstream genres, for the former embeds a love story within the context of a political thriller while the latter focusses on the crime-solving activities of Maj Sjöwall and Per Wahlöö's detective, Martin Beck. Arnfred has in the course of his long career made TV films as well as TV series, and his talent for directing actors makes him an important resource person. He has, for example, assisted Lars von Trier on *Breaking the Waves* (1996) and co-directed *The Kingdom* and *The Kingdom 2* (*Riget* and *Riget 2*, 1994/1997).

### Feature films
1975, *Let's Do It* (*Måske ku' vi*, co-director with Lasse Nielsen and Morten Bruus)
1977, *Me and Charly* (*Mig og Charly*, with Henning Kristiansen)

1979,  *Johnny Larsen*
1983,  *Land of Plenty* (*Der er et yndigt land*)
1988,  *Heaven and Hell* (*Himmel og helvede*)
1993,  *The Russian Singer* (*Den russiske sangerinde*)
1994,  *The Kingdom* (*Riget*, co-director with von Trier)
1996,  *Breaking the Waves* (assistant director to von Trier)
1997,  *Night Vision* (*Beck 2 – Spår i mörket*)
1997,  *The Kingdom 2* (*Riget 2*, co-director with von Trier)

## TV productions

1978,  *Power Cut* (*Strømmens dag*)
1985,  *Professional Confidentiality* (*Tjenstlig tavshed*)
1985/1986,  *Refugee Portraits* (*Flygtningeportrætter*)
1989,  *Hansen & Nielsen*
1989,  *Nielsen Broadcast*
1994,  *The Kingdom* (*Riget*, co-director with von Trier, episodes 1–4)
1996,  *Taxi* (*Taxa*, episodes 4–6)
1997,  *The Kingdom 2* (*Riget 2*, co-director with von Trier, episodes 5–8)
1999/2001,  *The Hotel* (*Hotellet*, main director and creative producer)

**Hjort:** Like many other important directors of your generation, you learnt how to make films, not at the National Film School,* but in the context of a small production company. What, for you, are the advantages and disadvantages of these two quite different ways of learning about film-making?

**Arnfred:** If you attend the Film School, you may initially get less experience on film productions. At the Film School you strengthen your intellectual readiness and acquire a lot of knowledge about, among other things, film history. If you're trained in the industry, your strength comes from having been able to try your hand at the many different tasks involved in film-making, but I would still have liked to have attended the Film School. At the time in question I didn't even consider applying because my former brother-in-law – who was the theatre director Finn Poulsen and someone I admired a lot – had applied and been refused. The Film School was even more elitist back then, and the admission standards were quite high. I had only the Danish equivalent of mediocre O levels to my name, so I started out as a camera assistant at Per Holst's. He and his wife had a small company. They mostly made advertisements and couldn't really afford to hire me, but I was hired nonetheless and received a very modest symbolic salary of 350 Crowns per month. Fortunately for me Per had just bought himself a new 35 mm camera. Per had no understanding whatsoever of anything having to do with technology, so I was told to play around with the camera, and after a while I managed to piece it together and got it working. So it was by trial and error that I discovered how the light metre, the F stops and the lenses worked. I then worked as a camera assistant for a while, primarily on advertisements, and that taught me a lot. One day Per gave me a roll of film, so that I could experiment on my own. I made my first little film, which was about a community in Sydhavnen that charted its own course, right in the middle of the capital. I haven't a clue where that film is today. I was gradually used more and more as a cinematographer at Per Holst's, and I worked as a camera assistant to a lot of talented cinematographers. I also did some editing, produced some sound and served as a commentator. I tried my hand at virtually all aspects of the film-making process, and at a certain point I felt there was nothing more for me to learn at Per Holst's.

I'd noticed that some of my colleagues were involved in feature productions and were earning significantly more money than I was. So I resigned and decided to free lance, which was a big step, but I was fortunate enough to be asked to work as a camera assistant on Gert Fredholm's first film, *The Case of the Missing Clerk* (*Den forsvundne fuldmægtig*). Henning Kristiansen was the cinematographer and I was his assistant. I was both proud as a peacock and extremely nervous at having been offered the job. It was the first time I'd been anywhere near the actors, and as a camera assistant you're in their face all the time, because you have to get them in focus. Every now and again I'd make a small suggestion to the director. I didn't really know how to behave yet, so I just proffered advice without realising that I might want to be careful about doing that. But Gert Fredholm thanked me afterwards because he felt that many of my suggestions had been helpful.

After that I worked as a cinematographer on some short films and documentaries. Then one day Steen Herdel contacted me and told me he wanted me to be the cinematographer on a youth film called *Let's Do It*. The director was called Lasse Nielsen, but it turned out that he had real problems communicating with the young people. Now, if I notice that things around me aren't functioning properly, I get involved, so I more or less ended up becoming the director of the film while also being the cinematographer. I felt a bit uncomfortable about that, because my aim hadn't been to take over the film. So I said I'd take charge of the shooting, but on the condition that we agreed that we'd made the film collectively. That's why the credits identify something resembling a collective. The film was an enormous success, although it's not a particularly good film. Back then, though, there was a need for that type of film.

**Hjort:** Films for children and young people have long been considered a defining feature of Danish film. The claim has been that this type of film-making has to be sustained if Danish children are to have access to narratives that reflect their national identities, realities and language. In a sense, the wave of Danish youth films can be traced to a couple of key films, including your own *Let's Do It*. As you point out, *Let's Do It* was produced by Herdel, whose interest in promoting realistic narratives about the lives of young people had a lasting impact on the genre. It's not uncommon for foreign audiences to be struck by the extent to which Danish children's films foreground the social incompetence of adults and the resilience and resourcefulness of children as they struggle to deal with the problematic realities that are inflicted on them. Could you describe the debates and visions that led to the production, for example, of *Let's Do It* and *Me and Charly* in the late 1970s? Is Danish children's film-making still largely motivated by the same kinds of questions as then, or do you see the genre as having evolved in a number of different directions?

**Arnfred:** It's true that there was a powerful youth film tradition in the 1970s. I find that things have changed a lot since then. In the case of *Let's Do It* we basically developed the story as we went along, because the script wasn't very successful. Back in the 1970s we'd organise a plenary session the minute we disagreed about something. Our discussions and decisions were always collective. Some people were, of course, more articulate or authoritative than others, but we'd been taught to listen to everyone, and that took a hell of a lot of time. I think that left it's mark on *Let's Do It*. The film was about a young couple who suddenly find themselves isolated and are taken hostage in connection with a bank robbery. However, it was, of course, also about the restlessness of young people and their relation to their parents, the lack of communication, the alienation, and the sense of being opposed to the grown ups. There was an element of Christiania and a bit of children power. The film was like a big thematic stew that combined all the topics related to the youth revolt.

*Let's Do It* had a contagious effect on a number of other youth films that were made during the 1970s and early 1980s. *Me and Charly* took up the same issues, and in a number of other films, including *Johnny Larsen*, I've similarly dealt with the question of the problematic adaptation process faced by adolescents as they make the transition to adult society. It was Henning Kristiansen, whom I'd worked for as a camera assistant, who called me and suggested that we make *Me and Charly* together. It's based on a novel called *The White Hands* (*De hvide hænder*) which isn't particularly successful, but I felt it had some interesting characters. It tells the typical story of the encounter between the highly maladapted boy from Copenhagen and the more well balanced boy from the provinces. Initially these two very different kinds of people meet as enemies, because the city boy steals the other boy's scooter. However, the film ends with the provincial boy giving his scooter to the city boy, so that he can get on with his life. That progression was in itself a very beautiful, self-contained story.

I don't feel that those kinds of stories get told anymore. In recent years there have been some youth films about girls, but I wouldn't say that they exactly continue the earlier tradition. I do think that *Let's Do It* provided the starting point for a lot of other films. Most of the established directors in Denmark today – not least Søren Kragh-Jacobsen – have paid their dues to youth films. They've done this in part because the money was available, since official film policy earmarks 25% of the available state funding for films targeting children and adolescents. If that rule hadn't existed I don't think as many films for children and adolescents would have been made, which may seem surprising, for children and adolescents are actually quite a good audience, as it turns out. Today the younger directors make films that find a starting point in their own generation, in their own alienation, and in their own curiosity about what's happening on the margins of society. Examples are *Portland* and *Pusher* but also a film like *Let's Get Lost*. I think the latter is a wonderful film, but it deals with the director's own generation. We didn't do that sort of thing back then, because we chose to focus on the younger generation. We were a bit older than our characters, but drew on our own experiences. All that's changed, but I still think the possibilities for making good films for children and adolescents are excellent in Denmark because we take the genre seriously.

Fortunately there are still a lot of people who feel like trying their hand at children's films, and it's important to ensure that good films for children and adolescents get made.

**Hjort:** *Johnny Larsen* was awarded a Bodil as Best Danish Film of 1979 as well as the LO prize, and a lot of people think of it as a kind of culmination of the youth films and social realism of the 1970s. This was the first film you directed alone. You yourself wrote the script together with Jørgen Melgaard. Yet, *Johnny Larsen* is also quite different from most of the youth films in that it provides a historical portrait of Denmark, a take on the plight of the Danish working class in the 1950s. What we have here is an image of the period just prior to the emergence of the welfare state. The film is based on John Nehm's books but nontheless has its own style and narrative mode. How do you see this film today and why was it so important to tell precisely that story at that particular point in time?

**Arnfred:** Personally I felt that *Johnny Larsen* was a natural part of my development as a film-maker. Yet, just as with all my other films, *Johnny Larsen* was a film I was asked to make. Some directors have ideas for films they'd really, really like to make. I've always been offered a lot of projects. So I've hardly had time to decide what it is I'd actually like to say. If you direct a successful film like *Me and Charly*, a lot of doors suddenly open up. It was the producer, Just Betzer, and the consultant Frits Raben, who's now deceased, who suggested that I might want to take a look at the proletarian writer, John Nehm. I read Nehm's books and I then wrote a script for *Johnny Larsen* together with Jørgen Melgaard in which we drew on Nehm's works. The film is a portrait of a period of which I had only the vaguest of memories. It takes place in 1951 during the Korean war, and I was six then. There were nonetheless a number of things that I could remember and I was fascinated by that, but other than that I wanted to recount a *Bildungs* story about this working class boy who had to live up to his father's expectations, but who also had to learn to set certain limits and to become his own person. The film also focusses on conflicts in his everyday life having to do, in part, with love and also with various authorities. I've had lots of experience with the authorities, and not least the military. The whole story about the military is actually a reconstruction of my own memories from a period in time when I found it really hard to understand why being a soldier had to be such a humiliating experience. I see this differently today, but I simply didn't understand it back then.

However, I felt like telling that story about a young person who matures and becomes an independent being at a time when something extra is required in order to oppose the authorities, in order, that is, not simply to follow in father's footsteps. The father is an example of a worker who survived the war, unemployment and so on, but who's still conditioned to do as he's told, to knuckle under and work like a dog. His dream of prosperity involves having his own fridge some day, his own car and summerhouse, after years of conforming and busting his ass. In that sense the father becomes a tragic figure. He becomes ambitious on his son's behalf and has to watch his own dreams of becoming foreman evaporate, which turns him into a defeated man. He's been kicked around his entire life, and happiness for him is to get a position that allows him to start kicking others around. For Johnny, though, it's more important to preserve his own integrity. As the film progresses he believes more and more in himself. That's why it's a story of an individual's process of maturation, but it's also a story about solidarity. In spite of his disagreements with his father, Johnny ultimately exhibits great solidarity with him. At the same time there's a strong bond between the generations. Although Johnny's relation to his father is strained, the boy has an excellent relation with his grandfather. I use Johnny's two friends as contrastive figures, for they each represent a different choice. There's the boxer who fights his way up through the system; and then there's the con-man who's so smart he's able to zig zag his way around all solid employment and manages to make a living conning people. Johnny could have made similar choices, but he doesn't.

**Hjort:** At one point, you were seriously considering becoming a farmer. Although you became a film-maker instead, you've always been attuned to this other reality, which you explore with great insight and feeling in your prize-winning film, *Land of Plenty*.

**Arnfred:** It's true that as a child I wanted to become a farmer. I must have seen a movie that made a real impression! But I did, of course, grow up in the country, and childhood experiences leave strong impressions, so I've always wanted to make a film set in the country. The project began when the Danish Broadcasting Corporation* contacted me because an author in Århus, Jørgen Ljungdalh, had written this enormous script. I was fascinated by the idea that someone had written a story with the intention of taking the peasants seriously. I proposed that we should make the film together, using cinemascope and stereo for the first time in Denmark. Nobody really believed in the idea and the producers I contacted, including Bent Fabricius Bjerre, were sceptical at first. As Bjerre put it, 'Who'd want to see a film about the peasants' problems?' We went ahead and wrote that story, which, as far as I can tell, is about the very things I've always dealt with. The key question in my youth films is whether one's life has meaning, and that's the issue that Knud (Ole Ernst), the farmer in the film, is grappling with. Behind it all there's a perhaps naive and romantic dream about family involvement, which is what our entire agricultural system builds on. However, reality isn't like that any more, and Knud is terribly naive in that respect, because his financial situation is such that his wife has to find work off the farm. She may also be more interested in finding inspiration in her work as a school teacher, although she's from the country too. If you're raising pigs in an industrial manner, the entire dream can be destroyed by the smallest problem, the tiniest grain of sand. A marriage like that isn't strong enough to bear the brunt of that collapse. At some level I think the film still works today. I have some contact with the agricultural sector because I'm a member of the Agricultural Cultural Foundation, so I participate in seminars from time to time on cultural politics and agriculture. I can tell that people enjoy seeing that film time and again and have it on video.

**Hjort:** You received a number of prestigious awards for *Land of Plenty*, which is a settling of accounts with the Danish heritage film tradition constituted by the many adaptations in the 1950s of the maudlin novels by Morten Korch. *Land of Plenty* explores the beauty of the Danish countryside in a series of intensely poetic images, but the ultimate message of this social realist film is that country living is anything but idyllic. The Korch adaptations seem, in some strange way, to be at the very centre of Danish film. Many Danish film-makers either engage critically with these films, as you do, or as Anders Refn did in *The Baron* (Slægten), or they feel compelled to remobilise the works in a series of ironic contemporary remakes. Here I'm thinking, of course, of Lars von Trier's Korch project. Why is the Korch tradition so central, and why was it important to you to correct his vision of things?

**Arnfred:** Because the Danish cinema public's knowledge of farm life is derived primarily from the Korch films. They retell the same story again and again, and it's always a matter of evil characters who are wholly evil and good characters who are entirely good. Korch chose a milieu that reflected the times he was living in. I wanted a modern milieu and the conflicts I deal with are of a somewhat different nature in that the evil characters aren't quite as visible. Evil is associated now with the large fodder companies and the banks, while Korch's stories focus more on the struggle of goodness against the evil within. I made *Land of Plenty* as an alternative to Korch, because when it comes to cinematic depictions of country life there's simply nothing else to square off against. The film is intended as a protest against the image that we Danes have of country living. Although the film is anchored in a rural family, it's just as much about the family as such. It could have been set in any of those places where there's a family that believes in the dream: a small electrician's company, a modest plumber's shop, a dairy or any of those small units that are so typically Danish. So I really used agriculture and the countryside as a backdrop for my story. I also did this because I think Denmark is a really lovely country. It's really very beautiful. That's why I insisted that the place where they lived had to be beautiful; there had to be something worth fighting for. I didn't want them simply to throw in the towel.

I did a tremendous amount of research and heard all about the difficulties that the farmers faced, and while we were writing the script I spent time on various farms and talked to people about how they were managing and why they didn't just give up. It was hard work getting them to tell me what their deeper motives for staying on were. It had something to do with the unpredictability of it all. You pretty much do the same things from year to year, but the results of your efforts are quite different. The way you live puts you in touch with nature in a different way; you're suddenly part of the cycle, of the seasons. Suddenly I understood what the motivating force was: expectations combined with a fateful gamble. Will we succeed or fail? A lot of what they do is trivial, but some things can't be determined in advance, and that's why these people persist. When I'd grasped this I thought, 'Now I understand my main character. Now I understand what it is, above and beyond pride, that he feels when he looks out over the landscape, what it is that's driving him.' I thought that was interesting. Another thing that was interesting about *Land of Plenty* was the casting. At first blush, you wouldn't think that Ole Ernst would make a convincing farmer. His earlier films had established him as a tough character from the Copenhagen region. Originally my idea was to find a real farmer, so I travelled throughout the entire country and saw a lot of amateur theatre, but I didn't find anyone. Ole was keen on the idea from the start and also agreed to prepare himself a bit

for the role by staying on the farm where we were going to be doing the shooting. The amazing thing was that as we were shooting we realised that fiction had become reality. The farmer we'd met was in exactly the same situation as my main character. His wife also worked off the farm and they had terrible financial problems. That's of course why he'd originally allowed us to shoot the film on his farm. He recognised himself in the story, could identify with it. As I was finishing up the film, things went from bad to worse, and they were finally forced to sell the farm and to move. It was a nightmare to watch this process unfold as we were shooting on the farm. The situation seemed absurd, but was also very moving.

*Harriet Andersson as Jasmin in* Heaven and Hell (Himmel og helvede). *[Photo: Vibeke Winding]*

**Hjort:** In 1984 the Danish Refugee Council invited you to shoot a series of documentary short films dealing with the plight of refugees around the world. Funding for this project stemmed from both Nordic sources and the Office of the United Nations High Commissioner for Refugees. You visited refugee camps in Nicaragua, Honduras, Mexico, Eritrea, Sudan, Kenya, Tanzania, Pakistan, Hong Kong, Thailand and Palestine, and the result is a number of intensely personal cinematic testimonies, many of which were shown on Danish TV (Danish Broadcasting Corporation) in 1985/1986. The narrative approach in each of the documentaries is the same: the camera situates a group of refugees politically and geographically and goes on to focus on the plight of one particular individual. Women provide the focus for many of the films. I am thinking, for example, of the quietly charismatic Cambodian midwife, Kol Som, or of the Afghan woman named Giul. Your feature films reflect your interest in social realism, a style that is not that distant from certain documentary practices. Yet, the refugee films are your first real documentaries. What, exactly, were you trying to achieve with these films and how are these intentions expressed cinematically?

**Arnfred:** I was unsure about how to tackle the assignment. I told the Danish Refugee Council that if they were looking for a series of journalistic documents about the plight of the refugees and the political situation more generally, then they should contact a journalist. I made it clear to them that what was of interest to me was the individual, and they accepted that. I found all the impressions overwhelming, though, for whom was I to choose? Every time we got to a refugee camp, we realised that the people running the place had been informed of our arrival, and they all had ideas about whom we should choose, namely, the model refugees, if you will. We said 'no' every time. However, my producer, Erik Crone, and I were a bit at a loss as we travelled around the world together during my first research trip. You see nobody could guarantee that a given situation would be unchanged when we returned with a film crew, that the refugee we'd chosen would be alive still and in the camp. So for me the trip was primarily educational and a source of a lot of very powerful experiences. However, once I'd returned home and had had time to collect my thoughts I found a key to the project, which I could use as my starting point: every refugee has a story, so my task must be to use the skills I have to draw out what is interesting about this person, without constantly wondering whether the person sitting next to him or her has an even more powerful story. Once I'd made that decision, everything became a lot easier, because then we could just walk around the camp and find people whom we wanted to talk to. My cinematographer, Dirk Brüel, and sound technician, Niels Arild, would drive around the camp with me for a day or two without filming; we simply absorbed as many impressions as we could. We took a few stills, asked a few questions, and listened, so that the refugees could get used to us before we returned with all our equipment. We lived with them, and under the same conditions. We ate the food they offered us. My task was to create trust and to get people to open up. The key to those films – above and beyond my regular curiosity – was thus this idea that was constantly in the back of my mind, namely, that the person before me had a story to tell. 'This person', I'd remind myself, 'is as interesting as everyone else in this world.' The task was to get that person to recount something about herself, to articulate her life goals, fears and dreams, and to depict this person in her reality. We were surrounded by death, yet we learnt something about the affirmation of life and about what it is that allows people in desperate situations to survive. The project was an incredible experience and I know it's left a lasting impression on those of us who were part of it. I remember a situation in which we were on our way home after a difficult trip to the border between Sudan and Eritrea, where 50 thousand refugees were gathered in a big camp. On the plane to Denmark, I was enjoying my first gin and tonic in a long time and reading a Danish newspaper. There was an article about some conflict in Kalundborg. Some citizens had decided to demonstrate against the local authorities' decision to equip a small number of refugees with bicycles. I was really ashamed of being Danish and discovered that my perspective on a lot of things had really changed.

**Hjort:** You were co-director, with Lars von Trier, of the successful hospital series, *The Kingdom* and *The Kingdom 2* and you played the role of assistant director to von Trier on *Breaking the Waves*. In Denmark you're perceived as the film-maker who taught von Trier to make full use of his performers' acting abilities. Outstanding acting is a recurrent feature of your films. Could you talk about the methods you employ in directing actors?

**Arnfred:** Let me just make one thing clear: at this point Lars is very good with actors. He's always been a brilliant film-maker, but working with actors wasn't his strength earlier. If he's learnt something from me, that makes me proud, but he doesn't need me any more. He now makes masterful use of all the medium's keys. As a director I think of myself as a kind of conductor of an orchestra. I have a whole lot of musicians, each with a score, and they have to play in tune and with the right rhythm. This conception holds both in front of, and behind, the camera. I suppose my method first and foremostly involves creating so much trust that the actors feel they can let themselves fall backwards and can count on my catching them, figuratively speaking. They also have to trust me enough to make it possible to pull out some of the drawers they normally don't use. Actors are in many ways like a dresser. They have lots of drawers which they can pull out as needed. They've learnt how to do that both with experience and as part of their technical training. This is typically fairly uninteresting, because Denmark is such a small country, so we've seen the actors in all kinds of connections and know what's coming. For me things become really interesting when I'm able to elicit something I know I haven't seen before, especially if I feel the actor is exploring a space where he hasn't been before. However, I can't achieve this unless the actor trusts me unconditionally. Now, it's not the case that you as a director always see the larger picture, but you have to pretend to see it and to be in control. I'm often driven by doubt, but that's something I can't reveal. I have to pretend to know what's going on, I have to pretend to know exactly what I want, not least in relation to the actors, but I'm often in doubt. Another strength I have is my ability to identify false notes. If I know the actors, I'm also usually able to indicate how some authenticity might be achieved.

During my first meeting with an actor I simply absorb as many impressions as possible in an attempt to figure out what kind of tone the actor has and which chords we should be using. I speak in musical terms because I find that being a director is like being a musician. I'm a former musician myself and I frequently use musical terms to describe the process of directing. It's a question of intuiting the actor's potential. Once I've 'read' my actor, I'd of course still like to be surprised, and fortunately I am every now and again. There are different ways of working with actors. If I don't get quite what I want, I might say the lines for them. Nils Malmros consistently does this with his actors, and most of them don't like it. I might nonetheless choose to do this in order to suggest a certain rhythm. I might actually go so far as to tell the actors where they should build pauses into their lines, when they should scratch themselves and where. We're talking about the nitty gritty of facial expressions and body language. I know that this attention to detail will give the final product the kind of spice that makes for authenticity. As a director you do everything to make the actors feel safe, and this includes making sure that the framework and props are just right, but sometimes actors focus on externalities because they're insecure. So you also have to prevent the actors from assigning blame in symptomatic ways. Directing is also a matter of praising the actors, of being loving, funny, and ironic, of tickling them in the right places. Film-making should be fun. Actually, that's probably my secret weapon. When everything comes together properly then there are a few moments in the course of a film that are positively divine. There may only be two or three of these moments in the whole film, but that's enough.

**Hjort:** Your most recent feature film, *Night Vision*, is a detective drama centred around a series of brutal subway murders committed by estranged youths as part of an ongoing computer game that occupies so central a place in their lives that the boundaries between virtual and actual realities are effaced. *Night Vision* is a Swedish film in both cultural and economic terms. Although the film is not an adaptation of a work by Maj Sjöwall and Per Wahlöö, it does focus on the detective, Martin Beck, who's a central figure in these authors' much-loved crime novels. The idea of having a Danish director make a film based on popular works that are widely regarded as part of the Swedish national heritage is, as you've remarked elsewhere, likely to be met with a certain resistance in some quarters. There's much discussion these days about whether films are or should be national in some usually unspecified sense of the word. Could you talk about some of the different ways in which issues of national culture impinged on the making of the transnational film, *Night Vision*?

**Arnfred:** Like most Danes I used to read Sjöwall and Wahlöö with great pleasure, back in the days when they published a new book almost once a year. Back in the 1970s it was almost like waiting for the new Beatles record. The Martin Beck books were the first Nordic attempt at, not just crime fiction, but detective fiction with a social perspective that embraced both the lower and upper echelons of society. That's why I immediately said 'yes' when I was asked whether I'd be interested in being part of the project. *Night Vision* hadn't even been written yet, but the idea was there. *Night Vision* is just one of a series of eight films, the first and last of which are feature films and the rest TV films. The films had limited budgets, so there wasn't much time for shooting. The script for the story I worked on was the result of collaborative efforts, via email, between my script writer in Sweden and myself.

You might wonder why on earth they'd ask a Danish director to make a Sjöwall and Wahlöö story. I think I could defend the idea that it's quite healthy to get a foreign director to tell a story that's based on what you might call the Swedish crown jewels. It is, of course, an original story and not an adaptation of the novels, but it's still a Swedish story that takes place in Swedish society. In my mind, though, that wasn't particularly important. I think of the film as almost an allegory of alienation in modern society, and in this case alienation causes a number of young people to seek shelter in a place where they're left entirely to their own devices. People have accused me of being hostile towards youth, which isn't at all true, and I'm not opposed to technology or anything like that either. I'm just trying to point out that loneliness exists in modern society as a result of a lack of contact between the generations. That's why young people seek out the various subcultures that exist all over the world, including Denmark. In Denmark we've fortunately dealt with our subcultures in a fairly reasonable way. We have Christiania, and the members of the anarchist movement have also somehow found a space where they can remain visible. It's incredibly important for a society to be aware of its subcultures and to relate to their members in a way that involves a good deal more subtlety than simply beating them up, because that just makes things much worse. In that sense *Night Vision* is much more of an allegory than a story about Swedish realities.

Perhaps the Swedes contacted me because they thought of me as the right director for this particular story, but I do think there was also a more prosaic reason, namely, that my being the director made it possible for them to get money from the Danish Film Institute.* Opting for a Danish director enabled them to put the final pieces of the financial puzzle together, because suddenly this was a feature film with a Danish director, a Danish cinematographer and a Danish producer. This meant that we were able to get the money we needed from the Danish Film Institute. I found it challenging to work in a less familiar context and with an all-Swedish crew (with the exception, that is, of my cinematographer and his assistant). It was a wonderful experience, because they do things differently over there, not worse, just differently, so I found myself having to adapt, but I also ended up teaching them some things. What emerged was a kind of transnational way of making films, for there was a reciprocal process of adjustment, both at the level of language and work habits.

**Hjort:** There's much talk these days of the need to internationalise Danish film. Proponents of this process argue that expensive international co-productions provide a means of ensuring the survival of the Danish film industry. Yet, directors of co-productions clearly encounter a number of specific problems that are interesting in the context of reflections on national and transnational identities. The problem of language resurfaces again and again, as does the divergence of acting styles rooted in national traditions. Most Danish co-productions involve collaboration between the Nordic countries. You, however, ventured onto largely unexplored terrain with *The Russian Singer*, which is a Danish-Russian co-production. To what extent were you concerned about issues of cultural verisimilitude and coherence while directing this adaptation of Leif Davidsen's popular novel?

**Arnfred:** *The Russian Singer* was once again a film that I was invited to make, but in this case the pre-history is a little unusual. One day Lars Kolvig, who's the film's producer, called and asked me whether he could send over a script by taxi. When I asked why he couldn't just mail it to me, he said that suddenly an opportunity to do this project had arisen, and he needed to go to Moscow. So he needed a quick response. I wasn't actually that thrilled with the script. The story in the original novel is quite good and takes place in the former Soviet Union in 1991, but the film script showed signs of having been reworked again and again. There had also been an attempt to update the action to the present, and that didn't really work. Still, I thought the project was exciting. My philosophy is that every now and again it's good to dive off the ten-metre diving board without knowing whether there's enough water in the pool. So I accepted the challenge and took the plunge. I went to Russia to do the casting. I decided very early on that Ole Lemmeke would play the Danish lead, but we still needed to find the Russian actors. I was over there five or six times before I finally found someone whom I thought could play the female lead, but then she fell ill and was hospitalised, and although she showed up for a number of the rehearsals, she didn't get better, so that didn't work. So there we were without a female lead and we were supposed to start shooting the next day. We were in a total panic and ended up shooting and casting at the same time. We shot some of the scenes that didn't require the presence of the female lead. Then one evening I settled on a new actress, did some video takes with her, and flew back to Copenhagen in order to show them to Ole Lemmeke. I returned to Moscow the next morning and gave her the role, which was fine. She was a pretty good choice.

However, the mere fact of making that film was an achievement in itself. The crew was largely Russian, but there were quite a few Danes too, including a sound technician, a cinematographer and a script writer. Every evening we reminded each other that the main challenge was not so much that of making a good film as that of simply completing the project we'd undertaken. We were actually incredibly impressed by the fact that we managed to make a bit of progress every day. The casting alone had been an absolutely incredible process. I'd said that I wanted actors who spoke English so that I'd be able to communicate with them, but my first assistant director, as well as most of the actors who showed up for the casting, barely spoke any English at all. So I had an interpreter, who was very good and now teaches at the European Film College. She was actually a script editor and she'd translated the script from English to Russian, so that the Russian actors and the Russian film crew would be able to understood what it was all about. I was so thrilled with her that I ended up hiring her as my personal assistant and translator and she did a terrific job. The actors who showed up had learnt a few English phrases, but that was really about it. Even the man who plays the old colonel, which is after all a major role, didn't know English. He didn't understand a word of what he was saying. He had to learn his lines phonetically, so his script was covered with phonetic signs. He was also a vodka enthusiast and he was constantly plastered. He had memory problems and simply couldn't remember his lines. So every time we shot a scene with him, we had five assistants standing around with these huge cards that had his lines written all over them. In Russia they call them 'idiot cards'. What's remarkable is that when you see the film you actually think he understands what he's saying. We gradually developed our own home-grown language. That's the kind of thing I was talking about earlier when I emphasised the importance of trust. We had a lot of fun together although I didn't understand what he was saying. He talked Russian to me all the time and I'd respond in Danish. It was amusing because I do think that he understood some of what I said. I gesticulate a lot and rely on body language quite a bit, and in that regard he was an incredibly musical person. He was a big star in Russia and was delighted to be part of the film. He came to Denmark for the premiere and gave a speech in Russian of which nobody understood a word.

I found the film challenging, in part because the story, which is about Russia, is written by a Dane. As a director I think it can be a real advantage to be an outsider because this may enable you to see a given country in a different light. I was praised for the authenticity of the film. The story may be questionable, but people felt the images were authentic. Indeed, the Russians agreed that they themselves wouldn't have been able to capture this authenticity because they would have opted to shoot in some quite different milieus. I was drawn to milieus that I found exciting and authentic. As a Dane my antennae were out and my eyes were wide open. That kind of fundamental openness is, I think, characteristic of the outsider who's just arrived in a foreign country. I have no problem with the idea of working in another country. In my mind it's an advantage. Nor do I have a problem with the idea of foreigners shooting Danish stories in Denmark. I'm much more sceptical about the 'Europuddings' that seem to result from attempts to piece together the financing for those big co-productions. *Breaking the Waves* is a good example, although that film is quite successful. However, for financial reasons there had to be a bit of Norwegian, some English, a touch of Swedish, a bit of Dutch, a little German and some French. I find that sort of thing a bit tiring. At that point I'd rather make films that cost less. I don't feel the need to make any of those big expensive films.

**Hjort:** In an earlier interview you drew attention to the galvanising effect that the Oscars garnered by Gabriel Axel and Bille August (for *Babette's Feast* [*Babettes gæstebud*] and *Pelle the Conqueror* [*Pelle Erobreren*] respectively) have had on the Danish film industry: 'The intense international focus on *Babette's Feast* and *Pelle the Conqueror* has meant a lot to Danish film people: it's boosted their national sentiment; and from now on it will be easier to get co-productions off the ground. At the same time Danish directors can't help but think "The international attention could just as easily have been focussed on me and my films", because the differences among us just aren't that great. That optimism is very positive' (*Månedsmagasinet IN*, June 1989). This optimism is, if anything, stronger than ever at this point. The 1997 Film Act* led to a number of radical institutional changes, most of which seem to have strengthened the position of Danish film, both nationally and internationally. What's your take on Danish film at this point?

**Arnfred:** I'm delighted that Danish film is thriving. And I find what Thomas Vinterberg is doing particularly exciting. However, I do feel that the younger directors tend to focus excessively on the margins of society. It's as though they don't really dare to tell stories about ordinary people. I'm still hoping that someone will have the courage at some point to make a film about perfectly ordinary people, and some fundamental issues, of course. I don't know how to explain the tendency to focus on the dramas that arise on the margins of society. Perhaps our day-to-day lives have just become so dreadfully boring, regimented and predictable that there aren't any interesting stories to be told about everyday life in Denmark. I don't know, but that wasn't the case earlier. We didn't shy away from stories about marital problems or familial problems. However, those kinds of films aren't being made any more, which is a pity, I think.

# Søren Kragh-Jacobsen

## 1947–

Like other influential Danish directors, Søren Kragh-Jacobsen is a versatile figure who has contributed to Danish culture in diverse ways. Just as Gabriel Axel trained as a carpenter before taking up film-making, Kragh-Jacobsen completed an apprenticeship as an electro-mechanic before turning to the arts. Kragh-Jacobsen studied documentary film-making at Prague's renowned FAMU (1969–70) and subsequently worked for a number of years in the Children and Youth Department at the Danish Broadcasting Corporation and as a musician. Although the documentary genre figures centrally in Kragh-Jacobsen's formal training as a film-maker, his name is associated with fiction film. More specifically, Kragh-Jacobsen is one of the leading Danish film-makers within the nationally and internationally recognised, social and psychological tradition of film-making for and about children and adolescents. Kragh-Jacobsen's first feature film, *Wanna See My Beautiful Navel?* (*Vil du se min smukke navle?*, 1978,

*Søren Kragh-Jacobsen.*

with music by the director) established a new tone in Danish film. In *Rubber Tarzan* (*Gummi Tarzan*) – which won a Bodil* as Best Film of 1981 and is based on Ole Lund Kierkegaard's novel by the same title – Kragh-Jacobsen demonstrated a fine ability to combine realism and comedy with aspects of the fairy tale genre in his depiction of the world of children. *Thunderbirds* (*Isfugle*, 1983), which is a dramatic socio-psychological portrait of two young men, is characterised by a visually more inventive style. The same can be said of *Emma's Shadow* (*Skyggen af Emma*, 1988), which won a Bodil as Best Film of 1988 and focusses on an imaginative upper-class girl and her encounter with the Copenhagen working class in the 1930s. In both *The Boys from St. Petri* (*Drengene fra Sankt Petri*, 1991) and the English-language *The Island on Bird Street* (*Øen i Fuglegaden*, 1997), Kragh-Jacobsen takes up themes related to the Second World War, which he explores through the eyes of children and adolescents. Kragh-Jacobsen's major international breakthrough was *Mifune* (*Mifunes sidste sang*, 1999), which is part of the Danish Dogme* project.

## Feature films

1978, *Wanna See My Beautiful Navel?* (*Vil du se min smukke navle?*)
1981, *Rubber Tarzan* (*Gummi Tarzan*)
1983, *Thunderbirds* (*Isfugle*)
1988, *Emma's Shadow* (*Skyggen af Emma*)
1988, *Shower of Gold* (*Guldregn*)
1991, *The Boys from St. Petri* (*Drengene fra Sankt Petri*)
1997, *The Island on Bird Street* (*Øen i Fuglegaden*)
1999, *Mifune* (*Mifunes sidste sang*)

## TV productions

1979, *Good-bye Lulow* (*Farvel Lulow*, episodes 1–3)
1984, *Life is a Good Reason* (*Livet er en god grund*)
1986, *Shower of Gold* (*Guldregn*, episodes 1–6)
1993, *The Corsican Bishop* (*Den korsikanske biskop*, episodes 1–4)
2000, *D Day* (*D dag*, collaborative Dogme project)

**Hjort:** Whereas older generations of Danish film-makers had no choice but to go abroad if they wanted to be trained formally in film, you had the option of remaining in Denmark. Why did you choose to study in Czechoslovakia, rather than at the newly established National Film School of Denmark?*

**Kragh-Jacobsen:** Because I saw myself becoming a documentary film-maker. I'm a trained artisan and you don't normally apply to the National Film School of Denmark with that kind of background. The National Film School of Denmark had a very literary orientation back then, so it seemed natural for me to apply to FAMU, particularly since I was interested in the Czech documentary film-makers. At that time I also had a deep sense of veneration for Eastern Europe. It's a five-year program, however, and I never completed it. FAMU didn't operate in the same way as the National Film School of Denmark. FAMU was more like a university and a third of the students were foreigners. The Czechs were very tired of westerners by the early 1970s. We had money and different customs. We even looked different. The Czechs had a completely anonymous way of dressing; it was part of their communist tradition. The rest of us had long hair and wore gaudy scarves, and the Czechs didn't like that at all. They raised the fees in order to get rid of us, so suddenly the school was out of reach unless you were from a very wealthy family. So I returned to Denmark where I was a musician for a year before I started working for the Danish Broadcasting Corporation. After a couple of years, I got a job as a program director at the Danish Broadcasting Corporation.

**Hjort:** Although you were trained as a documentary film-maker, documentary film-making is not in fact what people associate with your name.

**Kragh-Jacobsen:** I started directing short fiction films for the Children and Youth Department at the Danish Broadcasting Corporation, because it was impossible to make documentaries all the time. Around the same time, a young producer called Steen Herdel started up a smallish production company in the private sector, and he became a kind of anchor for the youth wave, which, incidentally, has much the same origin as the low-budget film wave of the 1990s. Young directors wanted more elbow room and felt that film-making had become too costly. They started to use the modest amounts of money they were able to raise to make films with amateurs, which necessarily meant films for children or adolescents. I'd done a lot of writing together with the author Hans Hansen, and in 1976 he published a novel called *Wanna See My Beautiful Navel? (Vil du se min smukke navle?)*. Now, I'm also a composer and songwriter, and I'd written a song that resembled Hans' story quite a bit; I suppose we'd inspired one another. Then one day Steen Herdel announced that he'd like to make a film based on that story. Hans, who'd written the book, insisted that I be the one to direct it. There's a lot of luck involved in being a director, although it's of course also a question of talent. However, if you can contribute the right thing at the right time things often work out, and *Wanna See My Beautiful Navel?* became a huge success. If you've produced one major hit in Denmark, you're allowed to produce another one. In that sense there's a lot of inertia in the system. I usually tell young directors not to worry if their first film doesn't win all the prizes, because that kind of success can be very hard to live up to. In my case a more gradual development has been good.

**Hjort:** After FAMU you worked for the Danish Broadcasting Corporation. More specifically, you were part of the Children and Youth Department, which was run by the well-known Mogens Vemmer. Do you think your experience with this unit had a direct impact on your films? There's a lot of talk about the relationship between film and television. How would you compare television production to work in the film industry?

**Kragh-Jacobsen:** It's true that I'm part of that famous Children and Youth Department, which turned out a lot of people who've gone on to do any number of other things. That's clearly where I discovered that I had a certain talent for directing children. I didn't realise I had that ability until I started working for the Danish Broadcasting Corporation. I have children myself and I like children, but the reason children's films became so central to my career is that I enjoy directing children. There's an unpredictability to it that I like. It's a bit like pulling the pin out of a grenade, because you don't know whether that little 8 or 12 year old being will be able to stand the pressure for ten weeks. Nor do you as a director know exactly what you'll be able to do with him or her. When you hire a professional actor, you more or less know the person in question. My decision to continue making children's films was probably an expression of a kind of fatigue that I felt at seeing the same faces on the screen again and again. In a film like *Emma's Shadow* an established Swedish actor plays opposite an 11 year old girl, and I thought that was a real challenge, but I don't actually think there's a huge difference between directing films for theatrical release and for TV, or between directing children and adults. My level of ambition is the same whether I'm directing a TV series or a feature film. There's just less money available for TV, so you have to work faster and without as many detours.

**Hjort:** In a lecture delivered at the European Film College in Ebeltoft during the summer of 1997 you interestingly suggested that film-making involving children differs dramatically as a function of certain national traditions. Could you talk about some of the key differences in this respect between your earlier Danish films, such as *Wanna See My Beautiful Navel?*, *Rubber Tarzan* and *Shower of Gold*, and your latest, international co-production, *The Island on Bird Street*?

**Kragh-Jacobsen:** You get a different perspective on Nordic children when you work beyond our borders. I've only done this once, so I don't know whether my experience can be generalised. I imagine that working with American children would be yet another kind of experience. *The Island on Bird Street* has an English boy in the lead role, but it also has a number of German and Polish children as extras. English children approach a director and a job in a far more polished way than Danish children do. I was quite shocked to see how inhibited the children were and I found their tendency to behave like little grown-ups rather frightening. My aim isn't to find little grown-ups for the children's roles in my films. I look for a child whose innocence and naïveté are intact. Although I met some 800 English boys in little suits from various acting schools, there wasn't one I could use for the lead role in *The Island on Bird Street*. I could tell that they were all technically good, but so are a lot of other people. If you're going to make a film that depends 100 percent on a child, which is true of *The Island on Bird Street*, then the boy has to be really gifted, because otherwise the film won't be any good. Therefore I had to go beyond standard English casting practices. People were deeply shocked every time I suggested that we might try something other than a casting director. I'd say 'Why not have some open calls, why not try some of the other methods we use in Denmark?' Here we invite everyone, we open things up, because what you're looking for ultimately is a face and a gift.

Once I have the face, then it's my job as a director to get the person in question to feel at ease in front of the camera, because if someone feels comfortable and safe, he or she can do anything. In England we were told that a Danish director couldn't possibly stage an open call in London because parents would immediately associate a Danish film with pornography. I actually think the real issue was laziness. The casters simply found the task of having to go out and meet all kinds of children from all over London unmanageable, and to them the idea of dealing with children who didn't have agents was completely crazy. In the end we gave up on London and went to Manchester, where I organised precisely the kind of open calls that I usually have. What was remarkable was that of the 350 boys I saw, there were two or three who completely fascinated me, and none of them had ever been anywhere near an acting school. They had the real thing, the charisma and that screen personality. That's how we found Jordan, who plays the lead role in *The Island on Bird Street*. He was actually just as sweet and polite as all the others – he bowed to us, was dressed in his best, had had his hair slicked with water, and that kind of thing – but he also had something else. There was something genuine and incredibly luminous about him, and he had a mad streak that I hadn't seen in the others, many of whom concluded by reciting a poem by Shelley or Byron for me, which was charming enough, but didn't exactly stimulate my interest.

**Hjort:** Professional script writers were an important part of *The Island on Bird Street*. A key difference between Danish and Hollywood film-making has to do precisely with the question of film scripts and who creates them. Whereas Hollywood favours specialisation and professional script writers, Danish directors tend to write their own scripts. How do you see these two approaches at this point?

**Kragh-Jacobsen:** What happens in the case of *The Island on Bird Street* is that this book lands on my desk and I become completely fascinated by it. It's no secret that I also become intrigued by the idea of being able to make an English film. When you're in mid-career that's something you'd like to try. I thought it would be interesting to see to what extent there's a difference between shooting a film in English as opposed to Danish, but I discovered that there's virtually no difference at all. It's neither harder nor easier to shoot a film in a foreign tongue. I've also directed in Swedish. Experience now tells me that film-making is exactly the same everywhere. The joys and problems are identical, as are the techniques, and the tone is almost the same.

Returning to *The Island on Bird Street*, I became fascinated by that book. Everyone reads a book differently and what really struck me was the terrifying poetic universe in that terrible story. However, I was at the mercy of the producers because I didn't know any English script writers, and England is after all a country where there are thousands of writers. People recommended someone called John Goldsmith to me. We met, had a congenial time together and discovered that we were on the same wave length, and word had it that he was very efficient and good. He then went off and wrote a first draft, which I found extremely superficial, simply dreadful. So I insisted that we needed to start working more closely together. English script writers actually rely on the director a lot. The director just doesn't get credited, as he or she would in Denmark. Goldsmith was constantly on the phone with me, because I of course knew the book that he was to transform into a script ten times better than he did. I have a house in the country and Goldsmith and I spent a week there working through the script scene by scene. We also came up with some new scenes. I'd spent two months on the book before even meeting him, so I ended up simply pouring ideas into his lap. I'm not saying this in order to diminish John, for he certainly had skills of his own, but it was clear to me where he was headed. So I said, 'You're headed in a completely different direction from where I want to go. This is pure Walt Disney'.

**Hjort:** Could you give some concrete examples?

**Kragh-Jacobsen:** Yes, the film's ending. He proposed this heroic ending, in which the clever boy who's been hiding in the ruin takes revenge on the evil German for having completely destroyed it. It was right out there along with *Die Hard* and *Home Alone*. I jammed up at that point and suggested they should find themselves an American director for the film, because, as I've said, that just wasn't the direction in which I wanted to take the story. However, the American money men had clearly told John that this was supposed to be family entertainment and action. I have a lot of faxes in which they insist, for example, that the film's 'pacing' shouldn't be like that of *Emma's Shadow*. It had to be a lot faster. However, if the pacing is to be faster, I think there should be a reason for it. So that kind of thing just brought out my Danish stubbornness. I tell them that I won't direct a film unless I know exactly what shape it's going to take. The producers accept this and I then try to work with John again and to get him to understand that we're not making an American film. *The Island on Bird Street* is a European film because 85% of the financing stems from European sources. A lot of the money comes from Eurimages, from the Nordic Film and TV Fund, from the Danish Film Institute, and especially from Germany, so we at least have to be faithful to the story. We should also preferably be able to look Uri Orlev, who wrote the book, in the eye afterwards. John and I really disagreed and ended up quarrelling. He then comes to Denmark one last time and we're sitting in my country house when he informs me that he has two days left to finish the script and that's it. I tell him that that's not at all how we work here. I've spent a year on this, so I won't accept anything that's not right. I get him fired when he produces something minimal within a week. I have to inform the producer that I can't possibly work with John's script, and at that point I'm actually willing to withdraw from the project.

I then suggest that they have some scripts by a range of writers sent to me. I end up receiving ten scripts from various agencies in England and I become fascinated by Tony Grisoni. He wrote the script for *Queen of Hearts*, among other things, which I think is a really beautiful film. Tony understands exactly what it is I want. He then works his magic on the book's story until the coffers are empty. I think he could have done a lot more if we'd had more time and money, but during the time that we did have, we worked incredibly well together. He was to receive only a modest amount of money for minor revisions, but we actually sat there and rewrote the entire thing. All the visual aspects of the story are my work. For example, I was the one who thought of having the boy, Alex, make a calendar that would involve counting the days with matches, and I still think that calendar is a beautiful visual symbol, for in the end he incinerates his life. That's just one example of how I might visualise the cinematic universe for the script writer. The ruin is, of course, the other main character in the film. There's a boy and a mouse, and I have to live with the mouse, but the ruin is in my mind a real character. It has to do all kinds of things: it has to underscore the boy's mental condition, to be chilling, to be a cathedral, a cave, something poetic. It really has to do all kinds of things, and as a director you clearly have to get these kinds of images into the head of your script writer before he starts writing. I tell Tony that he doesn't need to use a lot of words, that I'll produce an image of that ruin that will say it all. Tony then writes a script that I can use and we're well into the process of constructing sets in Poland and Germany when the film suddenly shuts down. The film goes belly up and doesn't get revived until four months later. At that point all the producers are desperate to get the film finished, because they've already spent a lot of money on it and have half-finished sets scattered around Europe. I start over with a completely new film crew that is predominantly English. Originally I was supposed to have made *The Island on Bird Street* with a crew that was one third Danish.

**Hjort:** Do you use a particular method when you're directing your actors?

**Kragh-Jacobsen:** You can't simply present a method and then insist that that's how you direct. All directors use their personalities to create the kind of atmosphere they'd like to work in. I meet with my actors and say to myself: 'This is how I'll direct her and this is how I'll direct him.' You do, of course, have to be clear on how you're going to interpret the text, on where the drama and poetry should be, and it's also best to have settled on a particular style. In short, you need a general perspective and you really have to love the project. I don't turn the set into a cathedral when I'm shooting. Some directors turn their sets into sacred places. This is what Bergman does, and I suspect that Bille August does the same thing. It's that business of not allowing anybody to laugh or speak in a loud voice because the master is working. I do respect the fact that this may be the method that works best for them, but my own approach is different. I think life is too short for that and I don't think that the final goal is all-important. I'd also like to have some fun along the way. We laugh a lot when we're shooting my films. Some actors can't stand that, but others love it, and that's the way it'll always be. I can easily sense when a given actor needs some peace and quiet, and then I make sure that that's what she gets, but there are no cathedrals where I work. It's all very playful and we always have a lot of fun. I'm always really up when I'm shooting. I'm much less fond of the subsequent process, which involves sitting at the editing table and studying all the mistakes that were made earlier. I do quite enjoy the mixing, though, and I also like to be involved in articulating the music.

**Hjort:** You're an accomplished musician and have even composed the score for some of your films. You seem to have very definite ideas about film music and its place within a cinematic work. What role do you see music as playing in your various films?

**Kragh-Jacobsen:** Well, that depends on what kind of film I'm making. I more or less know where the music should be as I watch the film emerge. I have a very clear sense of the kind of music that's needed. Over the years I've worked with four musicians, all of whom have quite different modes of expression. My first films had music by a Danish composer called Kenneth Knudsen. A Swedish composer called Thomas Lindahl wrote the music for *Emma's Shadow*. I've collaborated a lot with Jakob Groth, who wrote the music for *Shower of Gold* and *The Boys from St. Petri*. Actually, he's also written the music for *The Corsican Bishop*. I worked with Zbigniew Preisner, Kieslowski's composer, on *The Island on Bird Street*. These four composers are clearly very different, and the ideal situation would certainly be one in which you were free to choose each time. But the Danish film industry is very small and people tend to be very loyal towards their collaborators. I actually think that it should be a matter of analysing the salient mode of expression, film by film, with a central question in mind: 'What should the music be able to achieve here?' I was absolutely sure that the music in *The Island on Bird Street* had to underscore the film's stillness and noise. I was fundamentally opposed to the American producers' idea that the music should be romantic/sentimental and 'wall to wall'. I actually quite like sentimental music, if the film is right, but in this case it wasn't. That's why I knew fairly early on that Preisner would be the right composer. I knew that he composed music that doesn't intrude on the film, but somehow envelops it. His way of

*Jordan Kiziuk as Alex in Søren Kragh-Jacobsen's adaptation of Uri Orlev's novel,* The Island on Bird Street. *[Photo: Astrid Wirth]*

analysing each individual scene was simply masterful. I have to admit that none of the other composers I've worked with – and they're all very good – have had the same ability to pinpoint exactly what was needed. I did have a lot of doubts about the music he composed and the almost tyrannical points of view he expressed, but I must say that the more I listened to it, the more convinced I became that it was in many ways brilliant. It had a certain minimalism to it that underscored the stillness. It was incredibly staccato, and very, very ugly and filthy when necessary and very poetic at other times. It had that mantra-like repetitiveness which I've actually never cultivated before.

You really have to try to identify precisely what music can do for a given film. If it can't do much of anything, then I don't think there should be any music. One of my favourite directors, Bo Widerberg, whom I've been deeply fascinated by, rarely used film music. *Elvira Madigan* is, of course, an exception in that the Mozart theme is central, but otherwise there's hardly any music in his films, other than what's part of the action and milieu. I think that there's an incredibly bad tendency worldwide towards noisy music. My favourite example is *Home Alone*, which I found extremely irritating. Every time a postcard drops through the mail slot the child goes into a panic that reverberates loudly in the sound of 111 musicians playing a score by John Williams. That's an excessive use of music and it has the effect of making us all more and more restless. It really dulls the sensibilities. Things were different in earlier periods of film history. Take the Czech wave, for example. On those occasions when there's music, it serves quietly and precisely to underscore something. Nowadays we're not allowed to have an independent thought or to make-believe anything on our own. Everything is pre-chewed for us. I think that's a real pity and I also believe that the day will come when audiences will long for a certain silence in film.

**Hjort:** The creation of the Danish Film Institute* in 1972 was a milestone in Danish film history. Indeed, from 1972 onwards virtually all Danish feature-length fictional films have involved state monies administered by the Danish Film Institute. The Film Act* that initially defined the mandate of the Film Institute was revised in 1982, 1989, and 1997. In 1982 a crucial clause was added which specified that 25 percent of the budget administered by the Danish Film Institute and National Film Board in support of the production and distribution of feature-length films and short films was to be reserved for films for children and adolescents. At first blush, the Danish Film Act, as revised in 1982, appears to create unusually favourable conditions for film-makers specialising in the relevant genre. Yet, you have on several occasions been critical of the funding arrangements in question. What, in your opinion, are the positive and negative features of the Act's provisions for youth films?

**Kragh-Jacobsen:** I think our Film Act is fantastic, and I think the 25 percent clause is a coup. The result is that we figure much more visibly on the children's and youth film map than we otherwise would have. The combination of that clause, a talent pool, a few Oscars, and a good film school is the reason why there's a certain international focus on Danish film. Our children's films and youth films win pretty much all the prizes. I think that our take on reality within the children and youth film genre is incredibly important, because we know what America produces in this respect. I don't, however, actually like the concept of children's film, because I'm sure that it keeps some adults from seeing the films in question. You'd never call *E.T.* a children's film; it's family entertainment, which just happens to sound pretty silly in Danish. The fact is, though, that people streamed to the cinemas in order to watch four small children chase around after a Martian. *E.T.* sold tons of tickets. Another example is Spielberg's *Empire of the Sun*, which features an outstanding performance by a child lead. 'Here's a new Danish children's film' may catch the attention of the single father who's eager to entertain the 11 year old daughter he sees only on week-ends. However, the concept in question puts any number of other adults off the film, because if they typically go to the cinema only twice a year, they're not going to opt for a children's film.

I don't happen to think that all of my films are children's films. I think it was a big mistake to promote *Emma's Shadow* as a children's film. It could easily have been classified as family entertainment. It was released around the same time as *Pelle the Conqueror* (*Pelle Erobreren*) which wasn't considered a children's story, although it had a child lead. *Emma's Shadow* then gets promoted as a children's film, and although it didn't do terribly at the box office, it certainly didn't draw the audience it should have. I think 100,000 people saw it, so my experience is that classifying a film as a children's film can have the effect of destroying the film's market. The term 'children's film' should apply to films with little poetic, educational, or exciting stories that are aimed at children who are eight years old and under. Eight year olds or six year olds also need cinematic experiences. I don't know what the better label would be. I think the Film Act should simply indicate that 25 percent of the money is to be spent on films with youthful themes that interest children, preferably with a child in the lead role, but that's really the only negative thing that comes to mind.

**Hjort:** In a discussion of your views and films, published in *Morgenavisen Jyllands-Posten* (September 1994), you were described as particularly interested in questions of national identity and culture. Per Callum, the author of the article, maintained that there's something undescribably Danish about your films. Do you think of your films as profoundly Danish?

**Kragh-Jacobsen:** It's absolutely true that I have a strong sense of Danish identity, but I don't think that I'm any more patriotic than eight out of the ten people you might meet on the streets here. I do feel very Danish, but in an open, accommodating way. I don't have any prejudicial attitudes towards foreigners, nor do I feel any hostility towards immigrants and refugees. On the contrary. I think we stand to gain from the recent wave of immigrants and refugees. In the long run these newcomers will invigorate our inbred Viking genes, which is fortunately something that has happened many times before. I do, however, believe that something called a 'Danish identity' exists. I become perfectly exuberant, for example, when I return to Denmark by ferry from some place in the South. Now, what kind of psychic feeling is that? How can I possibly account for it? For example, I think the Danish flag is beautiful. Today it's almost a heresy to raise the Danish flag. If you do you're stigmatised as a nationalist who believes that all foreigners should be thrown out of Denmark and that Denmark is for Danes only. I don't feel that way at all, but I think it's a pity if a certain sense of patriotism stamps you as belonging to the ultra-nationalistic right wing. I've included a number of Danish flags in my films. For example, there are Danish flags in *The Boys from St. Petri* and in *Rubber Tarzan*, where there's a scene with a cosy Danish lunch, because that's how I was raised. I become livid when I come across people who claim that Denmark is just a business operation. It's a hell of a lot more than that. It's where my roots are, it's where I resonate with others and feel a sense of community. This has to do with the effects of the climate, with the joy that certain landscapes, or cities, or buildings inspire in us, with the knowledge that our ancestors lived here and are part of our history, with the pleasure we take in the Danish language. Denmark is not just a business operation.

**Hjort:** A director like Bille August has talked a lot about Nordic identity. He's claimed, for example, that the music in *Pelle the Conqueror* is very Nordic. Is the concept of a Nordic identity important as far as you're concerned?

**Kragh-Jacobsen:** Absolutely, and I wish the five Nordic swans flew together more, but it's hard to say whether my films have a specifically Nordic tone. For example, *The Island on Bird Street* is simply a Søren Kragh-Jacobsen film. There's nothing the least bit Nordic about it, but I suppose *The Boys from St. Petri*, which is about the emergence of the resistance movement, has a Nordic tone. However, it's not a concept with which I've worked consciously. I don't think I've really produced realism, with the exception of

*Shower of Gold* and *Wanna See My Beautiful Navel?*, and the idea of a Nordic tone is probably fairly intimately related to realism. *Rubber Tarzan* is a fantasy, a fairytale. *Thunderbirds* is a series of moods and a description of two people's psychic condition. *Emma's Shadow* involves a kind of oblique realism and the same is true of *Mifune*. The universes in question here have all been tilted, by as little, perhaps, as eight degrees, but just enough to make them interesting. However, if the public wants to interpret my films as really Nordic, that's fine by me.

**Hjort:** In earlier interviews you've made a number of anti-American pronouncements. I'm thinking, for example, of some of the statements you made in an interview with Peter Øvig Knudsen (*Information*, January 1993). You claimed that the Danish nation is rather pathetic in the sense that Danes have a tendency passively to consume and accept whatever films are readily available. You went on to say that Danes 'are being inundated with American productions, with American attitudes that are more vulgar and less generous than those of Danes.' Danish film-makers, you suggested, should be providing a specifically Danish alternative to Hollywood. What, in your mind, would the defining features of such alternative film-making in a Danish vein be? Is it a matter of privileging the Danish language, Danish values, a certain cinematic style, what Christian Braad Thomsen calls a 'Danish cinematic realism'?

**Kragh-Jacobsen:** Yes, I think the Danish language is important, given that we're talking about a national film production and a language spoken by only five million people. One of the reasons we have a system of state support is to ensure that Danes hear their own language in films, and that's of course one of the reasons why Danes are fond of Danish films. However, Danes barely experience the American language as foreign any more. If I want to take my sons to the cinema, I encounter a certain resistance if I suggest that there's a really good Italian film showing or that we should go to see a Russian film, although they actually like all kinds of films. They have trouble with that kind of suggestion because to them these are foreign films. They don't think of *The Matrix* as a foreign film, and I understand why. The persistence of an American star system is enviable. We've, of course, completely exterminated stars in Europe. We had stars in Denmark until 1960 and those people really sold tickets. Today it's only Erik Clausen and a handful of actors who can draw people to the cinemas.

What bothers me the most about certain big American productions is the total absence of morality. There I sit having been persuaded to see *Independence Day*; and my sons think that having me along is just terrible. I tell them that it's not a film, but a stupid carrousel ride. Why should we compete with that? What's it actually about? It's about shooting aliens. It's completely pointless. I used to read a lot of science fiction when I was younger and I know where they stole most of the story – from a Robert Heinlein story, which is actually quite beautiful, but they've completely stripped Heinlein's story of morality and content. Why should we compete with that? Why not make something that's deliciously funny instead? Why don't we have a kind of Woody Allen tone here? We have the same milieu. The fact is that Danish directors don't make films about what happens behind the four walls of the home, but that's often precisely where the conflicts in Denmark are hidden. We live in a country where both parents work all the time and where the children are cared for here, there and everywhere. That makes for a lot of humorous and conflictual material. When Lotte Svendsen suddenly makes *Royal Blues* it's a complete revelation.

**Hjort:** *The Island on Bird Street* departs significantly from your earlier films. Whereas the latter are rooted in national contexts and traditions, *The Island on Bird Street* is an English-language, international co-production based on a novel by Uri Orlev. In some respects *The Island on Bird Street* is to Søren Kragh-Jacobsen what *House of the Spirits* (*Åndernes hus*) is to Bille August. If films such as *The Island on Bird Street* and *House of the Spirits* can be described as instances of the internationalisation of Danish film, then what is your view of the process in question? What are the negative and positive features of internationalisation?

**Kragh-Jacobsen:** I don't see this as internationalisation at all. The question has been put to me before and I usually compare the film-makers' situation to the world of sports. It's considered completely acceptable for our talented football players to play football in England. The implicit assumption, however, is that film-makers betray their art and somehow lose their integrity when they leave the country and make an English-language film. I think of that kind of project as something to be undertaken along the way, but I wouldn't dream of making a Danish story in English in Denmark. In *The Island on Bird Street* I'm dealing with a traditional genre. There are at least a hundred films about the Second World War in English. I'd actually have preferred to have made the film in Polish, but it's probably a good thing that I encountered resistance to that idea, because my Polish isn't what it used to be. When some of us venture beyond the country's borders, it's because we find it amusing and instructive to be part of the 'game'. There's not a lot of money available here in Denmark and you can't count on getting money from the Danish Film Institute all the time, so you have to try other things in order to maintain your skills and earn your keep. However, the fact that the Institute is somewhat involved in, and generally supports, our efforts at European production is, I believe, a good investment, because we undeniably return wiser. I think the Danish Film Institute's current stance is the right one, but obviously Danish-language film production should have the highest priority.

**Hjort:** In an interview published in *Kristeligt Dagblad* (May 1995) you claimed that all of your films essentially retell one and the same story. The message in each case, you said, is the one articulated by the dockworker, Ole, in *Rubber Tarzan* as he attempts to plant a grain of confidence in the bullied child, Ivan: 'You're surely good at something. You just have to figure out what it is.' Other similarities among your films could be easily identified. For example, it's frequently a matter of a young, neglected child turning away from the natural parents who have little or no understanding of the child's needs. The neglected child replaces the natural parents with a surrogate parent who typically belongs to a lower social class. In *Rubber Tarzan*, for example, Ivan frees himself from his father's infantile, macho fantasies by befriending the dockworker, Ole. In *Emma's Shadow*,

Emma moves in with the social outcast, Malthe, after having engineered her own abduction in a desperate attempt to awaken her distracted, wealthy parents to her existence. The message is indeed constant here and it would appear to be in some sense a political one. Are concepts of class central to the vision you wish to project through your films and is this vision in any way linked to the kinds of social and political traditions that are valued highly in Denmark?

**Kragh-Jacobsen:** It's absolutely true that I've frequently told the same story. I like stories about 'secondary characters' – stories about the little guy's victory. It may ultimately be a melancholic victory, but at least the person is able to move on. I think it's a beautiful theme, and I have no intention of setting it aside. Every time I sit down in front of the computer and say to myself 'now you're going to do something different', I inevitably end up grappling with the same issue. I don't know why. It may be that that's just how I'm wired. Without drawing any comparisons, it's worth pointing out that Monet painted a hell of a lot of water lilies, and I believe they got better every time. I like the theme and I'm very interested in the concept of charity. If there isn't room for a little sympathy amidst all our wealth then I think the humanistic foundation underwriting our democracy has disappeared. It may well be that there's some political thinking buried in the scripts. When I was invited to participate in the Dogme project, I was convinced that I'd do something completely different, something wildly experimental, but there it was again as soon as my pencil hit the paper. Lars and I had talked quite a bit about rekindling the desire to make films again; I was pretty burnt out after *The Island on Bird Street*, so I must say that it was that phrase 'rekindle the desire to make films' that kept my pencil glued to the page, for I did experience an overwhelming desire to make *Mifune* as the story started to emerge. That it ended up being 'my' theme again may, I suppose, have something to do with the fact that I'm a fairly faithful soul.

**Hjort:** The production history of *The Island on Bird Street* is riddled with strife that highlights the difficulties of intercultural film-making. I'm thinking, for example, of the controversy surrounding the film's ending. As I understand it, your feeling throughout was that your American producers were forcing you to cater to their conception of American audiences. How do you feel about the whole question of audiences? One could argue that film-making in a small nation-state such as Denmark to a certain extent must be a matter of devising strategies of multiple address. That is, the viability of minor cinemas seems to be linked to the possibility of reaching multiple audiences. Do you keep national or international audiences clearly in mind when you elaborate your scripts and shoot your films?

**Kragh-Jacobsen:** Yes, I certainly do. I think all directors do, but I don't cater to the audience. There's something called a collective education of the audience, and I think about that a lot. In that respect I think American film is in the process of completely destroying people's taste. For example, a happy ending is almost a requirement at this point. But why? My greatest cinematic experiences involve unhappy endings. A film like *Death in Venice* (*Morte a Venezia*) is fantastic. An American film like *Love Story* didn't have a happy ending, but it was nonetheless a huge box-office success. And what about *Seven*? I don't understand the happy ending requirement. I don't think you can have a happy ending in a film that ends in 1943, because the two worst years of the war are yet to come. Who's to say that they survive? You can train a nation to believe that everything should have a happy ending now, but I'm not interested in being part of that. I think there should be many more colours on the palette, and I think most members of the audience would agree if they were allowed to express their views.

*The Island on Bird Street* admittedly found a pathetically small audience in Denmark, but it was also released at the wrong time. Also, it's not clear that its topic is of interest to very many people any more. However, two million people saw it on TV. It will be shown three times in all, so people will end up seeing it, so I'm glad I insisted on that ending, even if the Americans did change it immediately. There's a version that's ten minutes shorter, that is, a version that ensures that you never experience that desperate atmosphere of death in which the loneliness really stings, but in every great experience there's a moment of boredom, so I've consciously toned the film down, both at the level of sound and image, so that the viewer really feels the boy's loneliness. This is at odds with the times, for the tendency today is to provide the audience with facile entertainment, accompanied from beginning to end with loud film music, and then to send it on its way. Who the hell knows what the audience really wants? The claim is that they want films with a broad appeal, but what's that and why should we suddenly have to think in terms of breadth? *Breaking the Waves* and *The Celebration* (*Festen*) are two of the most successful films in recent times; they've sold to the tune of millions worldwide. Yet, in a traditional sense they're anything but films with a broad appeal. That's why I always say that narrowness can be a form of breadth.

**Bondebjerg:** You've recently enjoyed a great deal of success in connection with your involvement in the Dogme project, for *Mifune* has been acclaimed internationally. Have *Mifune* and the whole Dogme concept allowed you to explore a new type of story and a new visual style, or would you be inclined to see continuities between *Mifune* and your earlier films?

**Kragh-Jacobsen:** As I said earlier, I can't get around my heart, which really steers me a lot, so I think of *Mifune* as a natural continuation of my earlier work, but I haven't become any worse at telling the same story, and I actually think it's very liberating to have joined the ranks of the adults, because it's so much easier to make films for adults than it is to make children's films. It's wonderful to work with professional actors. Suddenly you're not holding your life in your hands any more, because they really know their stuff. I've accumulated quite a bit of experience over the years and I've now acquired some new instruments in the form of professional actors, so I look forward to playing a lot of 'concerts' in the many years to come.

# Bille August

## 1948–

Bille August was trained as a cinematographer and photographer at Christer Strömholm's photography school in Stockholm where he focussed on documentary film-making and news photography. He further pursued his training as a cinematographer at the National Film School of Denmark* from 1971–73. Prior to establishing himself as a film director in 1978, August worked as a cameraman on both Danish and Swedish short film, documentary, and feature productions. August's background as a cinematographer and news photographer is clearly evident in his films, especially in the Danish and Nordic productions which aim at psychological authenticity and realism. In his early film and TV productions, which include *In My Life* (*Honning måne*, 1978) and *Maj* (1982), August focusses on family life, the fate of women, and alienation in a modern, welfare society. In *Zappa* (1983), *Twist and Shout* (*Tro, håb og kærlighed*, 1984) and *In the*

*Bille August. [Photo: Rolf Konow]*

*World of Buster* (*Busters verden*, 1984), which are all based on novels by Bjarne Reuter, the emphasis shifts to the lives of children and adolescents. These films all provide a critical take on the psychological and social mechanisms governing the relations among the young people in question and their families more generally. August's international breakthrough came with *Pelle the Conqueror* (*Pelle Erobreren*, 1987). This adaptation of the canonised novel by Martin Andersen Nexø won both the *Palmes d'or* at Cannes and the Oscar for Best Foreign Film. The film is at once a social and historical epic about the transition from a feudal, agrarian society to the beginnings of a modern, industrial society, and a moving psychological portrait of a young boy and his father. After this major breakthrough August pursued an increasingly international career involving both Nordic and English-language productions. The script for August's film and TV series, *The Best Intentions* (*Den goda viljan*, 1992), was written by Ingmar Bergman and focusses on a key period in the lives of Bergman's parents. *The Best Intentions* masterfully explores the passionate relationship between two people with deeply different temperaments while convincingly evoking a certain period in Nordic history. This film was awarded the

*Palmes d'or* at Cannes in 1992 and was followed by another adaptation in 1996, *Jerusalem*, which is based on a novel by Selma Lagerlöf and takes place in Dalarne in Sweden around the turn of the century. The focus here is on inter- and intra-familial feuding as well as on a deep conflict between love and religion. August subsequently turned to the adaptation of modern best-sellers, starting with Isabel Allende's *House of the Spirits*. The film appeared in 1993 and was followed by August's adaptation of Peter Høeg's international best-seller, *Smilla's Feeling for Snow (Frøken Smillas fornemmelse for sne)* in 1997. Both films feature a star-studded cast, as does August's most recent film (1998), which is an adaptation of Victor Hugo's literary classic, *Les Misérables*.

## Feature films
1978, *In My Life (Honning måne)*
1983, *Zappa*
1984, *In the World of Buster (Busters verden)*
1984, *Twist and Shout (Tro, håb og kærlighed)*
1987, *Pelle the Conqueror (Pelle Erobreren)*
1992, *The Best Intentions (Den goda viljan)*
1993, *House of the Spirits (Åndernes hus)*
1996, *Jerusalem*
1997, *Smilla's Feeling for Snow (Frøken Smillas fornemmelse for sne)*
1998, *Les Misérables*

## Short films
1969, *The Wrestling Club (Bryderklubben)*
1970, *The Excursion (Udflugten)*
1975, *Kim G. – A Cyclist on the Ordrup Track (Kim G. – en cykelrytter på Ordrupbanen)*
1981, *The Heart of Gold (Guldhjertet)*

## TV productions
1978, *A Couple of Days with Magnus (Et par dage med Magnus)*
1980, *It's a Wide, Wide World (Verden er så stor, så stor)*
1982, *Maj*
1984, *The World of Buster (Busters verden, episodes 1–6)*
1991, *The Best Intentions (Den goda viljan, episodes 1–4)*
1992, *The Young Indiana Jones Chronicles (two episodes)*
1996, *Jerusalem (episodes 1–4)*

**Hjort:** Critics have been inclined to divide your career into at least two stages. Your early films make use of a realist aesthetic and focus predominantly on dysfunctional family dynamics in an emerging Danish welfare state. *Pelle the Conqueror* marks the turn towards earlier historical settings, epic narratives and mythical frameworks. *Pelle the Conqueror* is also the first in a series of binational or multinational co-productions. What remains constant throughout your career, however, is the asceticism and minimalism of your narrative approach. You've collaborated extensively with the legendary editor,

Janus Billeskov Jansen, who uses the image of an iceberg to describe your characteristic aesthetic. The idea is that in your films the image depicts only part of what must be inferred. Could you talk a little about what, for you, is at stake in this art of understatement that has become one of your trademarks?

**August:** It's true that several of my earlier films focus on people living in modern times and provide a take on what it means to be human in a society such as ours, whereas you might say that my later films tend to be set in various historical milieus. There's no particular reason for this. Coincidence has always played a crucial role. It's always the psychological dimension that draws me to a story. Whether the story takes place in the stone age, some Viking milieu, modern times or outer space is completely irrelevant as far as I'm concerned. What determines whether I throw myself into something is the actual chamber play, the story's inner drama or core. There's nothing more dramatic, in my view, than the psychology that can exist between people. As far as I'm concerned, action films are deadly boring. When I think about a film and start working on a story, I never start with the outer frame; the form is for me mere packaging. It's a way of enhancing and strengthening the inner dramatic conflicts. Once I've identified the film's psychological core and source of suspense, I start to dress up my story with the elements of form: a cinematographic form, a scenographic form and an editing style, all of which help to create a certain rhythm and together constitute a specific mode of narrative expression. A couple of times I've inverted the order somewhat. I would start with some visual idea and then try to force the psychological drama into that frame, but this always involved poor judgement on my part and has never worked for me. The process has to unfold in the opposite direction.

As for the minimalism, it's clear that once I've figured out what the dramatic conflict is about and have developed some sense of the appropriate mode of cinematic expression, I begin to aim at a certain balance that involves being very aware of the fact that I'm communicating with an audience. I do, of course, think about how best to express myself clearly, how best to make myself heard. It makes sense here to speak of a kind of ethics, an ethics of manipulation, where it's a matter of deciding how forcefully you should express yourself. When is a scene honest and organic and dramatic? At what point do you become melodramatic? When are the audience's true feelings being prompted? At what point are you being seductive or quite simply banal or vulgar? More generally, when does the magic trick work? I've tried to favour an approach that involves respecting the audience with which I'm communicating. I think that on the whole members of the audience are very well educated when it comes to film. They're so used to visual communication and their powers of comprehension are highly developed as far as cinematic expression is concerned. That's why I try to work with a mode of expression that is very subtle. I prefer to be suggestive rather than to spell things out.

**Hjort:** In previous interviews you've stressed the importance you attribute to notions of authenticity and purity, particularly in relation to acting. Actors who've worked closely with you have invariably claimed that you have a special ability to foster the kind of tranquillity and trust that leads to more authentic acting. How, exactly, do you achieve the kind of purity of expression that characterises, for example, Mads Bugge Andersen's performance as Buster in *The World of Buster* or Pernilla August's performance as Karin in *Jerusalem*?

**August:** I think that the work involving the actors, or the work involved in making a character or role believable, already begins during the process of script writing. It then intensifies once the script exists and it's a matter of beginning to think very concretely about a specific actor. I begin to fashion an image of very specific kinds of actors very early on inasmuch as I'm also involved in the script writing process. 'What do these people look like?' 'Which established actors could embody this role?' These are the kinds of questions I ask myself. In the case of *Pelle the Conqueror*, I wrote the role for Max von Sydow, although I had no idea whatsoever whether he'd even be interested in it. I couldn't think of any other actor in Scandinavia capable of playing that role, so I had Max von Sydow in mind constantly, and fortunately he wanted to play the part. If I don't have a specific actor in mind while writing, then I start very early on to think about who could possibly play the role in question, especially if it requires an adult. If it's a matter of finding a child, it's especially important to have some kind of image in mind of the character in question, because you have to comb various schools and institutions, and for that matter, streets and alleyways, in order to find the right person.

The actor and I constantly discuss the role in very, very concrete terms, from our earliest conversations to the more detailed discussions of various scenes with regard to something as apparently superficial as make-up and in the context of the dress rehearsals. Suddenly the role becomes very, very tangible and very concrete, and what you're really talking about in those situations is the psychology of the character whom you're beginning to understand. Another important stage in the process is the arranging of reading rehearsals with the actors. I never do full-fledged rehearsals, but I think the reading rehearsals are important. This is when we discuss the psychology of the various roles and the dramatic conflict more generally. Also, this is the actors' chance to try out their lines. We read through the script, so that I can hear what the various lines sound like. At that point I can still work on them and even rewrite them. The actors can also make suggestions. It may be a matter of proposing to rephrase a line so that it corresponds better to the nature of the role. I'm very open to that sort of thing, but above all else, these reading sessions provide an excellent opportunity for the actors and I to discuss the characters' reasons for reacting as they do and for saying what they say. You can basically discuss the deeper causes of, as well as the more immediate reasons for the characters' actions. On those occasions when I didn't organise these sessions, I had the unpleasant experience (on the first day of shooting) of facing an actor whose sense of her role was completely different from my own. You then have to spend many a precious hour trying to pull the person in a completely different direction while a film crew of some 100 people simply waits and waits. I make sure the actors know how they're to understand and play their roles well before we begin shooting, and I do this precisely in order to avoid the kind of situation I just described, as well as to make the work of preparing a given role easier and more efficient for the actor. So the reading rehearsals are very important. In Hollywood it's not uncommon to rehearse entire scenes for as long as three to four weeks. I never do that, however, because I feel that a lot of the spontaneity evaporates. The scenes end up being so over-rehearsed that you get only a mere reproduction on the actual day of shooting. I like to reserve the spontaneity for the camera, and I also like the kind of openness and vulnerability that characterises actors on the set when they know they haven't yet tried fully to act a given scene. I also have a particular way of dealing with unusually difficult scenes, scenes that may, for example, be decisive for a given character in the story. I always try to do these shots early in the morning, first thing, because I want to capture that naked, unspoiled look. If there's a scene like that, I usually start with a close up of the relevant actor at nine o'clock in the morning, first thing. I tend to organise the day around the scenes with a lot of character work, and I like to do the longer, more technical shots that don't require as much acting later on in the day.

**Hjort:** You're a great lover of music and the musical elements in your films are chosen or composed with great care. I am thinking, for example, of the fact that you asked Stefan Nilsson to compose properly Nordic music for *Pelle the Conqueror* and *The Best Intentions*. Could you describe some of the most basic principles governing your thinking about music in film?

**August:** Film music is a very important cinematic element as far as I'm concerned, because film music can stimulate and support a feeling; it can enhance a feeling to the point of perfection if it's chosen with care and is properly integrated into the film. If, on the other hand, it is used poorly, then film music can totally destroy a scene. You see that a lot in American films, where there's wall-to-wall music throughout the entire film, because the producers don't believe the members of the audience are capable of thinking an independent thought or having an independent emotional experience, but instead need to be led by the hand and stimulated all the way through. However, on numerous occasions I've realised that the composers I was working with simply didn't understand the mode of expression or psychology relevant to the story or scene in question. They simply got it wrong and couldn't get it right, so we finally had to replace them. Film music is a very special and tricky thing and requires a certain amount of experience, training and discipline on the part of the composer. Take, for example, any scene from *The Best Intentions*, which Ingmar Bergman presumably has written with great precision and conviction, and in all likelihood also with a great deal of subtlety. In that kind of context, the composer needs a good deal of humility if he's to get the tone right. If, however, it's used properly, then film music can, as I said, help to enrich a scene, because music, much like film, has that special ability to trick our intellect and to speak directly to our feelings. That's what's so unique about music and that's why it's so important that it be 100 percent right.

My most recent Scandinavian films are the result of my collaboration with Stefan Nilsson. I chose to work with Stefan because he's the composer who best understands that specifically Nordic mode of expression. I've talked at great length with Stefan about what it is that makes our Nordic music so special. He himself is from Northern Sweden and he says that for him – just as for many great Nordic composers – the Nordic spectrum of sounds is influenced by the migratory birds that are a central part of Nordic nature and the very special sounds that they make, which frequently involve a minor key. I think there's some truth to this. Nordic music is very, very special, and I think you have to have been born and raised here, to have experienced the very special atmosphere that exists in the Northern countries, if you're to understand what it's all about. I think that Stefan has a profound sense of all this, but as soon as he starts to compose in a more international vein, to write Hollywood-style music, things go completely wrong for him. His strengths lie where his roots are.

**Hjort:** You wrote the script for *In My Life* yourself and you collaborated with Bjarne Reuter on the scripts for *Zappa* and *Twist and Shout*, both of which are adaptations of novels by Reuter. You wrote the script for *Pelle the Conqueror* and a Danish script for *House of the Spirits*, which you then had translated into English. You also produced the remarkable script for the adaptation of Selma Lagerlöf's award-winning novel, *Jerusalem*. *Smilla's Feeling for Snow*, on the other hand, represents a real departure from your standard practices, for in this film use was made of a series of professional script-writers. What we have here, of course, is a contrast between European and North American film-making traditions. What, at this point, is your view of the relative strengths and weaknesses of these two, quite different approaches?

**August:** Most directors nearly always make the same film, in one way or another. You seek out the same topics, even when it's a matter of different stories and styles of work. You can, of course, explore these topics in different ways, sometimes with and sometimes without a literary text as a starting point. I should begin by pointing out that I don't at all subscribe to the idea that directors necessarily should write their own original scripts. As far as I'm concerned it's irrelevant whether a script is based on a dream, a real event, a poem, pure fantasy or a literary work. What matters is being able to produce a good film. In the case of *Smilla's Feeling for Snow* I had enormous difficulties, for the first time in my career, in trying to extrapolate a decent script from the literary text. What we discovered as we were writing the script, but also while we were shooting, is that Smilla actually is a literary condition. Unfortunately, I discovered this too late, and the train had already left the station at that point, so I couldn't very well get off. The crime story's entire plot – which is about a deadly parasite or worm and about how a meteor brings this deadly arctic worm back to life – is a literary condition too. Since the film had to make not only Smilla but the entire plot concrete, we suddenly discovered just how serious the problems we were facing were, quite simply because film is so damned concrete compared with literature. It was actually the first time I'd ever come across a literary work that simply couldn't be adapted to the screen, and that was quite a shock.

I love being involved in the writing process, and I always try to be part of it to the extent that that's possible. I have a lot of colleagues, especially abroad, who are extraordinary directors, but have neither the ability nor the desire to write their own scripts. They're very good, on the other hand, at collaborating with script writers. There's a special tradition in Europe that creates the expectation that a director also should be able to write scripts himself, but as I said earlier, I think that it's completely irrelevant who writes the script, and I don't think that a film is a greater work of art just because it's a piece of auteur work created by a script writer and director who are one and the same person. Sometimes that kind of fusion is interesting and sometimes it actually works, but it fails just as frequently as it succeeds. I think we've inherited that tradition from many of the old masters such as Bergman and Fellini, people who really mastered both tasks. However, it's not every director who's as good a writer as Bergman is, or who has as interesting a background as he has. That's why I think it's important to get beyond that kind of issue, so that you can team up with a script writer, should that be necessary. In Hollywood there's a huge team of script writers, and they all regard script-writing as a profession, as a good, solid job. My sense is that in Europe the attitude is that good authors don't write scripts because they write books. I don't know whether there's a certain amount of snobbism involved here, or whether writers simply feel that they can maintain control over their writing if they write books. Nobody, other than the author, can make any major changes to a book, whereas any number of people can change a film script significantly. In the US, however, the profession of script writer is very much respected, and there are a lot of truly outstanding script writers. Part of the explanation is, of course, that good Hollywood script writers get paid enormous amounts of money for their work and therefore feel valorised and respected. That's probably the big difference between Europe and the US, although this is changing. Film schools in various places in Europe now offer a script-writing option. That is, there's an awareness now of the fact that a good film presupposes a good script.

**Bondebjerg:** Your first feature film, *In My Life*, provides a visually minimalistic, but psychologically very powerful portrait of two young people living in Denmark in the 1970s. You have on previous occasions claimed that the film draws on your own experience of mind-numbing factory work and your encounter with factory workers. The film is not an instance of social realism, nor does it convey an explicit social critique. Would you nonetheless say that the film contains a political and social message which is inspired by the wave of socially committed films that was part of Danish film culture in the 1970s?

**August:** I've been very intent on *not* making political films, because I think 'politically correct' films are one-dimensional, and oftentimes simplistic and lacking in nuance. The idea was to create an emotional portrait of two people, two individuals, which would comment indirectly on our welfare society. As you already mentioned, part of the film's prehistory has to do with the fact that I worked in a lot of different factories during my years in Sweden because I needed money to live on and with which to finance my studies. What I simply could never understand was how the people I met could stand to spend their lives on something so meaningless, and I found myself wondering whether this was really the point of our entire welfare society. The lot of the working class had improved over the years and this class had gained access to certain goods, to the point where it basically became part of the middle class, and social democracy had itself made it possible for workers to have a say in the development of society more generally, but the emphasis throughout had been uniquely on material goods, and there was a high price to be paid for this. Whereas workers previously had been involved in somewhat meaningful work involving genuine skills, they were now reduced to mere support mechanisms, to machines. That was basically what I wanted to get across. I didn't understand how people could stand to live a life that involved spending eight hours on some totally meaningless job, at a conveyor belt, for example, in order then to spend the rest of the day at home firmly planted in front of some bovine TV program. I then discovered that the whole set-up was governed by expectations about the future. Perhaps you'd have plans for the week-end and then when the week-end turned out to be a lot less successful than you'd anticipated, then you could still hope for a good vacation. The future was always full of promise. The point apparently was that expectations about the future were much more important than the present itself. It was never a matter of living here and now. Instead dreams were constantly used as a means of escaping from the present. I think the film provides a critical and to some extent melancholic commentary on those kinds of attitudes. By the way, I don't think Danish society has changed one iota.

**Bondebjerg:** Your debut did very nicely in box office terms and sold almost 110,000 tickets. *In My Life* was also praised highly by critics. It won a Bodil* prize for Best Danish Film of 1978 and was the occasion for Kirsten Olesen's cinematic breakthrough. Indeed Kirsten Olesen and Grethe Holmer both won Bodils for their performances, the former as Best Female Lead and the latter as Best Supporting Actress. Nonetheless, five years would go by before you'd make another feature film (*Zappa*, 1983). In the intervening years you made a number of very fine, realistic films for TV. Of your earliest films, *Zappa* stands out somewhat in that it is characterised by dramatic conflict, a spectacular cinematic language and rather violent scenes (including, for example, the one in which there's a settling of accounts between Bjørn and Steen). You yourself have mentioned that the film was intended to depict a 'fascist microcosm'. *Twist and Shout* also seems to be governed by a more intense and pronounced dramaturgical drive than your earlier films. Were these two films a conscious attempt to get beyond a more descriptive and episodic realism and to explore a more dramatic type of narrative film, or do the differences in question have to do primarily with the nature of the films' themes?

**August:** It's definitely true that *In My Life* and my TV films were much less intense dramaturgically and foregrounded the description of unremarkable lives. The stories in both *Zappa* and *Twist and Shout*, on the other hand, involved a powerful dramaturgical drive. Once again, this was simply something that I'd become interested in and that I felt like experimenting with. And if I could do that without sacrificing what was the essence of the story, namely the characterisation of those people, then I felt it might be worth trying. In the final analysis it's a matter of fiction, not documentary film-making, so the optimal mode of narration involves, after all, a strong, believable drama. Some of my favourite films are films that are able to embrace both these dimensions. For example, *One Flew Over the Cuckoo's Nest* includes an extremely violent drama as well as perfectly unique descriptions of certain psychological conditions, moods and characters. There are so many examples of films that are able to do both things, and these films are

*Björn Granath as Erik incites the other peasants to attack the overseer in* Pelle the Conqueror *(Pelle Erobreren). [Photo: Rolf Konow]*

psychologically sophisticated and subtle, but they also have dramas that are powerful, believable and properly balanced. I think that it's this combination of elements that helps to ensure that film can bring together quality, substance and good entertainment values. I think that my ultimate goal is to make films that deal with something worthwhile, that can involve viewers in a mood or psychological condition that may be new to them. I want my films to be able to take the viewers on a psychological journey which they've never been on before, but in the context of a drama or frame story that is in harmony with the basic chamber play. I think that's essentially what I'm always after. Those are the stories that intrigue me and that I want to film. If it's only a matter of packaging, then it makes no sense to me. Yet, at the same time, if you have nothing but descriptions of people, if there's no drama, then it doesn't work either. So the ideal, as far as I'm concerned, is a combination of these two things.

**Hjort:** You've always emphasised the popular nature of the cinematic medium, and your self-understanding throughout your career has been that you make films with a broad appeal. I take it, then, that it's a matter of appealing to viewers across the divides of class, gender and nation. I'm curious to know how, specifically, your self-understanding as a popular film-maker enters into your thinking about a given film. In the case of *Pelle the Conqueror*, for example, there's a marked difference between the film and the novel in terms of geographical references. Unlike the novel, the film is virtually devoid of specific geographical markers, which presumably makes it more readily accessible to international audiences. Which concepts or principles guide your attempts to reach a large number and wide range of viewers?

**August:** When I'm in the process of choosing my subject matter or of working on a script, or when I stand there on the set, I don't think about communicating with an audience. To opt for film, however, is to choose a mode of expression that is complicated, involves a lot of people and, most importantly perhaps, is extremely expensive. However, at the same time you also know that film is a medium that potentially allows you to reach a very big audience. At some level all directors are aware of these different elements although they may try to deny this, and if they happen to have forgotten about these basic features of film-making, they'll surely be reminded of them when it's time to finance their films. Besides the audience simply has to be part of your awareness during the editing phase, for example, when it's a matter of working very concretely with a particular conception, of trying to convey a given thought. You've worked through all these different elements and you've thought long and hard before choosing what for you is the right mode of expression, and to what end? In order to convey something to other people. That's why the audience necessarily is part of your consciousness during the film-making process. That simply has to be the case, otherwise I've understood nothing. You sit there carefully editing a scene and you constantly try to clarify your mode of expression, so that the person on the receiving end will be able to understand what you're trying to say. You structure your communication in a way that avoids misunderstanding and that ensures that your message gets across, but during your day-to-day work, you cannot, as I said, think about the viewer. That's when you have to follow your own intuitions, your own precise sense of how best to articulate the drama, and so on. At the same time, what's so wonderful about film, and which no other medium really has, is that if all your efforts are optimally executed, then you're able to reach a very, very large audience, not only nationally, but also internationally. However, I don't, for example, engage in a calculation that says that if I edit an image of a snowstorm into a given scene because there's nothing like that in Italy, then the film suddenly becomes international. That's not how it works. In the final analysis it's all about performing a magic trick, but for whom? An audience, of course.

**Hjort:** *Twist and Shout* was the last August film produced entirely with Danish monies, for the Danish-Swedish co-production, *Pelle the Conqueror* marks the beginning of a process of internationalisation. Indeed, all of your subsequent films are categorised as off-shore co-productions, with Danish monies providing only a fraction of the total budget. Although you at a certain point ceased to produce films that qualify as Danish according to the Film Law, Danish audiences gravitate towards 'foreign' films such as *House of the Spirits*, precisely because they perceive such works as an important instance of Danish national culture. *House of the Spirits* received mixed reviews, but was nonetheless seen by approximately one fifth of the entire Danish population (940,605 viewers). How would you describe the role played in Denmark by English-language films connected somehow to Denmark, such as *House of the Spirits* or *Smilla's Feeling for Snow*?

**August:** I've explored a number of different avenues in the course of my professional career because I'm essentially curious. I started out with *In My Life*, which provided a critical take on our welfare society. I then made those youth films, including *Zappa* and *Twist and Shout*, and then later there was *Pelle the Conqueror*. The prospect of making films that would allow me to explore non-Scandinavian topics and to work with actors who weren't part of the Scandinavian framework seemed like a challenge to me. I was deeply fascinated by *House of the Spirits*, by its story and dramaturgy, by its ephemeral, supernatural elements. I saw a challenge in the idea of entering that universe and somehow testing it. I was virtually able to finance the film in exactly the way that I wished, and what is more, any number of Hollywood stars were eager to be part of it. As a director I did, of course, find that flattering, although I've never thought in terms of the cash value of film stars, having always simply emphasised quality. But there was something very challenging about the whole project, and I found the thought of getting going on it very exciting and stimulating.

However, there was something I hadn't fully grasped, namely that my first film in English – and working in a different language is always different – was a production that involved my dealing with five or six major film stars simultaneously. I met with a number of colleagues in Hollywood who said that I was simply out of my mind, and that I'd break my neck on that project. Well I didn't, but it was admittedly a very big mouthful to chew, and I ended up spending a lot of time and energy taking care of all those stars, so much so that I perhaps forgot to tell the story. I simply made one compromise every single day, and if you're shooting over a 40 day period, then you end up with forty compromises. I'd like to underscore that none of this had anything to do with the actors. They were in no way difficult, on the contrary, they were extremely cooperative and wonderful to work with, but they required more attention than I perhaps could muster at that particular point in time. I think the film's real weakness has to do with my failure to deal properly with the supernatural elements, although they were precisely what I'd been fascinated by, what I'd felt was challenging about the whole project. However, there's no going back – it was a process and I undertook it. It's certainly not the film that I'm most proud of, but it's meant a lot to a great many people, not only here in Denmark, but throughout Scandinavia and also in South America. Until *Titanic* it was the most widely seen film ever in South America. So it must have some positive features. I think *House of the Spirits* has a good dramatic structure and is a fantastic saga that focusses on a specific family while also recounting aspects of a country's history. I also like the way the lives of the characters involved intertwine, the way in which fate plays a trick on them, the way in which everything somehow has a higher meaning.

**Hjort:** Isabel Allende had refused to sell the rights to *House of the Spirits* to any number of interested parties, but succumbed to you when you screened *Pelle the Conqueror* for her in a rented theatre in Los Angeles. One of her conditions was that the magical realism of the novel be played down in the film, for she perceived the magical realism in, for example, *The Incredible and Sad Story of Innocent Erendira and the Heartless Grandmother*, an adaptation of a chapter from Gabriel García Márquez' *One Hundred Years of Solitude* as deeply problematic. Your adaptation of Selma Lagerlöf's novel, *Jerusalem*, is challenging in similar ways, inasmuch as supernatural elements also play a key role in this film. Could you describe your cinematic approach to the supernatural in *Jerusalem* and *House of the Spirits*?

**August:** That's a fascinating comparison, but I hadn't really thought about this or understood the parallels in question until I met Isabel Allende. She pointed out that South American culture has a lot of supernatural elements, just as the narrative art of the Nordic countries does. This may have something to do with the fact that both these parts of the world are so peripherally located. In a sense these are the ends of the world, where people live very isolated lives. What is more, nature plays a very significant role in those lives. In the North there are those dramatic seasonal shifts: the long, cold winters, during which people are very isolated and develop strange thoughts about the supernatural, and the summers when exactly the opposite is true. I think that in the course of thousands of years, the accumulated experience of living on the margins and in so violent a natural setting has conditioned us to reflect on the role that demons and certain supernatural forces may play in our lives. It's incredibly difficult to describe supernatural forces cinematically. It's much easier to do so in a literary work, because you can move around in time and space. The cinematic medium represents much more of a challenge in that respect because film is always so damned concrete. If a person dies and reappears as a ghost in a cinematic context, then the very same actor actually has to reappear, but in a different capacity. The situation is quite different if it's a matter of reading, for example, that 'the person's presence suddenly could be felt in the room.' In film, on the other hand, the person has to kind of wander into the room, and you have to discuss whether she should be wearing shoes, which clothes she should be wearing, and so on. What should her hair be like? How exactly does she come into the room? Does she appear as a vision that suddenly becomes manifest, or does the door simply open, or what? You end up having the most absurd discussions about issues that you have to resolve and to which the audience ultimately will respond very powerfully if you fail to do so in a credible way. The only person in the history of the art of film who has managed to do this kind of thing in a more or less convincing way is Ingmar Bergman. What's needed in the final analysis is something quite different from what I came up with. I think you have to try to explore that no-man's land between dream and reality, what I call the third dimension, and this is precisely what Ingmar is able to do. He's virtually the only person who's been able to do this with any kind of facility. It's not a matter of simply saying, 'I'd like a ghost here', or 'The dead should come back as ghosts', or 'Certain supernatural elements play a key role here.' All of this has to be integrated into the chamber play in a completely different way if it's to work. The best example of this in the history of film is the last fifteen minutes of *Cries and Whispers* (*Viskningar och rop*). As far as I'm concerned those sequences are some of the greatest moments in the history of film art.

**Hjort:** *House of the Spirits* was perceived as controversial and received somewhat disappointing reviews. Some critics took issue with the extent to which the film foregrounds Esteban (Jeremy Irons), rather than Clara (Meryl Streep) or Ferula (Glenn Close). Other critics felt that you failed to provide a sufficiently developed social or historical context for the story, but some of the objections were more overtly political in their thrust. I'm thinking, of course, of the fact that Latin American actors in the US demonstrated against your casting for the film, which placed non-Latin Americans in the leading roles. I'm interested primarily in the criticisms having to do with issues of cultural identity. How do you respond to the objections having to do with social context and casting? Were your intentions, in this film, primarily to use historical materials for fictional purposes, or did you see yourself as shedding light on certain historical events?

**August:** For me the most fundamental element in *House of the Spirits* was once again the chamber play, that is, the family drama. What's important is the relationship between those six or seven people who are involved in the actual drama, and also the theme about how the past is likely to catch up with you if you at some point commit an offence against someone or hurt another person deeply. Often that very same person will come knocking on your door, and that's exactly what happens in *House of the Spirits*. Everything has consequences and a deeper meaning, no matter what happens in the lives of the different people. You can't run away from your past, and this is especially true of Esteban. He mistreats people terribly, not because he's evil, but because that's his way of life, but the past resurfaces and ends up having catastrophic consequences for his family. I think some of the descriptions of the characters are wonderful, as is the contrast between the male and female universes of Esteban and Clara. The story paints a very grand, beautiful and colourful picture of some people and their family life. It is, of course, situated in a larger political or historical framework, because Esteban is involved in politics and Blanca falls in love with a young revolutionary. The combination of these social and essentially human contrasts creates a very beautiful and powerful story. Although the story takes place in South America we decided very early on that the film would be in English. I wouldn't have been able to direct the film in Spanish and we hoped and believed that the audience would accept our use of English-speaking actors. That kind of thing has, after all, been done before in the history of film, with audiences accepting the relevant convention. I screen tested I don't know how many South American actors, who were living in the US, but I found that none of them was suitable or good enough for the role in question. It's important to point out that as far as I was concerned it didn't matter whether these actors were stars or not. I came from Scandinavia, where I was used to working with first class actors, Max von Sydow, Pernilla August, Ghita Nørby, and all the others I'd worked with. In that sense I was very spoiled and used to working with first-rate actors. And I simply transferred that background directly to *House of the Spirits*. That's the full story behind the star-studded cast. There are those who've criticised me for not working with actors who looked sufficiently South American, but I have to say that if you've ever been to Chile, then you'll know that the county is much more European than South American and very different from, for example, Brazil or Bolivia. In that respect Chile is quite unique in

South America. However, the real problem was – and this is what film critics in England and the US really had trouble with – that the father in the story had a British accent, the mother an East Coast American accent, and the daughter a West Coast American accent. In addition we'd decided that the actors who were to play the roles of the poor Hispanics should have a Hispanic accent, but Antonio Banderas had a Spanish Hispanic accent and his father was from Mexico and had a Mexican Spanish accent and the servant girl was from Puerto Rico. It was a mess. The film critics who were native English speakers were so irritated by this linguistic confusion that they had trouble finding the story believable.

**Hjort:** In your adaptation of Peter Høeg's award-winning novel entitled *Smilla's Feeling for Snow*, you ventured onto what, for you, was unexplored territory: the thriller genre. Interestingly, *Smilla's Feeling for Snow* belongs to the category of films with a number of unused, but cinematically complete endings. Could you describe some of the different endings you toyed with, and reconstruct your reasons for opting for the one we know?

**August:** When I first read Peter's book, I was deeply fascinated by Smilla and the entire plot, the mystique of it and then that woman who has the courage to stand in the way of corruption and take on the steely grey world of male domination in which she finds herself. I was intrigued by that whole mystical universe, in which there's a little boy who has become the victim of a cynicism that only Smilla can penetrate. Then there's Smilla's relation to the fact that she's from Greenland. She grew up, of course, in a world that has that totally unsentimental relation to life and death that is so typical of the Arctic. There were a lot of things in the book that I found deeply fascinating, including the way in which Høeg makes use of certain philosophical profundities that are integrated perfectly into the literary context and keep the reader from questioning the plausibility of the plot. If you're going to make a film, you have to clarify the linear story, you have to make up your mind what the plot is. What, in very concrete terms, is Smilla actually like as a person? What is it that she uncovers? You also suddenly find yourself facing the questions that Peter leaves unanswered in the book because they simply don't interest him. That's fine as far as his book is concerned, precisely because it's a literary condition. However, we *do* have to answer all those concrete questions, and the result is something that's strangely unresolved, a series of half-baked explanations that virtually end up becoming excuses for all the things that don't add up. That's why we produced a number of different endings, in a desperate attempt to come up with something that made some kind of sense. In that respect the difference between literature and film is simply enormous. In literature the plot doesn't have to be clarified for the reader in the same way that it does for the viewer of a film. We came up with a number of different solutions and the one we chose is probably the best one we could think of at that particular moment.

**Hjort:** You've frequently said that you perceive your films, particularly *Pelle the Conqueror* and *The Best Intentions*, as very Nordic. Indeed, it's your view that *Pelle the Conqueror*'s international success can be explained in part by the way in which Jörgen Persson's images convey the moving beauty and rhythms of a typically Nordic nature. The mesmerising beauty of the natural landscapes does indeed seem to play an important communicative role. A seductively beautiful natural landscape can be expected to appeal not only to Nordic audiences, but also to other national audiences, who may at times feel distanced from the Nordic narrative by certain culturally opaque elements. Could you talk a little about the way in which you and Persson approached the filming of nature in your most Nordic films?

**August:** As I said earlier, I see nature as a very, very important element in our entire Northern culture. I'm thinking again of the light that changes so frequently, so rapidly, and to such a great extent. The dramatic seasonal changes are also a significant part of our culture, in literature, music, and all our other modes of cultural expression, and they've clearly coloured us as a people and are an integral part of us. That's why it was important to me in *Pelle the Conqueror* and *The Best Intentions* – but also in *Jerusalem*, where nature plays a key role in the whole narrative – to try to capture nature and the characters' place in nature so that I could shed light on their psyches and the circumstances of their lives. I put a great deal of effort into this while we were actually shooting the films and I insisted on shooting during two different seasons. This did, of course, make the projects more expensive, but I also think that the narratives are more powerful as a result. What's also interesting is that when these films are shown outside of Scandinavia people really experience this aspect of the films as truly exotic. It's different and it's part of our culture, and people understand this. People elsewhere in the world are very intrigued by this dimension, precisely because it's so different and exotic.

**Hjort:** *The Best Intentions* brought you into close contact with Ingmar Bergman and is a film that explores aspects of this film-maker's family history. The film was a great success and won the *Palmes d'or* at Cannes. We've already talked about the Nordic dimension of your films, but the meaning of the term 'Nordic' is perhaps a little more ambiguous than we've been suggesting. As far as I recall the reception of *The Best Intentions* was quite different in Sweden and Denmark, in part because of the role that Bergman plays in Sweden. How would you describe the experience of working in Sweden and your relation to Bergman? Is he an example of a Nordic director to whom you look, or have looked, for inspiration? Have any other Nordic directors been important to you?

**August:** It's clear that when I was offered the opportunity to make *The Best Intentions*, I thought, 'So now I'm going to go to Sweden in order to make a film about Ingmar Bergman's parents that is written by Ingmar Bergman; this is an incredibly risky affair. I'll immediately be compared with Ingmar, and I'll never ever be able to live up to the expectation that this is supposed to be a new Ingmar Bergman film, because I can't possibly make an Ingmar Bergman film and that's not what I want to do anyway.' The fact is that I knew in advance that a number of the Swedish film critics would be sceptical of what I'd done, but no sooner had I articulated my fears than I went on to reject them as completely irrelevant. I was so deeply fascinated by the story and the script that I knew that I would throw myself into the project and make the film. However, more important from my point of view was the fact that I'd been assured, especially by Ingmar, that my hands were completely free. I didn't want to become a kind of puppet or Ingmar's assistant director. I certainly wasn't interested in that. At that point in my career I'd found my own mode of expression and I'd established myself as a director in my own right. During my very first meeting with Ingmar, before I'd even had a chance to bring any of this up, he said that he knew from experience just how important it was for a director to retain his integrity, and that he wanted me to know that he was the script writer and I was the director. It would be my film, should I decide to make it. He anticipated and answered my question in a way that was decisive for me. Then later when the film premiered there were, of course, certain critics who started analysing my relation to Ingmar Bergman. As I said, I knew that this was coming, and there it was.

**Hjort:** Would you care to talk about the origin of your Victor Hugo film, *Les Misérables*, and about the challenges involved in adapting a French literary classic to the screen?

**August:** *Les Misérables* came to me as a very concrete offer from Hollywood. I knew nothing about the earlier adaptations that had been made, nor had I seen the very famous musical. The only thing I knew was the novel, which I'd read many, many years ago, and which I'd almost forgotten. I read the story in a completely unprejudiced frame of mind, and I thought the script was very good and that the story was fantastic. It's about some of the things that are very important to me, and which I've taken up in many of my films. The story involves themes having to do with forgiveness and love, which are important topics for me, and I found that they were developed in this instance in a wonderful and very dramatic manner. The story shows, in powerful dramatic terms, that human beings can change and that love and forgiveness can triumph, and this is, of course, the main point. In the end the policeman captures Valjean and realises that sometimes a human being really can change. He encounters goodness and realises that love is the only hope for mankind. Without going into the details of the ending too much, I can say that it's about the power of love, and one of the most beautiful expressions of love is forgiveness. This is what drew me to the story, and not so much the historical milieu, which I felt was less important. I tried to foreground the psychological drama and the relations between the different characters in my version of the story, but at the same time I did of course situate these elements in a rather spectacular milieu.

# Jon Bang Carlsen

## 1950–

Jon Bang Carlsen graduated from the National Film School of Denmark* in 1976 and has since directed a wide range of features, short films and documentaries, as well as a number of TV productions. His earliest work is intimately connected with the alternative political theatre of the Chariot of the Sun (*Solvognen*)*, but his most significant cinematic contributions take the form of careful explorations of the boundary between fiction and fact. Indeed, the concept of staging facts occupies a central place in Bang Carlsen's cinematic production from 1977 onwards, and he has described the relevant documentary method in the metafilm entitled *How to Invent Reality* (1996). Bang Carlsen's documentary films are often visually and symbolically powerful staged portraits of marginal figures and milieus that involve compelling stories, be they about a farmer's wife of Grundtvigian inspiration, as in *Jenny* (1977), or rich, eccentric foreigners, as in *A Rich Man (En rig mand,*

Jon Bang Carlsen. [Photo: Rigmor Mydtskov]

*1979)*. From 1980 onwards Bang Carlsen has increasingly sought out international milieus and stories linked to the US, Germany, Ireland and South Africa, where he has remained faithful to his method and characteristic themes. Examples here are the portrait of an Irish bachelor in search of love, *It's Now or Never* (1996), or *Addicted to Solitude* (1999), which is set in South Africa and depicts the lives of two lonely white women rather than the culture of black South Africans. Bang Carlsen's features typically cultivate an experimental visual style; this is particularly true of his moving film about a widow's experience and intense recollection of love in *Next Stop, Paradise* (*Næste stop – Paradis*, 1980), as well as of his visually compelling depiction of a Danish village with its curious customs and stories in *Ophelia Comes to Town* (*Ofelia kommer til byen*, 1985). In *Baby Doll* (1988) Bang Carlsen probed the psychological depths of the thriller genre in a story centred around a mother's childhood traumas and post-natal depression. His most recent feature, *Carmen and Babyface* (1995) draws on his own memories of childhood and adolescence in the 1950s and 1960s and explores a young boy's experience of divorce and sudden displacement from Copenhagen to the provinces.

## Feature films

1977,  *A Fisherman from Hanstholm (En Fisker i Hanstholm)*
1980,  *Next Stop, Paradise (Næste stop – Paradis)*
1985,  *Ophelia Comes to Town (Ofelia kommer til byen)*
1988,  *Time Out*
1988,  *Baby Doll*
1995,  *Carmen and Babyface (Carmen og Babyface)*

## Short films and documentaries

1972,  *Retarded Sara (Åndssvage Sara)*
1974,  *White Man's Seed (Hvid mands sæd)*
1975,  *The Santa Claus Action (Dejlig er den himmel blå)*
1976,  *Sand and Roses (Sand og roser)*
1977,  *Jenny*
1979,  *A Rich Man (En rig mand)*
1981,  *Hotel of the Stars*
1984,  *The Phoenix Bird (Fugl Føniks)*
1986,  *Before the Guests Arrive (Før gæsterne kommer)*
1986,  *The 16 mm Film-Maker's Son (Smalfilmerens søn)*
1987,  *I First Wanted to Find the Truth (Jeg ville først finde sandheden)*
1990,  *I'm Also a Berliner (Ich bin auch ein Berliner)*
1991,  *Yesterday's Heroes*
1993,  *Life Should be Lived: Letters from a Mother (Livet vil leves – breve fra en mor)*
1996,  *It's Now or Never*
1996,  *How to Invent Reality*
1996,  *My Irish Diary (Min irske dagbog)*
1997,  *Strange Fruit*
1997,  *Through Irish Eyes*
1999,  *My African Diary (Min afrikanske dagbog)*
1999,  *Addicted to Solitude*
2000,  *Return to Sender*

## TV productions

1981,  *You're Beautiful: I Love You (Du er smuk – jeg elsker dig)*
1983,  *The Ticket Collector (Kontrolløren)*
1984,  *The Longest Day of the Year (Årets længste dag)*
1984,  *The Silent Struggle (Den tavse kamp)*
1984,  *The Goddess of Freedom (Frihedsgudinden)*
1990,  *And the Sun Goes Down Singing: A Portrait of Sussi and Leo*
         *(Og solen går syngende ned. Et portræt af Sussi og Leo)*
1992,  *Blinded (Blændet, episodes 1–4)*

**Bondebjerg:** Having completed the Danish equivalent of 'A levels', you moved from Jutland to Copenhagen. Here you quickly became involved in the alternative art scene, and especially with the artists' collective called 'Solvognen'. You made your first film in 1972, namely the documentary *Retarded Sara*, and in 1974–75 you produced the two films entitled *White Man's Seed* and *The Santa Claus Action* in collaboration with the Chariot of the Sun. During this period you were also accepted to the National Film School of Denmark. What drew you to film and how do you see your early films at this point? Do you see them as articulating aspects of your characteristic style or as the mere beginnings of a career that subsequently developed in other directions?

**Bang Carlsen:** I come from a family of artists, for my parents were trained at the Royal Academy of Art, one as a sculptor, the other as a painter, so I grew up studying paintings. Whereas other people would play picture lottery, we'd look at paintings and try to guess who'd painted them. I thus grew up with images and with the stories that the adults would tell while we drew, and in a way, I suppose, that's also a kind of film. In the beginning I drew and painted a lot, and I think that my cinematic style was very much defined by my drawings. *Retarded Sara* already had some of the elements that would come to characterise my later work. I'm thinking, more specifically, of some of the images of nature and some of the street scenes. What I found fascinating in that film was the idea of defining a visuality for someone who couldn't see the world clearly in any of the standard senses of the term. Sara couldn't move and could only react to the world with her face. The most interesting shots in that film are some very long, very static takes of that retarded child's facial expressions, her responses, for example, to the music of the Rolling Stones and the wind coming off the Sound. There we already have what has somehow always been characteristic of my work, that enormous visual patience. I like to leave the camera on. Viewers with short attention spans are unlikely to find my films interesting. I like long takes. I like to keep on looking at something long after most people would have looked away. I have a lot of time, typically much more than the members of my audience do.

Solvognen is in my mind a crucial part of my early career. It was the first group I'd ever really felt part of. *Solvognen* was my only experience of working collectively, because otherwise I've always worked on my own. The key thing about *Solvognen* was its rejection of standard theatre life. Our claim was that the most important stage was out in the streets, because that's where we could reach people in their daily lives and without their defences up. Our main achievement with *Solvognen* was that we forced society to participate in our plays. We constantly found ourselves in that no-man's land between our daily lives and our thoughts about quite different daily existences. Sometimes we used dramatic action to force society to react to these visions, thereby, at least in our mind, helping the relevant agents to make themselves visible. That strategy is a key feature of my documentary style, for I've always claimed that the truth isn't necessarily what's most truthful. A lie may be much more truthful than the plain truth. That's why *Solvognen* was such an incredible source of inspiration for me. One of the reasons I left *Solvognen*, aside from the fact that my politics were at odds with theirs at a certain point, was that I became tired of not being able to control the visual side of things.

**Bondebjerg:** In watching both your features and documentary films one is often struck by your tendency to seek out figures on the peripheries or margins, and this may be linked to your own personal background. Your work, it seems, draws on a strong attachment to a given region as well as on a powerful urge to travel and experience other parts of the world. Your films express a genuine attachment to Danish culture and nature, but also an openness towards other cultures. Is this regionally anchored cosmopolitanism precisely what allows you to articulate the soul, culture and nature of other destinies and worlds?

**Bang Carlsen:** It probably is. I grew up in Vedbæk. My parents were drop-outs from a rich family that owned a factory called 'Carlsen's Cliché Factory' as well as a press, 'Carlsen's Illustrations'. My maternal grandfather was President of the Western High Court. It was an upper-middle class family straight out of a Herman Bang novel, and my parents were drop-outs because in the bourgeois world in question wanting to become a sculptor was a bit like wanting to become a prostitute. I was about 11 when my parents got divorced in Vedbæk and my mother fled in panic to some village or other in the middle of Zealand. She later married a doctor from Mols, where we've always had a family cottage. I think of Mols as home.

One of my memories of Vedbæk concerns an American man who worked in my father's workshop. We were out on the Sound together in a rowboat and he and my father decided to tease me. They agreed that the American would buy me and take me to America. I swallowed this hook, line and sinker, and I remember feeling a little sad about having to leave my mother and father, because I was very fond of them, but what had been decided also seemed to me to be my fate. That was the way it was meant to be. I was meant somehow to leave. That's been the story of my life. I don't think I'll ever settle down, unfortunately. I'm almost 50 now and I still experience that powerful longing to leave, although when I do I also miss certain smells and human traits. My homesickness is very much tied to certain landscapes. I don't know whether there's an element of cultural longing here. I think it's striking, for example, that I've never been particularly inspired by Danish film. I respect many of my colleagues, but I've never belonged to any particular group. I have a much more intimate relation to Danish literature and painting, for they're part of my inner decor and I would never dream of redecorating. I just love classic Danish songs and music, Carl Nielsen, for example, and the works of Johannes V. Jensen, Herman Bang, Axel Sandemose and H.C. Andersen are always in my suitcase.

**Bondebjerg:** A film like *Life Should be Lived* is very concretely about your mother, but it's also about the relation between the local and the global. Yet, the film consists only of letters being read aloud, photographs and images of landscapes. As a result it somehow becomes a very extreme expression of something that is constant throughout your films, namely, your tendency to use landscapes as mental images.

**Bang Carlsen:** That's absolutely true. Tarkovsky is one of the few fellows I really like. When I first saw some of Tarkovsky's work I felt I'd somehow already experienced the relevant film. What I like about his films is that no matter where his camera goes, there's that sense of a blind man feeling his way through the world. You get the feeling that everything is meaningful. Tarkovsky doesn't have that quite common and rather arrogant stance towards the visual that involves construing the world as a mere backdrop for some more or less interesting action. In his films the world is also an actor. It's all about sense perception, and there's a religious element here, what you might call a third dimension, and it's when that element is brought into play that it becomes really interesting, I think, to make and see films.

**Bondebjerg:** I'd like us to talk about your cinematic method. Your short films and documentaries from 1977 to 1984 establish you as one of contemporary Danish cinema's most artistically independent directors. I'm thinking of *Jenny* (Bodil* as Best Documentary Film of 1977), *A Fisherman from Hanstholm, A Rich Man, Hotel of the Stars* and *The Phoenix Bird* (Bodil and Robert* as Best Documentary Film of 1984). Thematically these films are wide-ranging, for they tell a number of very Danish stories, set in Fjaltring and Hanstholm, as well as some American stories that take place in rather unusual milieus. Yet, the informed viewer immediately recognises these films as works by Jon Bang Carlsen, for they all have a particular style and aesthetic. You've described your particular method, which involves a staging of documentary material, in the meta-film, *How to Invent Reality*. How exactly did you develop the method in question in the course of the films I just mentioned?

**Bang Carlsen:** I developed it quite concretely during the preparatory work for my first film after film school, *Jenny*. I've always travelled a lot, hitch-hiked a lot, and I've always loved hiking. I've always been in the process of leaving my own milieu. I encountered Jenny's milieu on one of those trips, and her environment became my own milieu in my autobiographical films, in *Life Should be Lived*, for example. It's a very striking milieu in Denmark because it has an air of total innocence; green fields, a house, a dairy, a road sign, a church, and then suddenly, brutally, there's the sea. All this is intimately connected to what is probably my central dramatic point: the red brick house that just sits next to the road that leads towards the horizon. Nowhere is the sound of the passing of time louder, nowhere is the demand to use your life on something meaningful more intensely expressed than there. In Copenhagen there's always a lot of pseudo-activity going on, so I don't notice those huge mental cliffs beneath my feet when I'm there. That's why I'm so fond of the landscape of western Jutland, around Bovbjerg. That's where the clay earth and the dream of lasting prosperity reach as far as the ocean before the dream is exposed. That's where I met Jenny and she agreed to let me study her daily life, and my work method, which is actually very simple, grew out of that process. I moved in with her and her son, who ran the family farm, for about six weeks. I experienced the stillness of their daily lives and the nervousness underlying that stillness, their humour, and how the light came in through their windows. I soon became part of their reality, a strange man, who didn't leave like other guests would have, but who stayed on, even while they slept. In the end they barely said 'hello' to me. After all, there's no need to say 'hello' to the furniture. I'm not a journalist, nor am I a school teacher. I've never had any particular need to be more intelligent than the people in my films. I'm just a storyteller. There's some aspect of their lives that I can use to tell some story or other, a story that isn't necessarily about them, but the story in question does emerge out of my encounter with them. Once I was back in Copenhagen, I wrote out all the small sequences that had made an impression on me. They were just little things, but I felt like using them to mediate the story. Obviously I could never simply shoot the sequences in question as pure documentary footage. The very presence of a large film crew would have completely distorted them, so I had no choice but to stage the fleeting moments in question. In order to make a film that was my personal take on a reflection of part of the world incarnated in their persons, their daily lives and rituals, I had to have complete visual control over my images, so I wrote a very precise script which included every single edit, and then I simply shot the film. With time I've become much more audacious in the sense that I don't feel obliged to respect whatever they happen to do in their daily lives. If I think that their mental architecture makes x or y plausible, then I have them do it. I did that sort of thing already in *Jenny*. There's that dream sequence in which she gets up in the middle of the night and milks the lace on the table cloth in the living room that's reserved for special occasions. That's not something she normally does, but I think the activity falls within the scope of her character, and helps to define it.

In *Hotel of the Stars* the element of staging is pronounced in the sense that those people weren't even living in the hotel. I had a job as an extra in Scorsese's *Raging Bull*, where I appear as a policeman. During that month I found the people I needed and then I had them all move into that hotel. *Hotel of the Stars* is the biggest lie, or one of the most staged films, you can possibly imagine. *The Phoenix Bird* was another story. Before I can work with a figure, I have to find a common emotional landscape between myself and the person in question. James Jarrett, the right wing fighter and I understood each other perfectly. He has exactly the same fear of that red brick house and the road that never contracts in happiness or fear and which will survive us both. However, when it was time for me to shoot the film, when we showed up with the camera and he suddenly had to do something completely new, namely get in front of that camera, that big, weird, eyelid-less eye of publicity, he became completely passionate. It provoked a rush of adrenalin much like the one he'd become addicted to in Vietnam when he was set down behind enemy lines in the 'last light'. He constantly wanted to redo the film completely in order to intensify the rush. He wanted to dramatise things, so my job became somehow to restrain him in ways that were consonant with the script I'd written.

**Bondebjerg:** *A Rich Man* is in many ways a classic of staged documentary film-making. Indeed, it's probably the Bang Carlsen film that involves the most staging. You wrote out lines for the rich man, which he duly delivers in front of the camera. You've just said that having an emotional angle on your central figure is crucial. What was that angle in this case?

**Bang Carlsen:** It seems like the most staged of my films because he's the worst actor. *The Phoenix Bird* is just as staged, but James Jarrett is a good actor and he was able to absorb things and recreate them in front of the camera, so that the viewer had this sense of life unfolding itself. Jenny is also a good actor, but Hans Schmidt is not an actor. The reason *A Rich Man* seems so staged is that I never found a key to his character. He was the only problematic case, by the way, and I'm distanced from him throughout. There are hardly any close-ups of him and that's because in that film the best close-up is the long shot. That's the best close-up I can produce, because he's the rich man who can stage himself and his environment 100 percent, nothing in his world is coincidental. All his statements are deliberate, as are his signals, his requests, and so on. When I approach his face nothing new happens. What normally happens when you shoot a close-up simply doesn't occur. There's nothing that contradicts his utterance. The expression as a whole is completely unidimensional, he's completely in control. So close-ups were useless. I couldn't get close to him emotionally. There were no cracks, and as a result the film has a certain distanced quality which I think is actually a strength. The whole set-up became a bit pop art-ish and really involved a lot of staging. Hans Schmidt was very fond of the courageous involvement and dare-devil attitudes of the main character in *A Rich Man*, which is a very abstract reflection of someone in our shared landscape. He provided us with the best imaginable work conditions, because here you have this man who has time enough on his hands to fool around with his daily life in the presence of a film crew. It can be quite amusing to watch your life get dissected as though it were a puzzle, and we, of course, also functioned as his court jesters. However, I suppose an important part of the portrait painter's work is the ability to entertain the person being depicted.

When you choose to tell your story in documentary form you encounter a central problem, which is that you have to make your films with far less money. There's simply no comparison between the budgets of my documentary films and those of features. If you focus on the production values of what you see on the screen the differences aren't that great, but there's an enormous difference at the level of the budgets. The fact that money is administered in this way within the world of film has been a big problem for me. There's no such discrepancy in the world of painting or literature, but in film there's this idea that the fiction film somehow is more prestigious than the documentary film. You can pay a trained actor an excellent salary for playing the role of a washer woman, but you can't pay a real washer woman for spending exactly the same amount of time in front of the camera. This idea that the reflection is worth more than what casts the reflection is very strange and has a real impact on my daily work. For example in *A Rich Man* I had to give up on an expensive scene in which the main character, once dead, is blown sky high on his yacht in the Mediterranean. That scene was really central and full of symbolic value, and had it been a feature film it would never have occurred to anyone to do without it.

**Bondebjerg:** Your documentary films are characterised by a very powerful use of visual devices, including, for example, atmospheric landscape images that virtually become mental metaphors. This is true of *Jenny*, *It's Now or Never* and your most recent film, *Addicted to Solitude*, which includes some amazing images of African landscapes. At the same time you seem to use objects and interiors symbolically, and your editing style is very pronounced. In your hands editing becomes a symbolic instrument that helps to characterise a given universe. A good example is *A Rich Man* which involves a very effective and deliberate to-and-fro movement between milieus that are made to seem adjacent. You also use tableaux a lot. Examples would be the staged images of people

Addicted to Solitude.

speaking directly into the camera in *A Rich Man* or *A Fisherman from Hanstholm*, or the shots of Jenny (in *Jenny*) singing in her frost-covered garden and milking lace in her dreams. Could you talk about your editing principles and your relation to Alexander Gruszinski and Anders Refn who've frequently functioned as your cinematographer and editor respectively?

**Bang Carlsen:** Visuality is my instinct. I can articulate myself verbally too, but I've always been very confident about my visuality. I'm hardly ever in doubt about where the camera should be. I do the writing myself, and if I fail to write a scene properly in relation to myself as director, then I can't figure out where to put the camera. Even when I'm just reading a text I have to know where the camera is, where the sense perception is coming from. A very central feature of my visuality and editing style, my rhythm, is my complete lack of respect for all action that lacks a genuine emotional base. I like to watch things fall apart. I like it when people are too late for something, when something doesn't work out. I like watching a given plan of action fall to the floor like some tattered old hat that wasn't any good after all. Suddenly, during that momentary pause that these discrepancies produce, the face, skin and soul stand out in all their nakedness. I think pauses are incredibly fertile. I grew up in times when the pause was treated with extreme disrespect. I'm thinking of TV and the tendency constantly to edit even faster, impatient as the legs of a junkie before the next fix. Most of the conversations we see are completely uninteresting. We see more or less educated people repeating the same old banalities in more or less nicely turned phrases, but what is extirpated from our culture is the interesting space of doubt, the power of the pause. The result, in my mind, is not only boring, but dangerous. In all my films, especially my most recent one, *Addicted to Solitude*, the camera continues to gaze at a given person even after there's nothing more to be said, because it's in those moments following speech that something might emerge that essentially tells it all.

Film is not something that should be dictated by words. I have a very passionate relation to visuality and I find placing a camera to be an incredibly amusing, interesting, even physical process. I don't have the same kind of intimate relation to editing. I don't trust my own sense of rhythm as a performer, only as a listener. I have, of course, spent years of my life editing. I end up doing battle with editors the minute they start to continuity-edit. I've had huge fights with Anders Refn about this, who is much more at home with mainstream film-making than I am. We had huge fights while we were editing *Ophelia Comes to Town*. Our most passionate discussions have to do precisely with pauses, and my claim is that the editing shouldn't coincide exactly with those moments that in some banal sense constitute a full stop. Instead it should be a matter of prolonging things just slightly. We had a lot of fruitful discussions about this issue, because I do, of course, have a tendency to go too far in the other direction, so I need some kind of dialogue. As for my cinematographer, Gruszinsky, I've frequently joked that I'm a better cinematographer than he is and he's a better director than I am. He's much more structured than I am, and a much better intellectual. He knows a lot more about film in all the standard senses than I do, whereas I'm much more focussed on visuality, but we've worked very well together. I also think Tom Elling is a wonderful cinematographer. He's also a painter, so he has a great deal of respect for a visuality that isn't framed by action. I've been incredibly irritated by a lot of cinematography over the years, because it's all so respectable. It's clear that the cinematographers haven't been given the time or haven't taken the time to digest what they have to 'see' with their cameras. In order to be on the safe side they simply tell too much, and thereby end up telling too little because they're not involved deeply enough in the story. But in the European tradition of things, cinematography is of course to a very great extent the director's responsibility.

**Bondebjerg:** I'd like to talk about your features, using an interview from 1997 following your participation in an Equinox course as a starting point. Although you're not wild about American film, your encounter with American screenwriters was an eye-opener that led you to reflect on differences between Scandinavian/European and American film art: 'I have the same kind of relation to American film as I do to fast food – I feel something while consuming it, but the feeling doesn't last. We have to learn from their ability to accommodate an audience, while retaining the poetic kernel that often exists in European film.' You further remark that film, for you, is a game: 'Perhaps it can become art, but initially at least it's a form of play. In Scandinavia we approach film in a very formal way – we're constantly pretending it's art, although it might be perfectly obvious that it isn't.' You also claim that feelings are absolutely central in your films, whereas much of Scandinavian film privileges the intellect. Could you try to unpack the strengths and weaknesses of American and European/Scandinavian film as you see them?

**Bang Carlsen:** I have a love/hate relation to the US. There's a sense of freedom there, which has also had an impact on film, and at some level film is an American art form.

Film in the US has never been enveloped in that rather dusty art aura that we have here. It's better now, but when I first started out in Danish film it was incredible. The distance between the commercial entertainers and the artists or intellectuals was simply enormous. In the US there's always been a much more fruitful form of collaboration between the intelligentsia and the commercial fellows. Take Arthur Miller, one of my heroes, he's an example of an intellectual who's worked with some very commercial figures. That's one of the things I like about American film. American film is marked by the dreadful vulgarity of capitalism, and its lack of personal ethics. It also derives tremendous strength from the logic of capitalism, which favours renewal and innovation. American film has to take chances, to be open towards new tendencies, because it can't afford to bore its customers, so it has to make room for new players. Our world is, or was, organised in terms of exclusive groups because we've been far less dependent on market mechanisms. I don't of course mean to suggest that I'm in favour of American relations of production. Culture is much too important to be abandoned to raw market forces, but a mixed form, like the Danish or French model, has been very successful. The Americans, however, still end up selling more hotdogs. It's important to recognise that film can be put to a wide variety of uses that needn't be mutually exclusive or compete with each other. I've made films since I was 21 years old, and I could never have done this in the US. I was able to survive because I'm part of a system that can afford to have a number of marginal players like myself. In the short run I would never have survived as a film-maker in a commercial system, but I do think that my films have managed to reach an audience in the long run. Here in Europe we have our auteur tradition, which I of course support 100 percent, and I suppose that it's the auteur films that deserve state support, that is, films where it's a matter of some person authentically trying to articulate a particular story world. If the films then go on to attract a large audience, then that's of course wonderful, but the anticipation of that kind of success shouldn't be a precondition for making the films.

**Bondebjerg:** Now that we're talking about Europe/America, we might want to refer to *Time Out*, which is certainly your most American film, for it's set in the US and features American actors in the leading roles. You yourself have said that you don't think the film is particularly successful, but I sense an encounter here between American and European traditions. *Time Out* has both a bit of David Lynch and Wim Wenders about it. It's as though you were trying to combine aspects of the action genre with visually poetic dream images and sequences. What we have here, it seems to me, is very much a mixture of Danish, European and American elements.

**Bang Carlsen:** Well that's me isn't it? I'm a European in America. However, absolutely everything went wrong during that production. I usually co-produce my films because that gives me more of a say, so I was involved in the decision to hire an American script-writer. And that was our first bad decision. Every time I've employed a so-called professional script-writer, it's been a complete farce. When I gave him the script it had one murder in it, and by the time he returned it to me it had 27, and all of the victims were women. Every woman who appeared in the film was murdered after two minutes.

Not long before we were supposed to start shooting I realised the script was junk. I should have gone back to my very first script, which was rather good, I think, but that wasn't on the cards, unfortunately. In my mind writing and directing go together. I have trouble separating the two activities and functioning only as a director. I've enjoyed working with dramaturgists, but every time I've tried to work with a writer, the film has become completely alien to me.

**Bondebjerg:** Your features are frequently about rather seedy people who are searching for love or an identity. I'm thinking of the character played by Karen Lykkehus in *Next Stop, Paradise*, but John and Molly in *Ophelia Comes to Town* also come to mind, for John is intent on finding both love and a father. In *Time Out* John searches for his father while travelling the road that leads to what is referred to in the film as 'the Capital of Dreams'. You frequently use dreams and religiously charged symbols to comment on these characters' pursuit of happiness. Do you see these films as exploring essentially the same themes and issues or are they in your mind quite different?

**Bang Carlsen:** *Next Stop, Paradise*, which in a way is my most traditional film, was inspired by the story of my own paternal grandmother. I like that story about the flower that doesn't blossom until the day before the frost sets in, the day it's destined to die.

That provided me with a very clear poetic angle on the whole film. As far as the other films are concerned, I'd want to point out that I have a problematic relation to father figures. I've always had trouble with groups; and I have a lot of problems with authority although it's also been a focus of longing for me. This has something to do with God and religiosity, and the figures in question are all in some way moved by these issues.

I'm personally very fond of *Ophelia Comes to Town*. Every time I see it I'm struck by how well it works in places, but when I pay attention to the dramaturgy I can't help but notice the most elementary mistakes. For example, the two corpses in the film are interchangeable, although the story depends on the audience being able to tell them apart. I invest so heavily in other kinds of visual details that I sometimes neglect certain narrative imperatives.

**Bondebjerg:** *Baby Doll* is your only attempt so far at a real genre film. It's a psychological thriller, but not in the tradition of Hitchcock. In this case the script was written, not by you, but by Lisbet Gad. Was *Baby Doll* an attempt on your part to reach a different kind of audience? How would you describe the relation between the themes and style of this film and those of your other films?

**Bang Carlsen:** I made it six months after *Time Out* and I enjoyed telling a story that required unity of place, since I'd just finished traipsing around New Mexico and California. It was one of the few scripts I'd ever read that had a distinct visual tone.

I subsequently rewrote some of the scenes in relation to ideas that were prompted by my choice of location. I'm thinking of the way in which we used the farmyard; those shadows that expand and contract in connection with the main character's spiritual dissolution. I also conceived of the business with the swing towards the end, but Gad had really produced one of the most visually interesting scripts I'd ever read. The one problem with the script was that it was unrelentingly sombre. It didn't define darkness in relation to light, but I still think the film functions well in visual terms. The visual choreography really works, but it's not powerful enough as a monologue. I believe it was Bergman who once said that 'Without a you, there can be no I' and this holds for monologues too. The film needs a number of substantial secondary characters, but I didn't make *Baby Doll* in order to reach a new audience. I just felt like making that particular film.

**Bondebjerg:** *Carmen and Babyface* is clearly in many ways a very autobiographical film, but it's also a somewhat realistic youth film with a more traditional narrative structure. Do you see yourself as pursuing this kind of realism of contemporary life with an emphasis on more readily recognisable stories in the future?

**Bang Carlsen:** *Carmen and Babyface* originally had a lot of dream sequences that involved John F. Kennedy becoming a father figure for that boy. There was even a scene in which John F. Kennedy had a one-night stand with the mother, and during that scene the boy experienced something I've experienced too. He wakes up and hears a male voice in his mother's bedroom, and this in a house in which there's normally no adult male voice to be heard. This is something every male child of divorced parents dreads. Before actually seeing the male in question, he looks out the window and notices an enormous limousine and lots of policemen and bodyguards. The mother has met J.F. Kennedy. Subsequently it becomes apparent that he's in the middle of a dream. The DFI consultant* and I ended up eliminating that scene because I couldn't defend its dramatic necessity. We needed to cut the budget slightly, so we had to sacrifice something, and unfortunately we hit on one of those crazy scenes that can really define a film, but which seem dispensable because they're not dictated by standard dramaturgical rules. That's another reason why I love documentary film-making. In that context of production I get a certain amount of money, and then I go out into the world and shoot my film. I have much more freedom when I'm working within that kind of economic framework. My only restrictions are my own sense of artistic discipline and the amount of money that's available for the film. When I make features I'm not the (sole) producer, which means that some production company is involved, and this in turn means that I have to be able to defend my choices verbally. The result is that it's the most boring scenes that tend to survive. Every time I see *Carmen and Babyface* I miss those dream sequences, that element of craziness. And a poor choice like that early on in the process clearly had catastrophic consequences for the film, but I have only myself to blame.

**Bondebjerg:** You're very much an auteur in the sense that you tend to function as script writer, director and producer in a given context of production. Do you feel any affinities for other film-makers? How would you describe your relation to Danish film history and to Danish cinematic traditions?

**Bang Carlsen:** I don't think Danish film history has had much of an impact on me. When

I was growing up in Vedbæk, there was a cinema on just the other side of our garden. It was always showing films like *Jules and Jim* (*Jules et Jim*) because that was the kind of thing that upper-middle class Danes living in Vedbæk liked to see. Those kinds of films meant a lot to me, as did some of the American films, *Rebel Without a Cause*, for example, and John Ford's films. I hardly ever saw Danish films. I've subsequently found some of Dreyer's films, and especially their visuality, to be extremely inspiring. Dreyer's films are wonderful. Then I have clear memories of a delightful scene from *Summer in Tyrol* (*Sommer i Tyrol*) in which the drunken and depressed character played by Dirch Passer dances intimately with a camera. Films by the great Swedish directors have also been important to me: Bergman's *Sawdust and Tinsel* (*Gyklarnas afton*) or *Summer with Monica* (*Sommaren med Monika*), and Jan Troell's *Here's Your Life* (*Här har du ditt liv*), which combines narrative and visual elements in the most amazing way; and Widerberg, of course, who had a special ability to create the most incredible moments right in front of the camera. Those moments that had us spellbound as we watched his films on the hard wooden benches in the local Vedbæk cinema. I recently saw *Raven's End* (*Kvarteret Korpen*) again, and I felt I was seeing those very moments for the first time, amazing.

**Bondebjerg:** You've made three films that centre on children and their perception of the world: *My Irish Diary*, *My African Diary* and *The 16 mm Film-Maker's Son*. What is it about the world of children that you find so intriguing?

**Bang Carlsen:** My first child was born when I was 21. He spent the first few years of his life in a basket under an editing table at the National Film School. Children have meant a lot to me, because they have that ability really to see and to wonder at the world, and that's a gift that anyone who works with film needs to have. In that respect we can really learn a lot from children. Children are also much better than most grown-ups at philosophising about what they see and experience. In many cases grown-ups have spent so much time trying to subordinate their thinking to rules and norms that half their brain is tied up in knots. It's an extraordinary experience to discover new worlds in the company of children. They're much more attentive to all the different variations on life. That's why it made sense to me to shoot those film diaries about the daily lives of my children in Ireland and South Africa, where I was shooting my other films. It was fun and extremely stimulating to return to my cinematic point of origin, to be an eye behind a lens that looks out at the world with a sense of wonder.

# Lars von Trier

## 1956–

Lars von Trier is without a doubt the director who has contributed most to the renewal of Danish film. Of the directors who have drawn attention to Danish film internationally, he is the one who has had the greatest impact on the new 1990s generation, not least because of his central role in Dogme* 95. His cinematic work ranges from avant garde films to innovative explorations of some of the classical film genres. Before his directorial debut, Lars von Trier studied at the University of Copenhagen's Department of Film and Media Studies (1976–79), where he was a member of the experimental Film Group 16 (1977–79). He was subsequently admitted to the Director's Stream at the National Film School of Denmark,* where he studied from 1979–82. His earliest short films were stylistically inventive explorations of themes and symbols which would later play a central role in his feature films. In his much-praised graduation film *Images of a Relief* (*Befrielsesbilleder*, 1982), von Trier developed a mode of cinematic expression that was heavily symbolic and emotion-laden. Critics noted that there had been nothing comparable in Danish film since Dreyer. Von Trier established himself both nationally and internationally with the so-called 'Europe trilogy', which embraces his first three feature films, *The Element of Crime* (*Forbrydelsens element*, 1984), *Epidemic* (1987), and *Europa* (1991). The trilogy is characterised by a personal, experimental cinematic style, by a creative exploration of historical and existential themes and taboos, and by an

*Lars von Trier shooting his Dogme film,* The Idiots (Idioterne)*. [Photo: Jan Schut]*

208

innovative use of existing genre formulae. *Breaking the Waves* (1996), which is an erotic melodrama, marks von Trier's turn towards classical genres, and this interest is further pursued in the musical, *Dancer in the Dark* (2000). In his experimental, self-reflexive Dogme film, *The Idiots* (*Idioterne*, 1998), von Trier paints a moving portrait of a group of young people in pursuit of an inner authenticity, their inner 'idiots'. Von Trier has also left his mark on TV, in part with *Medea* (1988), which is based on Dreyer's Euripides-inspired script, and with the TV series *The Kingdom* (*Riget*, 1994) and *The Kingdom 2* (*Riget 2*, 1997), which masterfully combines elements of horror, playful humour and biting satire. This series was von Trier's big popular breakthrough.

## Feature films
1984, *The Element of Crime* (*Forbrydelsens element*)
1987, *Epidemic*
1991, *Europa*
1994, *The Kingdom* (*Riget*, co-director with Arnfred)
1996, *Breaking the Waves*
1997, *The Kingdom 2* (*Riget 2*, co-director with Arnfred)
1998, *The Idiots* (*Idioterne*)
2000, *Dancer in the Dark*

## Short films
1977, *The Orchid Gardener* (*Orchidégartneren*)
1979, *Joyful Menthe* (*Menthe – la bienheureuse*)
1980, *Nocturne*
1981, *The Last Detail* (*Den sidste detalje*)
1982, *Images of a Relief* (*Befrielsesbilleder*, graduation film)

## TV productions
1988, *Medea*
1994, *The Teachers' Room* (*Lærerværelset*, co-director with Rumle Hammerich, episodes 1–6)
1994, *The Kingdom* (*Riget*, co-director with Arnfred, episodes 1–4)
1997, *The Kingdom 2* (*Riget 2*, co-director with Arnfred, episodes 5–8)
2000, *D Day* (*D dag*, collaborative Dogme project)

**Bondebjerg:** You're perceived both nationally and internationally as playing an important role in contemporary Danish film, but if we examine that role closely an important shift becomes apparent towards the end of the 1990s. At the outset of your career, your films bespoke an avant-gardist, individualistic, enfant terrible-like intention constantly to displace the norms of artistic production. This innovative dimension still characterises your work, but your role in Danish film is now that of the gentle, almost avuncular enabler. We're sitting in the middle of the film town in Avedøre, which was inaugurated last week. Originally Zentropa was a company designed to give you full artistic control over your films. Today Zentropa is an open-ended, collectivist and multifaceted project. Your last film, *The Idiots*, and the Dogme concept itself, are reminiscent of the collectivism of the 1970s. What's your own take on this shift and what role do you see yourself and Zentropa as playing in contemporary Danish film?

**Von Trier:** Peter Aalbæk and I created Zentropa so as to be able to produce my films. It was to be a 50/50 company that involved our having to agree about everything. This quickly changed, as Peter went his way and I went mine. On the whole it's functioned well, and Peter has been a good producer, but there have been a number of crises and the idea of my having full control over my films has at times been a total lie. For example, Aalbæk and Vibeke Windeløv allowed filters to be used during post-production of *The Idiots*. That was an insane cock-up, but it may have involved a break-down in communication on my part. Part of the problem with the Dogme concept has been that nobody has taken it completely seriously. It's been viewed as a bit of a joke, like the ones in the satirical 'Just imagine' rubric on the back of the newspaper *Politiken*. Why would anyone in his right mind impose such ridiculous restrictions on himself? It's the equivalent of making fire with two stones instead of a Ronson lighter.

**Bondebjerg:** What exactly has happened here? The emphasis now is on collectivism, on community, and you yourself have become some kind of enabler.

**Von Trier:** That's partly coincidence. There's a parallel shift in my relation to actors, for now I engage in an almost hysterical dialogue with them. I'm just interested in different things nowadays. Actually, whether Danish film is able to do x or y doesn't really mean that much to me, but I feel quite at home in these surroundings, and I'm comfortable with that collectivist spirit. At my age it's quite common to revert to the opinions and standards of one's parents, so that's where I am right now, and at some later point I might twitch my tail one last time and land somewhere else. This business of establishing collectives and cooperation is very much in line with my parents' way of thinking, but I'll happily stab them in the back any time, of that you can be completely sure. In that sense it's hard to predict where I'll go from here.

**Bondebjerg:** To what extent are you personally involved in the development of Zentropa? I'm thinking, for example, of the internet experiments.

**Von Trier:** Those kinds of initiatives normally come from me. The 'Open Film Town Project' is my initiative. The document describing it does indeed prepare the ground, not only for a collectivisation, but also for a demystification of the film medium. If you read my document closely ('Project Open Film Town', January 1999), you'll see that I talk about the 'democratisation' of film and the audiovisual mass media and about opening up the closed film milieu to the surrounding world, both locally and globally. One aspect involves making use of the internet, but in such a way that the virtual community combines with concrete communities and activities related to local creative talents and schools, and to foreign speakers who might be invited to offer seminars and master classes in production. We're talking about the old collectivist ideal from the 1960s and

1970s, but rethought in relation to new technological possibilities as a 'vision for the new millennium' – and Dogme 95 fits in here quite naturally.

**Bondebjerg:** In *Lars von Triers elementer*, Peter Schepelern (1997) suggests that you grew up in a very liberal and culturally radical family environment and had serious problems adapting to school and tolerating authority. In what way has this personal background affected your stance more generally?

**Von Trier:** Paradoxically enough that anti-authoritarianism probably makes it easier to become an authority figure oneself. I recently talked about these issues with Klaus Rifbjerg, whom I've interviewed at some length. We talked about how we'd both been bullied in school, and we virtually decided that the way we'd organised our careers and lives at some level expressed a desire to control the bullying. If you can't beat the bully with physical strength, then you have to think of something else. We're really talking here about some kind of deeply primitive survival strategy. That makes it all seem rather impoverished.

**Bondebjerg:** Schepelern identifies a lot of literary and cinematic projects that you were involved in at a very early age. For example, you dictated a short crime novel to your parents as a seven year old, and you conducted your first experiments with eight mm film between the ages of 11 and 15. A lot of artists probably draw creatively on their memories of childhood and adolescence, but in your case the fertile connection between art and life seems to have been established very early on. How do you see the relation between these early years and your later development as a film-maker?

**Von Trier:** That really depends on how you look at it. Some people have pointed out that even Napoleon's mother was terribly fond of her son; she thought that whatever little Napoleon did was wonderful. My mother was like that. If I drew a squiggle on a piece of paper, she'd think it was absolutely wonderful. That kind of response encourages you to do things. That's one side of the story. At the same time, like all families my family had a lot of skeletons in the closet, and I was a sensitive child with intense angst as far back as I can remember. The childhood influences that caused me to develop in an artistic direction are probably a combination of constant praise and a kind of escapism, because art, for me, was a universe that I could control. Control means a lot to me, and to all people, I think. I'm very envious of people who have the courage to allow themselves to be controlled. It must be wonderful not to fear that, but in my case the aim was to construct a universe that I could control. That's why the practice of my art has never been a source of angst. I've never feared I might produce something that wasn't good enough. There's no guaranteeing that I won't ever feel that way. Whatever I'm involved in may turn out not to be viable in audience terms or in any number of other respects, but I've never questioned the deeper qualities of my work. This has nothing to do with talent. It's just a question of personal disposition. The fact of not being nervous frees up a lot of productive energy, because it's common to think: 'It's not good enough, I can't live up to the expectations.' I've never felt that way. I can't say I'll never feel that way, but this ability simply to regard those who don't appreciate your qualities as stupid is a tremendous strength. Success is dangerous that way. It's like the standard of living. It's easy to raise your standard of living, but it's very hard to lower it.

**Bondebjerg:** Most of your early films involve experiments with narrative form, genre and visual style. You're also interested in painting and your own paintings range from an almost uncanny hyper realism to something more playful, and this range is itself reminiscent of that of your cinematic oeuvre. This emphasis on powerful visual experiments has been coupled throughout with a choice of provocative themes. We might refer here to the epigraph in Schepelern's book: 'Great art is always flanked by its dark sisters, blasphemy and pornography.' Your early experiments, both as a member of Film Group 16 and during your first years at the Film School, certainly cultivate certain perversions and fantasies, just as they bristle with references to the cinematic avant garde and various literary provocateurs. This is true of *The Orchid Gardener*, *Joyful Menthe* and *Nocturne*. What's the significance of these films for your subsequent development as a film artist?

**Von Trier:** I remember showing *The Orchid Gardener* to a dumbfounded audience in the Department of Film and Media Studies, which back then was housed behind the Saga cinema. There was total silence afterwards. Then someone said: 'Why?' I didn't think it was so strange when I made it, but maybe it is. *Joyful Menthe* was more of a study in style, because I'd seen too much Marguerite Duras, but *The Orchid Gardener* was more interesting. I always tell young people that it's very important to make a fool of yourself in the beginning. It's always interesting to see precisely that film in which a director makes a fool of himself, and this holds for virtually all the directors whose films are worth seeing today. In some ways, that film always has a special place. At the very least we want to be able to see it afterwards. Somehow those moments of stupidity contain the essence of it all. After all, it's because you expose yourself that you make a fool of yourself.

**Bondebjerg:** Do you regard those early experiments as stylistic exercises?

**Von Trier:** I've never undertaken stylistic exercises in order to practice something. I've just made things the way they needed to be made. The themes and styles reappear in my later work, but those early films did allow me to experiment with certain techniques. It was fun to have a go at a tracking shot and a freeze frame. I also worked with masking, both horizontally and vertically. The result wasn't bad and it was damned interesting work, but it wasn't just a stylistic exercise. My first film, *The Orchid Gardener*, was quite good, and I used any number of different cinematographers. I haven't seen it in a long time, and it's excruciating to watch it because I've exposed myself in it. As the years go by you become better at not exposing yourself quite as much, at exposing yourself only as much as is required. At that point there's an element of control, whereas earlier there was no control. *The Orchid Gardener* was virtually psychotic, the expression of a young man who was in really, really bad shape. As for the provocative themes, in that respect I haven't changed at all. I still deal with exactly the same things, but in a more controlled way. The problem is that you become better at what you're doing, which means that you more easily satisfy any number of different standards, but I constantly try to force myself to undertake things I don't yet master. That sounds very snooty, but it's really true. You can become so good at producing things that they become nauseatingly boring to look at. That might have happened had I continued to make the same film again and again, as some people do. In the case of *Europa*, I really felt that I'd come to the end of the tracks. Everything had become so aesthetic and was so cleverly made, relatively speaking, that something new had to happen. I feel the same way about *Dancer in the Dark*.

**Bondebjerg:** The connection between perversion and art, which Schepelern underscores in his book, is apparent in many of your films, where an intense and hauntingly expressed sexuality often plays a central role. Schepelern goes so far as to claim that 'all in all Trier's universe represents an unmistakable forum for sexual perversity' (1997: 207). Do you accept this characterisation of you artistic universe?

**Von Trier:** A provocation is nearly always implicitly understood to be other-directed, but that's not necessarily the case. No matter what I'm dealing with, I nearly always try to provoke myself and to see the issue from a new perspective. In the case of *The Orchid Gardener* this is all very extreme, but it's true that my attempts along these lines often involve the same things: different kinds of sexual perversion, the entire gamut of disorders. Like Freud I see sexuality as a drive that really means a lot to humans. There's probably a close connection between sexuality and art, but I can't really expand on the point. Schepelern's statement sounds just fine. Whether the connection is particularly strong in my work, I don't know, but it may be that I, just like Rifbjerg, live out a lot of my sexuality through my films, instead of behaving promiscuously. There are different ways of doing things, and some people do precisely the opposite.

**Bondebjerg:** You're often described as the internationally oriented loner in Danish film. At the same time you're the director who has had the strongest impact on the widely discussed Danish new wave of the 1990s. What's your relation to Danish film and culture? You've pointed to Dreyer as a source of inspiration on numerous occasions. More recently, you and Zentropa have helped to revive the Morten Korch* film tradition, which simply couldn't be more Danish. What we have here are two extremes in Danish film culture, and to the best of my knowledge you've rarely referred to any other figures in the Danish film tradition. Do you on the whole find the Danish film tradition uninteresting and have you looked primarily to foreign directors for sources of inspiration? Is the concept of Danish culture and identity essentially of little interest to you?

**Von Trier:** I don't know what the Danish film tradition is. Is there really anything that characterises the Danish film tradition? When I was at the National Film School, we reacted violently against the Danish films that were being made at the time. We thought they were absolutely putrid and that there was no reason at all why we should want to deal with them. In that sense I've referred to Danish film a lot, but always in an inverted, negative way, but our film landscape is much more interesting today than it was back then. I have a very loyal relation to a few of the old directors. Dreyer, of course, but Kubrick was also one of the good guys. No matter what he came up with, I simply had to prostrate myself before it and see it.

Korch was yet again an attempt to provoke myself. In some sense you need to discuss the extent to which form and content are involved here, what's what. Maybe it's the case that all stories actually can be found in the Korch stories, that we're dealing with something very basic that all stories and all films necessarily build on. Maybe it's also the case that all the other things that are pumped into the other films actually are a kind of style that makes it all bearable to people like us, so that we dare to cry and to let ourselves be moved. We rely on this huge superstructure consisting of all kinds of artificial crap. If you look at my own films, then *Breaking the Waves* clearly belongs in the sentimental department. That film's synopsis outlines a story that not even Korch would have been able to accept. It's really far out, almost in the ladies magazines genre. Having read some Korch books – which I doubt my parents or anyone else ever did because he was almost automatically regarded as something negative – I couldn't get around the fact that some of the stories were really skilful and had a fantastic set-up, but Korch has always had a problem with endings. They're always weak, as though he suddenly had to bring things to a close, but I think his stories have some real qualities if you read them without prejudice. I was interested in doing some cultural slumming. I recently saw *The Red Horses* (*De røde heste*, directed by Alice O'Fredricks, based on the novel by Morten Korch) and *Ditte, Child of Man* (*Ditte Menneskebarn*, directed by Bjarne Henning-Jensen, based on the novel by Martin Andersen Nexø), and the parallels are far more pronounced than the differences. If you look at them in terms of an earlier perspective you can't fail to notice which of the two would have been viewed as good taste and which as bad. Viewed in a larger historical perspective the stories are surprisingly similar. The key difference has always been the ending, whether it's happy or sad. We have a concept of what we think is unsophisticated, but frequently it's a matter of what we with reference to others would call a style. We've somehow agreed that certain things are unsophisticated, but why are they unsophisticated? Why is the one better than the other? I did work on that TV series, but we didn't end up producing a genuine Korch film, which I still think would be an interesting thing to do. I would have liked to have made some genuine Korch films, but cooperation is difficult and people have divergent interests. I've never worked on something written by someone else, and it's a little much to have to make an entire film just to prove my point about Korch.

**Bondebjerg:** Your graduation film from the National Film School, *Images of a Relief*, created a stir and was also released theatrically. You wrote the script yourself and you worked on the film with two of your earlier collaborators, the cinematographer Tom Elling and the film editor Tómas Gislason. The film, which cultivates death and decline during the days of liberation in 1945, is full of pathos and is very powerful stylistically and symbolically. It's intentionally controversial inasmuch as it focusses, not on the liberation itself, but on the suffering of the main character, who is one of the German losers. The film doesn't resemble other Danish films, or, for that matter, other Scandinavian films. Many critics have pointed to Tarkovsky's influence. Could you talk about the origin of the central idea here, your key source of inspiration and your general approach?

**Von Trier:** I was very inspired by Tarkovsky. I won't make any bones about that. I saw an excerpt from *The Mirror* (*Zerkalo*) on Swedish television once, just a travelling shot around that house, and that was one of those 'I'll be damned' experiences. It was overwhelming, so I was very much on that wave length. But the film has other things too. It's not just Tarkovsky. However, we were certainly playing around with his artistic devices. At the same time, it was clear that I had to privilege the German point of view, since I'd been raised against the grain. I've always found it odd that our open-mindedness doesn't extend to the Second World War. When the war comes up, people suddenly become almost nationalistic. It's strange how the philosophy changes just because the times change. That oughtn't to be the case, for the philosophy should be a constant. That's why I adopted that angle in the film, but there were also Nazi allusions in *The Orchid Gardener*. There was everything. I don't think I would have been allowed to adopt children right after that film. There was talk of my adopting a child back then. It's probably good that we didn't include the film as part of our application!

**Bondebjerg:** You further refined the visual style and themes of your graduation film in your next three films, which make up the so-called 'Europe trilogy': *The Element of Crime*, *Epidemic* and *Europa*. This trilogy is also the beginning of your lengthy collaboration with the script writer, Niels Vørsel. Although the three films are stylistically connected, they are also very different, both thematically and in terms of their modes of production. *The Element of Crime* was a relatively cheap English-language production funded by Danish sources, and you've described it as a 'modern film noir'. *Epidemic* is a meta-film and very much a low-budget production, whereas the melodrama, *Europa*, is a big, international co-production. Why did you decide to refer to these films as a trilogy? What, for you, is the connecting thread in these labyrinthine films?

**Von Trier:** Niels later characterised the theme of these three films as 'the dangers of nature', and I think this is pretty accurate. In *The Element of Crime* nature encroaches on the human. In *Epidemic* the dangers of nature are represented by the plague-like illness. I just saw a program about jungles, which was very interesting. If I try to imagine the most comforting image in the world, I see a forest lake with a bellowing stag, a waterfall in the background, and some mossy remnants of tree trunks. What's amusing about precisely that image in relation to the jungle is that the latter involves an ongoing struggle for survival, whereas there's hardly any struggle connected with the kind of forest we have here, because we know who the winners and losers are. It's interesting that what we find most soothing is an image that points back to the worst thing of all. Had it been people instead of trees and animals, it would have been a Hieronymus Bosch image, humanity as a battlefield. I don't know whether this is especially related to Europe, but Europe is, if nothing else, where I'm from. The trilogy is all about that play of forces, about longing,

*Poster for* Europa.

and about nature over and against culture, that's what we felt held the Europe trilogy together. It's the same story in each of the three films. The inquiring humanist who leaves his home terrain and journeys out into nature ends up going to rack and ruin. In *Europa* nature, the jungle, was a wartorn Europe, and in penetrating it the humanist ends up succumbing to its laws. You find the same story in the other films, for in each of them people end up being trapped and destroyed by the very search in which they're engaged.

**Bondebjerg:** *The Element of Crime* initially received mixed reviews and sold only 37,000 tickets. Johs. H. Christensen claimed that it was a 'conceited and pompous' film with 'aesthetic' and 'moral' standards well below those of cheap pulp fiction. The Danish Film Institute had simply 'poured its money down the drain' (*Kristeligt Dagblad*, May 1984). Henning Jørgensen's review was more favourable, for he noted a strangely 'decadent, jarring beauty' (*Information*, May 1984). *The Element of Crime* went on to win the *Prix technique* at Cannes, as well as a Bodil* and a Robert* as Best Danish Film of 1984. During the film's promotion, you violently attacked the banality of the Danish realism of everyday life, and you wrote the following in connection with the premiere: 'We won't settle for "well-meaning films with a humanistic message". We want more – the real thing, the fascination, the experience – childlike and pure as true art. We want to go back to the time when love between film-maker and film was young, when the joy of creating oozed out of every frame. Substitutes cannot satisfy us any more. We want to see religion on the screen. We want to see mistresses of the screen vibrant with life: unreasonable, stupid, stubborn, ecstatic, repulsive, wonderful, but *not* tamed and made sexless by a moralising grumpy film-maker, a stinking puritan, cultivating the moronic virtues of the nice facade.' Is the film an expression of a youth revolt oriented towards Europe and against the dominant tendencies in Danish film at that point in time?

**Von Trier:** It's probably just an expression of what we were just talking about. It's a revolt against well-meaning humanistic pieties, and I still feel that way, for I have little use for niceties and good intentions. I'd like to see all kinds of films, including Nazi films, as long as they have something to say. I belong to the school of thought that believes that people are able to draw their own conclusions. That's always been very important to me, and it's essentially my stance towards life. It's an anti-pedagogical stance, because I believe that if people are presented with information they themselves can decide what to do with it. The information shouldn't come in the form of a textbook, or involve the kind of pedagogy that relies on the idea that you can produce virtuous people by administering the proper dose of information. I think that things find their natural balance, and I believe that it's very important that Nazis be allowed to demonstrate in Denmark. That was also my parents' position.

**Bondebjerg:** Up until 1991 your films are anchored, not so much in stories, as in specific scenes or ideas concerning the composition of images. *Images of a Relief* involves three strikingly different locations (a dilapidated factory, an opulent upper-class villa and a forest). In *The Element of Crime* there are three guiding scenes, which you have described as 'the harbour scene', the 'foot-and-mouth disease scene' and the 'rope jumping scene'. In an exchange with your former teacher, Martin Drouzy, you said the following: 'I choose a theme in order to have an excuse to produce certain images. The first thing I think about when I'm opting for a milieu and temporal framework is whether they enable me to produce the images I want to produce' (Drouzy 1991). Does this mean that up until 1991 the images are everything, while the story and perhaps even the acting are nothing? Were you a masterful manipulator of images rather than a cinematic storyteller during those early years?

**Von Trier:** It's hard to make that distinction. It's true that at that point I didn't want to engage in a dialogue with the actors about their views on the psychology of a given character. I had my own, very precise interpretation of what I wanted, but that doesn't mean that I considered the acting negligible. The actors' presence was just as important as in other films, but the psychological dimension was of no interest to me. I don't know whether I was particularly focussed on the image; if I was, then sound was important too. If, however, you mean image as a more general concept, then yes, but the images also tell a story. It's just a question of what we mean by 'story'. A story in a single scene can be just as important, if not more important, than the story understood as what somehow can be boiled down to Korch-like formulae. If you take all the great stories and boil them down to the bare bones, then there are five to ten basic stories in the world. Should we only, then, allow ourselves to explore images if the film is governed by those kinds of stories, and should we have to refrain from exploring images creatively if those bare bones are absent? That would be a little too restrictive. At some level this has to do with the audience's expectations. The audience cannot be allowed to unplug, but in order to avoid that only the most minimal skeleton is required. The skeleton is much more pronounced in my films now than it was earlier, and I'm not worried about that because I feel as though I'm able to put ornaments on the skeleton. However, even back then I was aware of the fact that a more general audience would only sit through a film if that skeleton was there. I may have felt that it was cheating to stick it in when what was important, in my mind, was something else, and generally speaking I'm not really in favour of cheating.

**Bondebjerg:** Your stylistic and thematic universe is characterised by European themes, references and sources, and it's tempting to interpret you as representing some of the most vital elements in what we think of as the European film tradition. This is a tradition that sees itself as violently opposed to dominant American film art, that is, narrative genre films. What's your own relation to European and American cinema and film culture?

**Von Trier:** That's hard to say. It's true that I'm not as crazy about American film as a lot of people are. I remember that there were quite a few people in the Department of Film and Media Studies who really cultivated American film. I've never had that kind of relation to action films and gangster films. I thought Huston was good and I quite liked the various Humphrey Bogart films, but they never meant a lot to me, whereas I was wild about the neo-realist films. I'm thus most inspired by the European tradition, but this is also because we're constantly exposed in various ways to the narrative model that the American directors employ, and as a result it's just not that interesting.

**Bondebjerg:** Would you say that you have become more interested over the years in narrative genre film?

**Von Trier:** We're now trying to make some films that are so sentimental that even the Americans would be ashamed to make them, but the relevant American films have never interested me that much. I've watched Douglas Sirk's films, but that was mostly because you were supposed to be interested in him as a student of film. I feel the same way about Sirk as I do about Korch. It's a matter of provoking yourself. Sirk is, of course, much worse than Korch, but I'm now trying to be very sentimental in my films. I've had good experiences with that. I think that I'm good at being sentimental, even if sentimentality is something that people tend to keep at arm's length. However, we can't help but be influenced by American film, for it's all we ever see during childhood and adolescence.

**Bondebjerg:** The TV series *The Kingdom* and *The Kingdom 2*, which you provokingly claimed to have made with your 'left hand', was a major popular breakthrough. Before then you'd made the stunning TV film, *Medea*, which was based on a script by Dreyer which he himself never shot. The stylistically innovative von Trier remains present in *The Kingdom*, which playfully mixes various genres. At the same time you quite consciously chose to work with the most popular of Danish actors, many of whom were known from the earlier TV series, *Matador*. The critics emphasised the radical, hand-held style (inspired by various American TV series), the mixture of mysticism and horror, the contagious sense of narrative *jouissance* and the exuberant satire. That narrative *jouissance* was viewed as introducing something new into what had previously been a rather sombre universe in decline. Your famous left hand seems to be quite capable. What's the origin of this transformation?

**Von Trier:** We had to do something to ensure Zentropa's survival. That's how I remember it. We talked about producing a gigantic TV series. I've always dreamt of making *Berlin Alexanderplatz* which would probably kill me if I ever did. We then decided we'd use a hospital as our setting, and this worked nicely. I've always thought that 'the kingdom' was an amusing and somewhat blasphemous name for *rigshospitalet*. That business about the left hand refers to the fact that we did our utmost not to become too academic about it all. We didn't read through the scripts in a series of rehearsals; we just barrelled along guided by the principle that any idea whatsoever was good enough. If we liked an idea, we didn't stop to think about it, but simply proceeded at top speed. That's what's meant by 'left hand'. It's not the work of a fine hand, which is also a way of provoking yourself, if you're used to writing with your right hand. I'm sure the graphologists would get something quite different out of the left hand compared to the right hand, but I circumnavigated that cultured right hand. It used to be tremendously important to me not to imitate others. If I was going to make use of various effects, then I'd want to refine them, so they'd become my own. In *The Kingdom* we just appropriated the whole kit and caboodle and stole widely from the entire genre film tradition. We appropriated what we needed from Brian de Palma, for example. We asked ourselves what would be most effective, and then we simply did it that way. The second part was by far the silliest and the most fun to write. There was something Finn Søeborg-like[1] about it. Some of the lines were added afterwards, including the ones where Moesgård walks around with a phallus in his hand and talks about how a ship's entire crew was saved by a big turd. I just found that amusing.

**Bondebjerg:** You've flirted with melodrama in your earlier films, but with *Breaking the Waves* you take the leap, for this is a full-fledged melodrama about love, intense sexual passion and religious sacrifice. This powerful cocktail of sex and religiosity is explored by means of a classical dramaturgical structure involving a realistic psychological dimension. Compared with your earlier films the actors also seem to be foregrounded more. Critics around the world responded enthusiastically, but there was also a sense of bewilderment. Feminists were puzzled by the representation of women and others wondered whether you'd seriously embraced religion. Do you see the film as a religious film, or at least as a film about religion and the close connection between erotic obsession and religious obsession? Does *Breaking the Waves* mark a departure from your earlier thematic and stylistic choices or is there a deeper continuity here?

**Von Trier:** The film expresses a negative interpretation of religion. I'm a Catholic, but I'm an auto-didact when it comes to religion. I was baptised, but I don't know anything about anything, precisely because I'm from a family of atheistic believers, in the sense that for my family the idea that religion was deeply prohibited was itself a religion. That's why those religious phenomena are as lacking in nuance in my mind as the inhabitants of Duckburg might be, but to me it's precisely the fact that the story is told in an unschooled and naive way that makes it so beautiful. I know that Schepelern is opposed to seeing the film as genuinely religious and believes that religion is merely an image I use in order to express something else, but it's a film about a religious problematic. Although the film isn't an introduction to religion, it is an expression of my religiosity, but it's also, once again, an attempt to provoke myself. I establish a problematic and take things to their logical conclusion, which involves asking whether a sacrifice could be sexual. We know about the sacrifices of saints, so why couldn't a sexual sacrifice be a saintly sacrifice? That's precisely what Bess' sacrifice becomes, for she fucks her way into heaven, as Aalbæk puts it. Yes, this is powerful stuff, but it's all very consistent.

**Bondebjerg:** And what was your response to the feminists' objections?

**Von Trier:** They don't worry me at all, because deep down I feel I'm more feminine than most women, so all that feminine sensitivity doesn't threaten me. Whether the characters in my films are male or female isn't decisive. Also, you could say that Bess acts of her own free will. In that sense her actions aren't a sacrifice, or rather, she herself performs the sacrifice, so at most we're dealing with a masochistic image of women, if we need a label. What is more masochism comes just as easily to men as it does to women. The renowned feminist Marie Marcus wrote about this at one point. I forget whether two thirds of us are masochists; it's something along those lines.

**Bondebjerg:** *Breaking the Waves* was an expensive film by Danish standards, and you've claimed that in this film you wallowed in some of the values, cheap tricks and effects that you'd always been taught to avoid (*Politiken*, 1996). However, in March 1995 you'd made an about-turn, advocating a back-to-basics approach in the Dogme 95 manifesto that you presented together with Thomas Vinterberg, and in 1998 you released your own Dogme film, *The Idiots*. Control and chaos are the conceptual cornerstones of your artistic strategy, for even your wildest and most experimental films early on involved specific concepts, stylistic ideas and principles that governed extensive preparations at the pre-production phase. Dogme 95 articulates a strict 'Vow of Chastity' pertaining both to the technological bases of the relevant films as well as to their thematic content. These rules foster a renewed authenticity and spontaneity not only in the actors, but also in yourself, for your diary and Jesper Jargil's film about the making of *The Idiots* both document a certain self-exposure to the point of vulnerability. Dogme, we know, is a film-historical rebellion, an attempt to regain control over the technological apparatus of film. Is your own Dogme film also an effective means of living out an inner chaos?

**Von Trier:** Yes, I tried to use my left hand a bit there, but the whole idea behind the rules is that we, in setting limits to freedom, enhance freedom within circumscribed limits.

**Bondebjerg:** So you've used the Dogme concept as a personal inroad to something that has to do with your childhood and background. There's a good deal of self-exposure at key points, particularly because you've also published your film diary. This is a package deal that reveals many sides of you. Was this planned from the outset?

**Von Trier:** No, but I felt that it was only reasonable to let down my guard since I required as much from the actors. The diary springs from the fact that I frequently find myself wishing that there were diaries documenting, for example, the production of Bergman's films; they'd provide such insight. What does he think about a given performance? Where are the weaknesses? Did he shoot that scene on a good day or a bad day? The point wasn't necessarily that *my* document would be something special, but rather that the idea of a diary was interesting in and of itself.

**Bondebjerg:** One of the Dogme rules specifies that the director can't be individually credited, and there's an aspiration here towards collective authorship. Yet, in practice this seems to be hard to realise. The Danish Dogme films are profoundly different and very much an expression of their respective directors, instances of individual authorship. What's the motive for this rebellion against individual authorship? Is individual expressivity not in many ways the very basis for significant art?

**Von Trier:** Yes, it's easy to see who's made what. That's the paradox. We talk about putting the films in uniform and we create uniform rules, but the paradox is – and this is also the point – that the first three Dogme films very much reflect their individual directors. It's amusing that this should be the case, but then why would talk of uniformity destroy individual qualities? That's precisely what hasn't happened although there's been an imposition of uniformity and an emphasis on the collective.

**Bondebjerg:** So in protesting against auteurism, you end up reinforcing it?

**Von Trier:** The uniform rules are our only protest against the auteur idea. There's something healthy about the idea of not crediting the directors, for it's the work that matters, not the man behind it. A little humility in that respect is healthy and suits the whole project. Otherwise there's not much humility in the Dogme project. Specifying all those things the directors aren't allowed to do is in itself a provocation, and the business of not allowing the directors to be credited was like a punch in the face of all directors. I quite liked that, but while there's an externally directed provocation here, there's also an even stronger inwardly directed provocation. What provokes others also provokes me. I've used my name a lot in promoting my films, just as David Bowie – of whom I'm a great fan – has allowed his person to fuse with his work. That's why I decided to provoke myself in this way, just to see what would happen. The provocation is always initially inwardly directed, and then it becomes other-directed as a side effect.

**Bondebjerg:** At this point a number of transgressions of the Dogme rules have been noted. Vinterberg has openly confessed to six transgressions and the recent crisis surrounding your own film, *The Idiots*, was widely covered in the press. The claim was that Zentropa, allegedly without your knowledge, had engaged in light manipulation in the laboratory. You've now thrown yourself into a mega production to the tune of 100 million Danish Crowns and some of the other Dogme brethren are working on completely different films. At the same time, the Dogme concept seems to be spreading to other countries. Is Dogme a manifesto with only a specific, punctual function, or do you see the principles in question as continuing to play a role inasmuch as they respond to an ongoing need for a specific kind of film?

**Von Trier:** I do believe there's still a need for that type of film. I don't think it's necessarily crucial that the Dogme rules be followed. I think the issue of whether you can gain something by throwing away total freedom in exchange for a set of rules is worth discussing, and it's interesting to see whether some of those rules might be of use to others. I've created rules before, so I think I've demonstrated that rules can lead to something positive. I think the need to go back to basics, which the rules are a response to, is more urgent now than ever before. I would find it amusing if Dogme could continue to exist like a little pill you could take when there was too much of the other kind of thing, too much refinement and distanciation. You'd then take a little Dogme pill and feel much better afterwards, because you'd be grounded again. I also think Dogme could provide an amusing form of discipline if it could exist as a kind of test that even the experienced directors would have to take every now and again, but I don't know what will happen to the Dogme concept. I've only seen those three films, but in my opinion they're all much too respectable. Mine is too. That wasn't my intention, but it's nonetheless the case, in part because it was tampered with. Now it's not quite as respectable. We've now produced a copy without optical manipulation, but the difference isn't that great.

However, we're in no way involved in the Dogme films being produced in various places around the world. We have no control over them whatsoever. I think our certificate was a mistake because even if we'd wanted to police the films, we wouldn't have stood a chance. All those things really take place in the director's mind, and that's something we can't control. I still think that Dogme might persist in the sense that a director would be able to say, 'I feel like making that kind of film.' I think that would be amusing. I'm sure a lot of people could profit from that. At which point you might argue that they could just as easily profit from a different set of rules. Yes, of course, but then go ahead and formulate them – ours are just a proposal.

**Bondebjerg:** The public is eagerly awaiting your next film, *Dancer in the Dark*, which you've finished shooting and are now editing, and if all goes well, it will be shown at the Cannes Film Festival in the Spring of 2000. This film continues your exploration of classical film genres, for it's a musical, a genre which has been mobilised only rarely during the last two decades of European film history. Indeed, in Denmark the last musical (Rifbjerg and Balling's *Annie Cat/Jeg er sgu min egen*) dates from 1967. Why have you turned to precisely this genre and what's your relation to some of the classical European and American musicals?

**Von Trier:** In this regard I'm influenced by the Americans. The musical is, of course, an American genre, one that I've always been very fond of, even as a child. I've always been crazy about the Kelly films, and I thought that *West Side Story* was a good film. Musicals have always interested me and suddenly it was possible to raise the money needed to make one. I don't know what it'll be like as a musical, but it has a lot of song and dance. What I'm trying to do in this film is to preserve certain sentimental qualities, or emotion-laden qualities more generally, in the context of a musical. This can be very hard because the songs are so stylised, if only because the actors regularly stop talking and start singing. In the history of film, musicals have often been mediocre works at the level of feeling. You don't exactly walk around weeping after having seen *Singing in the Rain*. I think that's actually a pity, because I know that it was once the case that opera audiences would leave the theatre in tears, and opera involves even more stylisation than the musical, because there's only singing. So I'm interested in seeing whether it's possible to combine affect and song.

**Bondebjerg:** Normally you yourself define your future film projects, although you've made a few things on request. What are the genres and cinematic challenges that you're eager to take up now that you've tried your hand at avant gardism, Dogme, film noir, melodrama and the musical? Where will the next challenges and provocations come from?

**Von Trier:** You can always keep on provoking yourself. That's the advantage of that approach. If that's the strategy here, then it can still be used in the future. Right now I don't know whether there's a genre that I'd find challenging, but I suspect I'll think of something. I think Kubrick was interesting that way because he was able to keep on redefining the genres. That's really brilliant. I think I'd like to make something that is extremely violent.

---

1   Danish writer, born in 1916. Breaks through in 1950 with the novel *That's Life* (*Sådan er der så meget!*) which was noted, not so much for its realism, as for its rather ironic and somewhat grotesque depiction of city life with an emphasis on the petite bourgeoisie and low-level bureaucrats.

# Project 'Open Film Town'
## Visions in connection with the film town in Avedøre

Film production has always been shrouded in a veil of mystery. Studios, artists, and production environments have done all they can to remain inaccessible to outsiders. These attitudes can probably be traced back to the days when the moving image was equated with magic. As everyone knows, the magicians' secrets must be kept, or their lack thereof obscured; but then again, magic tricks are very traditional affairs, for they practically never evolve ... and from society's point of view they're pretty insignificant.

Yet, that's not what film is like!

We're dealing with part of the most important mass medium of our day ... the audio-visual. Film is the subspecies that provides a vehicle for fiction, the form of individual expression that has been the unsurpassed medium for commentary and vision. Whether fiction or nonfiction, film provides an increasingly important tool for global communication.

In the case of developments in film, television, images and sound, the message equates with the development of civilisation for better or for worse. We cannot permit these developments to take place in dusty rooms, behind closed doors; nor can we leave them in the hands of the chosen few!

Fortunately technological progress is on our side. In the old days you could hide behind a mountain of expensive equipment, behind insurmountable financial obstacles. In those days you could point out with a certain amount of accuracy that the medium was such a costly affair that it was not for the man in the street. Today progress is undermining this argument. Soon everyone will be able to produce on cheap but fully professional equipment.

Film is not something that can be kept locked away, and nor can the secrets of the trade, the knowledge of how to use the equipment or the rules that are a prerequisite for the use of this form of communication, for at the same time that progress has been made the rules have fortunately – and quite understandably – crumbled. A genuine democratisation is on the way. At the end of the 1990s the lie of inaccessibility is being totally refuted by time itself!

What can (and must) we do in this time of change, those of us who are involved in film production and who are still regarded as the 'official' or 'professional' film-makers? One thing and one thing alone: we must work with progress in the hope of fostering what remains the most important element in communication, the very element that was initially forgotten in the heady rush of liberation: thoughtfulness!

We must open things up ... nothing less. Freedom of information must be a minimum demand ... a more logical one would be actual participation, or at least understanding!

As the elders it is our duty to hand things on, so as to allow new generations to continue them or reject them, so as to liberate the medium in a dignified way, but the relevant practices mustn't be transmitted in rooms that are as inaccessible as those we used to produce in. They must not be restricted to the chosen few ... or to the few who manage to navigate through the labyrinths and sites where the knowledge happens to be available. Discussion and sharing of experience must not take place at film schools or in small groups selected by the elders. Reaching the information must not be a struggle in itself ... the information must be freely available to all ... because that's the only way of securing the process of democratisation that technology has already begun.

Among these amateurs – the 'un-chosen' – we may find the loyalty that has been so seriously ignored by the old hands, the thoughtfulness, the discussion about goals and means and ways that is indispensable to a living medium and has been neglected due to self-righteousness.

Let's think of the creation of the Film Town as an opportunity to do things differently: Its very location outside the prestigious neighbourhoods and among the people might in itself seem portentous enough. Let us gather all the visionary talent and the very industry associated with cinema here! Let's construct the Film Town wisely, using contraries, so that art and industry can fertilise each other. It shouldn't simply be a matter of a professional partnership of interests, but of bringing into play the entire range of companies, artists and artisans from all aspects of audio-visual activity in a concerted effort aimed at opening the doors wide. All the knowledge and discoveries associated with the Film Town must be to everyone's benefit. All the ideas to be found in this business must be examined thoroughly and must be made accessible to anyone who might possibly put them to use.

As mentioned, it is important to exercise care when envisaging the Film Town during the early design phase. We want as many different units as possible in order to achieve the breadth necessary to invest our outward-facing activities with authority. People from as many different relevant lines of work as possible must be given the chance to join in: actors, technical staff, computer people, writers, music-makers, advertising people, etc., and preferably also media researchers and representatives from the state film bodies. Most importantly, the place shouldn't be dominated by a single company, not by Zentropa or anyone else.

The Open Film Town project is an extension of production activities and internal communication into the establishment of a centre for external, non-commercial, open discussion and studies designed to benefit the medium at every level. The aim is fully to meet the needs of the relevant people who are not typical applicants to, or students at, film schools or universities, and by whom the medium will be borne to a greater and greater degree in the future.

## What we shall do:

### At the local level:

We wish to establish a form of production that is as open as possible, i.e. visible to all interested parties, and that provides good opportunities for outsiders to become practically activated users of the Film Town's resources. In addition, we want to explore the medium in the context of a number of get-togethers involving comprehensive, unrestricted access; most importantly, we aim to arrange a monthly masterclass with a leading international figure who happens to be working in the Film Town at the time in question (Film Town contracts should all include a commitment, on request, to give a masterclass while working there).

The masterclass is a phenomenon known from music and involves a master teaching a small number of students how to play an instrument in front of an audience. The virtue of this arrangement is not so much the fact that the few who are taught profit (though they often do), but rather the fact that the master cannot help but pass on his knowledge, experience and philosophy to the larger audience in a way that is different from and far more vital than a traditional lecture.

## What's needed in practice:

A large venue, since the turn-out is likely to be significant in the event of appearances by leading international figures. Resources for organising the events. The necessary technology (sundry production gear and equipment for projecting the work to a large audience). Staff to plan and organise the events and to liaise with the public about them. Funds to develop new local contacts with the Film Town.

### At the global level:

Progress has, of course, provided us with a remarkable tool: the Internet. What could be more logical than distributing and promoting the theoretical aspects by the same means that will soon provide the vehicle for all the products that the whole thing is about? We can concentrate all our efforts there: the various masterclasses, available in English transcripts (with some attached images), and followed by a chat with the teacher; this will then be included in the data base. Soon the server will contain practical and theoretical information of a volume, variety and accessibility that no textbook can compete with.

This open context, with its rich contents, will attract interested, qualified contributions from all over the world (I'm not aware of a similar forum anywhere else).

That we have every chance of becoming the central site for the discussion of film theory and practice is clear from the vast interest generated in connection with the Dogme 95 manifesto and films. It is acknowledged internationally that Dogme has resulted in the first interest in and discussion of media theory (a discipline that one would otherwise be inclined to call 'extinct') among artists and professionals for decades.

This internet site would be a natural home for a conference on Dogme 95, one designed to sustain the project's positive influence, to provide a meeting place for those already making new Dogme films, and to exploit the international awareness Dogme 95 has attracted as a way of foregrounding the site's other functions. If an up-to-date forum for discussing the medium belongs anywhere in the world at present, it is surely in the home country of Dogme 95!

One obvious move would be to place large quantities of otherwise inaccessible material from Film Town productions at the site for study purposes. This would really be a provocative move, considering the secrecy with which the game used to be played. All the material from my next film, *Dancer in the Dark*, could be placed there to be viewed at will – including all the miss-takes and cut scenes (material like this is very useful in stimulating serious discussion when seen in relation to the finished film).

It goes without saying that the creation of this kind of Internet forum would lead rapidly to links with other relevant environments all over the world. Links to these sites should also be provided and collaboration encouraged.

The possibilities on the web for a platform like 'Open Film Town' are unlimited.

### Practical requirements:

An extremely powerful Internet connection. Room and resources for work on graphics and content. Management and expansion of the various discussion fora (including the continuation and further development of the Dogme conference at an international level). It is vital that visitors clearly sense that a web-site like this is staffed; if it is to have the desired prominence, top priority must be given to maintaining and developing the site. Extensive server storage space will also be required to accommodate all the materials that are to be made available on the site for free perusal and the purposes of discussion.

These outward-looking activities would give the Film Town every chance of becoming the long-awaited link between the theoretical and practical dimensions of the medium! (For too long it has been popular among film professionals to look down at, not to mention reject, the existence of any kind of justification for a theoretical dimension.)

The Film Town, then, houses an enormous potential for the development of the cinematic medium; and it also opens up great social, pedagogical and creative opportunities – both locally and globally.

Open Film Town is a vision ... we owe it to the Millennium to realise it.

**Lars von Trier** – (Avedøre 1999)

# Ole Bornedal

## 1959-

Ole Bornedal started out in radio and TV before breaking into film-making. At the outset of the 1980s he produced a series of remarkable radio montages, and he played a key role in the renewal of Danish TV satire. *The Good, the Bad and the Really Funny* (*Den Gode, den Onde og den Virk'li Sjove*, 1992–93) is an example of his contribution along these lines. Bornedal has also written and directed a number of plays and is part of the influential, trend-setting milieu associated with the 'Dr. Dantes Aveny' theatre group in Frederiksberg. But Bornedal's real breakthrough came in the form of TV plays and TV series. *Masturbator* (1993) is important in this respect, as is the women's road movie series, *Charlot and Charlotte* (*Charlot og Charlotte*, 1996), which represents an effective visual mixing of genres and affords the viewer an unforgettable journey through Denmark. Between 1993–94 Ole Bornedal found time to serve as Director of TV Drama for the Danish Broadcasting Corporation, a

*Ole Bornedal. [Photo: Rolf Konow]*

position from which he resigned following the remarkable success of his first feature film, the thriller *Nightwatch* (*Nattevagten*, 1994). This film established Bornedal as one of the innovative directors of the Danish new wave of the 1990s, a tendency that has significantly expanded the generic range of Danish film. *Nightwatch* also sparked interest in the US, and an American remake, *Nightwatch*, was released in 1998.

### Feature films
1994, *Nightwatch* (*Nattevagten*)
1997, *Mimic* (producer)
1998, *Nightwatch* (*Nattevagten*, American remake)

### TV films, TV series and other TV productions
1988, *The Dreamer* (in collaboration with Liselotte Winkler)
1989, *Under the Clock* (*Under uret*)

1992–93, *The Good, the Bad and the Really Funny* (*Den Gode, den Onde og den Virk'li Sjove*)
1992, *Somewhere in the World* (*I en del af verden*)
1993, *Masturbator*
1996, *Charlot and Charlotte* (*Charlot og Charlotte*, episodes 1–4)
1998, *Deep Water* (*Dybt vand*, episodes 1–2)

## Radio montages
1982, *I Found a Whale in Texas* (*Jeg fandt en hval i Texas*)
1986, *The Motorbike Accident* (*Knust, kværn og kvæstet*)
1987, *Moriendo*
1989, *Treblinka*

## Plays
1993, *Oh Happy Day* (*Den dag lykken*)
1998, *Macbeth – Two Words and a Coincidence* (*Macbeth – to ord og et tilfælde*)
1999, *God Bless Denmark* (*Gud bevare Danmark*)

**Hjort:** You grew up in a small provincial town in Jutland, where you were raised by a single mother who, although she influenced you positively in many ways, had little to do with stimulating your interest in film. The provincial cinemas in Nørresundby and nearby Aalborg first provided you with a point of access to the world of film. What, aside from your talent and perseverance, made it possible for you to break into an industry centred largely in Copenhagen and associated closely with a number of established family traditions and names?

**Bornedal:** I often think it's good to grow up in the vicinity of cement walls and in polluted air, because the dreams people have in these kinds of places necessarily have to be that much more powerful. I have the feeling that if you grow up in the most beautiful places in the world, close to a beautiful coastline and surrounded by the most beautiful people, with a garden full of the most fertile trees and luxurious red fruits, then you don't experience the same need to dream of beauty, you're not driven by the same type of longing. Instead the opposite frequently happens, inasmuch as you start to long for what is ugly.

I grew up in a place where people needed and were allowed to give free rein to their dreams. I can remember sitting in the garden together with my little friend, who didn't get enough to eat, because his father gambled away his wages. There we sat fantasising wildly about jaguars and women. We hadn't even reached puberty yet, and there we were talking about women, luxury and cars. Socially and statistically I had the odds against me, and that gave me an incredible kind of freedom. I didn't have to deal with the weight of certain expectations. All my mother ever said was: 'You have a special gift, and you're special. Think hard and make sure you make good use of your talent.' The teachers in school, where I was viewed as a very unusual child, actually said pretty much the same thing. That's why I was able to move to Copenhagen and to set myself the impossible goal of making some kind of career for myself in the film business, and although I couldn't get into the National Film School,* I could get into the University of Copenhagen. Our system is so Danish, because there's just no competitive spirit in Denmark. It's virtually against the law to be competitive. In principle it's also against the law to be ambitious in Denmark. That's why the universities have become dumping grounds for people with good grade point averages, who have the liberty to approach everything they do in the most unambitious manner imaginable. They can park themselves in the universities for a few years and run around saying that they're studying psychology although they never open a book.

That's exactly what I did, and I quickly ground to a halt because it was all too intellectual and academic. Also, I already had a feeling that the favoured academic approach to the language of art was contrived. I could just tell that my expressive gene lay elsewhere. Milos Forman's *One Flew Over the Cuckoo's Nest* wasn't constructed in terms of some book of symbols that he tried to integrate into the story in order to make it more compelling. Forman was driven rather by a strong, intuitive sense of how to tell stories. That's the simple truth, but the intellectual's use of the language of interpretation involves trying to systematise Forman's mode of expression. We're supposed to believe that he actually mastered the relevant system at an intellectual level, which he didn't.

I started doing radio completely by accident, but I was extremely good at it, and it boosted my sense of self-confidence enormously. It probably gave me the confidence I needed to believe that it was only a matter of time before I'd be making films. I besieged Per Holst Film and tried to convince him that I was a talented director. He partly believed this to be true. At some level he could tell that I had some kind of talent. He gave me a monthly salary which was to keep me at Per Holst Film, where I was supposed to generate some ideas, but none of them ever went anywhere, and he never asked me to direct a damned thing.

I was actually having a good time with radio, but then I started writing for TV, and I did this because Per Holst started to challenge me. The second time I presented him with a project, he leaned back in his chair, listened to my idea, and said the following with his inimitable sense of authority: 'Ole Bornedal may well be incredibly talented, but how typical it is of him to be blustering around and to show up without a finished script. ' I was mortified, because he was absolutely right. That's why I started writing a script and that's also why I started working for TV, and I virtually forced a TV film down the throats of the people at the Danish Broadcasting Corporation. I was in charge of one of the most popular satirical programs on Danish TV, so I knew that we'd set aside ten days for the purpose of shooting a new trailer for the program, but I basically decided that we didn't need a new trailer. Instead I said that I'd use those ten days to shoot a short fiction film. At first the response was, 'That's impossible. You can't make a film', but I said, 'If you don't give me those ten days, I'll leave the Danish Broadcasting Corporation, and you'll never hear from me again.' I ended up making the TV film *Masturbator*. I haven't seen *Masturbator* in a long time but I still think it's pretty good.

It's always been a struggle. I've never been given anything on a silver platter, and I think that's made me a very strong director, because I've had to function as both a producer and a director. I understand the Machiavellian system, I've learnt the art of diplomacy, I know how to meet a deadline, I understand money matters, and so on. I've absorbed all that by simply being involved in so many aspects of this line of work. After *Masturbator* I was approached by Bo Leck Fischer, who was a producer for the TV drama unit and who's always been a bit of a madman. He's facilitated the production of some of the most challenging TV programs, and he basically threw another little TV film into my lap. It ended up being called *Somewhere in the World* (*I en del af verden*), and although it's just a lot of primitive video nonsense, it worked pretty well. As a result of those two TV productions, people at the Danish Broadcasting Corporation suddenly realised that I had some sense of how to make films for TV. *Masturbator* got pretty good reviews and was described, among other things, as the most important event in Danish TV since Lars von Trier's *Medea*. After that I started to write *Nightwatch*, which Michael Obel had agreed to produce. He's a very commercial film producer, very admirable in many ways, but not the most intellectual person in the world.

**Hjort:** You're very fond of Ingmar Bergman's films and in your immensely successful road movie, *Charlot and Charlotte*, you nod to the Swedish film-maker in a lengthy and rather unusual re-enactment of a scene from *Wild Strawberries* (*Smultronstället*). Bergman is a controversial figure in the Scandinavian film world and some film-makers, such as Søren Kragh-Jacobsen, go so far as to claim that his presence has been so overwhelming as to have had a suffocating effect, if not on Scandinavian film as a whole, then on Swedish film. What, exactly, is the function of the re-enacted sequence? How would you describe your relation to Bergman and his films?

**Bornedal:** Now, I happen to think that *Wild Strawberries* is one of the greatest films that has ever been made. It's in many ways the ultimate film, because it's touching, moving, frightening and poetic, and because it celebrates life in spite of life. It basically depicts some frighteningly cynical people. If you were to propose a story like that, people would think 'What a sinister, depressing film.' It's a story about an old man who realises that he's wasted his life. He's been cold as ice his entire life because he once was rejected by his great love, and as a result his son has become just as cynical as he himself used to be. Within that general theme Bergman manages to celebrate life and the idea that people can change. That man, who has caused so much unhappiness, nonetheless learns so much from his life journey that he is able to smell the scent of fresh strawberry blossoms on his clean bed linnen.

    *Charlot and Charlotte* was a study in clichés. I was in the kind of mood that made me want to travel around Denmark for a couple of months together with people I love and a film crew I liked. There's a circus-like quality to film-making, which has to do with coming together like a family for a certain period of time and exploring some sensuous spaces that are largely without limits. That's incredibly fascinating. My goal in *Charlot and Charlotte* was really only to play around freely and to carry out an experiment for myself, and that experiment was defined by questions such as: 'What would happen if I were to close my eyes and make a film? What would happen if I were to write this film without serious reflection, if I were to coast my way through it, without respecting my art, without having any particularly great artistic ambitions?' I remember that Trier said that he'd made *The Kingdom* (*Riget*) with his left hand. I made *Charlot and Charlotte* with my left foot. The entire process was very casual, and it was a very cheeky undertaking on my part, because I knew that I had an entertaining story. I'd been producing satire long enough to know whether the coin would drop, and I just knew that the story would work. I could tell that people were amused when they read the script. I was fairly sure that something really dreadful would have to happen for it not to turn out reasonably well.

I simply played around with a number of clichés, and in that respect the road movie provides a wonderful dramaturgical tool. You get away from the chamber play, and you don't get tired of the main characters, because you can keep replacing them. The dramaturgical elements are very underdeveloped, because that's what a trip is like. If we were to head south together, we would meet a lot of interesting people, and we would easily be able to turn that into a story. It was really just a question of mobilising a lot of clichés. Now, I just happen to love the classics of the Danish cinema, which meant a lot to me as a child. We used to queue up in front of the cinema in order to see the newest Dirch Passer film. Unfortunately Dirch Passer died before I hit the scene, Poul Reichhardt died before I hit the scene, and Poul Bundgaard died the other day. I'd offered him two film roles over the years. I really worship those old Danish luminaries and Ove Sprogøe is one of the ones I love the most. So I called Sprogøe, whom I'd met a few years earlier, and he was very eager to be part of *Charlot and Charlotte*. That's why that sequence we were talking about, the one that resembles Bergman, was made with Ove Sprogøe's sense of inwardness and poetry. I hadn't consciously thought of Bergman and *Wild Strawberries* in connection with the scene, but I suddenly realised that we were dealing with a Bergman cliché, just as there are so many other clichés in that film. There's nothing more to it than that. *Charlot and Charlotte* is just a joke. However, Bergman is probably the person who has influenced me the most, along with the neo-realists. They're the directors who have moved me the most.

It's true that Bergman has had a suffocating effect on a lot of mediocre directors in the Scandinavian countries and elsewhere in the world, because film art suddenly came to be viewed as something highly intellectual. Every film-maker has his or her own unique language, a unique mode of expression that draws on a very personal source of inspiration. Ingmar Bergman draws on one of the most unique sources in the entire world, because very few people have been locked in that closet and beaten by pappa the priest. Bergman creates a film style based on silence and whispers, on a denial of God's existence, all of which he redeems, of course, through the very aesthetic that he masters so brilliantly. Bergman wouldn't be able to make a thriller, for example, but he's a master at what he does. To all those little boys, which is what directors mostly are, Bergman's film art clearly represents both a potent source of inspiration and a challenge, for he's a film artist who not only feels what he describes, but is able to communicate it. That's why they're so eager to imitate him, and that kind of imitation is one of the greatest catastrophes in film history. Not clichés, not the mobilisation of clichés, but the kind of copying that involves believing that the relevant feeling somehow can be imitated.

It's clear that a strong and talented director may well have a suffocating effect, just as Lars von Trier might have today, because he's become an idol for so many people. If I didn't know Trier well enough to know that the Dogme* concept springs from a satirical and provocatively idiotic way of thinking, then I would start to fear its dominance. There just might be some people out there who are stupid enough to think that Dogme ought to become the new style. If a producer had proposed the Dogme concept, he would have been collectively slaughtered by every director in the country, but the proposal just happened to come from an artist, so now suddenly it's brilliant. It's that simple.

Bergman's great impact has to do with his deep and provocative psychological insights. I don't remember a lot of the images, but the ones I do remember have a kind of caustic power to them, and at times I use them myself. There's especially one effect that I use from the end of *Summer with Monica* (*Sommaren med Monika*). I think that was the first Bergman film I ever saw, and it completely took my breath away. I was just entering puberty and I thought Harriet Andersson was the most wonderful woman in the whole wide world. There's a scene in which she leaves her husband and child, and the camera moves up a side street in a sleazy part of Stockholm and seeks out a pub. The camera comes to a standstill outside the pub, and we all know that she's sitting on the other side of the window drinking beer with some bastard. We know that she's to be condemned now for having let down and betrayed the wonderful man she'd found, for having thrown away all that happiness. Then she turns her face towards the camera and looks straight at us, and she's as cold as ice and completely proud of herself; she just couldn't care less. That kind of simple, minimalistic provocation is brilliant film art. That's what film art is all about and that kind of effect is best attained, not by means of that bloody hand-held camera that's so popular at the moment, but by means of clean, simple choreographic moves in a dance between a camera and an actor. That dance, unfortunately, is all too rare.

**Hjort:** Contemporary Danish cinema is surrounded by optimism, and this optimism is generated, not only by the emergence of internationally acclaimed film-makers, but by the growing interest in Danish film in Denmark, where American film for decades has held sway. Recent figures indicate that Danish films generate about 30 percent of Danish ticket sales, which is a significant increase compared to earlier years. Your work has contributed directly to this renewed indigenous interest in Danish film, and I'm thinking here, of course, of the thriller *Nightwatch* and of the popular road movie, *Charlot and Charlotte*. In an interview with *Politiken* (August 1996) you criticised earlier tendencies within Danish film as follows: 'Anything that even remotely resembled a commercial success was slaughtered, and the Danish film industry became a playground for spoilt intellectuals.' What, in your mind, explains the radical shift away from art-cinema productions to popular films, which clearly marks the landscape of contemporary Danish film-making? *Nightwatch* was funded through the 50/50 policy introduced by the Film Act* of 1989. Is the 50/50 policy, which has since become the 60/40 policy, in part responsible for what is being hailed as the renewal of Danish film?

**Bornedal:** I definitely think so. *Nightwatch* was funded by means of the 50/50 policy, because none of the relevant members of the consultant* system wanted to fund it. I think *Nightwatch* had a much greater impact on Danish film than you actually might think at first – although it may be rather self-centred of me to talk about this. There had been two big box office successes before *Nightwatch*. One was *House of the Spirits*

Nightwatch (Nattevagten). *[Photo: Rolf Konow]*

(*Åndernes hus*), which was the film that our parents and grandparents went to see. That film was able to appeal to everyone, because it was a Bille August film with lots of big stars. The other film, *Waltzing Regitze* (*Dansen med Regitze*), was classic Danish film art at its best. It effectively conveyed a fine story that simply appealed to a wide audience. *Nightwatch's* impact was somewhat different. It was in many ways more modern and appealed to a younger generation. *Nightwatch* made use of a contemporary cinematic language while mobilising the classic thriller genre, and it was driven uniquely by a strong sense of narrative desire, by a tight dramaturgical set-up. What is more, it pursued certain entertainment values almost shamelessly. I don't think the film is a great work of art, but it did help to legitimate the idea that even European film art can make good use of generic stories.

In Hollywood there's been a long tradition of this kind of thing, and there's also a good deal of respect for, and interest in B films. The film milieu is extremely liberal, and the dominant motivating force is an intense passion for film-making. It's clear that the Hollywood system with all its commercialism also has its limitations. However, the director's sense of narrative pleasure is completely uninhibited; it's unconstrained by intellectual requirements having to do with what might be considered proper or a matter of good taste. You see the same kind of phenomenon at various film festivals around the world, where one cinema might run a Bergman retrospective, while another shows horror films. One of the interesting things about the French film milieu is that although French film is highly intellectual, attitudes towards the various film genres have been very liberal. In France people also talk about *le film d'action* as great art. It's possible to publish an interview with Jean-Claude van Damme in a serious film journal. People know full well that Jean-Claude van Damme films aren't serious cinematic expressions that are designed to save the world; they're ballet and nothing more. As instances of the genre, though, some of them are really quite good. They meet the genre's requirements, as well as the expectations of their intended audience. That's a lot more than can be said of so many of the more intellectual films, or of the kind of intellectual film art that seems intent on saving the world. 'Art as weapon' was after all one of our battle cries in the 1960s and 1970s. Naturally that meant that a lot of bad, intellectual directors took over the medium and made films that were essentially hostile to the audience. The money in question should have been used on more artistically innovative projects. Cinematic technology is outstanding today, and that's where the Dogme concept comes into the picture. Now all those experimental film artists, and all those people with a story they're dying to tell, can go out and make the relevant films for virtually no money at all, with two hand-held cameras. In that sense the Dogme concept, in combination with new technologies, might just be the salvation of European film art. That is, now all those chamber plays that previously would have been fairly expensive to make can be made digitally.

**Hjort:** Your thriller, *Nightwatch*, was an enormous success and sold some 465,344 tickets in Denmark alone. The film's strict adherence to certain generic conventions, combined with its emphasis on a tightly constructed narrative, recalls certain American film-making practices. The concept of American film, interestingly, is also explicitly evoked in the course of the film. The main character, Martin (Nikolaj Coster Waldau) asks his lover, Kalinka (Sophie Gråbøl), whether he can say 'I love you' without sounding like a 'bad American movie'. During the closing moments of the film, Martin looks teasingly at his friend, Jens (Kim Bodnia), as they await their brides before the altar, and he says: 'If this were a film, it would be called *Nightguard*.' Could you talk a little about the interpenetration of Danish and American elements in this thriller?

**Bornedal:** As a film-maker I've simply studied my masters, and I've also seen a lot of dance. Making a thriller has a lot to do with dance, choreography and music. It's a question of timing and movement, of the extent to which one builds up and comments on a mood. I think that's all just a matter of talent; you either have it or you don't. Bille August doesn't have it. He was unable to pull off *Smilla's Feeling for Snow (Frøken Smillas fornemmelse for sne)* as a thriller because it was so obvious throughout that he was dancing a dance that he just didn't know. I'm not saying this in order to criticise Bille, who's someone I'm very fond of and who's a talented film-maker. The point is that he just doesn't have the knack when it comes to that genre.

When you make a film nowadays, there's always some kind of meta-level, a film within a film within a film. When you write a dialogue nowadays you frequently refer to other films. The universe of film or images is a very large part of our everyday world. If Freud were to write his interpretation of dreams today, it would be very different, because we get most of our symbols and images, not from our dreams, but from the media. At some level, art believes it has a certain integrity. At some level the dull actor believes that drama is just drama and that focus is just focus. Bad directors, bad actors and especially bad script writers believe in the idea of truth. They believe that our task is to represent the real, a naturalistic universe, but any naturalistic universe is simply a construction. That's why it's often so boring to watch Chekhov or Ibsen nowadays. Their plays tend to be staged very naturalistically and the directors don't allow themselves that ironic distance.

**Hjort:** *Nightwatch* made Danish film history when you, shortly after its release, found yourself being courted by Miramax, who were interested in purchasing the rights to an American remake. You accepted a tempting contract with Miramax and the terms specified that you would direct three films for the company, the first of which was to be *Nightwatch*. As you, of course, know, interest in this remake process has been intense in Denmark, and a number of publications have made a point of keeping Danes up to date on what has become the saga of *Nightwatch*. You were required to change the film following a test screening that suggested that American audiences would respond poorly to certain religious elements. Miramax postponed the film's release on more than one occasion, and when *Nightwatch*, with its stellar cast (including Nick Nolte, Patricia Arquette and Ewan McGregor), was finally released in April 1998, it received mixed reviews. What did you learn from your experience with Miramax? Are there lessons here from which young Danish directors more generally might profit?

**Bornedal:** A lot of interesting experiences followed in the wake of my collaboration with Miramax, especially on account of Bob and Harvey Weinstein, who were in charge of the project, and with whom I actually became very good friends. The actual shooting of *Nightwatch* was terrific, everything was totally wonderful, and I was free to do as I pleased, but everything suddenly became extremely complicated during the post-production phase. The real difficulty was ultimately that *Nightwatch* would never become a box office hit in the US. The film was too European and too different. Americans like to view death as a spectacular show, as a dramatically exaggerated element that creates a motive for revenge and leads to some kind of resolution, but American audiences typically lose interest the minute death, or the silence of death, are represented as almost a fundamental element in a film. I think that the most important difference between European and American film has to do primarily with the difference between silence and noise. Compared with the American norm, *Nightwatch* is a very quiet film. It draws heavily, I think, on Bergman's stillness. It relies on a choreography of stillness, as I like to say. I found the media attention rather irritating. I didn't think that either I or the film *Nightwatch* deserved much attention. It's clear, though, that in a country the size of Denmark, it's terribly interesting if someone goes abroad, just as people in Nørresundby were fascinated by the idea of my studying at the University of Copenhagen. The problem was that the Weinstein brothers expected *Nightwatch* to become a huge box office success. They kept trying to build up the film, to turn it into something it was never meant to be and couldn't possibly be, and I'd been telling them this for two years. At the end of the day, they nonetheless expected it to do just as well as *Scream*, which was unthinkable.

**Hjort:** In an earlier interview, you made a number of fascinating, but tantalisingly obscure pronouncements about *Charlot and Charlotte*. You said, for example, that the series creates 'a kind of strangely popular, modern Morten Korch* landscape, that otherwise has nothing to do with Korch. It is grotesque, witty, ominous, dark – it's Fellini in Danish' (*Ekstra Bladet*, May 1995). It seems to me that it's important to clarify these remarks. The Morten Korch films constitute a corpus of popular heritage films that were reviled by film-makers of an earlier generation, and this tradition is now being resuscitated, perhaps in an ironic mode, by film-makers associated with Lars von Trier and Zentropa. Why, exactly, does *Charlot and Charlotte* have everything and nothing to do with Morten Korch?

**Bornedal:** Probably because the story didn't have much to do with Morten Korch, while the scenographic design did. With reference to Danish film traditions, it's interesting to note that a lot of recent films take place in urban environments, whereas Morten Korch is all about rural environments. I was surprised to discover how easy it was to use the Danish landscape as a cinematic cliché. Denmark has some of the most beautiful landscapes in all of Europe. There's almost nothing like it. Southern Europe becomes dry and boring in the course of the summer, whereas Northern Europe retains a certain freshness. Together the colours, the sun and the landscapes make for an extraordinary scenography, one that has been used very, very little in modern Danish film. Those directors who have attempted to mobilise it, have done so poorly. I'm surprised that the Swedish landscape figures only as a minimal aesthetic element in Thomas Vinterberg's *The Greatest Heroes* (*De største helte*). My cinematographer, Dan Laustsen, and I, on the other hand, shamelessly sought out the most picture-perfect images. The Korchian element in *Charlot and Charlotte* is really a matter of fully utilising the landscape's scenographic potential.

**Hjort:** In an interview with *Berlingske Tidende* (August 1996), you suggest that *Charlot and Charlotte* was designed specifically to appeal to women: 'It's a very feminine series.' That women constitute a significant percentage of a film's potential audience is a fact that critics regularly remember with surprise when they need to explain certain cinematic successes. The phenomenal success, for example, of James Cameron's *Titanic* has once again placed the issue of a female public on the agenda for discussion in the popular press. You are clearly a film-maker who thinks carefully about the issue of audience appeal. You seem to be intent on developing a strategy of multiple address, for your films seem to appeal explicitly, not only to male and female publics, but to a national as well as a series of regionalised audiences. How, exactly, do you approach the question of audience appeal?

**Bornedal:** The underlying principle is really just my conception of myself as someone with really ordinary tastes in film. My films are based on that assumption and they're rooted in the kinds of stories that I myself would feel like seeing. That basic perspective does, of course, need to be broadened a little once questions of financing and marketing enter the picture, but I don't think there are huge divergences at the level of what large numbers of people in various western societies like to see. For example, I was sitting in my office some time ago and I thought to myself: 'I haven't seen a story about an unlikely couple and their love for each other in ages.' In a flash I'd written a story called *The Lady and the Thief*, which is about a 55 year old aristocratic lady and a 22 year old thief who end up getting involved. She's dying of cancer and he takes her on a journey which ends with him dying and her being cured. When I start telling that story, people sit up and listen. A good film is already a good film the minute you can sense that enthusiasm while recounting the story. Not the kind of enthusiasm that has to do with people noting that Ole has decided to tell a story, but genuine enthusiasm. For example, when people start to cry while I'm telling the story, that's when I know it really works. At that point, the film is off to a good start.

**Hjort:** You're a versatile and energetic figure. At this point you've written and directed radio plays, TV series, shorts and feature films. You've also written and directed a number of plays. You staged *Oh Happy Day* in the well-known Frederiksberg theatre, *Dr. Dantes Aveny* in 1993, *Macbeth – Two Words and a Coincidence* in Gladsaxe Theatre in 1998, and *God Bless Denmark* in Østre Gasværk Theatre in 1999. It could be argued that this kind of versatility partly reflects the economic realities of artistic production in Denmark. As Søren Kragh-Jacobsen points out, the number of feature films produced annually in Denmark is significantly smaller than the number of talented Danish directors. The tendency among contemporary Danish film-makers is thus to combine film-making with a range of other activities. One senses, however, that your wide-ranging activities are based, not on purely pragmatic considerations, but on the conviction that experience with a range of inter-related media ultimately strengthens one's abilities in each of the relevant areas. Has your work in radio and theatre made you a better film-maker?

**Bornedal:** Very much so. I'm definitely a much better director as a result of my theatre experience. You can cheat constantly in film. You can sit a hundred metres away from the actors and still get something out of them, or, rather, they can be forced to produce something worthwhile themselves. You'll always get something on film and the camera is brilliant at cheating, and if you shake the camera, then, funnily enough, the performances always seem to improve, because a shaky camera lends a certain documentary quality to the scene. Even you and I, who probably have only average acting skills, could produce a vibrant scene on film if we were filmed with a hand-held camera.

What's really a challenge for the actor/director is the kind of situation in which an actor stands frozen in front of the camera and has to make a given scene work, has to bring to life the very character that the scene is all about. That's when the real demands get made concerning what exactly is to be expressed in front of the camera; and we're talking here about a camera that exposes and reveals things, instead of shakily obscuring them. There's nothing more static than theatre, because the basic box-like structure is almost a given, and it takes extraordinary discipline to bring it to life. Bergman was able to create the most powerful and vulnerable of characters because he knew so much about theatre. Many of the directors who are especially gifted at working with actors have had a lot of experience with theatre. There are, of course, lots of outstanding directors who've had no experience whatsoever along those lines, but that also shows in their films. Their films are frequently in many ways very effect- or plot driven – and I'm thinking here of John Ford, William Wyler or Hitchcock for that matter.

I don't take on lots of different jobs on account of monetary considerations, and I'm not sure that Søren Kragh-Jacobsen is really right when he claims that there's more than enough talent around. The fact that audiences have ignored Danish film for so many years suggests rather that there isn't enough talent around, or, at the very least, that there wasn't enough talent around earlier. There may be enough talent to support twelve feature films a year, and the talent pool is probably big enough to support twelve 'new technology films', aka Dogme films. That means that there's room for the production of expensive films with a broad appeal, as well as the kind of experimental, elitist films that are also necessary if directors are to become better and more intelligent film-makers.

# Susanne Bier

## 1960–

Susanne Bier graduated from the National Film School of Denmark* in 1987. Bier's reputation as one of Denmark's most talented young directors is based in part on a couple of features – *Freud Leaving Home* (*Freud flyttar hemifrån*, 1990) and *Like It Never Was Before* (*Pensionat Oskar*, 1995) – that are classified as Swedish rather than Danish. Bier is nonetheless perceived by Danish audiences as a quintessentially Danish film-maker whose films appeal to a broad spectrum of the Danish public. Bier won international acclaim for her work

*Susanne Bier.*

already as a student. *Island of the Blessed* (*De saliges ø*, 1987) won a series of prizes, including the prestigious American Academy Award for Best Student Film. The romantic comedy, *The One and Only* (*Den eneste ene*, 1999) was a major breakthrough and is one of the most widely seen films in the entire history of Danish cinema, having sold 850,000 tickets in 1999 alone. Susanne Bier's films successfully combine technical inventiveness with a focussed narrative centred on dialogue and outstanding performances. Bier's systematic interest in issues having to do with multiculturalism and complex identities makes her a unique figure in Danish film-making.

### Feature films
1990, *Freud Leaving Home* (*Freud flyttar hemifrån*)
1993, *Family Matters* (*Det bli'r i familien*)
1995, *Like It Never Was Before* (*Pensionat Oskar*)
1997, *Credo* (*Sekten*)
1999, *The One and Only* (*Den eneste ene*)

### Short films
1987, *Island of the Blessed* (*De saliges ø*, graduation film)
1991, *A Letter to Jonas* (*Brev til Jonas*)

### TV productions
1992, *Luischen*

**Hjort:** Having completed the Danish equivalent of 'A levels', you spent three years at the University of Jerusalem studying comparative religion and set design. You also studied architecture in London for a couple of years. These different interests are, I believe, reflected in your films. Much like Antonioni, you tend to use architectural constructs, not simply as a means of establishing a physical context for a given narrative, but as a way of actually generating the fiction and its various meanings. I'm thinking, in particular, of the Swedish film, *Like It Never Was Before*, which begins with a series of lurid images of perfectly maintained suburban dwellings that are filmed in fast motion and strikingly contrasted with rat-infested garbage. The film seems in many ways to be posited on the assumption that there is a significant correlation between buildings and modes of life. In a sense, *Like It Never Was Before* is a story about the houses we see during the opening moments of the film. What role does architecture play in your thinking about film?

**Bier:** I too believe that the buildings or physical spaces have an important bearing on the characterisation of the characters' concerns. At times it's as though they're trapped in what they at some level see as a safe haven or basic framework, although it doesn't in fact make them that happy. This is very much the case in *Like It Never Was Before*. In my case what happened was that as an architect student I would fantasise about the people who were to live in the houses I was trying to design. I became more and more intrigued by this and actually started designing specific things for specific characters that I had in my head. Then I suddenly realised that you just can't make buildings that way. Personally, I prefer architecture that doesn't impose its life on mine. I like something that is, if not neutral, then at least reserved. Personally, I like something that is distinctive, but doesn't tell me how I should live, but as a film-maker you of course inevitably describe how people live. That's essentially what made me shift from architecture to film. It was a very organic shift for me.

**Hjort:** A salient feature of your films is extraordinary acting. Could you talk about your approach to acting?

**Bier:** My starting point is a firm belief in the idea of very specific and clearly defined characters. I've never been interested in people who are a bit anonymous, and I would never be able to describe someone who is very anonymous. If you look at the characters in all my films, you'll notice that they're all very clearly defined; they're very extreme, for better or worse. I suppose that that is what interests me about them, and this is probably also true of my own personal life. It's also the case that if the character is very clearly defined and extreme, then everything having to do with the description of that character has to be equally definitive. That's essentially how I work with actors, because I think things become very clear that way. My feeling is that in Scandinavia there's been a tendency to emphasise a certain naturalism, and I must say that I don't actually experience the naturalism in question as particularly true or as particularly descriptive of how people really live together. My characters are always a little more crazy. I'm sure that other people wouldn't describe them as naturalistic characters, although they *are* authentic, because they're emotionally authentic.

Now, I know I'm getting myself into something that can be a bit difficult to grasp here, but I frequently experience naturalism as an attempt to produce something that looks like reality, instead of focussing on some characters with specific problems and working on their relevant emotional realities. In Scandinavian film, for example, a sad woman is typically described by means of a series of very direct indications. The woman might be made to stand in a certain place, and perhaps there's a little tear in the corner of her eye. It's apparent that it's a matter of a kind of suffering that involves accepting the pain. She might be standing by the window, peering out and watching her lover leave without doing anything. I would never ever be able to describe a woman that way, because I don't think that's how women react. That doesn't mean they have to shout and scream or be generally hysterical, but I think it's much more interesting if the woman walks out the door, pretends that she isn't the least bit sad, and stands in the farmyard waving good-bye. At the same time the viewer should sense that her composed exterior conceals deep unhappiness. As far as I'm concerned that way of depicting sorrow is much more true and interesting. I have absolutely no relation to the Scandinavian tradition of cinematic representation, with its very direct correlation of inner feeling and external appearance.

**Hjort:** There's been a good deal of talk about making room in Danish film for marginalised voices. For example, Christian Braad Thomsen claims that his aim in *Wellspring of My World* (*Herfra min verden går*) was to record the lives and regional dialects of people living in Jutland. In a similar vein, Lotte Svendsen, who is from Bornholm, has said that she intends, not only to make use of a particular regional dialect in her films, but to focus on the lives and concerns of the lower class. What has been interestingly absent from the discussion so far is the idea that Danish film-making also needs to reflect the multicultural dimensions of contemporary Denmark. It seems to me that your films contribute considerably to Danish film-making in precisely this respect. I have in mind your first feature film, *Freud Leaving Home*, which is based on a manuscript by the Jewish-Swedish writer Marianne Goldman. The film's story is not only about a Jewish family attempting to deal with illness and death, but also about competing notions of Jewishness. In a review of *Family Matters*, Dan Nissen (November 1993) correctly points out that you've systematically demonstrated 'an ability to depict temperaments that depart radically from the insipid dispositions typically attributed to Danes.' Do you see yourself as exploring typically Jewish realities, or is Jewish culture a privileged means of thematising the more general question of what it means to belong to a culture and a community?

**Bier:** I would love to make a film with a Jewish theme again at some point. It's clear that I know that world concretely and can easily describe it as a result. In my mind having a definitive cultural background and also a very strong family background is a source of tremendous strength. The implications of this milieu for my work as a film-maker are probably that I'm able to draw on certain styles of communication. The way that my family communicates is reflected again and again in my extreme characters. With reference to the contrast between naturalism and the idea of making feeling central, I think I've been fortunate to be part of a family that has been incredibly interesting to observe in that regard. I do think that I, as a modern Dane, at times end up feeling fairly alienated from certain typically Danish ways of relating to other people, particularly when it comes to family. I feel much too young to be able to speak of the films I've made in terms of the notion of an oeuvre, but one could certainly argue that there are some recurrent themes in my work. I can certainly see that that's the case, and frequently my films are about feeling alone while being surrounded by a lot of people. I don't think this is a particularly Jewish or particularly ethnic theme, but I do think it's something that is salient in a culture where there's a hell of a lot of communicating going on. For example, in Sweden, where I've worked a fair bit, they have a film art that builds enormously on silence and the unsaid. Swedes are like that to a certain extent. They live out in the country and nature is tremendously important to them. I, on the other hand, can easily construct the stillness I need in a lot of noise. This is a completely different way of doing things and reflects, I think, a different cultural background.

**Hjort:** Your second feature film, *Family Matters*, involved multiple sources of funding and is classified as a Danish/Swedish/Portugese co-production. Some critics have argued that *Family Matters* suffers from many of the problems that typically plague co-productions, that it's an example of a Euro-pudding. The claim is that the somewhat far-fetched nature of the story may be dictated in part by funding arrangements, which are also apparent in the rather different acting styles of the Portugese, Danish and Swedish actors. What, at this point, is your own view of *Family Matters*? Do you agree that European co-productions, to date, have been shaped largely by strategic thinking and purely financial concerns? Is it indeed necessary to pay greater attention in the future to questions having to do with a film's cultural coherence and identity?

**Bier:** I think the situation has really changed. When we made *Family Matters*, co-productions were very much in their infancy and I have the feeling that a different co-production model has emerged in the meantime, one that involves emphasising one particular place. That is, if it's a matter of two production companies collaborating, then a certain amount of alternating occurs. One might prefer, for example, to emphasise Denmark in the first instance, and subsequently Holland, instead of producing something that is bound to be diffuse and unclear. I don't believe in writing stories aimed at co-productions, but I do believe, on the other hand, that there's a much greater degree of exchange now than there used to be and that many more things get off the ground than just ten years ago. So at this point I think there are a lot of stories involving elements derived from various countries.

I'm very sceptical of the kind of new nationalism that insists that we must protect everything Danish. I don't think Danish culture is in any way threatened. Cultures have to be strong enough to resist an encounter with other cultures. If they aren't, then there's no reason to sustain them. I'm convinced that whatever is worth preserving in Danish culture easily can accommodate a significant degree of inspiration from, and interaction with, lots of other cultures.

I can see lots of weaknesses in *Family Matters*, but at the same time I'm also very fond of that film. The films that work easily and do well, the successful films one makes, have a life of their own. It's true that you can be more or less involved in promoting them, that you can be more or less committed to attending various festivals with them, but at some

*Sidse Babett Knudsen and Paprika Steen in the romantic comedy,* The One and Only *(Den eneste ene).* [*Photo: Ole Kragh-Jacobsen*]

level they actually have a life of their own. You feel a much greater degree of responsibility, on the other hand, for the films that aren't quite as successful. Perhaps you even have a strange kind of soft spot for them. That's a bit how I feel about *Family Matters*. We could have done a lot of different things with that film. To start with, it would have been a good idea, for example, to decide whether it's a tragedy or a comedy. All those comments about the extent to which some of the acting styles diverged, or the confusion surrounding the combination of Danish and Portuguese elements, have something to do with the fact that it's simply not clear whether the film is a comedy or a tragedy. Had it been either one or the other, we would have been forced to make some radically different decisions about the story itself, and then the other elements would have fallen into place much more easily. It's clear, though, that that film was an attempt to do a lot of different things all at once. With time and experience, one learns how to keep things separate. Before making *Family Matters*, I had made *Freud Leaving Home*, which was a major success, and that kind of major success so early on in one's career is actually quite problematic, because it interferes with one's ability to judge things properly. I've learnt more from *Family Matters* than from any other film I've ever made, because it taught me that it's not enough simply to floor the accelerator, as it were. At some point, one has to ask oneself a lot of very basic questions, and I simply hadn't done that. At the same time, I do think there are some wonderful scenes in that film, but if I were to make it today, I would structure it very differently. I don't really think the problems that have been identified stemmed from weaknesses in the script. They were linked, rather, to my own basic naïveté about how many different elements a single film actually can sustain.

**Hjort:** Your husband, Philip Zandén, has acted in virtually all of your films. For example, in *Family Matters* he plays the role of the cook, Jan Borelius, who learns late in life that he was adopted as an infant. Traumatised by his discovery, Jan goes in search of his biological mother who unwittingly leads him to his sister with whom he falls in love and has an incestuous affair. Philip Zandén's role in this film is particularly important, for he also wrote the script, together with Lars Kjeldgård. In an interview published in *Politiken*, Zandén makes the following remark about the film: 'It includes the best of American film and television – that which is effective and different – as well as elements from classical European drama' (November 1993). What, exactly, is your relation to American cinematic traditions and film-making practices?

**Bier:** I've learnt a lot from American film of the 1970s, Coppola, Scorsese. In a way I'm drawn to realism, but I probably feel emotionally closer to southern European film, that is, Spanish film. In some strange way, I'm especially drawn to Spanish film, more than to Italian film, for example. I do, of course, learn from observing the Americans. I just happen to have seen Almodóvar's latest film, *All About My Mother* (*Todo sobre mi madre*) which is different from his earlier films, and which is much less extreme and more emotional, at least that's how I experienced it. I simply feel at home while sitting there watching it in the movie theatre. He describes certain situations and feelings that I can identify with, although the world in question of course also is completely different. There are a lot of Scandinavian film artists whom I admire enormously, but I don't actually feel a deep sense of belonging in relation to the community in question.

**Hjort:** Your film *Freud Leaving Home* was praised by critics and much loved by audiences. A key term used to identify the film's virtues was 'popular', which, as Jens-Martin Eriksen remarks in an interesting essay published in *Politiken* (October 1997), is anything but a precise term. Following Eriksen the popular is often associated with 'What expresses the nation's true spirit, its real essence or the specificity of what is Danish.' As a result, he claims, the term 'popular' easily becomes 'a Danish euphemism for nationalism.' What is striking is the desire, on the part of critics and reviewers, to categorise a film such as *Freud Leaving Home* as popular. *Freud Leaving Home* is anything but a matter of further entrenching existing ways of imagining a people or nation, for what is brought into focus here is the question of complex identities, the cultural reality of citizens whose modes of belonging to a nation are complicated by religion and exile. In this sense, it is not surprising that *Freud Leaving Home* won a Special Mention at the Montreal Film Festival in 1991. The compelling way in which *Freud Leaving Home* explores the boundaries between, and tensions within, cultural and religious communities would hardly have been lost on Montreal's intensely multicultural audiences. Do you think of yourself as a popular director? To what extent do you keep the audience in mind when you develop your film projects?

**Bier:** I think that popular film, in a positive sense, is the ultimate goal. I do, of course, have a positive, inclusive sense of 'popular' in mind here. I don't think that one should talk down to people, although this really happens a lot. However, if you have something to say and can express it with such precision and simplicity that it moves a lot of people, then I think you've achieved something important, especially in the case of film, for film is, after all, a popular medium. I don't think there's anything particularly attractive about the idea of making films that nobody wants to see. Or at least in that case, the films would have to be very, very cheap. I do respect the film artists who make that kind of choice, but then you have to be sure that you're willing to restrict yourself to a particular category of budgets. As far as the audience is concerned, I believe that I always try to encourage an ongoing discussion with myself and other members of the film crew about basic questions of comprehension: How will this be understood? What kind of experience will this prompt? Who is likely to understand this? For example, when I was shooting my most recent film, *The One and Only*, we were discussing the characters and realised that although I and a couple of the other female members of the crew might find it amusing when a given character does such and such, there are a lot of people, who don't happen to live where we live or eat the kind of food that we eat, who simply won't get the point. It's easy to get trapped in a kind of internal code, so in that sense I certainly do think about the audience, and in any event these issues really interest me. I think of film as a type of mass communication and I care about reaching a lot of people, or particular kinds of people. Admittedly, this is all very complicated and it's frequently a matter of speculation. If you read the relevant American studies – and they're based on a lot of experience in the area of audience research – you'll see that they're also wrong sometimes. It's really a question of being very clear and of breathing life into what you create. That's what excites people, and their responses aren't necessarily governed by a lot of deep reflections. If the film has some life in it, then it's off to a good start.

**Hjort:** Many of your films deal with sexual conflict and transgression. Your much praised student film, *Island of the Blessed*, tells the story of a priest who, inspired by Abraham's sacrificial attitudes towards Isaac, kills the child who is born to his wife as a result of her adulterous relation with his brother. In your short film, *A Letter to Jonas*, you focus, among other things, on adultery and serial monogamy. In *Freud Leaving Home*, Freud (Gunille Röör), a passionate student of psychology, decides to discover sex as her mother dies of cancer. Freud's brother, David (Philip Zandén), confronts his parents with his homosexuality, while her sister, the orthodox Jew, Deborah (Jessica Zandén), has both an affair and an abortion. In *Family Matters* Jan (Philip Zandén) has sex with his sister, Constanza (Ana Padrao), first unknowingly and then in full knowledge of the transgressive nature of the relationship. There's the suggestion earlier on in the film that Jan also has an affair with the male taxi driver who drives him and his mother, Lilli (Ghita Nørby), from Copenhagen to Portugal. In *Like It Never Was Before* a frustrated husband played by Loa Falkman has a homo-erotic affair with a fire-breathing magician figure called Petrus (Simon Norrthon). *Credo* is all about psychological manipulation, sexual exploitation and self-identity. What explains the recurrent emphasis in your films on sexual conflict and transgression?

**Bier:** I'm enormously interested in eroticism at all possible levels, and this is reflected in everything I do. I don't mean sex, but rather a kind of underlying erotic drive or erotic frustration, which I think is very important. I think this interest perhaps also sets me apart from what is traditionally Scandinavian. My characters are far more erotic than those you typically encounter in Scandinavian film. This is also why I feel such an affinity for Spanish film, because Spanish film makes this erotic dimension completely central. In Spanish film you might have a conversation between two people, who are sitting in a train, an elder and a younger woman. The situation might be one that wouldn't typically be experienced as erotic, and yet, the scene might nonetheless be extremely erotic because both people are so clearly driven by their erotic longings. I think all my characters have this dimension, and I suspect that I have it too. I can't help but cultivate this side of the characters I deal with. I think erotic longing is one of the most salient factors in our lives. We can suppress it and do all kinds of things with it, but I think it's decisive for who and what we are.

**Hjort:** Early on in your career, critics hailed you as the outspoken, forceful, female director who was needed in Danish film. In a discussion of *Credo*, you foregrounded the strength and resourcefulness of the two central, female characters, Mona (Sofie Gråbøl) and Anne (Ellen Hillingsøe). Although they're up against a powerful sect, Mona and Anne manage to engineer their own escape. Are you particularly interested in dealing with questions of gender in your films?

**Bier:** I've been fortunate, for a lot of women have paved the way for me. As a result of their efforts I've never had to fight for the right to be a woman *and* a film-maker. So in a certain sense I'm not preoccupied by feminist issues. I don't make films because I want to make some political statement about women. I do make films in which I say a lot about women, because they're what really interests me. If I were to identify an issue on which I take a radical political stance, it would be nationalism, and that issue can of course hardly be said to be irrelevant for gender politics. I can hold forth at length about racism and the government's policies on refugees and immigrants, and I probably find those problems more acute and urgent in a Danish context than gender-related issues.

**Hjort:** In an article published in *Politiken*, Helle Hellmann (1991) cites you as having said that whereas concepts of nationality can be mobilised in unappealing ways, some form of shared cultural identity is crucial. I'm interested in this regard in your interpretation of the shifts in the Film Act's* definition of Danish film. The Film Act of June 7, 1972 provides an explicitly cultural definition of Danish film. More specifically, to qualify as a Danish film, and for support from the Danish Film Institute, the language of the film must be Danish. At the same time, the film's technical and artistic crews must be made up predominantly of Danish nationals. A rather different definition of Danish film is introduced by the Film Act of 1989 which specifies that the film *either* should make use of Danish *or* should contribute in some significant way to 'film art or film culture in Denmark.' Should the state be in the business of promoting a national, cultural identity?

**Bier:** I think the existence of a vibrant cultural life is important. I think culture is important. I think it's important that children learn that when they express themselves artistically they're also exploring life and death, and this can only occur if a stimulating cultural life exists. In that respect I think the Danish film industry is a very positive force, and, all things considered, very much on the right track. I have the feeling that the view is – also amongst members of the Danish Film Institute – that films should have a certain breadth, in the sense of being able to draw an audience, but should also, if possible, be about something worth talking about. The question is how does one talk about that balance, which is very much like the balance involved in gourmet cooking. It's a matter of getting it right, of acquiring the relevant skills, of course, and of being as aware as possible of the various constitutive elements. The advantage of film is that it's able to speak to a lot of people, including children and adolescents. I don't know what it's like in the schools today. I don't know whether the Danish literary canon is perceived as a series of anachronisms, but film, it could be argued, can help to solve certain problems in that respect. However, films also have to talk about something that has a certain depth, a certain significance. When I was getting ready to make *The One and Only* I had to situate myself in relation to the requirements of comedy, and comedy is supposed to be funny. In the case of a romantic comedy you end up mulling over questions like: Do I really have the courage to be that straightforward? Do I really have the courage to be that sentimental? I think it's incredibly liberating to be allowed to pursue precisely those qualities, because they're what we sometimes long for. We would like life to be simple. Frequently it isn't, but it's incredibly liberating when it is, if only for a couple of hours.

**Hjort:** *Credo* is in many ways a radical departure from your earlier work. How would you characterise the key differences between your earlier films and *Credo*? Where does *Credo* figure in your ongoing development of a personal cinematic style?

**Bier:** My greatest strength has to do with characterisation, with my understanding of people and my ability to convey that understanding cinematically. Deep down I just know that I have a gift for understanding people and their relations to each other, and that this is why I'm able to make films that are moving. I don't know that the thriller is really my genre. The thriller is by definition not a character-based genre. If I were to come across a character-based thriller I'd be really intrigued, but I'm convinced that what I have to say, what I want to say, has to do with personal relations. I don't think I'll be making any films that consist of cars chasing other cars, people talking on mobile phones, shots being fired through windows, and that sort of thing. I like that kind of film, but I think they're better made by others. I'm drawn to stories about people and that's what I would like to continue to immerse myself in. I'm also able to do something with humour, but those two things are related. I often think that I have a tendency to find a lot of situations a little bit funny – including situations I might find myself in – even though they're in fact deeply serious. I think that duality will always be there in everything I produce. I think that I'm a bit of a chameleon when it comes to style. I don't think that I have a particular visual style. I suspect that I'd always want to subordinate stylistic considerations to the specific story at hand, to the specific theme.

# Jonas Elmer

## 1966–

Jonas Elmer graduated from the National Film School of Denmark* as a director in 1995. Elmer has yet to make a lot of films, but he established himself so definitively with his first feature film, *Let's Get Lost*, which was awarded the Bodil* prize for Best Danish Film of 1997, that he is considered one of the most promising directors of the Danish new wave of the 1990s. Elmer's special angle and invention is a poetic, improvised depiction of everyday life.

### Feature films
1997, *Let's Get Lost*

### Short films
1995, *Debut* (graduation film)
1998, *The Art of Success* (*Det sublime*)

*Jonas Elmer. [Photo: Anders Askegaard]*

**Hjort:** The release of your first feature film, *Let's Get Lost*, was a major event in the history of Danish film. The film received both a Bodil and a Robert* prize as Best Danish Film of 1997, and your achievement was further rewarded with prizes from the Edith Aller's Foundation and the Carl Dreyer Foundation. *Let's Get Lost* focusses on four main characters, the psychology student, Julie (Sidse Babett-Knudsen), Mogens (Bjarne Henriksen), Thomas (Troels Lyby) and Steffen (Nicolaj Kopernikus). Julie, who has recently been abandoned by her lover, struggles to deal not only with her grief, but with the fact that her apartment has essentially been taken over by her friend, Mogens, and his football-loving friends. Critics hailed *Let's Get Lost* as a breath of fresh air. They were fascinated by the fact that the film cost a mere 3.2 million Danish Crowns to make, took only 12 days to shoot, and was the result primarily of improvisation. There is no question that your film is innovative for a number of reasons in a Danish context. You yourself have emphasised the notion of innovation in relation to *Let's Get Lost*, for you've claimed that your only rule in making this film was that rules should be broken. What are the rules that *Let's Get Lost* breaks?

**Elmer:** I think that my stance on rules can be traced to my childhood, to the fact that I grew up in a hippie family and went to a hippie school. I've always had a lot of trouble with those very rigid rules that one was supposed to follow. It was very difficult, for example, to get around the rules at the National Film School; and it's important to know the rules, so as to be able to break them. I decided very early on in the process of making *Let's Get Lost,* before I even knew what the story would be, that I wanted to make a film that provided a perfect framework for the actors. In other words, every single decision I made was made in order to create the best conditions imaginable for the actors and their work. That's essentially how I constructed a set of rules for the film. It was actually quite easy to establish them, because I simply filtered all ideas in terms of whether or not they were desirable seen from the perspective of the actors. Keith Johnstone's book, *Improvisation for the Theatre* was my bible for years and years, and has had an enormous impact on my work. In improvisation there are no rules, only frameworks. Over the past ten to 12 years I've been involved almost continuously with improvisation groups that I'd establish and which would allow me to work intensely with actors. In that context much of what we did was of course aimed at live performances, and the latter were purely a matter of entertainment, nothing more. These improvisation groups provided a wonderful opportunity to work with actors. I have to admit that I was personally much more interested in the rehearsals than the live performances, because during the rehearsals we were able to work towards certain goals that weren't dictated by the presence of an audience that had to be entertained. The idea motivating *Let's Get Lost* was to make not just the actors, but the entire film crew part of the actual improvisation process. Everyone was forced to be fully present. There was no manuscript to rely on, so everyone was forced to become involved in the project. This approach is, I believe, the main reason why people responded so positively to the film. They sense that it has life in it, and that is, after all, what this is all about, creating life on the screen.

**Hjort:** Could you talk about the elements that were *not* improvised and that provided a certain framework for the process of improvisation?

**Elmer:** I'm very interested, for example, in how differences in status affect relations between people. I think the balance of power between people, and the way in which it shifts, are central elements in all theatre and film-making. I started our rehearsal sequence with a lot of technical exercises that are designed to make actors conscious of status mechanisms, thereby allowing them to play with them. What is involved here is very much like a game in which one has to reach a shared goal, but without any given individual being in a position of control. It's a fascinating way of working because there really aren't very many situations in life – with the exception of being newly in love - in which one has that kind of faith in others. It's a matter of allowing yourself to be led somewhere that you haven't completely defined. We emphasised technique for a very long time, so that I could discover the actors' strengths and limitations. In so doing we constructed a universe together that was meant to compensate for the script that we didn't in fact have. My goal during those rehearsals was to ensure that all the actors knew their parts so well that I in principle could have them act the relevant parts in any kind of situation.

**Hjort:** How did you organise the story's elements while you were shooting?

**Elmer:** I actually cast the four main actors before I knew what the story would be all about. The idea was that *Let's Get Lost* would be an ensemble film. That is, there was no main role as such. Instead each of the four characters figured centrally in his or her own little integral story. I actually wrote out the four stories for the four characters separately. That's why I ended up spending a good deal of time with my editor, Mette Zeruneith, with whom I created a structure for the entire film by literally cutting out scenes and placing them in a sequence from beginning to end. The entire film was organised in such a way that a given actor, who plays the lead in his or her own story, suddenly can appear as a secondary character in one of the other actors' stories. This approach created a strange, fluid structure, with the characters sliding in and out of each other's unfolding stories. After the first day of rehearsal I had something resembling a half-finished structure. I then constructed a notice board that was six metres long and two metres wide, and covered it with information that essentially outlined the entire film. I'm the kind of person who has to see things before understanding them. That's why I really insisted on being able to see all the locations on the notice board. I constructed the board in such a way that all the scenes from one to thirty nine were situated on the horizontal axis and all the characters on the vertical axis. I devised a variety of systems. For example, there was one system that involved assigning each character a particular colour of tape, so that I, at a purely visual, graphic level, could see whether a given character had been excluded from the story for too long. There were also stills on display and they provided another important source of inspiration for the various scenes, which I wanted the actors to have. So I spent a good deal of time familiarising them with the board, and they used it a lot. For example, they would experiment with moving scenes or entire acts around, in order to determine what might be gained by restructuring the story. The result, from my point of view, was a group of very engaged actors, who weren't interested only in their own characters, but also in the entire story, and how it was told.

**Hjort:** What about the dialogue? Were any of the lines determined in advance?

**Elmer:** Some of the lines that were really central to the story were. The most important of these lines was the one in the scene where Julie falls apart, when she asks her ex-lover how he could possibly have stopped loving her. That was determined in advance. It wasn't actually in the script, but I had talked to Sidse Babett Knudsen, who knew that the relevant scene was to be constructed around that line. The characters are all very lonely, which is why it's so important that that line be included. Other than that there were a few lines here and there, which, again, were necessary for reasons having to do with basic story-telling principles. One of them figures in the beginning of the film, when Julie throws the three guys out of her apartment. Her comment makes it clear that although she's only given Mogens permission to crash in her apartment for a week-end, he's actually lived there for two and a half years. I wanted to include that line because it somehow tied the characters together. By the way, I stole the idea from Vittorio de Sica. I've stolen shamelessly from any number of films. I and many other directors from my generation are very good at stealing. The video machine, which is an extraordinary invention, has meant a lot to me. I spend an enormous amount of time watching films, looking at clips and scenes again and again, and studying lighting and particular gestures. Equipped with my remote control, I can go on and on cultivating a given detail that interests me, without having to see the entire film. I see many more films than I read books, and it's clear that when I'm working on a film myself I tend to allow myself to be inspired by this aspect of my life. However, it's important to add something to what one steals, so that one somehow appropriates it fully. I'm completely without scruples in that respect.

**Hjort:** I find that very interesting. The older directors with whom I've spoken don't foreground their debts to other directors in the same way that your generation does. What's your relation to other contemporary Danish film-makers?

**Elmer:** In my mind Nils Malmros is the director who's most willing to expose himself, who's the most honest. I have enormous respect for that, but I don't really find Danish cinematic traditions particularly inspiring for the simple reason that for the time being I'm interested in making comedies, and the Danish comedy tradition is shamefully poor. If you look to Britain or the US instead, you find comedy traditions that are taken as seriously as tragedy. That's not the case here. Comedy in this country is synonymous with putting on a ridiculous hat and behaving like an idiot, and I'm really not interested in that sort of thing. I'm much more influenced by American and British traditions, because in those countries there's a clear understanding that characters can be deep and complex, even in comedies. I would like to aim at creating some believable and interesting characters while respecting a fair number of the basic rules of comedy. My greatest example is Fellini, although his films are very far removed from what I do. I find it fascinating when the screen somehow pulsates with life, and I think this is really true of his films. I'm happy to admit that I steal from any number of genres broadly distributed across the film-historical spectrum.

**Hjort:** We're of course also interested in how exactly you broke into film-making. In earlier interviews you've emphasised the fact that you were raised by parents who themselves were cinephiles. Could you talk a bit about how you got started?

**Elmer:** I was raised on film at home. My father is a great film enthusiast and I went to the movies a lot when I was younger. I also happened to take a screen test when I was 14, and I ended up getting a tiny role in a short fiction film. In the following four or five years I managed to get a series of very small roles in different films, and the advantage of having a very small role is that you're free to walk around and talk with other members of the crew, because you're forever waiting. I was absolutely fascinated by the way in which films were made, and when I was 18 I decided that I would go to London because

*The psychology student, Julie (Sidse Babett Knudsen) with her football-loving friend, Mogens (Bjarne Henriksen) in* Let's Get Lost. *[Photo: Anders Askegaard]*

I felt that English actors affected me much more positively and powerfully than Danish actors did. The idea was to move to London for a while in order to learn more about how English actors worked. At that point in time I dreamt of becoming an actor myself. So I moved to London and lived there for seven months. During that time I happened to discover an improvisation group that was very committed to the ideas of the improvisation theorist, Keith Johnstone. Within a very short period of time I was involved in any number of improvisation groups in London. I travelled around London and trained with these groups several times a week. To me it was an absolute revelation to discover that stories could be told that way, and I suddenly discovered that there were any number of things that I was capable of doing. I then returned to Denmark where I set up my first improvisation group. It turned out, however, that I was more interested in making films, and I decided that it had to be New York. I didn't really have any contacts, so I simply went over there with an open return ticket and got involved in various student productions via the film school at New York University. I made coffee and walked the dog! However, the smaller the productions, the more influence I was given and the higher I was able to rise in the hierarchy. After a while, I was also able to work on the larger productions, but I think I learnt more from the small productions, because on the large productions I couldn't get close enough to the director and photographer; I just had to do all the boring things.

**Hjort:** Some Danish directors have had the privilege of working in Hollywood and in some cases the results have been favourably received, in other cases, less so. What would you say that you learnt from your experience of film-making in a North American context?

**Elmer:** People were very passionate about film-making and had a lot of fun doing it. I worked mainly on art film productions, and people were very committed to making the films in question. No matter how strange or weird the films were, the attitude on the part of the crew members was that they were in the process of making something absolutely wonderful. Instead of being paid, I was allowed to query all the crew members about the bases for the decisions being made, and everyone was incredibly generous about sharing his or her knowledge and insights with me. As a result I was of course more involved and engaged than I would have been had I simply been required to fulfill some peripheral function or other. I think that in general the Danish film milieu is much more closed. People are more possessive and don't really involve others in what they're doing. That kind of attitude is very limiting and I really don't see how anything the least bit positive can come of it.

**Hjort:** You're currently under contract with the producer Per Holst, along with four other promising young directors. Per Holst commands a great deal of respect and is widely perceived as a man of integrity and vision. What exactly is the nature of your contract with Per Holst? What, for you, are the appealing aspects of the framework that Per Holst provides?

**Elmer:** My contract simply consists in my making films with him, and I'm paid a certain amount of money for doing that. He's the only producer I've ever met who is more interested in film than money. That's sometimes a problem for him, but it's truly wonderful to work with that kind of person, with someone who's so passionate about film, and who also has an incredible storehouse of experience, which I can then draw on. I'm given a lot of responsibility as a director, and I do of course have to live up to certain expectations. We've made one film together and so far he's never imposed his vision on mine. He's suggested a lot of changes and adjustments, and in some cases I've incorporated them, in other cases I haven't, but he leaves it to me to make the decisions that need to be made, and then I have to try to do the right thing. It's wonderful as a young director to sense this kind of support and trust coming from a producer who is known to have produced some of the best films that have been made in Denmark over the past 25 years. I'm delighted with the partnership and I hope it will last some 20 to 30 years.

**Hjort:** *Let's Get Lost* was repeatedly praised for its style, and a number of critics have suggested that you in your first feature have developed a distinctive, personal cinematic style. On the whole this black-and-white film relies on the conventions of realism, but there are a few sequences that depart radically from this framework. I'm thinking, for example, of the highly stylised shots of the narrative being imagined by the frustrated would-be writer, Thomas (Troels Lyby). Another example, which is perhaps a citation to

Busby Berkeley's musicals, would be the aerial shots of the young soccer enthusiasts performing a kind of soccer ballet that corresponds to the rhythm of extra-diegetic jazz music. How would you describe the cinematic style of *Let's Get Lost* and do you envisage further work in the same style?

**Elmer:** Every story has to be told in whichever way suits it best. When I was working on my graduation film for the National Film School, *Debut*, I put an inordinate amount of energy into the purely stylistic side of things, and I feel that I did this at the expense of the actors and their characters' presentation. They were very much subordinated to the camera work. I tried to do something very different in *Let's Get Lost*, where the emphasis throughout was on the actors, but I think that film can do so much; or, there's so much that one can do with film. The point, I believe, is to create a universe that fits the story. I'm very fond of Dennis Potter myself, and he's worked a lot with the idea of narrating at different levels and in different ways within the same stories. I've never found that approach problematic, because every time he shifts to a new style, it seems absolutely right to do so. My aim, ultimately, is to be able to unite what happens at the most intimate level between characters in the film with a story world that is somehow bigger than life, but it will probably take me a really long time to achieve that goal. When I watch films from the twenties and thirties, I always notice that, with a few exceptions, they're a lot more interesting to look at, in purely visual terms, than what gets produced today. Stylistically I'd like to move in that direction and to combine that kind of visuality with my way of developing characters. The point is to create a universe that isn't real, one that isn't afraid of revealing that it isn't real.

**Hjort:** Whereas policy-makers typically assume that producers and directors should have a clear sense of a given film's target audience, European directors frequently claim to consider such pragmatic considerations secondary to the primary task of telling a story that is compelling in and of itself. There are, of course, exceptions, and I am thinking here of Ole Bornedal's interesting interpretation of *Charlot and Charlotte* (*Charlot og Charlotte*) which he sees as being addressed specifically to female audiences. You've made a number of similar remarks about *Let's Get Lost*. In an interview with *B.T.* you say the following: 'My philosophy is that if I can just lure women into the cinema, the men will come too' (September 1997). I think you're right to see *Let's Get Lost* as a film that intelligently explores discourses and realities associated with women. I'm thinking, for example, of the marvellous and already classic scene in which Julie (Sidse Babett Knudsen) discusses with a friend (Mette Horn) the injustice of being jilted by a lover who owes the very erotic abilities that make him appealing to rival females to her careful guidance and training. Could you say a little more about the way in which the concept of audiences, and particularly female audiences, figures in your thinking about film?

**Elmer:** When I make films I think first and foremostly about my own tastes and interests, rather than those of some possible audience. I would like to make mainstream films, but what I focus on is the story. I do, however, believe that if a particular story excites me, then there's a strong likelihood of others finding it interesting too. *Let's Get Lost* was aimed at a female audience, because the narrative itself has a kind of poetry that women understand. Perhaps that's a theory based on my own lovers!

**Hjort:** Although the situation has improved markedly in recent years, it's still the case that Danish screens are dominated by American, rather than Danish images and stories. Not surprisingly, then, the 'Four Year Plan,' released by the Danish Film Institute makes the following claim: 'It is important to ensure the existence of a national film culture that expresses and sustains Danish values, Danish culture, language, and identity' (1998, 3). In many ways this policy statement corresponds to the view you expressed in an interview with *Politiken*: 'In the final analysis it's also a matter of accustoming the public to seeing Danish films in the cinemas' (September 1997). What, more specifically, are you driving at here, and how do you see yourself contributing to the process in question?

**Elmer:** I think it's important that films be made that allow children to discover from the outset that it's also interesting to see stories from their part of the world, but this does presuppose a much higher standard generally. After all, children and adolescents opt for what's most vibrant. However, I do think we have certain traditions in Denmark that provide us with something to build on, and I believe that we actually can create some stories that are capable of capturing the imagination of younger audiences. It is of course the commercial films that carry the greatest economic weight and make it possible for other directors to make more experimental, art house films, but I think it's sad that some of the commercial films one sees so clearly are attempts to follow some American model. I think these films are profoundly uninteresting because they can't actually hold a candle to the American films. I intend to try to keep on growing, to explore territory that is unknown to me and where things can happen that may be either totally wonderful or completely catastrophic. That's what's interesting, but I think it's incredibly important to have a set of priorities that ensures a broad range of offerings, so that people become accustomed to seeing Danish films.

# Lotte Svendsen

## 1968–

Lotte Svendsen graduated from the National Film School of Denmark* in 1995 and has, as a result of both her public self-presentation and films, established herself as an outspoken representative of a new generation that is leftist, politically engaged and socially aware. Svendsen's first short films distinguished her as a satirist with a probing grasp of some of the class differences and social contradictions at the heart of the Danish welfare society. *Cafe Hector* (1995), for example, is a serio-comic exploration of conflicts between Danish yuppies and social outsiders, and of the dynamics of social hierarchy. Svendsen's breakthrough came with *Royal Blues* (1997), which paints a more detailed portrait of the lower and upper classes in Denmark and effectively introduces a new, more colourful style to Danish social comedy. Svendsen's first feature film, *Gone with the Fish* (*Bornholms stemme*, 1999) also attracted large indigenous audiences and is

*Lotte Svendsen. [Photo: Jan Buus]*

a film that draws on the Danish comic tradition of political and social satire associated, for example, with Erik Clausen, and on the new British socio-realism of Mike Leigh. The film focusses on the fishing crisis of the 1980s seen from the perspective of a fishing community on the Danish island of Bornholm. *Gone with the Fish* brings together socio-realism, comic farce, melodrama and at times magical realism. This kind of blending of genres is unusual in the context of Danish film and bespeaks great promise and talent.

## Feature films
1999, *Gone with the Fish* (*Bornholms stemme*)

## Short films
1995, *Harmony* (graduation film)
1995, *Cafe Hector*
1996, *Mother's Day* (*Mors dag*)
1997, *Royal Blues*

**Hjort:** In his preface to Martin Dale's *Europa Europa* (1992), David Puttnam praises the author for having suggested that 'European film-makers may have lost touch with their natural audience and that any renaissance in European cinema must necessarily be built around a re-creation of trust.' You've frequently mentioned your admiration for British film-makers such as Ken Loach and Mike Leigh. What's more interesting, perhaps, is the inspiration you've drawn from Danish directors such as Erik Clausen and Erik Balling, both of whom are key figures within the tradition of popular Danish comedies.* Whereas many film-makers in the 1970s reviled the popular comedies of the 1950s, especially the idyllic representations of country life found in the Morten Korch* films, younger film-makers such as yourself and Thomas Vinterberg see the relevant Danish tradition in a quite different light. Is your interest in this tradition in part motivated by the kinds of concerns articulated by Dale and Puttnam?

**Svendsen:** I've experienced a rather frightening, but probably quite typical tendency for people to adopt certain positions without in any way questioning them. When I first started at the National Film School in 1991, the term 'popular comedy' was reviled by both teachers and students. If the students happened to propose something funny, the immediate reaction was: 'Fine, as long as it doesn't involve the kind of slapstick and generalised idiocy we associate with popular comedies.' It's not uncommon for fairly sick norms concerning what's in and out to emerge. I have to admit that I've always been rather sceptical about those norms. As the Danish author, Soya, once put it, any idiot can be self-important and serious, but you need a sense of humour, an ear and real talent to make people laugh. The problem is that we end up losing our audience if we choose to favour arcane psychology, instead of having the courage to work with and bring to life certain archetypes. Why would it be wrong to produce popular comedies and to construct archetypes? In the old variety tradition the relation between artist and audience was very straightforward and pragmatic. I think our task as directors is to take a close look at the world our audience lives in, to caricature that world, turn it upside down, question it. This is why I have such respect for both archetypes and popular comedy. They can be very thought provoking and can be effectively used to stimulate political debate and to raise probing questions. I think the popular comedy genre has enormous range, but at a certain point, Danish directors became almost fearful of content-related issues and very preoccupied instead with formal issues, which were considered trendy; and this development had a clear impact on the fate of the popular comedy genre in Denmark. The emphasis in the 1970s and early 1980s was entirely on content understood in political and ideological terms and there was no room whatsoever for formal, aesthetic concerns. The reaction in the late 1980s and early 1990s was to equate content with politics and to construe form and aesthetics as incredibly exciting in and of themselves. We've lost something very basic here as a result of this way of thinking and in my mind it's very important that we don't allow ourselves to be intimidated by the 1970s and the fact that everything went wrong back then. It will never be old hat to talk about content, quality, society, social stratification and hierarchy. After all, that's us, that's our life. *We* are society. I think there exists a very concrete form of social theatre that film-makers would do well to draw on, but in this respect I'm terribly old fashioned, at least compared with my peers, for I insist on the right to feel a certain social outrage. The fact is, of course, that the liberals with their philosophy of the survival of the strongest have been gaining considerable ground, and that's why I'm concerned in my films with questioning authority and carefully examining status distinctions among people. I want to reach a lot of people, because I feel that I want to move a lot of people. I've never experienced, while writing, that I had to compromise myself politically or in terms of the story I wanted to tell. I don't know whether this is because the film consultants haven't entirely grasped what I want to say, but they've never told me that what I was doing was too radical, rigid or acerbic. I've never had to deal with that kind of censorship, but then I don't think I'm really the kind of person anybody is going to want to censor. Hopefully the many political ideas I have in connection with what I do don't amount to raised fingers, but are played out, rather, in various grotesquely comical situations. The goal of entertainment will always be more important to me than my political stance. In fact, I would much rather entertain than preach and I think it's a crime to be boring. The contempt that people feel for popular comedy ultimately has to do with questions of self-confidence. Making popular comedies is apparently not quite as distinguished an activity as producing art like Kieslowski's. The sense of cultural inferiority that attaches to popular comedies accounts for the need to entertain that is so central to the genre. Entertainment, after all, is what justifies its existence.

**Hjort:** Scathing, satirical wit is one of your trademarks, and you use a wide range of devices to create the ironic tone that is a salient feature of your work in both film and theatre. In *Mother's Day*, for example, you mobilise a variety of genres to great ironic effect. The domestic conflict between a jealous, possessive mother and her son is thus explored in terms of conventions associated with detective and crime genres. The most important element, however, of your ironic cinematic style is a particular mode of acting, which is exemplified beautifully by Malene Schwartz' characterisation of the mother Margit in *Mother's Day*. How would you describe the acting style that is favoured in your films? Could you talk a bit about how you achieve the style in question?

**Svendsen:** In that regard my theatre group, *Emma's Dilemma*, is incredibly important, because I work with the actresses Helle Dolleris and Sofie Stougaard in both contexts, in film and on stage. *Emma's Dilemma* is our private stage. We do, of course, stage performances, but the space in question is very much our own as we receive no salary and don't have a producer breathing down our necks. What matters is quite simply the character work we're able to do. There are a couple of things I'd like to clarify in connection with the question of irony and parody. *Mother's Day* is a parody of a symbiotic relation between a mother and her son, but the Belinda figure in *Royal Blues* is not a matter of parody. Belinda is a real person. I was very much aware of not wanting to make her an ironic figure, because in my mind irony easily becomes a form of cynicism. In that sense, I have to admit that I find my own sense of humour worrisome at times. In a film like *Cafe Hector*, the male hero figure is almost too ironic. I would have liked to defend him a bit more, because in the final analysis ironic distancing can be a way of evading responsibility. As far as my preferred acting style is concerned, I think some of the young actors were rather shocked when they first met me and discovered how different my views are from those of many other directors. They've gone to acting schools and have learnt a lot about method acting and Stanislavski. They've been taught that authenticity is tremendously important, and that if it's authentic in here, then it's not necessary to try to project a lot. If you simply think, 'I've lost my best friend', then we'll be able to tell whether the feeling is somehow true by merely looking into your eyes. That kind of acting style moves from inner to outer realities and is very much based on Stanislavski, but I'm much more interested in ancient Greek tragedy and its use of masks. In that context, actors were humble extras who were hired in order to present certain characters to an audience. One finds resonances of this tradition in Shakespeare's approach to acting, for he also makes ample use of caricatured archetypes: the little funny figure, the tall, evil person, the pretty girl, the nasty witch. However, because Shakespeare has expressed it all so beautifully and with such intelligence, these archetypes are given an incredible range and lives that really move the audience. As far as the English realists are concerned, I would want to call Mike Leigh a social realist, rather than a realist. I'm not interested in being a social realist, but I'm very interested in being a social *sur*-realist. One does sense this kind of distinction in the case of Mike Leigh, but not in the case of Ken Loach, which is why I find myself moving further and further away from him. In Loach's world things are too politically correct, too pure and authentic. There's no madness, nothing that somehow says, 'This is what the world I'm postulating looks like'. That's why I've come to appreciate Mike Leigh more and more, because he combines a certain madness with realism. I've also become fascinated by Emir Kusturica, who made *Underground* (*Bila jednom jedna zemlja*) and *Arizona Dream*, brilliant films, also in terms of their acting styles, which are very caricatural. However, if we trace a line from certain ancient Greek acting styles to Shakespeare, through to what some of the British directors are doing today, we find incredible humility. The actors in question efface themselves. They think of themselves as mere craftsmen, as tools, and it's with this kind of attitude that they explore external reality, pubs, busses, whatever. It's as though they say, 'Now I'm going to photograph the world with my mind and then I'll put the character on, from the outside.' That's how I work with my actors. I find myself telling Sofie Stougaard to forget her hyper-stimulated, privileged potter home, her almost exhibitionistic self-confidence, to efface herself and go out into the world in order to observe the more invisible people whose stories also deserve to be told. It's your duty to photograph those people and to assume the roles they suggest, from the outside as it were. This is exactly the opposite of what Stanislavski had in mind. I would like us to feel a certain humility that stems from the idea that we merely mediate a surrounding reality which we have to try to penetrate. I don't think of myself or actors as great, sensitive artists. In that respect there's an enormous difference between me and Jang Refn and our respective ways of working with actors. He requires his actors virtually to become their characters. In *Royal Blues*, for example, we precisely used this idea of assuming a role externally by mentally photographing someone or other on the street and then deciding that the person in question would be one of our characters. *Royal Blues* is all about various individuals we met in the Vesterbro neighbourhood of Copenhagen. When we first start working on the characters, I say 'Let it all hang out, exaggerate, be theatrical.' I never work from the script itself, but focus instead on what happened prior to what the script describes and what will happen to the characters afterwards. I create situations in which the actors meet as characters, which allows us to talk psychology and to figure out what works and what doesn't. After that we identify the best moments, which we then purify and hone. When we're improvising I always have my hands on the steering wheel. We think of some situations, the actors shout and scream, I provide critical comments and then we start to tighten things up. Once the psychology is more or less right and we have a clear sense of the relevant status relations, the actors know their characters so well that they don't have to worry about being able somehow to prove who they are. At that point the characters start to become smaller and smaller and more and more real, because I do of course want these figures to be believable. I want the audience to recognise them and understand them, but I always work from something big and exaggerated to something small.

**Hjort:** The stories you tell are very much anchored in material culture. Indeed, your cinematic approach is characterised by a recurrent use of objects and domestic interiors as a means of exploring conflictual human relations. The importance attributed to objects in your stories effectively reflects the claustrophobic universe of the lower class and *petite bourgeoisie* that provide the focal point for your films. It's no accident that Stella (Maria Karlsen), the wayward and free-spirited girlfriend in *Mother's Day*, should be unable to negotiate the cluttered and carefully arranged home shared by her boyfriend, Martin (Jacob Weble), and his mother, Margit (Malene Schwartz). In a brilliant scene, you have Stella burst into Margit's living room, where she wreaks havoc with a pole lamp as a result of her uncoordinated gestures. Something similar occurs in *Royal Blues*, where the drunken and unemployed loser played by Sofie Stougaard destroys a royal bust cherished by her law-abiding, royalist mother. Fetishistic attitudes are also attributed to the characters in *Harmony*, who are shown poring over carefully prepared photographic records of the coffins used to bury family members. In your feature film, *Gone with the Fish*, the impact of diminishing fish stocks is expressed in socially significant, material terms. The main character, Sonja, is, for example, forced to relinquish the very kitchen appliances that once were the source of status and prestige. Declining fish stocks require Sonja to invest her libidinal energies in a quite different set of objects, and she thus finds herself decorating countless replicas of typical local churches for German tourists. What is your view of the role played by objects, and material culture more generally, in your films?

**Svendsen:** I intentionally allow material values to govern those scenes, as a passion in and of itself. We're one of the richest countries in the world; poverty really doesn't exist in Denmark any more. The problems that do exist are more psychological in nature: loneliness, a sense of inferiority, isolation. These are the problems that certain social groups have to grapple with. In this sense the focus on objects and material goods in my films is meant to comment critically on a situation that is clearly getting out of hand. Danes are so consumer-oriented and busy accumulating things that they don't even have any respect for the unions anymore. The unions have undermined the very solidarity they were supposed to promote. There's a group of people in this country, who live on transfer payments and can't hope ever to be taken seriously. Those people just don't figure in the social consciousness of the unions. They've been written off and statistically it's just a matter of throwing them out. What matters is accumulating stuff. Perfectly ordinary lorry drivers, street workers and store assistants, people whose relation to the unions is secure, enjoy a standard of living that is absolutely absurd in comparison even with southern Europe. Everyone owns a video machine and television and people shop at Bilka every week-end. It's fucking American. The only thing people want to see is *Wheel of Fortune*; that's what's left of culture and humanism these days. We've foregrounded the consumerist tendencies in society and have construed everything in terms of winning and hoarding. Everything has become one big competition. What matters today is accumulating things, and then you die and leave behind piles of junk. What kind of life is that? Accumulate and die. Even in the area of culture we've accepted this idea of maximisation. The Film House, Holmen, Copenhagen Cultural Capital – what we're talking about here is monuments. The money for culture is used on monuments, instead of on films and books and the kind of creative fringe environments where people are able to start up a rock band with no more than unemployment benefits. So what I see is a really frightening consumerist tendency in society. That's at least part of the explanation for the central role that material goods and objects play in my films.

At the same time it's also the case that I think that a scene works better if the action is centred on one particular thing and the sub-text on something quite different. That is, I'm not interested in seeing a film about some couple, a man and a woman, and she says: 'Why don't you ever praise my work?' He says: 'Because you haven't let me screw you in ten years.' I'm not interested in watching that kind of dramaturgy, but I *am* interested in seeing a scene in which there's a woman who says: 'And then I painted this picture on Thursday.' And somebody else says: 'It's wonderful!' And then the husband says: 'Yeah, you got lucky there.' And she says: 'I didn't get lucky. I did a good job.' 'No, you got lucky.' 'No, I didn't get lucky, I did a good job.' He won't praise her because he hasn't been laid, and she won't give him pussy because he won't praise her. What this is really about is whether he will say that she's talented rather than just lucky. It's a matter of getting the sub-texts into the picture, while letting the scene be about something very concrete.

**Hjort:** Could you talk a bit about your approach to set design and your use of props?

**Svendsen:** I'm unbelievably demanding in that respect. I know exactly what I want. I think there are a lot of set designers who think it's incredibly trying to be part of my crew. A lot of them would call my films kitsch and bad taste with an emphasis on weird settings and milieu, but for me it's really important that there be an aesthetic dimension, some form of beauty. The last thing I want is some stag antlers on the wall. I'm not seduced by clichés and I have very clear ideas about what I want to achieve. I just want to show you this book, which I shared with the crew I made *Gone with the Fish* with (*Ray's a Laugh* by Richard Billingham). This is a really tough book and my film isn't this tough. What we're dealing with here is really English poor white trash. What I find

*Poster for* Gone with the Fish
(Bornholms stemme).

amazing about the couple whom this book is about is their way of decorating their apartment. There's a kind of scenographic beauty here, and as a result these people in some strange way seem beautiful in that context. An artist like Francis Bacon, for example, deals with the most brutal feelings, and the most brutal images, people who are completely destroyed, but at the same time he was an indoor architect and aesthete. The richest people had him design their homes for them, and you can see all of this in his paintings. He works in a way that I would like to, focussing on human brutality and human beings' inability to talk properly to each other. However, he situates this brutality and lack of communication within some form of beauty and order. Billingham's book involves the same collision between brutality and beauty. If a set designer had put this book together, I'd praise her to the skies. I can't get enough of this book and keep finding new things in it. So in that sense I'm in the process of trying to become more aware of how my at times very symmetrical long shots might be made more lively and contradictory. I don't move my camera much, so I'm very grateful to my set designer for having helped me to sharpen my cinematic aesthetic, to strengthen it. People have said that I don't use the language of cinema enough, and there may be some truth to this, but I'm trying to develop an aesthetic. I'm not there yet, but I'm working on it. In *Gone with the Fish* I consciously worked more on the images in an effort to create an off-beat aesthetic. I'm not after side-lighting here, which gives everyone a tanned look and makes them seem lovely and glamorous. It's the compositions themselves and the way in which they're framed that should do the narrating.

**Hjort:** You're from Bornholm, a small Danish island close to Sweden. During a talk at the European Film School in Ebeltoft in 1997 you made much of the fact that you intended to use the regional dialect, *bornholmsk*, in your first feature film, *Gone with the Fish*. The Danish film industry is, and has always been, very much centred in Copenhagen, and as Erik Clausen has argued eloquently, Danish film-makers have tended as a result to focus excessively on the lives and concerns of privileged Danes living in and around Copenhagen. Could you talk a little about your understanding of the relation between centre and periphery in Denmark? What are some of the challenges involved in renegotiating that relation through the mobilisation of a regional dialect's expressive range?

**Svendsen:** I've consciously wanted to get away from the narrow-minded self-importance of the capital. I completely agree with Clausen and I think it's wonderful that he never tires of saying these things. In my case the decision in question has nothing to do with a politics of film, because even if I'd grown up in the middle of Copenhagen, I'd still want to tell the same stories. What interests me in the case of *Gone with the Fish* is the family psychology, the inner story. That is, what happens between a man and a woman when the woman suddenly becomes the breadwinner – and this is, of course, very much a current conflict in central Copenhagen. Ultimately my stories are driven by existential concerns. That being said, my desire to tell this particular story has everything to do with the transformation that I and my actors, who are also from Bornholm, undergo the minute we get to the island. We change quite automatically the minute we begin to speak our local dialect. We become islanders again. We efface ourselves and become something else. We're able to do the most exquisite character work in no time at all the minute we can make use of our dialect. We become more primitive, more funny, more surrealistic. Something happens that makes it all a lot more enjoyable. That's one of the reasons why I simply have to make use of *bornholmsk* in this film. Another reason is that I've always been very proud of the fact that I'm from Bornholm. Being from Bornholm was very much my own thing; nobody could compete with me in that regard. In fact that's something I learnt during my years with the BZ movement: whether you're unemployed, poor, unknown or ugly, there's nothing to be ashamed of. On the contrary, for if you're part of the BZ movement, it's what makes you different that defines your strength. As a result I've felt a certain pride about being from Bornholm, although I'm from a family that has had its share of misfortune. I think most people would be ashamed of belonging to my family, because it includes a lot of egomaniacs and alcoholics. However, the anarchistic, anti-authoritarian stance that lies at the heart of the BZ movement really reorganised things for me in such a way that I am able to feel a certain pride about things that are actually quite untrendy. I'm also quite proud of the fact that I'm so damned politically outraged in this age of self-centredness. I hate trends and tendencies. I grew up in an environment that taught me that only dead fish swim with the current, and that idea is really quite characteristic of how I've chosen to work with film.

I was terribly ashamed of my family background until I was about 14. I went to a private school where I was together with a lot of very well balanced children, the sons and daughters of potters, artists and teachers, who were not islanders, but had moved to Bornholm at some point. These kids spent their time horseback riding or learning to play the violin. When it was my turn to bring someone home, there was goulash and farting family members and grandad with his big mouth who'd announce that he didn't like tit ointment, and grandma would sit there crying because she had cancer, and so on. I was terribly traumatised by all of this until I joined the BZ movement and suddenly realised that all of this weirdness can be viewed with so much love that it acquires its own existential justification. I find that I'm constantly returning to that family space, to the feelings and experiences I associate with it. No matter how different the films might seem, the conflict is repeatedly being played out in that living room at home.

**Hjort:** *Gone with the Fish* makes constant reference to local lore and popular folk wisdom. There's a debate throughout the film about martens and whether they exist on Bornholm, and characters furtively dispute the existence of humanoid beings living underground. At one point, Sonja, the main character, chases a little man from her house with shouts of 'Bobærakus, may the devil take you.' My suspicion is that these elements do more than provide the film with a certain *couleur locale*. How do you see these elements as functioning within the film? Do you think they're readily accessible to all audiences or do they rather presuppose an audience with a certain kind of background knowledge?

**Svendsen:** You're asking whether I have some kind of hidden agenda. It's, of course, true that I had ten thousand hidden agendas when I wrote *Gone with the Fish*. Nothing is a matter of coincidence, but you see the thing is that you're not allowed to talk about the people who live underground.

**Hjort:** And do all Danes know this?

**Svendsen:** No, not at all. I'm going to have to be a bit affected here. As an islander you're not allowed to talk about the subterranean people. At the same time, it's clear that I have to do precisely that inasmuch as they're part of my story. It's all about a myth that claims that there are people living down beneath the cliffs and that it's important to remain on friendly terms with them. I should say right now that I wouldn't mind at all if spectators were to have the feeling that they're looking at a world they don't entirely understand. I make very precise use of the subterraneans, for the point is that they take us back to some important ancient stories. If you as a woman gave birth to a child with a hare lip, it wasn't your child. Instead it belonged to the subterranean people, who had somehow surfaced in order to exchange their child for yours. Then you'd have to take the child and throw it into some chasm. That way they would get their child back and you would simply have to hope that they might also return yours. The subterranean people thus serve a particular function having to do with good and evil. That is, we need evil too, but can't ourselves be evil, so we end up hiding the relevant phenomena underneath rugs and beneath cliffs.

To return to your question, I'd say that a film like Kusturica's *Underground* was one of the greatest cinematic experiences I've had in the last three years, in part because he makes use of such straightforward symbols. In the film they convince people that the war is still going on; they stage false alarms and lock people in the basement. That's an incredibly powerful symbol of East block ideology, but at the same time I also sensed a certain integrity that had to do with the fact that the film didn't cater to me as a member of the audience. The message was: 'We make the rules here. We're Yugoslavs, we play noisy bugles, and you can either take it or leave it.' The fact that the film was so integrated and so uncompromising at the level of its expression allowed me to experience something very pure and uncompromising, and I found this fascinating. I think we lack this kind of thing in Danish film. At times things are reduced here to storytelling for midgets as a result of the privileging of a certain dramaturgy and the infernal meddling of consultants.* I mean in a social context it's always interesting to talk to someone who seems to have some secret. One probably loses interest a lot faster in the person who is unconstrained and blurts out everything all at once. I hope and believe that people will remain curious, even though the world being shown in some weird way is a very different one. That's why it's really important to me that the all of the actors in *Gone with the Fish* speak *bornholmsk*.

**Hjort:** In previous interviews you've emphasised the centrality in your films of marginal figures, losers and outcasts whose lives matter very little to anyone. What has not been sufficiently underscored, in my view, is the fact that your films explore the nature of the boundaries separating different social classes, as well as the bases of group cohesion. *Cafe Hector* is probably the most interesting of your films in this respect. In this short film, two outsiders, Uffe (Lars Mikkelsen) and Thorvald (Jesper Asholt), independently decide to use violence to force yuppies in a chic cafe to take them seriously. The impossibility of justifying the violence of exclusion, or hierarchies of being, is underscored in the final moments of the film, when Uffe, who entered the cafe in order to hunt yuppies, finds his plans thwarted by the unexpected arrival on the scene of Thorvald, and instead kills the intruder. With that improvised gesture, Uffe transforms himself from an object of yuppie derision to an object of yuppie veneration. Would you agree that your films deal with the arbitrary and irrational dynamics of exclusion and inclusion?

**Svendsen:** Exactly. You're the first person to have talked about this dimension of my work, and it's really crucial to me. It has something to do with my upbringing. I was raised by a man who was an anarchist and an alcoholic, so there was simply no basis for a smoothly functioning, middle-class set-up. When we went to the supermarket, he might decide to knock over a stand of tomato cans, that is, make a scene, so there was no authority figure to look up to: he wasn't the powerful father and I the little girl. Things were constantly being inverted, and seen from the perspective of standard middle-class conceptions about child-rearing, this did, of course, make for a good deal of uncertainty. We lived in a cute little Lilliputian town on Bornholm where everybody would fly the Danish flag. My father would fly pirate flags, he'd walk around barefoot, and liked to play Béla Bartok and Mahler at three o'clock in the morning, with the volume turned way up and the windows wide open. He was self-destructive, but he was also extremely vivacious. I did get a certain strength from him on account of his intelligence, when he wasn't walking around feeling drunk and weird. He didn't have any inferiority complexes. On the contrary, he flaunted his desperation. I've set my own limits since I was four. Because I was raised in this kind of anti-hierarchical way, I've always questioned authority. Why should somebody be an authority figure? Why should someone have power over me? As a result I'm not the least bit overawed, for example, by the hierarchical way in which the film industry is organised.

**Hjort:** You're one of five promising young Danish directors who have been contracted by the producer, Per Holst, to develop a series of film projects. There has been much talk, within the context of the Media Program, of the relation between European film and standard European conceptions of the producer. More specifically, the claim is that the survival of European film, and the creation of New European Cinemas, depend on the possibility of replacing the European view of the producer as simply a fund raiser with an understanding of the producer as a creative figure capable not only of developing a project with the director, but of mediating successfully between the director and the targeted audiences by means of intelligent marketing and publicity. When Per Holst decided to support five directors, he was once again hailed as a bold and innovative figure within the Danish context. Are Danish conceptions of the producer's ideal function and role changing?

**Svendsen:** Per Holst is not some capitalist pig disguised as a high school teacher. He fully assumes his role, and dresses like an old-fashioned capitalist. He takes us out for good lunches and has a bigger office than the rest of us. He insists on rank. At the same time, he also has everything that's needed to meet with the people from the E.U.. You can trust him, because what motivates him is the desire to make films, not the desire to make money. That's the key difference between a good and a bad producer. That's of course why he's been willing to take the greatest risks. He's the producer who got all the young Danish directors going. He produced von Trier's first film, Bille August's, Nils Malmros', Helle Ryslinge's. He's always had a good nose for quality and he hasn't produced many flops. So what's essential to the role of the producer is the desire to produce films coupled with a stubborn ability to be a damn capitalist. I become very nervous when I hear the word 'creative producer', because I can't help but think: 'If you're so creative, then why aren't you a director?' I've worked with some very ambitious producers, who didn't have the necessary self-confidence to become directors. And during the development phase they desperately fought to impose some of their own values on the story. At that point you're suddenly dealing with a compromise between two voices, but you can't have two voices narrating the film. There has to be a single voice. In that regard at least I'm an auteur. Producers should be crazy about producing films, but they shouldn't actually make them themselves.

**Bondebjerg:** *Gone with the Fish* received predominantly positive reviews and will in all likelihood become a big box office success. *Information*'s Morten Piil went so far as to call it the best film of 1999 and one of the best films of the 1990s. He claims among other things that *Gone with the Fish* marks a breakthrough for the kind of socially oriented film-making that might be able to create a much-needed alternative to a very male tendency in contemporary Danish film to focus on rather desperate urban men. Other reviewers have, however, suggested that you failed in *Gone with the Fish* to achieve a proper balance between comic and socio-realistic elements, and you have been quite critical of the marketing strategy that launched your film as pure comedy. How would you classify the film generically and what were your guiding intentions in this respect?

**Svendsen:** I think it's really important to draw certain distinctions and I've had a lot of doubts about the way in which *Gone with the Fish* was promoted. My sense is that the marketing experts in some unfortunate way wanted to construe my film as a kind of extension of Susanne Bier's *The One and Only* (*Den eneste ene*), as the same sort of comedy. But I really think it's a matter here of the most extreme form of false advertising, for *Gone with the Fish* and *The One and Only* are polar opposites. They're radically different although they perhaps both deal with confused people who are having trouble figuring out what love is all about. My film has a lot more in common with a heavy, serious film than it does with pure comedy, so I didn't agree with the marketing strategy that was adopted, but at the same time I haven't really been able to challenge it effectively, because I find it hard to describe what I do. My films seem to fall between stools, between the serious and the comic, and I'm slowly beginning to realise that this is exactly what I want them to do. *Harmony* was criticised for falling between stools, and the same thing happened with *Royal Blues*. I seem to have to hear this about nearly all the films I make. The only thing I haven't been taken to task for is that maudlin *Mother's Day*, which is terribly sweet and works quite well, but doesn't in any way go against the grain. I'm working on becoming better at doing what I think is my own thing: precisely situating myself between those two poles.

**Hjort:** How would you situate yourself in relation to the predominantly male new wave in contemporary Danish film?

**Svendsen:** I think it's rather amusing to note just how much attention the eternally pubescent 35-year-old male on his interminable inter-rail pass gets these days. You have to get the audience to swallow the following premise: you're 35, you're told that you're going to be a father, and suddenly your entire world collapses! You can get the audience to accept this, but only if you have some kind of unwritten agreement here in the late 1990s that there's a generation that will never ever grow up. It's one unending children's birthday party! It's true that the number of people living alone is probably very high and that people cultivate their bodies as never before. At the same time the media and culture more generally have a tendency to focus on precisely those people who have these kinds of values, people who somehow have the energy or some reason for cultivating their egos in the most extreme ways imaginable. The covers of *Euroman* and *Eurowoman* encourage what I'm talking about, and there are lists all over the place of what is in and out. The media are playing a fairly monotonous tune, which is all about eternal youth. This is where I want to respond: 'There's still the remaining 85% of the population, the people who got married, had some kids, go to work, contribute to their pensions, attend some sports event on Saturday, and the rest of the time they're together with their kids.' I think the media tend to downplay this aspect of reality these days. Critics claim that I have a special talent for describing people on the fringes of society. That's such garbage! The way Sonja and Erik live is a whole lot more representative of the population generally than Rikke Louise Andersson and Kim Bodnia tearing each other apart somewhere in the Nørrebro neighbourhood of Copenhagen.

# Thomas Vinterberg

## 1969–

Thomas Vinterberg graduated from the director's stream of the National Film School of Denmark* in 1993. The breadth of his talent was evident already in his graduation film, *Last Round* (*Sidste omgang*, 1993), and in the short comic film, *What's Your Guess?* (*Slaget på tasken*, 1993). *The Boy Who Walked Backwards* (*Drengen der gik baglæns*, 1993) won numerous prizes both in Denmark and abroad and is a probing psychological story, involving a pregnant mixture of realism and symbolism, about a nine-year-old boy's traumas and dreams in connection with his older brother's death. Vinterberg's first feature film, *The Greatest Heroes* (*De største helte*, 1996), established him as the most talented of the young male directors associated with the Danish new wave of the 1990s, which draws its inspiration, in part, from American film-makers, particularly Martin Scorsese, Francis Ford Coppola, and Quentin Tarantino. *The Greatest Heroes* is an independent Danish take on a road movie and focusses on an escaped bank robber, his desperately romantic, heroic flight through Sweden, and his attempt to rescue his daughter from her violent stepfather. In 1995 Vinterberg, together with Lars von Trier, articulated the Dogme* concept that was designed to renew Danish film, and by the same token he cemented his reputation as one of the most important figures of new Danish cinema. His Dogme film, *The Celebration* (*Festen*, 1998), won the Jury's Special Prize at Cannes and was a major international breakthrough. This film is an intense and relentless drama about child abuse and the questioning of parental authority. It is characterised by a new, spontaneous acting style and visual aesthetic, and reveals Vinterberg to be something of a Danish Bergman in modern Dogme garb.

*Thomas Vinterberg. [Photo: Robin Skjoldborg]*

## Feature films
1996, *The Greatest Heroes (De største helte)*
1998, *The Celebration (Festen)*

## Short films
1993, *The Boy Who Walked Backwards (Drengen der gik baglæns)*
1993, *What's Your Guess? (Slaget på tasken)*
1993, *Last Round (Sidste omgang, graduation film)*

## TV productions
2000, *D Day* (*D dag,* collaborative Dogme project)

**Hjort:** You're one of a number of young Danish film-makers who were raised within non-traditional families. More specifically, you grew up in Nordkrog, a commune known for the intellectual bent of its members. Nordkrog is, for example, associated with your father, the literary critic, Søren Vinterberg, as well as with the science journalist, Tor Nørretranders, and the musician Henrik Strube. You're said to have discovered film as a 14 year old. What, for you, is the origin of your commitment to film? How would you describe your point of entry into the world of film?

**Vinterberg:** It's quite a banal story. I started making my first film when I was 16, and it may well be that I had plans along those lines already as a 14 year old. When I was studying for the Danish equivalent of 'A levels', I played a lot of music together with my friends, but I was the only one who'd stayed in school. The others left school earlier so as to have more time to practice their instruments. The result was that I couldn't keep up with them musically and this bothered me. I was frustrated by not being able to keep up on my guitar and decided to throw myself into film-making instead. Together with a very good friend, I started writing a film script for a 45 minute film called *Snowblind (Sneblind)*. It was quite ambitious, and we spent four years making it. As soon as I started working on that film, I could feel that film-making clicked for me, that it involved skills I'd be able to master, that I'd found my vocation, if you will. I liked the aspect of film-making that made me the connecting link between a whole lot of people. I really enjoyed shooting a film together with 30 other people, where I was kind of the lynchpin. This may have to do with my experiences living in a commune. I also enjoyed scripting the stories. I was also affected enough to find the prospect of a lot of media attention appealing. At that point I was very young, so the idea of fame was very enticing. I no longer feel that way at all. *Snowblind* turned out to be a really bad film, a catastrophic film, but there were 30 of us involved in that film, and none of us had any prior film-making experience. Yet of those 30, 25 now make a living as professional film-makers, and the film got me into the National Film School.

**Hjort:** In previous interviews you've mentioned your admiration for directors such as Martin Scorsese and Francis Ford Coppola. You've also expressed some concern about the influence of Quentin Tarantino. Indeed, you went so far as to suggest that we'd all be better off if he were hit by a truck! Now, what is striking is that your list of favourite films and directors includes some Scandinavian names and titles, Ingmar Bergman, for example, and his *Fanny and Alexander* (*Fanny och Alexander*). Older Danish directors, such as Christian Braad Thomsen or Søren Kragh-Jacobsen, tend to situate themselves in relation to non-Scandinavian directors and films. In the early 1970s, Danish film was a project that had yet to be realised as far as many Danish directors were concerned. Your stance seems to be quite different. Have the achievements of a Lars von Trier, Bille August and Gabriel Axel had the effect of making Danish film a tangible reality to which one can relate positively as a budding young Danish film-maker?

**Vinterberg:** I don't look to the old Danish directors because their films were successful. I love the Danish popular comedies* and the Olsen Gang films and am very much inspired by them. I love the nostalgia that surrounds them. They strike a memory chord from my childhood. People saw them a lot, and they combine a certain naïveté and precision in a way that I really like. The stories are actually extraordinarily well told while being extremely naive. I like that combination a lot. I have a sentimental relation to that part of the Danish film heritage, and I feel a certain fascination for the crime films from the 1970s, *Per*, for example, and the films with a certain social-realist flavour. I also like those a lot. I've actually derived a lot of inspiration from earlier Danish films. The real low point in Danish film, I think, occurred during the 1980s. As far as I'm concerned only a tiny number of interesting films were made during that period. That's actually when the great directors emerged, von Trier and Bille and so on, but at the same time it's the least vibrant decade in the history of Danish film. The films being made now are all part of a big reaction to the films that were produced during the 1980s. With regard to the role played by Lars and Bille, it's clear that they've significantly expanded the stage for Danish film, and I think that was really necessary. I think that at an unconscious level that has affected us all a lot; the fact that Danish film now figures on the world map. The claustrophobic feeling that accompanies the thought of being financed by the state, of being guaranteed only a tiny audience, and of being part of a small industry is compensated for by the circus that those directors are able to generate. I think that's very important for Danish film and for the self-conceptions of those of us who are part of the relevant industry. We've always been very hard on ourselves in terms of self-criticism, and the bar is set quite high in Denmark. If you look at what gets produced in the US, perhaps only 4 percent of the scripts that are initiated actually get produced, and those are the films that we see, and of those films only a third are good. We probably make two good films for every ten films that get produced, so my self-esteem on behalf of Danish film is quite high.

**Hjort:** You're very interested in music. Indeed, for many years it looked as though you were destined to become a professional musician. Francis Ford Coppola's *The Godfather* is one of your favourite films, in part because of the way in which it uses Nino Rota's memorable music. I'd like to talk about your views on film music, perhaps in relation to *What's Your Guess?*. In this short film, Louise (Ann Eleonor Jørgensen) and Christian (Ulrich Thomsen) are threatened with eviction by Dan Lethner (Bjarne Henriksen), who works for a real estate agency. The narrative unfolds according to some of the basic principles of comedy, and music is used throughout as a key structuring device. The credits list Nikolaj Egelund and Bernhard Hansen as responsible for the film's music. What, exactly, were the three of you trying to achieve with the music in *What's Your Guess?*?

**Vinterberg:** I'm glad you chose to focus on that film, because I actually think that as far as the narrative use of music is concerned it's one of the best films I've ever been involved in. First of all there's a direct reference here to the Olsen Gang. *What's Your Guess?* is closely related to the Olsen Gang genre, and this is true not only of the music but of the whole way in which the story is told, the editing, the use of wipes and that kind of thing. Jesper Klein's character is also a nod to the past. The film's music ended up in a really interesting place somewhere between Bent Fabricius Bjerre and Nino Rota. It was something like the Olsen Gang theme meets the Nino Rota theme. That's what we aimed at during the editing. I think that Nikolaj Egelund, who incidentally has been my best friend since childhood, got it just right. We attributed a narrative dimension to the music, thereby making it part narrator. In fact, that's what I always do, when I use film music. In the other more sentimental films I've made, the music is there to express the feeling that ultimately is the very theme of the film although it isn't explicitly described on the screen. When I make a film about a boy who is stricken by grief, or, as was the case in my graduation film, a man who is profoundly sad, I have him spend approximately 90 percent of his time talking about the opposite, about partying. At four particular moments the viewer is given insight into his deeper concerns, but throughout the entire film the music recounts his deeper concerns, so that the four moments actually give us access to his interiority. In that way the music takes on an extremely important narrative dimension, one that constantly reminds us of the deeper forces motivating our main character. In this respect *What's Your Guess?* is somewhat different, for although the music is narrative in its thrust it is perhaps a little more superficial and tends to serve a more mechanical function aimed at generating suspense.

**Hjort:** Grief and loss are at the heart of *The Boy Who Walked Backwards*. In this film, the nine-year old Andreas (Holger Thaarup) dreams of moving backwards through time, to a point when his older brother Mikkel (Rune Veber) is still alive. The film was very well received and critics, impressed by your ability to work with children, drew parallels between yourself and the young Bille August. The praise is entirely deserved, for the roles of Andreas and Mikkel are in many ways very challenging. The Andreas character, for example, involves considerable range, for the young boy's experiences include getting drunk on Martinis, intense grief at the death of his brother and a moving conversation with the dead Mikkel in the final scenes of the movie. How do you approach the challenge involved in directing young children?

**Vinterberg:** What first and foremostly fascinated me about working with Holger, as the boy who plays Andreas is called, was his personality. Here was a person who intrigued me, someone whose mind I wanted to understand. I became very fond of him, just as I did of Thomas Bo Larsen, who was in my graduation film. The principle guiding my casting was to choose people I wanted to spend time with, and they all became my friends. Holger had a lot of things that were closely connected with the film: pain, happiness, intense feelings. At the same time he had a very clear understanding of the world of the film with all its compulsive rituals and such. The actual technical dimension involved in working with children as actors doesn't interest me that much, because in many ways it's a matter of one-way communication. That is, I tell them what they should do, and they then do it. When I work with professional, adult actors, it's the other way around, for they present me with lots of ideas about how best to interpret their roles, and then I pick and choose. I actually think that the process in the case of children is a lot more mechanical and a lot less vibrant than people tend to think. The feelings that are represented in *The Boy Who Walked Backwards* are brought out primarily as a result of our interaction as private persons and Holger's interaction with, and understanding of the story, much more than through our actual method of working, which consisted largely of instructions such as, 'go over there, say such and such, and turn around.'

**Hjort:** You graduated from the National Film School in 1993, with the film *Last Round*. The story is about a young man, Lars (Thomas Bo Larsen), and the way in which he chooses to take leave of his family and friends when he learns that he has leukaemia and no more than three months left to live. The film received the Jury's Prize and Producer's Prize at the International Student Film Festival in Munich. Critics took note, among other things, of what they called your balanced film style and careful visual aesthetic. Do you feel that you've developed, or are beginning to develop, a particular cinematic style? If so, how would you describe it?

**Vinterberg:** Film aesthetics is probably one of the things I find most confusing, so I tend to be a bit flighty in that respect. I've always focussed much more on the script and the actors. When I was in film school, my Polish teacher used to say 'You're afraid of the camera.' That's been my weakness and I just haven't given priority to that side of things. That's also why I constantly accept challenges and make room for heated discussions with my cameraman. I'm not, of course, complacent about the weaknesses in question. I've now worked with some cameramen who have been very good at opening up a dialogue with me about visual aesthetics and I'm beginning to move towards a mode of narration that I like, but in the last film, *The Celebration*, I consciously blocked all kinds of aesthetic possibilities. That's why I currently find myself giving absolute priority, formally speaking, to the actors and the script, but I'm beginning now to work on questions of film style. I want to make publicity films so that I can practice what is called mise-en-scène. I've never focussed on mise-en-scène before, and when you're making advertisements you have to give priority to precisely that, because there's really not that much else you can foreground.

**Hjort:** You wrote the script for your first feature film, *The Greatest Heroes*, together with Bo Hr. Hansen and Mogens Rukov. Like many of the films produced by younger Danish directors, *The Greatest Heroes* focusses on the lives and concerns of criminals. Yet, the thrust of this film is quite different from that of, say, Nicolas Winding Refn's *Pusher*, for in your cinematic universe, it's the criminal element that embodies generosity and attempts to live by moral ideals. Carsten (Thomas Bo Larsen), a 31 year old criminal, embarks on a romantic quest to save his newly discovered 12 year old daughter, Louise (Mia Maria Back), from abuse at the hands of her stepfather, Allan (Bjarne Henriksen). You've claimed that this film targets a certain national trait: petty-mindedness. In the context of a discussion of *The Greatest Heroes* published in *Det Fri Aktuelt* (November 1996) you recount the following anecdote: 'I once asked an Englishman about his experience of Danes, and he claimed never to have met so petty-minded and rude a nation. And there's probably some truth to this.' Also, in an interview published in *Berlingske Tidende* (November 1996) you claim that the characters in your films are naive precisely because naïveté is the most effective means of challenging petty-mindedness. Will you continue to target the national trait in question? Other Danish directors have been critical of this trait too, but have approached the problem differently. What's the advantage of romanticism and idealism compared, for example, to acerbic social satire?

**Vinterberg:** Petty-mindedness, lack of generosity, claustrophobia and mendacity are traits that can't be avoided in a country the size of Denmark or in an industry as small as the Danish film industry. What we're talking about here are so many ways of protecting one's self-conceptions. There really isn't room for anything else; the pettiness is almost inscribed in the geography, which imprisons people, and that sense of suffocation is probably something that will always prompt certain reactions in Denmark. The fact that people constantly long to get out is probably something that fuels the flames of narrative desire in Denmark, and in a way the same is true at the level of emotion. *The Greatest Heroes* is about a man who is a social misfit because he doesn't have all those reservations, all those self-protecting and yet other-regarding mechanisms. He's completely without reserve, and he probably springs from my own intense need to free myself from all those formalities, from all the petty-mindedness, which, of course, are part of me too. Ultimately the hero in the film may well be just as much an expression of my own personal desire to free myself from that kind of pettiness, an expression of my own needs, as he is a commentary about my country. I'm drawn to people who have a certain openminded lack of reserve in my own personal life, which is why I end up writing about those kinds of people. The people I like have an openness, which doesn't necessarily make them naive, but which does make them courageous, passionate and honest. I seek out people who have those character traits, perhaps because I feel I'm somewhat lacking in that regard, and that's why my film heroes also have those traits. In more general social terms I would want to say that I think I'm a typical Dane, and I think there are actually a lot of Danes who have the same need to kind of escape. That's why so many people really could identify with the main figure in *The Greatest Heroes*, although he actually behaves in a completely irresponsible manner, lacks control and shoots things to smithereens. People really liked that kind of behaviour precisely because so many Danes experience a lot of pent up aggression towards all the formalities that are observed in Denmark. I come from an intellectual background where every topic of conversation involved so many filters and so much verbalisation that it at times was extremely difficult even to catch sight of the relevant feelings. A lot of feelings get cooped up in that kind of context, so in that sense the film is clearly also a personal reaction to my own background.

**Hjort:** The world of cinema is frequently represented as a polarised one involving only Hollywood and its Other. In the context of a minor cinema, the question of a director's allegiances is never unimportant. If the Danish film industry is to thrive, then at least some of its more successful directors have to be able to resist the siren song of Hollywood. Interestingly, you seem to refuse the standard way of construing a Danish film-maker's options. In an interview published in *Jyllands-Posten* (September 1994) you introduce a quite different set of geographical references: 'Right now my dream is to make films in the capitals of Europe. Mostly Copenhagen, but I like the idea of becoming part of the film culture that currently exists in London.' Some film scholars are quite excited these days about what they're calling New European Cinemas. What is it about, say, London, that appeals to you as a film-maker?

**Vinterberg:** I'll have to begin by identifying what repels me about going abroad, and that's the complete difference of mentality that I encounter. I've spent some time with agents in New York and that kind of thing, and, without wishing to give offence, I must say that I think what I saw was an expression of extraordinary superficiality. Now, fortunately I haven't been to Canada, which is where you're from, so I can talk freely about those living south of the border. Already after my visit to New York, after three days in that city, I could feel that it wasn't at all a place that I could really respect. There are a lot of fantastic people there, a lot of very different people, and New York is in some ways the capital of the world. At the same time there's a lot of superficiality, and there's a lot of faking going on, and I can't think of worse conditions for making a film, not, at least, if it's to be made the way I make films. I've been to New York five times, and every time I'm there I become more and more convinced that I'm really a European at heart. What I find attractive about the idea of working in London is the fact that the language barrier would be less formidable than the one involved in working in Paris, for example, and yet you'd still somehow have moved beyond that Danish sense of claustrophobia. However, I've been inspired by other things since then. I have to admit that my collaboration with Lars von Trier has taught me that he is able to make Denmark big, without leaving Denmark, and this, for me, is the ultimate ideal. The idea is not to go international and become famous, but to think oneself beyond certain typical Danish mentalities. The first thing that occurs to you is, of course, that you need to move to a new city, because you somehow assume that if you move physically your head moves too, and that may very well be the case. Yet the biggest struggle, the biggest challenge, is really a question of making the home terrain grow.

**Hjort:** In 1995 you and Lars von Trier embarked on a fascinating project, Dogme 95. The four directors participating in this project were asked to adhere to ten rules. The intention motivating Dogme 95 is to explore the way in which certain constraints provide the conditions of possibility for innovation and creativity. It's also a matter of resisting the technology-driven tendencies of contemporary film-making, for a small, state-supported industry simply cannot bear the kinds of astronomical budgets associated with use of the newest technologies at any cost. Finally, Dogme 95 is meant to counteract some of the negative effects of an increasingly democratised cinematic medium. What, exactly, is the relation between the democratisation of film and decadence? Is *The Celebration*, which was made within the context of Dogme 95, in your mind an antidote to decadence?

**Vinterberg:** In my mind there's a connection between my need to make a Dogme film and the main character in *The Greatest Heroes*. What was really satisfying about making the Dogme film was being able to break with convention, to throw off, as it were, that terribly heavy, suffocating blanket that covers all of Danish film-making, and for that matter, American film-making. Dogme breaks with the particular way of making films that has come to have the status almost of a given, and which you're expected simply to accept without question when you're about to make a film: there have to be a certain number of lights, so and so much make-up, and the idea is to get as far away from reality as possible in order to create a new and, it turns out, often uninteresting reality. It's probably that breach with ossified convention that explains why I loved making my Dogme film. The gesture is essentially that of the main character in *The Greatest Heroes* when he shoots the windowpane to smithereens in the weapon store, and it has the effect of cracking the layer of cement that covers the entire Danish film industry. The result is improvisation and a tremendous sense of release, but all within a carefully circumscribed framework, because a film is, of course, all the more inspiring to make if the basic production parameters have been clearly defined. That's obvious and anyone who is involved with something that resembles film-making just slightly knows this. The same holds for interviews: the more precise the questions are, the more precise are the answers. A painter relies on the four sides of his frame. If he didn't total chaos would ensue. The clearer you define a task for yourself, the more fun you have accomplishing it. That's what the entire Dogme project is about. If the Dogme rules specify that no sound effects can be used, then you're left with only your volume knob to work with, and suddenly there's a whole world in that one knob. Suddenly that volume control allows you to evoke a wide range of different moods. In that sense, it's very inspiring. Jørgen Leth once said to me, 'In restriction lies the greatest source of inspiration' and I think I've shown that to be true with *The Celebration*. You also referred to decadence and that kind of thing. Normally I try to avoid elaborating on that issue because I believe the point is stated clearly enough in the original document. I think it's expressed very precisely there and every time I try to expand on it, I feel it becomes more obscure.

**Hjort:** Like many other Danish directors, you're critical of some aspects of Danish film policy. More specifically, you've taken issue with the fact that only paltry sums of money are set aside for script writing. The result is that many film scripts are inadequately developed or simply based on pre-existing literary classics. In an interview published in *Politiken* (December 1993), you put the point as follows: 'I'm sure that Denmark is full of stories, but I don't think they're given enough space to develop.' Do you have particular stories, or particular Danes in mind here?

*Ulrich Thomsen as Christian, the abused son in Vinterberg's award-winning Dogme film,* The Celebration (Festen)*. [Photo: Lars Høgsted]*

**Vinterberg:** I think the situation has changed significantly since that interview. There are far better opportunities now for telling a wide range of stories and for focussing intensely on script-related work. The National Film School's script-writing stream is at this point one of the institution's most important and best supported programs. It's thriving and the interest in script writing is enormous. A new subculture of script-writers has emerged, and the people involved really know how to tell stories, and they're being remunerated for their work. People are also telling stories that have a broader appeal, so I think the situation has improved quite a lot. I've also acquired some insight into how people write elsewhere in the world, and this has opened my eyes to how well we actually write here in Denmark. I've also discovered just how many scripts it takes to get something good. I've read a lot of scripts, including foreign ones, and most of them, by far, are bad. That's why the American industry is organised in such a way that the vast majority of scripts end up being shelved. Only the good ones get produced, but they can also afford to pay for all those scripts. I don't think I can identify the kinds of Danish stories that aren't getting told. Because so many stories *have* been told since I gave that interview. There's a lot of experimenting going on and the number of original scripts being written is so great at this point that I'm almost tempted to say that adaptations of literary works have become interesting once again. Things have really changed a lot.

**Hjort:** I'd like to pick up on some remarks you made in the interview published in

277

*Politiken* (December 1993): 'How do we get at our generation's language? The language is rich enough, but the diction itself is flat, the music of the language isn't that vibrant. That's actually a real problem if you would like people to speak in an everyday language that is also comprehensible.' I find your remarks fascinating because they help to identify certain shifts within the history of Danish film. When Christian Braad Thomsen began making films in the 1970s, it was a matter of choosing what he perceived as a vibrant and in some instances regionalised vernacular over the stilted and artificial Danish spoken by professional actors. The situation today, you suggest, is rather different. The vernacular is now a recurrent feature of Danish film, but this vernacular is now deficient in some way. Could you elaborate on this point?

**Vinterberg:** I probably feel much the way that Christian Braad Thomsen did back then, because as far as I'm concerned there's something very liberating about the fact that actors have been given priority in Danish film and about the fusion of acting and script writing, which used to be separated in the most ridiculous of ways. You used to have people, who were completely removed from the story, communicating with each other via a beautiful theatrical Danish that had nothing to do with the situation at hand. That being said, I do think that one of the drawbacks of emphasising everyday speech in all contemporary Danish films, especially my own, is that the films become so colloquial as to seem almost linguistically flat, to the point where you begin to long once again for the language of the Royal Theatre. Now I've worked together with Henning Moritzon from the Royal Theatre in connection with *The Celebration*, and he's actually one of the few actors I've worked with who is capable of combining colloquial speech with the beautiful, acquired language of the theatre. But my goal is probably to enrich the language without making it a source of alienation for the audience or an obstacle to their identification with the characters. It's a difficult balance to achieve, but it's also a reaction to all the improvisation that's emerged and which I myself helped to initiate. I think there are a lot of superfluous fillers that in some way dull the point of the lines, 'uh' and 'man', for example. And I can feel that I'm at a turning point right now, because on the one hand I don't want to alienate or reject my audience, but on the other hand I don't want to render the lines superfluous by simply allowing people to blather as they wish. I think that contemporary Danish film has travelled very far down the road called idiomatic street talk or colloquial speech, and people respond by saying 'oh, what excellent acting', but there's very little commitment. I think actors have to ask more of themselves. I think we have to ask more of the written lines; we have to ask more of the value of a line.

**Hjort:** In 1997, Lars von Trier, much to the surprise of many Danes, bought the film rights to all of Morten Korch's* novels. Korch's romantic depictions of country life are the basis for the countless popular comedies produced during the 1950s. The renewal of Danish film is typically construed in terms of a rejection of these very popular comedies. You were asked to direct a new Morten Korch film within the context of von Trier's larger project. What, exactly, is the aim of this project, as you see it? What do you hope to achieve in your own Morten Korch film?

**Vinterberg:** I have to start by saying that I've declined that Morten Korch invitation, but I can, of course, talk about what I found appealing about the project and why I understand their reasons for undertaking it. I've never come even close to breaking with the tradition of Danish popular comedy. The people who broke with that tradition belong to a quite different generation, to my parents' generation, I think. I have, on the contrary, frequently referred to the tradition in question in my films, as I explained earlier. In that sense I felt that it was actually the right moment to revive the popular comedy tradition in as concrete a way as the Morten Korch project makes possible. There are a lot of great qualities in Korch's work. He has a very well oiled narrative machine and extremely effective stories. Then there's a sentimentality and naïveté at the level of expression, as well as a number of values that in one way or the other have been neglected in Danish film. I said 'no' to the project because I believe there's a great risk of people regarding the film I would make as an ironic work. There's a great risk of my regarding it ironically, and the reason is that we can't help but be very far removed from the world of Korch. That's why I don't think it's worth spending time on. It's simply not important enough to me, and that's why I've said no.

**Hjort:** Would you like to talk a bit about your Dogme film, *The Celebration*?

**Vinterberg:** I think it's the film I've most enjoyed making in a long time. I found making it very stimulating and I'm very pleased with it. In my mind it's an important film, in the sense that it's not just another film, but a film that distinguishes itself as something extraordinary, as a clearly defined experiment that succeeds. It's a film that transcends the ordinary, commercial ways of making films, and it has helped me to transcend the conventions of my own film-making. Making it was very liberating and opened my eyes to what it means to make films. When I'd completed my graduation film, *Last Round*, my wife and I agreed that it would take me another five years to make another film like it. The next few films might be good, but they probably wouldn't be able to achieve that same pure feeling of something big. I think that *The Celebration* is the closest I've come to that feeling.

**Bondebjerg:** You've said the following with reference to *The Celebration*'s theme and salient mode of expression: 'The film is an expression of the Denmark I live in and it expresses much of the hostility that I lie in bed dreaming about at night' (*Information*, June 1998). On previous occasions you've talked about your fascination for characters and individuals who acquire a certain problematic hero status as a result of their ability simply to let go and to allow chaos to prevail. Your remarks suggest that *The Celebration* touches on feelings and explores issues that at some level are related to your own experiences. At the same time, though, it would appear to bring into play a more general form of social symbolism. Is the image of the family in *The Celebration* a metaphor for society?

**Vinterberg:** Let me start with a very banal observation. What you're pointing to here is also the expression of a certain method. Opting to work with a figure who is intent on being in control, but suddenly is deprived of all control, is a way of gaining access to the real being who's been hiding all along behind a facade. This generates a kind of duality that brings the figures to life as real beings. I'm also personally very drawn to the idea of getting to the bottom of the world I live in. My Denmark, which includes the Danish film industry as well as my childhood experiences, is very much governed by reason. It's a world that in many ways is crippled by reason and an insistence on being mature. That's why I'm naturally tempted to let the characters in my films be directly, irrationally, in touch with their feelings. It's quite clear that the family in *The Celebration* somehow becomes a metaphor for aspects of Denmark, for that insistence on the need to be calm and reasonable, for the deft repression of many things, including, for example, agression. I didn't consciously choose to paint this image of Denmark; the image emerged in a much more intuitive manner. It's true that I thought to myself early on in the process that it would be wonderful if the film in some strange way could be a portrait of Denmark, just as *The Kingdom* is in its own way. How you then go about generating that image in the actual writing process is something I'm not entirely sure of. However, by including, for example, a foreign element – a black man who speaks a different language – it's possible, in a very banal way, suddenly to underscore the extent to which the film's depiction of the family functions as a portrait of Denmark.

**Bondebjerg:** The Dogme films have been applauded for the intensity and authenticity of the actors' performances, but have the Dogme rules also influenced your film aesthetics? At an earlier point in this interview you said that you hadn't previously emphasised the aesthetic dimension of film-making, but that you now stand at a crossroads in this respect. How would you characterise the visual and cinematographic principles that you and Anthony Dod Mantle worked with in this film? How did you and your editors, Jesper W. Nielsen and Valdis Oskarsdóttir, establish the film's particular rhythm? Would the film have been as strong, from a purely cinematic point of view, without the framework created by the Dogme rules, or are its salient cinematic properties, including the editing rhythm, very much elicited by the Dogme concept?

**Vinterberg:** The answer to the second half of that question is quite simply 'yes.' At the same time I would want to point out that people's goals and ambitions often grow out of their weaknesses. Stutterers often become good singers, just as people who are shy frequently become actors. It's very clear to me that my aesthetic ambitions are a direct expression of my own weaknesses. They're an expression of a profound lack of interest, which then blossoms when I feel a certain peace of mind and a growing sense of self-confidence. Film is, of course, my medium, but I'm a bit of a stutterer when it comes to my relation to the camera. It's actually rather strange, because when push came to shove, and I found myself working with my cinematographer, Anthony, I actually had a very precise and stubborn idea of the kind of look that I was after. What happened, very concretely, in the case of *The Celebration* was first of all that I experienced real irritation at not being able to culitvate a visual aesthetic because the Dogme rules literally prohibit that. Secondly, it turned out that in following the rules we were generating something that resembled an aesthetic in its own right, and as a result I virtually didn't have to think about that aspect of the film. Our films, that is, Lars's, Søren's, Kristian's and my own, are very different, but Dogme comes very close to being its own aesthetic. I did, of course, transgress the rules slightly, for as I stood there with Anthony I couldn't help wondering where I should place the camera, but that's really just an expression of the fact that you can barely avoid such reflections if you want to be able to make films. I did opt for a certain method that was to ensure that things emerged more or less spontaneously. I didn't spend any time preparing and, having observed the actors during rehearsals, I made sure to rely on my intuitions when conveying what I was after to Anthony.

**Bondebjerg:** The editing is also very interesting. There are a number of very fine aesthetic effects at various points in the film and they're linked to the actual method of editing.

**Vinterberg:** Let's start with the rules. They're very inspiring in that they call for brutality at the level of editing. They also call for a great deal of clarity, because you have to edit all reels at once, and that encourages you to cut out everything superfluous, to edit all the way to the bone, so to speak. However, that's also why it suddenly became very interesting to begin to look for a certain poetry in that very naked type of editing. It was wonderful to break the rules in that way without really breaking them, to draw inspiration from them and consequently experience a certain sense of freedom. In any event I'm like a fish in water in the editing room, compared with the handicap I feel I have when dealing with the camera. That's where you start to write the melody again. In this case it was also insanely easy to keep track of the entire process, because we simply edited everything at the same time. There weren't a whole lot of different reels to keep track of, so we were able to keep track of characters and themes instead and to produce those poetic effects you mentioned.

**Bondebjerg:** Critics have on the whole pointed to the fruitful way in which the film blends black satire with dramatic and comic elements. And Jonathan Romney (1998) even characterised the film as a combination of Buñuel's and Renoir's critique of the bourgeois family. Does the film, in your mind, draw on other films, or is it inspired, not so much by the history of film, as by other realities?

**Vinterberg:** I was very clearly inspired by other film-makers. At the time I mostly didn't know this, but it's very clear after the fact. There's one point in the film where we were aware of stealing. I'm thinking of the chain dance sequence. We stole that from Bergman. Our excuse for doing so was that he himself stole the idea from Visconti's *The Leopard* (*Il Gattopardo*). In that case, I have to admit, it was a matter of cynical theft. It's amusing that the films mentioned in connection with *The Celebration* all figure amongst the best films by my favourite directors. I saw their films while I was at film school, at a time in my life when I didn't have a clear sense of anything, and I saw all those films without knowing what I was seeing, but it's very clear that I've drawn on that cocktail of experiences. Buñuel made an enormous impression on me back then. I've also been told that there are

Shakespearean elements in the story, and traces of Bergman, and those are all people who've had a tremendous impact on me. The most direct influence comes from something as banal as *The Godfather*. That is, the whole family pattern and the premise about a difficult son and a quiet son who rebels. I actually told Thomas Bo Larsen to imitate the example of James Caan, but the other films are all films with which I'm familiar, and which have become part of my unconscious. As such they're bound to have left certain traces. With regard to the combination of satire and Norén-like drama I would want to point out that it's probably precisely this mixture that makes the film thoroughly evil. I think I used laughter as a way of undermining people's defence mechanisms. Brutality and aggression are a strong cocktail and it can be hard to see one tragic scene after the next. I know myself well enough to know that it doesn't take long to construct a certain defence mechanism against that kind of insistence on the tragic. In my opinion, given the tools that are available to me, the most effective way of undermining the relevant defence strategies is to make the audience laugh at what is in fact brutal and tragic.

**Bondebjerg:** Together with the three other members of the Dogme group, you've just recently carried out the TV experiment, *D Day*, which involved showing four films (one by each of the Dogme directors) simultaneously on four separate channels. In addition images from the actual production room were broadcast on a fifth channel, while a sixth channel showed all four films simultaneously in split screen and without sound. The plan is to edit all of this into a feature film at some future date. On the whole viewers and critics were rather disappointed with *D Day*. They claimed that it was difficult to choose among the channels and hard to find head or tail in the story or stories. What were the intentions motivating the experiment, and what's your verdict on the result?

**Vinterberg:** I was proud of that experiment, because I felt that in purely formal terms it points to some angles that are interesting and which haven't been pursued before. As Mogens Rukov said, it's interesting to think that we now can imagine covering the peace negotiations in Syria with a camera in each room, a TV station in each room, and the possibility of piecing together the general picture oneself. I felt that the form in question forced the audience, in a very concrete way, to participate actively in what they were watching. I liked the fact that it raised the question of what it is that we actually see when we watch a film. What is it exactly that we experience? I think there's something very lonely about the thought of sitting there and watching a film that nobody else sees. I think that's actually deeply problematic, just as it's problematic to deprive the director of the power to control his story. I think that it was incredibly interesting to raise the question as to whether people ever see the same thing, even in those cases when it's a matter of only one film being broadcast. I've travelled around with a copy of *The Celebration* and I've noticed that people have seen their own private film and have reacted in completely divergent ways at any number of points. Those are the kinds of interesting phenomena that are foregrounded by *D Day*. Less dramatically, I like the fact that it was an inherently risky project. Much as in the case of Dogme, we moved hand-in-hand and as a group onto territory that was unpredictable. I like that. Any number of amazing things can happen as a result. That's not what happened. I think the experiment failed, but I'm still in some strange way very proud of the fact that we undertook it. I suspect that one of the reasons it failed was that we abandoned two basic principles. First, we didn't create a common story; instead we each ended up messing around with our own story. People didn't get a shared sense of what was going on, for they didn't have access to any connecting information. That was a very serious mistake, and it's clear that we, as the directors, should have worked on the story together. The other very important mistake we made was that we allowed the need for planning to take over completely. This problem arose as a result of certain technical issues, the millennium celebrations, the police, and so on. That is, what one experienced was four characters who, because of us, weren't really capable of reacting to each other. The social dimension failed in that respect too, and I think that's one of the reasons why people simply unplugged.

# Glossary

Århusiansk. Accent associated with the town of Århus.

Bodil. Danish award established in 1948 and named after the actors Bodil Kjer and Bodil Ipsen. The winners are identified by an association of Copenhagen-based journalists (Filmmedarbejder-foreningen), and awards are distributed across a number of categories, including, for example, Best Danish Film, Best Actor, Best Actress and Best Cinematographer.

Chariot of the Sun (Solvognen). A group of radical performers opposed to bourgeois conceptions of theatre and closely associated with the Christiania colony in Copenhagen.

Consultant (Filmkonsulent). Danish Film Institute support for feature and documentary film-making was until 1989 allocated following an artistic assessment by one of six film consultants appointed for a three-year term. The 1989 Film Act provides an alternative route to DFI funding in the form of the 50/50 (60/40) policy (see below).

Danish Broadcasting Corporation (DR TV). State institution providing two public service channels in a context of state monopoly from 1951 until 1988, and since then within a more liberal economy. Home to the so-called 'Children and Youth Department' (Børne- og ungdomsafdelingen), a key producer over the years of children's and youth films.

Danish Film Institute (Det Danske Filminstitut). Established in 1972 and since 1997 an umbrella institution embracing the previously autonomous National Film Board (Statens Filmcentral), the Danish Film Museum (Det Danske Filmmuseum) and the Danish Film Institute. The mandate of the DFI is to support film art and culture in Denmark.

Danish popular comedy (folkekomedie). Examples include the Morten Korch adaptations (see below) and the Olsen Gang series (1968–81, directed by Erik Balling). The genre in question finds its roots in popular theatre and emphasises stark oppositions, clearly defined characters and elements of slapstick.

Dogme 95. Film Collective, members of which are Lars von Trier, Thomas Vinterberg, Søren Kragh-Jacobsen and Kristian Levring. To date four Danish Dogme films have been released: *The Celebration* (*Festen*, Thomas Vinterberg), *The Idiots* (*Idioterne*, Lars von Trier), *Mifune* (*Mifunes sidste sang*, Søren Kragh-Jacobsen) and *The King is Alive* (Kristian Levring). Four new Danish Dogme films by Lone Scherfig, Henrik Ruben Genz, Ole Christian Madsen and Åke Sandgren are in progress. Non-Danish films by Jean-Marc Barr, Harmony Korine, Daniel H. Byun, José Luis Marqués, and Vladamn Zdravkovic have been granted Dogme certificates, and requests for the relevant document have been received from an additional 14 film-makers with Dogme films in progress. See www.DOGME95.DK

50/50; 60/40 policy (50/50; 60/40 ordning). The Film Act of 1989 made provisions for a 50/50 policy that was designed to stimulate cinematic productions with popular appeal. The 50/50 policy enabled private investors to circumvent the authority of the consultants and to receive matching funds of up to three million Crowns from the Danish Film Institute with relative ease and speed. The percentages were changed to 60/40 in 1998, with the larger figure representing the contribution of state monies.

Film Act (Filmlovgivning). 1922, 1964, 1972, 1982, 1989, 1997. For present purposes, the key Film Acts are the Act of 1972, which has the effect of establishing the Danish Film Insitute and makes film art a matter of state support; the Film Act of 1982 which earmarks 25 percent of the budget for films for children and young people and introduces the 50/50 policy; and the Film Act of 1997 which has the effect of fusing three previously autonomous institutions into the Danish Film Institute (see above). It is also worth noting that the Film Acts of 1972 and 1982 emphasise the Danish language and define Danish film in ethnic terms, whereas the later Acts of 1989 and 1997 articulate a two-fold definition of Danish film that attenuates and makes possible the circumvention of previously required ethnic elements.

Folk High School (Folkehøjskole). A system of adult, boarding school education inspired by the teachings of the Danish theologian and nationalist, N.F.S. Grundtvig. The first school was established in Rødding in 1844. Although the initial intention was more inclusive, in practice the schools aimed primarily at members of the peasant class. At this point there are approximately 100 recognised folk high schools in Denmark.

Fynsk. Accent associated with Funen.

Jysk. Accent associated with Jutland.

Korch, Morten. Danish novelist (1876–1954) whose popular novels about rural life and conflicts between peasants and landed gentry became the basis for numerous widely seen adaptations during the 1950s and 1960s. *The Red Horses* (*De røde heste*), the first of these adaptations, was directed by Alice O'Fredericks and Jon Iversen and produced by ASA. In the mid-1990s Zentropa/Lars von Trier purchased the rights to Korch's work, and to date this has led to two productions: *Quiet Waters* (*Folkene i Dale*), a popular TV series, was shown on Danish TV in 1999; the first Zentropa-produced, Korch-based feature, *The Lady of Hamre* (*Fruen fra Hamre*), directed by Katrine Wiedemann, was released during the Spring of 2000.

National Film School of Denmark (Den Danske Filmskole). Founded in 1966, the school offers four-year programs in the areas of directing, cinematography, sound technique, editing, producing, and animation, and a script-writing option lasting 18 months.

New Fiction Film Denmark (Dansk novellefilm). Special funding program introduced in 1994 in order to promote the short fiction film as an independent genre. 'A joint production effort involving DR TV (the Danish Broadcasting Corporation), TV 2/Danmark, the National Film Board of Denmark and the Danish Film Institute, New Fiction Film Denmark budgets DKK 24 million annually to carry out its brief' (Alice Njor, 'Foreword', New Fiction Film Denmark 1996).

Rigsdansk. High Danish.

Robert. Danish film award granted for the first time in 1983 by the at that time newly established Danish Film Academy. Prizes are awarded in a number of categories, including Best Danish Feature, Best Actor, Best Actress, Best Editing, Best Music and so on.

# Bibliography

## Articles and Books

Billingham, R. (1996) Ray's a Laugh, Germany: Scalo.

Birkvad, S. (1992) Verden er Leth. En bog om Jørgen Leths film og forfatterskab, Odense: Odense University Press.

Björkman, S. (1999) Trier om Trier. Samtal med Stig Björkman, Stockholm: Alfabeta.

Bondebjerg, I. (1996) 'Between War and Welfare: Danish Documentary Films in the 1950s', Aura 2, 31: 30–56.

—. (2000) 'Film and Modernity: Realism and the Aesthetic of Scandinavian New Wave Cinema', in I. Bondebjerg (ed.) Moving Images, Culture & the Mind, Luton: University of Luton Press, 117–33.

Bondebjerg, I. et al. (eds) (1997) Dansk film, 1972-97, Copenhagen: Rosinante.

Braad Thomsen, C. (1991) Arv og gæld – hjemstavnsbilleder, Gylling: Hovedland and Narayana Press.

—. (1998) Sygdom forvandlet til skønhed. En filmdagbog fra optagelserne til 'Den Blå Munk', Århus: Klim.

Brink, L. and Lund, J. (1975) Dansk rigsmål. Lydudviklingen siden 1849 med særligt henblik på sociolekterne i København, Copenhagen: Gyldendal, 1975.

Carlsen, H. (1998) Mit livs fortrængninger. Erindringer (memoirs), Copenhagen: Gyldendal.

Conrad, K. (1991) Drengedrømme. Nils Malmros – en auteur, Copenhagen: Amanda.

Dale, M. (1992) Europa Europa, France: Académie Carat and Media Business School.

Daneskov, L. and Kristensen, K. (1989) Nils Malmros. Portræt af en filmkunstner, Silkeborg: Hovedland.

Degn Johansen, T. and Kimergaard, L.B. (eds) (1991) Sekvens. Filmvidenskabelig årbog: Lars von Trier (special issue on Lars von Trier), University of Copenhagen: Department of Film and Media Studies.

Dinnesen, N.J. and Kau, E. (1983) Filmen i Danmark, Copenhagen: Akademisk forlag.

Drouzy, M. (1991) 'Biografiske skitse' (biographical sketch), in T. Degn Johansen and L.B. Kimergaard (eds): 9–20.

Engberg, M. (1987) Dansk filmhistorie 1896–1985. Et kompendium, Copenhagen: C.A. Reitzels forlag.

—. (1990) Danish Films Through the Years, Copenhagen: The Danish Film Institute.

Finney, A. (1996) The State of European Cinema: A New Dose of Reality, London: Cassell.

Fisker, J. et al. (1997) Omkring Barbara, Frederiksberg: Fisker and Schou.

Gellner, E. (1996) 'The Coming of Nationalism and its Interpretation: The Myths of Nation and Class', in G. Balakrishnan (ed.) Mapping the Nation, London: Verso: 98–145.

Higson, A. (1995) Waving the Flag: Constructing a National Cinema in Britain, Oxford: Clarendon.

Hjort, M. (1996) 'Danish Cinema and the Politics of Recognition', in D. Bordwell and N. Carroll (eds) Post-Theory: Reconstructing Film Studies, Madison: The University of Wisconsin Press: 520–32.

—. (2000) 'Themes of Nation', in M. Hjort and S. MacKenzie (eds) Cinema and Nation, London: Routledge: 103–17.

—. (2001) 'Reflections on a nationalist style of film-making', in J. Holmgaard (ed.) Word and Image, Copenhagen: Medusa.

Hroch, M. (1985) The Social Preconditions of National Revival in Europe: A Comparative Analysis of the Social Composition of Patriotic Groups among the Smaller European Nations, Cambridge: Cambridge University Press.

Jeppesen, P. et al. (eds) (1993) Danske spillefilm, 1968–91, Esbjerg: Sammenslutningen af danske filmklubber.

Jørholt, E. 'Erfaringens filmiske prisme', in Bondebjerg et al (1997): 242–63.

Krarup, H. and Nørrested, C. (1986) Eksperimentalfilmen i Danmark, Copenhagen: Borgen.

Lee, B. et al. (1992) 'Critical Multiculturalism', Critical Inquiry 18: 530–55.

Leifer, A. (2000) Også i dag oplevede jeg noget. Samtaler med Jørgen Leth (interview book), Copenhagen: Informations forlag.

Malinowski, B. (1955) Sex and Repression in Savage Society, New York: Meridien.

Mogensen, J. (1981) Kundskabens træ – en film bliver til (on the production history of Tree of Knowledge), Trøjborg: Centrum.

Nørrested, C. and Alsted, C. (eds) (1987) Kortfilmen og staten, Copenhagen: Forlaget Eventus.

Piil, M. (ed.) (1998) Filmguide. Danske film fra A til Z, Copenhagen: Gyldendal.

286

Rasmussen, B. (1968) Filmens Hvem – Hvad – Hvor. Danske titler og biografer, Copenhagen: Politikens forlag.

Rex, J. (1972) Aske, tid og ild – fra et glemt terræn (photographs), Copenhagen: Brøndum.

—— (1972) Kvindernes bog (feminist interview book), Copenhagen: Gyldendal.

——. (1978) Jeg har ikke lukket et øje – en billedroman (a novel in images), Copenhagen: Borgen.

——. (1986) Stamtavler (paintings, photographs), Copenhagen: Eks-skolens forlag.

——. (1989) Figur og rum (paintings), Copenhagen: Brøndum.

——. (1995) Malerier og tegninger 1995, med tekster af Per Aage Brandt, Ole Nørlyng, Marianne Bech, Copenhagen: Brøndum.

——. (1996) Billedet bag billedet (photographs), Copenhagen: Fotografisk Center.

Riis, J. (1998) 'Toward a Poetics of the Short Film', p.o.v. A Danish Journal of Film Studies 5: 133–50.

Schepelern, P. (1997) Lars von Triers elementer. En filminstruktørs arbejde, Copenhagen: Rosinante.

——. et al. (eds) (1997) '100 års dansk film', Kosmorama 220 (special issue with extensive bibliographical references pertaining to the various decades of Danish film history).

Soila, T. et al. (1998) Nordic National Cinemas, London: Routledge.

Taylor, C. (1989) Sources of the Self: The Making of the Modern Identity, Cambridge, Mass.: Harvard University Press.

——. (1992) 'The Politics of Recognition', in A. Gutmann (ed.) Multiculturalism and 'The Politics of Recognition', Princeton: Princeton University Press: 25–73.

Troelsen, A. (ed) (1980) Levende billeder af Danmark, Copenhagen: Medusa.

Trolle, K. (ed.) (1980) Frøken Smillas fornemmelse for sne. Bogen om Bille Augusts film efter Peter Høegs roman (production history of Smilla's Feeling for Snow), Copenhagen: Munksgaard Rosinante.

Vinterberg, T. (1998) Festen (The Celebration), Copenhagen: Per Kofod.

Von Trier, L. (1996) Breaking the Waves, translated by Jonathan Sydenham, Copenhagen: Per Kofod.

——. (1998) Dogme 2: 'Idioterne'. Manuskript og dagbog, Copenhagen: Gyldendal.

——. and N. Vørsel (1995) Riget (The Kingdom), Copenhagen: Aschehoug.

Wolden-Ræthinge, A. (1993) Bille August fortæller om sit liv og sine film (interview book), Copenhagen: Aschehoug.

Zeruneith, I. (1995) Wide-Eyed: Films for Children and Young People in the Nordic Countries, 1977–93, Copenhagen: Tiderne Skifter.

## Newspaper articles, interviews, policy documents, reviews

Anon. (1996) New Fiction Film Denmark, Copenhagen: New Fiction Film Denmark.

——. (1972/1982/1989/1997) 'Lov om film og biografer' (Film Acts).

——. (1998) Det Danske Filminstituts 4-årige handlingsplan (The Danish Film Institute's Four Year Plan), Copenhagen: The Danish Film Institute.

——. (1998) Danish Feature Films, Copenhagen: The Danish Film Institute.

Arnfred. M. (1989) Interview with L. Dueholm, 'Jeg går i biografen for at blive forført', Månedsmagasinet IN, June 6.

Bang Carlsen, J. (1997) Interview with I. Carstensen, 'Dansk film savner legen', Berlingske Tidende, November 4.

Bier, S. (1993) Review by D. Nissen, Det bli'r i familien/Family Matters, Information, November 19.

——., and Zandén, P. (1993) Interview with H. Hellman, 'Det bli'r i familien – Susanne Bier og Philip Zandén om inderlighed – også i film', Politiken, November 14.

Bornedal, O. (1995) Interview with A.-M. Gregers, 'Bornedal flytter til Hollywood', Ekstra Bladet, May 29.

——. (1996) Interview with H.J. Møller, 'Mellem sortsyn og lalleglæde', Politiken, August 21.

——. (1996) Interview with D. Myhre, 'Syltet serie tegner til succes', Berlingske Tidende, August 21.

Braad Thomsen, C. (1966) 'Efterlysning af dansk filmrealisme', Aktuelt, April 28.

——. (1971) 'Frihed til blufærdighed', Fyens Stiftstidende, September 30.

——. (1983) Interview with bor, 'Filminstruktøren Chr. Braad Thomsen: Jeg vil gerne lave film om Karen Blixen', Midtjyllands avis, November 21.

Camre, H. (Director of DFI) (1998) Press release, 'Udfordring til dansk film' ('A Challenge for Danish Film'), The Danish Film Institute, August 25.

Clausen, E. (1986) Interview with H. Høgsbro, Land og folk, May 10.

—— (1987) Interview with B. Steinborn, 'Dem dänischen Film mangelt es an Anti-helden', Filmfaust 2, 62: 26–35.

——. (1988) Interview with H. Hellmann, 'Til kamp mod den danske leverpostej-nationalisme', Politiken, March 6.

——. (1990) 'Dans på blomstrende tidlser – Det er min egn', Kristeligt Dagblad, August 23.

——. (1991) Interview, Politiken, November 14.

Elmer, J. (1997) Interview with C. Hjorth-Knudsen, 'Jagten på øjeblikket', B.T., September 20.

—— (1997) Interview with P. Dabbelsteen, 'Bittersød hverdag', Politiken, September 12.

Eriksen, J.-M. (1997) 'Indespærringens ideologi – Et lykkeligt farvel til den kvælende og danske folkelighed' (on the concept of the popular and its relation to nationalism), Politiken, October 5.

Gerner Nielsen, E. (Minister of Culture) (1998) Press release, '75 pct. mere til dansk film' ('75 percent more for Danish Film'), Ministry of Culture, August 25.

Kragh-Jacobsen, S. (1993) Interview with P. Øvig Knudsen, 'Hovedet bliver ikke bidt af mange gråspurve', Information, January 29.

——. (1994) Interview with P. Calum, 'Filmfolk', Jyllands-Posten, June 13.

——. (1995) Interview with U. Poulsen, 'Der er altid noget, du er god til', Kristeligt Dagblad, May 6.

Refn, A. (1987) Interview with H. Holmberg, 'Vi skal lave mange danske film, der fortæller om os', Thisted Dagblad, October 20.

——. (1993) Interview with K. Apollo, Månedsmagasinet Agenda, November.

Svendsen, L. (1999), Review by M. Piil, Bornholms stemme/Gone with the Fish, Information, September 3.

Vinterberg, T. (1993) Interview with H. Hellman, 'Kunsten er at være sig selv', Politiken, December 5.

——. (1994) Interview with V. Andersen, 'Thomas Vinterberg går forlæns – med fuld fart', Jyllands-Posten, August 25.

——. (1996) Interview with J. Høyer, 'Jordemødre og andre helte', Det fri Aktuelt, November 2.

——. (1996) Interview with S. Frank, 'Tiden er den værste fjende', Berlingske Tidende, November 5.

——. (1998) Interview with Jesper Juul Jensen, Information, June 19.

——. (1998). Interview with R. Wood, 'Humble Guests at the Celebration', Cineaction 48: 47–54.

Von Trier, L. (1984) Press Release, 'The Element of Crime. Programerklæring', May 3, reprinted in T. Degn Johansen and L.B. Kimergaard (eds): 157–58.

——. (1984) Review, J.H. Christensen, Element of Crime/Forbrydelsens element, Kristeligt Dagblad, May 15.

——. (1984) Review, H. Jørgensen, Element of Crime/Forbrydelsens element, Information, May 14.

—— (1996) Interview with Christian Braad Thomsen, 'Kontrol og kaos', Politiken, July 5.

——. (1999) 'Projekt åben filmby' ('Project Open Film City'), January 27.

## Websites

www.dfi.dk
www.branchenyk.dfi.dk
www.d-dag.dk
www.zentropa-film.com
www.dogme95.dk